EVA TANGUAY
"*The Girl Who Made Vaudeville Famous*"
(Her billing)

AMERICAN VAUDEVILLE

Its Life and Times

by Douglas Gilbert

DOVER PUBLICATIONS, INC.

NEW YORK

Manufactured in the United States of America

Dover Publications, Inc.
180 Varick Street
New York 14, New York

This Dover edition is dedicated
to the memory of
DOUGLAS GILBERT
1891-1948
as a tribute to his contribution to
the history of the performing arts in America

Acknowledgment

MUCH of this book is largely due to the kindness of scores of persons in and out of the profession who contributed unstintingly their experiences and recollections. I am especially indebted to Jack Murphy, an observant trouper for fifty years, and to Edward V. Darling, principal booker of the Keith circuit, for information unlikely ever to have been disclosed save by their enthusiastic cooperation. Page after page I owe to the friendly interest of George M. Cohan, Joe Cook, Alfred Lunt, Ed Wynn, John Golden, Epes W. Sargent, John F. Royal, Charles MacArthur, Al Shean, Tom Fadden, George Middleton, Eddie Girard, Sam Curtis, Johnny O'Connor, William Morris, Jr., Jerome Wilzin, Frank Sullivan, and Nellie Revell. Use of the data with which they supplied me is, of course, my own responsibility. A mean job—tracing of copyrights of the old songs I have used—was lightened and often made almost pleasant by the helpfulness of E. C. Mills of the American Society of Composers, Authors and Publishers, and Walter

Douglas of the Music Publishers Protective Association. Some of my nicest pictures were supplied through the efforts of Mrs. Barrett from the Theatre Collection in the New York Public Library and Mrs. Lillian A. Hall, custodian of the Theatre Collection, Harvard College Library. My dear old friend Murdoch C. MacLeod not only read my proof but guided me countless times. Others, mindful of the vastness of my subject, and astounded at my challenge, may well ask of me: "Who has tied my son to this sword?" I shy from the query as though at the bar of justice. Its implications are dreadful.

DOUGLAS GILBERT.

Contents

Book III

THE GOLDEN DAYS

Book IV

THE REVELS END

BOOK I

Beer Halls and Slapshoes

Nostalgic Notes and
Spangled Origins

VAUDEVILLE was America in motley, the national relaxation. To the Palace, the Colonial, the Alhambra, the Orpheum, the Keith circuit and chain variety houses, N. Y. to L. A., we flocked, vicariously to don the false face, let down our back hair, and forget. Vaudeville was the theater of the people, its brassy assurance a dig in the nation's ribs, its simplicity as naïve as a circus. The two-a-day variety show all of us knew and many of us loved was a complete characterization of a pleasantly gullible, clowning America, physically bestirring itself, sunnily unsophisticated. Its social implications, reflected in the response of its audiences, are pronounced because its entertainment was largely topical fun. The trend of its humor was the march of those times. Thus, vaudeville is an important chapter, not only of the stage, but of Americana.

Its life was incredibly brief—some fifty or sixty years. For many of us the end came with the folding of the New York Palace as a two-a-day in 1932. No precise date can be fixed for its beginning. The specialty show has existed for centuries, and an imaginative mind may, with justice, seek its origin in the pagan rites of Isis, Bacchus, or pre-Christian Rome. "Specialty" shows apparently made an early appearance in this country. In I. N. Phelps Stokes's monumental "Iconography of Man-

3

hattan Island" there is mention of a "group of Philadelphia comedians" en route to New York in 1769, doubtless for the entertainment of bewigged and bibulous burghers.

The first "vaudeville" house in New York may have been opened by a William Valentine. The year is not known, but it was probably the late forties or early fifties. Valentine spoke one day to a friend of his plan for a theater and his difficulty in finding a suitable title for the sort of entertainment he contemplated. "Well, what kind of show are you going to do?" the friend asked. "Oh, a variety of entertainment," Valentine replied. "Then why not just call it a variety show?" was the practical response. Presumably he did—and there the record ends.

The first in this country to use the word "vaudeville" to describe a variety show was John W. Ransone who assembled a specialty group in the eighties and toured the sticks with it, himself playing the part of a Dutch comic. He may have borrowed the name from the "Vaudeville Theatre" which was established in San Antonio, Tex., as early as 1882, or may be it was the other way round. The word derives from the French Val de Vire (sometimes Vau de Vire), the valley of the Vire River in Normandy, where quaint and sprightly songs and ballads were sung. Tony Pastor, one of vaudeville's great showmen, loathed "vaudeville" as a sissy term for the correct "variety." It was the fussy and supersensitive Keith who appropriated it to bolster his vanity.

Pastor always insisted that variety shows stemmed from minstrels, a singular viewpoint in the light of his circus experiences in which he himself had taken part in acts closely akin to those of later vaudeville. He was right, however, in that a sort of vaudeville was part of the old minstrel show in which songs, clogs, ccmedy skits, and one-act abbreviations of musical farces were used to supplement Mr. Bones's ricochets with interlocutor and end man. Just before the outbreak of the American Civil War young women were drafted to enliven these shows for a touch of sex (most of the customers were men) and a show crudely comparable with modern vaudeville began.

Another influence derived from a man named Simmons, who starred his daughter in a touring company. In the early eighties Simmons conceived the idea of putting in comics and doing something of a sustained specialty show. It was an instant success, and he made much money. He may have cribbed the earlier efforts of Lydia Thompson and her British Blondes, a beefy sex show which Simmons developed further. He tighted his girls' legs, laced their waists to the waspish allure of the day, and inaugurated what was to become burlesque. This may have had some slight affect upon early vaudeville, but, on the whole, burlesque, in which the height of humor centered about the apertures of the human body, wandered to the Tenderloins leaving variety to work Main St. and Broadway. (Incidentally, it has been said, and might well be argued, that the strip tease is the only entertainment indigenous to America.)

Boat shows with their variegated bills were also a factor in the development of vaudeville, albeit of minor influence. These floating gypsy troupes maintained their character, and in American chronicles are allied with no other Thespian group. Playing the bayous and tributaries of the cotton country in the sixties, seventies, and eighties, they did a barter business, accepting merchandise for admissions. Hunting knives, molasses, berries, corn, yams, chickens, geese, and pelts were taken at the box office. The berries, tough chickens, and yams were fed to the actors, the corn to the fowl, and the surplus was sold in towns along the river. The crudeness and simplicity of the boat shows preserved their integrity. They were little affected by the notable early tours of Pastor and other managers, but they did serve to rouse show-minded people to feverish activity with regard to the variety show.

But all attempts to trace the origin of vaudeville (variety, the specialty show) are as profitless as they are fascinating. The reasons for its demise are as interesting as they are sad.

over

Obviously the murderer was mechanized entertainment. Yet the early managers saw no menace when motion pictures were introduced—on the contrary, welcomed the advent of the short-reel Biograph flickers as audience "chasers," never foreseeing the shadow of a photographed jazz singer coming to croon the death of vaudeville. And the *coup de grâce* of radio was beyond the imagination of a drug addict. There were other factors. The vulgarity of the last comics was one—a curious irony, for that is how variety started—a runny nose, a belch, and drunken laughter. Vaudeville's early humor was mainly physical; its comedy low. But it was rich, robust, unbuttoned, having little truck with subtlety or sly sophistication.

In the last few years efforts have been made to "revive" vaudeville. The Messrs. Olsen and Johnson, a team of knockabout zanies, characteristic of the muscular thrust that typified the heyday of American variety, were highly successful, 1938–1940, with "Hellzapoppin," the cast of which included some of variety's old-timers in fragments of their specialty acts. But "Hellzapoppin" was a freak, a bastard revue—mad in its humors, novel in its rib of the audience—a crazy but funny hodgepodge, a theatrical bishop's egg.

With less success in 1939 Kurt Robitschek, a manager wise in vaudeville lore, produced "Vaudeville Marches On" and Broadway thumbed it down, mostly because he sought to modernize—and Continentalize—his bill. Frank Fay, who followed with his own revival, was also unsuccessful. Both men may be complimented for bravery, but they should have known that today, with the great comics and song and dance talents mortgaged to the movies and radio, an acceptable vaudeville bill could not be assembled. Assuming the miracle, it could not be made to pay at an $11 top. Except for phenomenal novelties like Sarah Bernhardt, to whom Martin Beck paid $7,000 a week at the New York Palace, the highest salaries in vaudeville's golden age averaged $2,500 to $4,000 a week for two shows a day. These were paid only to the great box-office draws—Tanguay, Bayes, Janis—and in a number of

Hitherto unpublished photograph of Sarah Bernhardt arriving (1912) for her first vaudeville tour. That is Lou Tellegen partially eclipsed by Sarah's shako and at extreme right is Martin Beck, who imported her and whose courtesy released this picture. Also shown (next page) is the Divine One's financial acceptance of her contract. The receipt in dollars then approximated $14,476, or two weeks' pay.

instances the announced salary probably was a press agent's figure. Indeed, Edward V. Darling, chief booker for the Palace, was limited to $8,000 for his weekly winter billing budget, and in the summer months to $5,000.

Today Eddie Cantor, making personal appearances at the movie presentation houses with his unit show, has been paid $15,000 weekly for the act. And with whatever magic wand he wields, one can scarcely expect a manager to lure Ed Wynn, Jack Benny, Fred Allen, W. C. Fields, or Edgar Bergen (who was once happy to get $350 a week for his ventriloquial splinter), back to a two-a-day vaudeville revival when, in addition to their movie commitments, they can receive from $5,000 to $10,000 from commercial sponsors for thirty-minute broadcasts—once a week.

In the farther field of sociology it is the opinion of many that an authentic revival of vaudeville would be resisted today by an indifferent public that has learned to amuse itself with sports, automobiles, and cocktail parties; finds intimate entertainment in night clubs, or in its own living rooms where radio comics pathetically attempt a reincarnation with their who-

was-that-lady-I-seen-you-with gags. Joe Jackson, Charlie Case,
Bert Williams, Nora Bayes, Eva Tanguay, Elsie Janis, Vesta
Victoria, the Dolly Sisters, Irene Franklin, Duffy and Sweeney,
McIntyre and Heath, Collins and Hart, Gallagher and Shean
—these and several hundred others contributed something
that cannot be recaptured in motion picture or broadcast
studios. The setting is gone with the response.

Dumps, Slabs, and Honky-tonks

THE vaudeville we of this generation knew was sired by Tony Pastor who first played to a "double audience" (men and women) when he opened his Fourteenth Street house in Tammany Hall, New York, October 24, 1881. It was the first "clean" vaudeville show in America and to its bill, as Fred Stone used to say, a child could take his parents.

Only those blessed with the age to recall the very early days can appreciate the contrast of Pastor's entertainment with the general fare of the seventies and eighties when, in beer halls and for-men-only dives, roughhouse turns and afterpieces were smuttily "blued" to amuse the tosspots, strumpets, dark-alley lads, and slummers who in those years made up variety audiences from Boston to San Francisco. Indeed, one of New York's variety halls (said to have been Volk's Garden), which Pastor ultimately took over, fathered one of our oldest and most indecent gags which is still, with saloon humor, tied to the names of some of our loveliest stage and movie ladies. During the course of the bill, so runs the yarn, the manager announced to his beer-sodden patrons, "And now, gents, Miss Lillian McTwobucks will sing 'Love among the Roses.' " Whereupon a drunk arose and in stentorian tones replied, "She is a whore." The unabashed manager dismissed the interruption. "Nevertheless," he said, "Miss Lillian McTwobucks will still sing 'Love Among the Roses.' " Apocryphal or not, it is a perfect characterization of early vaudeville and its audiences.

Variety and its votaries were the pulp side of the slick picture of Edith Wharton's elegant eighties which, with a curtsy to the memory of that gentle lady, is a swish title for so lusty, gutsy, vigorous, and guzzling a decade. Variety halls with wine rooms and bars red-lighted every thriving town in America. Prostitutes were genuine sluts awash in carnation perfume, and Welsh and Cornish miners in the coal and iron warrens of Pennsylvania fought bare-knuckle bouts in the rear of the halls. The $15-a-week comics were harassed by a brawl a night in the beer-hall olios where the most popular afterpiece was likely to be "The Haymakers," a pantomime of midnight "blue."

For Men Only.

The curtain rose on a group of harvesters, boys and girls, busy about a haystack. Smirks and gestures of a purport easily grasped by those in the audience not too drunk to understand were a prelude to the exit of all but one couple. This couple repaired to the back of the haystack. Then the others returned, and the boys, one by one, with simpers, gigglings, and pointings and suggestive calls visited the girl behind the stack. As each returned to the stage his expression registered what had happened. The finale was the exit of one of the boys in disordered clothing.

This act was by no means universal, but it was played in such theaters as "Bottle" Koenig's in the Barbary Coast and the Haymarket in San Francisco, and in Kansas City. Frequently in houses where blue afterpieces were the rule the performers in the olio were forbidden to use risqué dialogue, double-entendres, or suggestive situations as a build-up for the smut at the end. There were a number of other obscene afterpieces in pantomime, but their titles were changed so constantly they cannot be pinned. Some may feel nausea at these, but a little revulsion should be saved against the fact that they still persist in recognizable forms and could have been seen within the last few years in Times Square burlesque houses.

Dan Manning, of Manning and Bailey, a frankly purple act, was a favorite in the blue houses where his song, "Hi Dinky Doo," was a nightly request:

Hi Dinky Doo

As Adam walked out in the garden one day
Singing Hi diddle diddle the cat and the fiddle,
His clothing was light—it was summer they say;
Singing Hi dinky doodle dum day.

He sat down in the shade to smoke and repose,
He soon fell asleep but when he arose,
There sat mother Eve, in very short clothes
Singing Hi dinky doodle dum day.

Now who are you? said Adam, then Eve quickly spoke,
Singing Hi diddle diddle the cat and the fiddle,
I'm one of your ribs—but he laughed at the joke,
Singing Hi dinky doodle dum day.
I saw you looked lonesome, and thought it no harm
To step in for a chat and walk over your farm.
So sit down by my side and don't feel alarm
At my Hi dinky doodle dum day.

Johnny Forbes, another blue performer, achieved beer-hall notoriety with:

Such a Delicate Duck

I once knew a girl so modest I swow,
(I can't remember her name just now).
She wouldn't touch a flower pot, oh, no, dod rot 'em,
For the nasty things had holes in their bottoms.
CHORUS: Such a delicate duck
I never did see.
She was too damned particular,
She never suited me.

I took her out one night for a walk,
We indulged in all sorts of pleasantry and talk.
We came to a potato patch, she wouldn't go across,
The potatoes had eyes and she didn't wear drawers.

Such passages in an otherwise honorable story of a lost art
were exceptions. But they did exist and, as chalkings on
vaudeville's stage door, reflect the humor of a soup-stain day,
picturing our grandfathers, horny-handed, in overalls and
jumpers and manure on their boots. The afterpieces as we
shall see, were not all so nauseating. Washed clean of their
smut, many were later built into full-length plays, famous
throughout the country. "The Parlor Match" returned the
team of Evans and Hoey a fortune. And one of the most
beloved dramas of past times, "The Old Homestead," was a
mint to Denman Thompson. They were based respectively
upon "The Book Agent" and "Joshua Whitcomb," both
filthy afterpieces.

The Caravan Players.

Pastor's initial ventures into the sticks in the sixties and
seventies with his compact variety unit offering comedy,
dancing, songs, and sketches must be credited as the major
influence in stimulating the rising American interest in the
specialty show, but there were other well-known traveling
units spreading word that money could be made on actors
who were not "Harolds and Arthurs"—as your specific
vaudeville trouper, who was one-part gypsy and born in a
suitcase, called the legitimate players. Most active of these
troupes were those of E. S. Washburn, Barry and Fay, M. B.
Leavitt, and Hyde and Behman.

A Hyde and Behman skit which achieved nation-wide
notoriety (and financial success) was "Muldoon's Picnic," referred to in a contemporary print as "this comical piece which
is now being played throughout the country with much success by Hyde and Behman's Combination." It was a dung-boot
comedy, amazingly daring in its religious slurs and walloping

humors; utterly incomprehensible to us who tread lighter than the angels in our approach to religion as theatrical material.

New York was well supplied with variety houses, all of them beer halls and "drop-in" places. Among those prominent in the decade between 1875 and 1885 were Koster and Bial's in 23rd Street west of Sixth Avenue, Miner's Bowery, the London Theatre, Parker's American Theatre at 443 Third Avenue, and, curiously, the "Aquarium," at Broadway and 35th Street, an astonishing uptown location for those times, as its managers doubtless found out, for the house does not seem to have thrived. More successful were the New National Theatre, 104–106 Bowery, managed by Michael Heuman; the Globe Museum, 298 Bowery; the New York Museum, 210 Bowery; and in near-by territory, Waldman's Newark Opera House. In Brooklyn there were Hyde and Behman's in Adams Street and Zipp's Casino; Winter's Grand Central Casino, 123 South Street, Trenton, N.J., and the historic Howard's Athenaeum in Boston.

The nucleus of the first "chain" was inaugurated around 1880 by Harry Miner and Thomas Canary, who operated Miner's New Bowery and the Eighth Avenue Theatre in New York. That their enterprises were more extensive is indicated by their announcements guaranteeing ten to sixteen weeks' playing time for "first-class talent." They conducted a management and booking office, bid for acts, and at one time managed Murphy, Mack, Murphy, and Shannon, one of the biggest of the "four" acts. Probably the first Southwestern chain was that of the firm of Holland and Bell which controlled My Theatre in Fort Worth, the Horseshoe in Waco, and the London in Galveston.

Irreverent Transformations.

The success of the shows that took to the road was followed by a miraculous mushrooming of variety theaters in the nation's towns. Throughout the country every barn and shooting gallery that had a roof over it with room for a bar and a hall in which 150 folding chairs could be assembled bid for "specialties" and advertised in the trade journals. They were variously called "slabs," "dumps," and "honky-tonks" by the performers who nevertheless played them gladly, for actors do have to eat, a necessity which John Henshaw and his partner, May Ten Broeck, a famous comedy team of the eighties, built into an amusing act.

With few exceptions, the rough-hewn "Palaces" where the shows were presented were makeshifts, as across the continent churches, barns, warehouses, dyeworks, livery stables, markets, and other abandoned buildings were converted into variety halls. Churches were readily transformed. Pews could easily be removed to make room for chairs and tables; balconies metamorphosed into private boxes for stouping and wenching. To make a stage and proscenium from pulpit and choir loft was but a carpenter's problem, and any competent nail thumper could, almost overnight, bedevil a Sunday-school room into a bar.

Enoch's Varieties, an important theater in Philadelphia in the eighties, had been an old church in Seventh Street below Arch Street. In fact Philadelphia, whose title as the cradle of vaudeville is handily supported by the number of first-class performers who made their debuts in that city, showed a surprising disregard of consecrated masonry. Two other churches, one at Third and Green streets, another at Eleventh and Wood streets, were similarly converted, their choir stalls turned into wine rooms, their pulpit platforms enlarged for buskined troupers who speedily unsanctified the atmosphere with shady afterpieces.

The first hootchy-kootchy dance to appear in this country was presented in the Eleventh and Wood Street house in 1876 when the church was taken over and run as a variety hall by Harry Drew. The troupe consisted of three men and two women; the men the musicians, the women the dancers. The men sat on the floor; one played an Armenian pipe, another a

kind of violin, the third a tabor or small drum which he beat
with his hands in the manner of a swing band bass-slapper.
The women wore short skirts, and a silken band bound their
breasts. Their feet, in fact the rest of their bodies, were bare.
They had originally been brought over for what may be called
the Centennial's "Midway." But the Turkish Theatre on the
Exposition grounds in which they were first billed was poorly
located and soon closed for lack of patronage. Although the
dance was sensationally sexual, it was received with apathy.
The cancan, with the girls kicking high in ruffled drawers, then
a novelty and soon to reach excessive popularity, was considered far more risqué. Near nakedness (then as now) verged
on an embarrassing affront, whereas a peep at panties, or
drawers as they were called, or a momentarily exposed three
inches of thigh was variety's acme of hotta-stuffa. At any rate,
the kootchy girls were a flop. Drew closed his hall, and the
kootch dance passed out of theatrical ken until 1893 when it
reappeared on Chicago's Midway where, our morals having
become more puritanical, the act was a sizzling success.

One of the queerest of the early theaters (they were all stag
houses) was the Academy in West Superior, Wis. It was
owned and managed by Fanny Prestige who ran a boardinghouse for performers in the same building with the theater,
tended her own bar, booked her own shows, and did her own
cooking. Beneath a wild toss of chemically blond hair she
dangled a pair of eight-carat diamond earrings. Her invariable
costume was a sealskin coat which she wore over a Mother
Hubbard. When Fanny closed for the night she went to the
bar and emptied all the liquor from the bottles into a couple of
jugs which she carted up to her bedroom. She was quite aware
of the proficiency of actors as sleepwalkers and took no chances.
A firm, but pleasant woman, she was well regarded by performers, who were genuinely sorry when she quit show business, married a mining man, and settled in Montana.

And at any gathering of gaffers one always recalls the Parlor
(sic!) Theatre in Duluth, Minn. This was a large store with the

front boarded up, the audience entering through the saloon next door which was operated by the owner as a part of the house. Kitchen chairs were the seats. Those placed in the space that had formerly been the front show windows were sold as choice locations. A piano furnished music. In the early eighties in Duluth it was illegal to serve drinks in places of amusement, so the astute proprietor knocked a hole through the wall separating the auditorium from the bar. It was just large enough for one person and at intermissions the line of thirsts extended nearly into the street. Although the intimacies of the Parlor were so pronounced as to discourage the best in make-believe, performers never regarded booking time there as too irksome. Duluth had a midnight closing law and shows were short.

Hash and Hall Bedrooms.

Quite a number of the managers operated boardinghouses in conjunction with their theaters. These varied from fair to frightful, but the whole business was so take-it-or-leave-it that nobody cared. Performers knew one another and the managers then were mostly friendly. When a performer arrived on Monday morning for rehearsal it was customary for the manager to greet him with a couple of dollars' worth of checks in five-cent denominations. These were good for drinks at the bar. The catch was that they were charged against the performer's salary. The manager watched how the bar bills were running and toward the end of the booking time was careful with his checks.

Oh, lovely were the boardinghouses. There was, for instance, Mrs. Patton's at 8 Oxford Street, Boston. Mrs. Patton, God rest her soul, in the late eighties was about forty-five, garrulous, and of so visitin' a nature her suffering house sat, like an unwashed child, awaiting the ministrations of stern authority. Her board rate was $5 a week and, as some old actors say, almost worth it. Motives never guided Mrs. Patton; her routine was impromptu. Did an actor ask for a cake of soap? "Well," would Mrs. Patton say, as though all the world but shared desires, "I'm after lookin' for a cake meself, I was. An' will ye have a dhrink?" It was her way of squaring all shortcomings; many, before and since, have invoked its benison. Mrs. Patton never kept an exact tab on her roomers, did all her bookkeeping in her head. An actor, renting a room of a Monday morning, hastily dumping his personal effects onto the bed, as likely would return from rehearsal to find it occupied by two strangers. Forthwith he would proceed to complacent Mrs. Patton who inevitably simulated utmost confusion at a problem beyond adjustment. "I'm sure I don't know what can be done about it. Maybe they will leave tomorrow, an' in the manetime come and have a dhrop o' th' cratur." It was so exquisitely a house of humors—Mrs. Patton's humors—that actors, however beleaguered by the mal-domestic lady, would return again and again, of course on the pretext that it was handy to Keith's Bijou.

Mrs. Irish's, on Dix Place, hard by Mrs. Patton's, was neater. Mrs. Irish, having a greater sense of order, never over-booked her house. A commendable housekeeper and a genial lady, she would send meals to the Bijou (as would Mrs. Patton, if she remembered) when extra performances required her boarders to remain at the theater or made it difficult for them to get out for food.

Two famous New York theatrical boardinghouses were Mrs. Scully's, at 311 East Fourteenth Street, and Mrs. Tobin's, also on Fourteenth Street a couple of blocks west. Among their regular patrons were Frank McNish, Tony Farrell, Fred Huber, Walter Deaves, Imro Fox, the magician, Pitrot, the man of many imitations, the Rooney Sisters, Delmore and Lee, Murphy and Willard, Monroe and Mack, Fox and Allen, Lawrence and Barrington, Daly and Vokes, Cruett, Beers, and Cruett, a "bughouse" contortion act, the Three Keatons (one of them was the kid named Buster), Hines and Remington, Barton and Ashley, the Barton being Johnny Barton, uncle of Jim (Jeeter Lester) Barton, whose act was "Canal Boat Sal."

Annie Ashley played the name part and she was terrific; in slapping Johnny silly she slapped the act into prominence. Still farther west on Fourteenth Street was Cook's place, which also had its regulars.

Two hotels catering exclusively to New York performers in the eighties and nineties were the Smith House and the Bussey House, adjoining properties in Great Jones Street. These were hutches of activity; many an act was bred in them or polished to ultimate importance. Almost any hour of the day or night acrobats shook the sturdy walls and floors practicing flips in the halls or limbering up with forward or back benders. Ocarina soloists, jugglers, and contortion dancers were always in action, while monologists spouted new routines. Most of the doors were left wide open and anyone passing along the halls could see a dozen acts in course of construction or undergoing repairs.

When $40 Was Tops.

The old-time variety actors took a lot for $40 a week, the standard rate for an established act. Some of the smaller houses—Lafayette, Ind.; Ashtabula Harbor, Ohio; Niagara Falls, N.Y.; Hamilton, Ontario; Butler, Pa.; Saginaw, Mich. —set a $30 limit. These salaries were for two; a single act received half. An act with three or more persons was not held to the limit for two but got what they could above $40. Animal acts, or acts with cumbersome gear and equipment, were also on the bargain basis. These salaries applied to the average variety house in the early eighties. Some years later the higher class houses paid well. Yet the actors playing the honky-tonks for meager wages, doing sometimes as many as five shows a day, rarely complained. And as a matter of fact, against the economic scale that prevailed in the eighties generally, they had small cause. A first-class carpenter, cobbler, house painter, or plumber received $12 a week. And the legitimate actors were scaled away below the variety trouper. Legit salaries ranged from $5 to $7 a week for juvenile and utility roles. Otis Skinner confesses receiving but $7 weekly even after starting his career.

Booking was usually from one to six weeks in a house according to one's repertory, reputation, or pull with the management. The numerous performer cards in the theatrical journals of the day indicate a lack of bookers and agents—a condition that was remedied when the smart boys caught up with the trend. Performers ordinarily did not make long jumps because it was possible to stay many weeks in a single town. Philadelphia, for example, had more than twenty variety houses in the early eighties; and from there it was only a short hop to Wilmington, Baltimore, Washington, Richmond, or New York. This brought about three different groups of performers: the Far Western, the Midwestern, and the Eastern. If an Eastern act went as far west as Chicago their friends gave them a farewell party and saw them off at the train.

The Murderous Museums.

In the eighties the appetite for diversion grew by what it fed on and enterprising managers like Kohl and Castle in Chicago and Austin and Stone in Boston, as well as B. F. Keith, albeit then in a minor way, threw the public added forage in museums which for a time were excessively popular. The museums were divided buildings, one part for the curio, or freak, exhibition and the other for the variety show. With no intent so to do they encouraged performers and developed acts. It was common practice for a museum to play five shows daily and sometimes more. Their stages being limited, they could present only the so-called artist act. They could not book big aerial acts with their heavy apparatus and revolving ladders, most animal acts were barred because of lack of room and the exhausting schedule, and spectacular acts and pageants were also unplayable.

This not only made a field day for the comic, the song and dance team, the seriocomic, the juggler, magician, crayon sketch artist, marionettes, et cetera—it put a premium on their

Façade and lobby of one of Keith's earliest Boston theaters. Its precise date is un-available but the leg-o'-muttoned lady in the foreground suggests the early nineties. Papa with the stick and topper would know. And note the prominence of the box office. Keith was fussy about such things.

acts. Museum time frequently paid from $20 to $30 more a week than the standard minimums on the straight time. But the performers earned it. With a strong attraction in the curio hall like Laloo, Bertha Mills, or Jo-Jo, the variety performers were forced to race their acts, crowding show upon show to disgorge one audience and cram in another.

Performers have been known to play as many as seventeen shows a day in museums when the curio freaks were as big a draw as the three aforementioned. And these three were terrific. Laloo was a young chap with a twin brother growing out of the top of his stomach; the growth had legs and arms but no head. Bertha Mills exploited her feet which were nineteen inches long and a big guffaw to gaping hicks. Jo-Jo was the celebrated dog-faced boy.

A standing "museum" yarn concerns a blackface song and dance team who were booked at the Clark Street Museum in Chicago when a freak attraction was packing immense crowds into the curio hall. Their act was the well-known "Arkansas," not to be confused with "The Arkansas Traveler." The first line of their song went:

"I'm going back to Arkansas tomorrow . . . "

The team began at nine in the morning and by noon had given five performances. With no time out for luncheon, by 2 P.M. they were exhausted and at 6 P.M. were silly with fatigue; still they kept going back to Arkansas. At 11 P.M. they staggered on for their last show. Washing up after, they somehow managed to get to their boardinghouse which, during the early morning hours, caught fire. Numb from exhaustion, they slept until firemen shook them roughly. Whereupon, half conscious, they   stood up and began:

"I'm going back to Arkansas tomorrow . . . "

They were removed to safety.

Other important museums were Epstein's in Randolph Street, Chicago, the Wonderland in Minneapolis, the Wonderland in St. Paul, Avery's Museum in Cincinnati, Conner's in Allegheny, Pa., Davis's in Pittsburgh, Bradenburg's in Philadelphia, Huber's in New York, and in Boston, Austin and Stone's and Pilling's.

Museum performances were almost always given before mixed audiences and blue stuff was banned. Most of the museums pasted warnings in dressing rooms that the words "slob," "sucker," "damn," "hell," and "socks" were forbidden. The ban on "socks" may seem unreasonable today but in the eighties crude jests—"stronger than father's socks," or "I threw my socks at the wall and they stuck"—were common gags. Reference to bedbugs, impurities in food, or questionable houses or streets was also barred, doubtless a relief to the actors, to whom they must have been vivid, personal reminders of uncomfortable nights in flop joints and boardinghouses.

Many entertainments were given in halls that had fair stage and scenic equipment; here beginners or talented amateurs could easily find booking for four or more nights weekly. The entertainments (this is in the seventies) were sponsored by lodges, clubs, store employees, churches, and politicians— media that were swelled by a dozen or more German societies, Saengerbunds, Maennerchors, Turnvereins, and Harmonie Bunds, all of which put on Sunday night shows. In addition, ambitious young managers were constantly organizing companies to tour near-by towns. (Most of these flopped, but it was good experience.) Moreover, anybody who could pay for the printing and hall hire could stage a benefit at which a new act was sure to appear among the "Host of Volunteers." For these performances even the amateurs were paid—"Amateur Night" had not yet become a racket. Thus a young dance act, probably after a fortnight's rehearsal in a grain car (a favorite "rehearsal hall" for dancers in those days; grain-car floors were hard, smooth, and clean), who had made their own equipment (as many were forced to do since apparatus was expensive), not only got the experience of facing an audience but received the equivalent of a night's lodging for the effort.

An interesting phase of the eighties varieties was the contests among performers. There were all kinds of matches between clog dancers, jig dancers, harmonica players, bone soloists, pantomimists—who competed usually for silver cups. A winner aided his booking time.

Most popular and most numerous were the clog-dancing contests: Lancashire clog, American clog, hornpipe clog, trick clog, pedestal clog, and statue clog. Dancing was judged according to time, style, and execution, and separate judges checked each feature. It was the habit of some judges to go beneath the stage and listen to the beat. Sand jig dancing was judged in the same manner. Possibly clog did not originate in America, but America made it its own, and our performers were unbeatable. A clog dancer named Queen electrified the English music halls when he went abroad for a tour in the eighties. They found his triples, rolls, and nerve steps uncanny, refused to believe he accomplished them unaided by tricks, and caused him no end of embarrassment by demanding to see his shoes. Queen stopped all that by making his entrance in slippers and passing around his shoes for the audience to examine, as proof that he used no clappers or other Yankee gadgets. When the shoes were returned he put them on in full view of the audience and went into his act.

"Father Was a Peculiar Man."

Variety was a curious hit-or-miss activity, a theatrical shot in the dark. It was of the stage, yet distinct from the legitimate theater whose "Harolds and Arthurs" regarded variety performers as low persons of no moment, yet were willing to act on the bills with them for quick "off time" money. Variety performers themselves were bedfellows in a definite alliance for a common cause. Yet many remained strangers to one another, so widely were they flung, so diverse were their professional interests, and so varied their itineraries. A variety trouper traveled more in a year than a legitimate actor did in a lifetime. He moved every week, and at each move met from twenty to thirty other performers, usually new ones. It was astonishing how old friends, through fortune's cantrip and the vicissitudes of booking, continually missed each other. About 1878 J. A. (Jack) Murphy, then of Murphy and MacReady, met a blackface comedy musical act, Bryant and Saville, while they were playing on the same bill in Philadelphia. Murphy and Bryant and Saville became friends during the engagement. Parting after it closed, they toured America, England, and the Continent ahead and behind each other for thirty-three years before they came together again in 1911.

No more typical variety performer could be found than Jack Murphy. A fine dependable comic, born to the motley of vaudeville, he devised his own material and contributed gags, lines, and comedy to other acts. His was a representative act for nearly fifty years. He covers the period of variety almost from its inception to its death, springing with it from the wine rooms and free-and-easies to the Albeean temples that today, like sprawling headstones, mark its demise throughout the land.

A high-school lad fond of clowning, Murphy broke in in 1876 at a Philadelphia free-and-easy which had sprung up to catch the overflow from the Centennial Exposition. (As a digression, it should be set down that more variety acts came out of Philadelphia than any other town in the United States; the city offered more chances to break in an act and smooth it up.) The show was billed as "The Log Cabin Varieties" and Murphy, besides appearing in a piece called "Love Among the Roses," did a fill-in turn playing the banjo, telling jokes, giving a short monologue, and doing a song and dance in blackface. Like this:

Father was a peculiar man, he was always getting into trouble. If you couldn't find him at home you could always find him at the police station or some saloon. They sent me out to hunt him one day and I went right to the police station. There I found him. There were two other cases that came up before father's. The first man was arrested for stealing a pair of pants. The judge discharged him; said you couldn't make a suit out of a pair of pants. The other man was charged with petty larceny. He stole three bottles of beer. Judge dismissed him, too. Said you couldn't make a case out of three bottles of beer. Then father came up. Judge said—what are the charges? Father said if you'll let me out of this I won't charge you a cent. Then the judge said haven't you been here before? And father said well, I come in now and then to get my mail. The judge asked father then if he had no permanent address and father said yes, but I'm here more than I'm at home. Then the judge said well, what is this all about, there must be some complaint? A neighbor then came in and said judge, this man came home the other night, took down the front door, and hit his wife over the head with it. No case at all, said the judge, any man has the right to a-door his own wife. Father was pleased to get out and said let's go have an oyster stew. That's what father called for, an oyster stew. What we got was an oyster's one. The water wasn't warm enough to kill the oyster. He kept hopping up to the rim of the bowl trying to bite the cracker I had in my hand. When I got the oyster it didn't agree with me. I went to bed and couldn't sleep for that oyster. I had the nightmare in bed, but the bed was a little buggy, so I hitched the mare to the buggy and drove out of town.

Well, there it is and you have to take it. That is what your grandpappies laughed at. The seventies were the cowbarn days of vaudeville. The audiences (all male) were none too bright, a mental condition hardly improved by alcoholic befuddlement. Jokes had to be sledge-hammered home. The days of personalities, subtlety, wit, expert dancing, and superb technique were to come.

Gaslight Days

T HE scenic equipment of variety halls in the seventies and eighties was not heavy or expensive. Nearly every house had an advertising drop which was let down during intermissions or between acts. These drops usually depicted a small landscape in the center, the balance of the space being taken up with ads for liver pills, big beers for five cents, trusses and rupture appliances, oyster houses, pile ointments, pool parlors, and low-priced funerals. The squares into which the drops were divided were each about six by two feet; and for each square the theater charged a rental of $2 a week. On a monthly basis an advertiser could get a double square for $3 weekly. If the pile ointment company discontinued, the theater painted out the ad and sold the space, say, to Hostetter's Bitters.

The stock sets were a kitchen interior with a "breakaway" window, a plain chamber with doors right and left, a dark wood scene, and a light wood scene. "Dark wood" meant a heavily timbered and foliaged spot with large tree trunks, fallen limbs, and general autumnal effects, usually sinister; a setting for villainous deeds in the curse-you-Dalton closing dramas. "Light wood" was the contrast. It was cheerful, usually of spring foliage, and brighter tree trunks were used such as white birch. Possibly a stream meandered gently through a rear meadow, and violet patches were often used—sylvan retreats for young love in the romantic scenes. There was a set cottage, and a street "in one," that is, a set or drop in the first entrance for conversation acts, comic turns, or monologues. Few drops were used except the curtain and the advertising drop. All other scenery was painted on rough burlap instead of the linen now used. The burlap was filled with heavy glue sizing for smoothness, necessary because it was so coarse. It was then painted in strongly contrasted colors. Soft tones would have been lost in the gaslight days. There were no pastels.

Make-up was crude. For character, eccentric, and dialect acts it began with a heavy foundation of flesh grease paint. Red for cheeks and noses was bright vermilion with no shading whatever. Solid black was used for wrinkles, expression marks, and eye shadows. Flake white was used for a prominent upper lip to contrast with the vermilion of the cheeks. Wigs of impossible colors could be used and whiskers were mounted with wires. Clothes were seldom cleaned. Comic pants were worn until strong enough to walk away unflung. With the advent of the electric light actors in such make-up and costumes became frights and scareheads and nose putty and vermilion had to be tossed from the make-up boxes. Wrinkles and expression marks had to be finely blended, the brown liner being used instead of the black. Bald wigs, too, had to be carefully blended, the blend band frequently being made of silk instead of the thick cloth permissible (because undetected) in the gaslight days. The old wire mounting for whiskers had to be discarded and in the new era crepe hair was attached by means of gum mastic mixed with ether. Collars and dickeys were changed more often, had to be. White spats were kept clean and comic pants were aired, naphthaed, and kept pressed, or new ones purchased. Patent-leather clog shoes came in and the old slaps were treated to a surprising number of shines.

Thunder-mug Scene Painters.

The wonder is that the "artists" of the gaslight days were able to accomplish as much as they did. The gasboard was located in the first entrance, where the electric switchboard is in the modern theater. At curtain time one of the stagehands lighted the borders with an alcohol torch attached to a long pole—a Thespic altar boy, as some impious actors dubbed him. Borders and foots were controlled by sets of levers which were generally too light or too loose. If they slipped they sometimes hampered performers severely, as when a scene, meant to be played in temporary dark, had perforce to be played dark throughout.

"Bunch" lights were obtained by grouping gas burners on a standard and reflecting them from bright new dishpans. For spots or floods the calcium, or limelight, was placed in the center of the balcony. The light was produced by jets of flame from two pressure gas tanks blown against two pieces of lime which were inserted one above the other into the lamp in vertical position, the flames being directed to their point of junction. It will not be necessary to remind old-timers how this apparatus hissed, sputtered, cracked, dropped sparks and fragments of red-hot lime, and often went out entirely, usually when most needed. Large squares of colored glass were used for media, instead of the gelatine now employed.

The more pretentious houses were equipped with paint frames located on the back wall of the theater and rigged to raise or lower by means of ropes and counterweights. On this frame the flats, wings, and set pieces were fastened. The scenic artist stood on a narrow platform high up in the flies, working by the light of a row of gas jets under a reflector. Dry colors mixed with glue were used and as these were required in large quantities (and tin cans were not then so plentiful), large, yellow chambers, family size, the kind known in England as "thunder mugs," were frequently used in laying out a "palette." The artist or house manager shopped around for them, obtaining chipped or imperfect pots by the dozen at nominal cost. Having convenient handles, they were ideal containers. Artists often worked at night while the show was in progress, and on a night in the eighties in an Omaha theater an assistant dropped a pot containing ocher; it crashed to the stage during an unhand-me-villain scene. The distressed actors ad-libbed themselves out of the mishap, but when they and the trembling assistant confronted the house manager, whose rage they expected would crumble the stage, all he said was "Keep that in. It's the best thing in the act."

In these initial houses the scenic artists were not regularly employed. They worked by the job and supplied special stuff or repainted old scenery for several houses.

Buying or borrowing props was unheard of. They were made by the prop man, a mad genius who worked in papier-mâché, wood, and plaster, supplied burnt cork and jig sand, created rain and water effects and thunder, and made "quick match" and lycopodium torches.

"Quick match" was a witch's brew, the base of which was powdered sugar and potash. Touched with a rod tipped with cotton dipped in sulphuric acid, it flamed instantly. It was used to set off powder trains in military sketches or to give the semblance of an explosion or the firing of a mine.

Lycopodium torches were used for conflagrations. The yellowish lycopodium powder was placed in a tin cup connected to an alcohol torch by a tube about three feet long. A vigorous puff through the tube would dust the powder into the alcohol flame producing an instantaneous brilliant flash three or four feet long—very handy for dashing out with girl in arms from "burning" buildings. The torch was also used in pantomimes to frighten the clown, by fire-eaters for sensational entrances, for revels of the gnomes in spectaculars, et cetera.

The property man made "breakaway" tables, hinged in the center so the legs would spread if weight was put upon them, and "breakaway" chairs, both for comic effects, as were the "breakaway" windows with glazed-paper panes. He made tree stumps out of nail kegs which he burlaped and painted; kept intact the supply of blown-up bladders for the low comic to bash in the face of the straight man, or "feeder," and slapsticks he made of all sizes. He made stone walls out of soapboxes painted gray; these were also useful as fortifications or ramparts to be knocked down by the capturing troops as the cavalry dashed in—tarantara. He made prop bricks and specialized in smoke pots, a hellish type of fireworks that spewed smoke in the required colors of oyster white, dark gray, or dense black. These were used for "faulty" stoves, and smoldering fires. Sometimes they were placed under a chair in which an old man was dozing, to choke him out and give the young lovers a chance. Sometimes they were fastened to the coattails of a schoolmaster.

Props supplied "fizz" bottles (before the days of siphons, wine bottles were used). He made stuffed clubs, dummies, and all necessary "art" appliances. If bundles of lath were needed for prison bars he borrowed a wheelbarrow from the grocer, hustled to the lumberyard and brought them back. He handled the offstage effects, pulled strings for trick stuff, took care of the guns and pistols for the military and Indian sketches, and often filled in on the stage (frequently with lines) as soldier, Indian, policeman, washerwoman, or other incidental character. The versatility of Tony Pastor's genial, bibulous prop man, Charlie Ludwig, was so well known that performers at the Fourteenth Street Theatre, instead of carrying an extra man or woman, would recruit him for a weekly tip of $1. Generous acts paid him $1.50.

In the vaudeville heyday to come the prop man was constantly tipped by performers (generally uselessly, for many of them grew into sluggards and gyppers), but in the seventies and eighties tips were unknown. The average weekly salary of the prop man was $12. Later the more pretentious houses paid as high as $25 a week.

The rest of the stage crew in the early variety halls consisted of two "grips," or scene shifters, and a stage manager. The stage manager acted as interlocutor in the minstrels (a feature of many bills), played "straight" in the afterpieces, and sometimes took on important roles in the dramas and sketches.

"A Chord in D, Professor."

The variety orchestras of the early eighties varied in size from one piece, a piano (and sometimes a banjo), to seven or eight pieces. A seven-piece orchestra usually consisted of violin, cornet, piano, clarinet, trombone, string bass, and drums. The general run of the theaters used three pieces—piano, cornet, and drums. Drums were highly essential. They crashed the bumps of the comics, played the long roll and crash for a sensational finish of the aerialists, slides for life on the wire, leaps through rings of fire, etc. More later about the banjo, an important instrument in the early days.

The orchestras in the best theaters were extraordinarily good. Actors almost never carried their own orchestration, except for a specialty. Music for end songs, singles, and fill-ins was left to the ingenuity of the orchestra. The absence of technique and the hit-or-miss attitude of the actor (based upon the belief that a mummer's life was but an interim of earthly ad-libbing) often taxed the abilities of the musicians. But your typical variety-hall musician could play from memory a vast repertoire of clogs, reels, hornpipes, sand jigs, and walk-arounds, and could fake a song in any given key. All of them had to be good readers and improvisers. Many of them were not only fine soloists, but well grounded in harmony, counterpoint, and form.

In the early days music cues were incessant. The actors were so continually spattered with them it was hard to deliver an important line or make a significant gesture without being slapped in the ears by one. The actors raged, for often the audience could not hear the lines, but the practice continued until the cues became such a nuisance they had to be restricted to precise business. This was one of the few "refinements" of Keith and his "polite vaudeville" colleagues that was really helpful.

Here is a typical first part (of the show) music cue sheet of the seventies and eighties:

At rise of curtain. . . . . .Orch. . . . . .(lively music).

Cue. . . It is good Squire Beasley. . . . . .   "   (jolly music for squire's
                                                     entrance).

Cue. . . (When comic falls down). . . . .   "   (Drum crash).

Cue. . . I feel like dancing. . . . .   "   (Specialty).

Cue. . . The villagers are coming. . . . . .   "   (Lively 6–8 time).

Cue. . . (Old man sits down suddenly). .   "   (Clarinet squeal).

Cue. . . While the villagers make merry   "   (Country dance).

Cue. . . I spurn you. . . . .   "   (Chord in D).

Cue. . . I am poor, and alone. . . . .   "   (plaintive music).

Cue. . . Try to forget my troubles. . . . .   "   (hornpipe by sou-
                                                     brette).

Cue. . . It contains dynamite. . . . .   "   (G chord—fortissimo).

Cue. . . (When burglars enter). . . . . . .   "   (Sneaky music).

Cue. . . (For knife combat). . . . .   "   (Allegro).

Cue. . . Will tell my sad story. . . . .   "   (Adagio with muted
                                                     violin).

Cue. . . (For change of scene). . . . .   "   (Waltz).

Cue. . . It is the cavalry. . . . .   "   (Bugle call).

Cue. . . The mill is on fire. . . . .   "   (Hurry music).

Cue. . . We must save her. . . . .   "   (Frenzied music).

Cue. . . Saved . . . . . , ...   "   (Joyous music until
                                                     curtain).

At the end of the first part the orchestra tore out in a body
to the bar to fortify themselves for the next act, sneaking under
the stage through a door about the size of a passbook, leaving
the bass fiddle to cover their retreat. Someone might save the
girl many times during the show, but the musicians, poor
chaps, had to save themselves.

Yet they were blessed with a condition for which there has
been no parallel since, save for the boom years of movie and
radio. A good theater musician in the early eighties was
virtually his own master. Liking not a house, he could thumb
his nose at the manager and be off. Several thousand variety
halls were functioning. There was ample employment nearly
everywhere.

"Gents, the Hand Is Quicker . . . "

Shows ran late. In some sections of the country, notably in the West and Far West, the program continued until daylight, or as long as anyone was buying wine or fancy drinks. But there were no matinees. The chief revenue of the house was derived, not from the show, but from the bar and the lunch counter where sandwiches, pie, oysters, fried chicken, chili con carne, and tamales were served, the menu varying with the geographical location.

Many of the houses operated gaming rooms. Faro and roulette were favorites, but spindles and eight-die cases were common. Spindles was played on a square table with numbers marked in a circle. An arrow pivoted to the center was spun. When the arrow stopped its point indicated the prize (if any). The game was played at a dollar a spin. Few won, for the arrow was controlled by secret mechanism known as the "squeeze." This was either a foot lever or a leverage operated from a corner of the table. Pressure by juggling a pile of silver dollars was an occasional method of control.

The eight-die game was played over a square shallow case with a glass top. Under the glass were displayed coin and currency ranging from 50 cents to a $100 bill. To these moneys were attached the numbers which must be thrown to win. The player paid his dollar, then tossed the eight dice across the glass top from a dice box. The operator helped the player to count, pointing to the different dice with a pencil. It was the operator's count that counted. If the miracle happened and the player threw eight aces he was tossed out for cheating. Some variety houses operated stud tables, and in the Southwest Mexican gambling games were frequent.

Theater admissions were nominal. Bartenders often distributed tickets to good spenders. In an audience that might number two thousand persons during the course of a long Saturday night (the shows being continuous), there would be a few hundred paid admissions, generally at 25 to 50 cents a ticket. The bar, the wine room, the gaming tables, did the business.

The wine-room girls, though they appeared on the stage at the opening, were not performers. They worked on a drink percentage basis, the standard rate being 10 cents on a dollar bottle of beer. This contained about a fifth of a gallon, about as much as most gin and Scotch bottles today. It was usually served with glasses scarcely larger than a whisky jigger. The girls also received five cents on each fancy drink and 50 cents for each $4 bottle of champagne. As the drinks were served the waiter gave the girl who had ordered them a check which she cashed with her evening take at the bar after closing. Most of the champagne was carbonated pear cider, beautifully bottled and labeled, and costing the house 64 cents a bottle in case lots. The managers carried out the Tex Guinan touch, proceeding on the assumption that each hello-sucker would not know the difference between the fake and the real Rheims which they probably did not. But imported champagne of the best vintage was stocked in special compartments for the important town officials, traveling men, politicians, cattle kings, and mine owners who often attended the shows.

The female performers also worked the wine rooms and boxes; in fact, it was obligatory for them to do so when not appearing on the stage or changing costumes. Often this plagued the performance, as when an actress entertaining a couple of good spenders was needed on the stage. In such instances it was the policy of all variety houses never to mess up a party. If a girl performer overheard her cue while she was arching up to a cowhand (in from the range with six months' pay) she just forgot it, and the actors ad-libbed themselves out as best they could. If the girl was a single, that is, if she appeared in a specialty of her own, a substitution was made.

The "boxes" were interesting hideaways and rather quaint. They were small compartments fitted into both sides of the balcony and draped with lace curtains caught up at the sides—

more like a boudoir than a rendezvous. To these the boys with big money and extensive thirsts were escorted and the curtains drawn so they could cuddle the girls and see the show in privacy.

Although the nature of their work made for looseness, few of the actresses and wine-room maidens were promiscuous. Ladies of the evening had their own racket, picking up where the wine-room girls left off. As a matter of fact (and convenience), few prostitutes attended the Western variety shows. Their hours of work coincided with those of the performers. Moreover, especially in the West, brothels were the rule and streetwalkers rare.

Sometimes the wine-room girls had difficulty in frustrating the advances of the brawny lumbermen, cowpunchers, gun fighters, and "long riders," as the train bandits were called. A favorite ruse was to give the explorer a key, purring, "This is the key to my room. I want you to keep it for me until I go and change. Now don't lose it. I'll be right back." A large box of assorted keys was kept under the bar for this purpose; stock equipment. Tragically stock. The trick was worked so often the men became aware of it and some bloody rows resulted— once murder. One night in the eighties a lumberjack waited for his slippery companion at the stage entrance of the Alcazar Theatre in Hurley, Wis. When she appeared he split her in half with an ax.

The girls could not, of course, drink against all customers. Most of them drank little at any time. They signaled the waiter to bring cold tea for whisky, or nonclaret lemonade. If real liquor was served the girl could secretly empty her drink into one of the palm-filled jardiniers which had been placed here and there for decoration. To the girls wine-rooming was a job, no more disreputable than hat-checking in night clubs today. Some of them bought property and retired; some married well; some . . . they are all gone.

The Show Is On

Many houses furnished no programs. They advertised with an A sign—two boards placed outside the theater in the form of an A—upon which the talent of the show was listed. Gaudy hangers were distributed to saloons, pool parlors, and barbershops; and the names of prominent actors were occasionally written in soap across the mirrors over the bars in the local pubs.

Frequently the musicians played on the street in front of the theater before the show opened. Sometimes the property man or a stagehand played the drums and cymbals while the drummer confined himself to the snare drum, an instrument requiring skilled application. When this barkerfest was over, the musicians repaired to the orchestra pit and blared out a semiclassic like "Poet and Peasant" or the overture to "Massaniello."

Then came the show. Bills averaged from twelve to fifteen numbers and lasted longer than an English week end. The "first part" usually ran forty-five minutes. Next came the olio, that is, the variety acts of song and dance, comic skits, acrobats, afterpieces, closing dramas, and what not.

At rise all the performers, including the wine-room girls, sat on the stage as in a minstrel opening and remained there during the first part. The girls were clad alike, usually in white

37

dresses with red or blue stockings and a sash. Sometimes they
formed a semicircle, sometimes they were in swings, swaying
rhythmically, or in raised tiers of seats, or perched around on
rocks or camp stools carrying garish parasols or fans. The inter-
locutors, in whiteface, sat in the center of the semicircle and
two blackface comics occupied the ends. Comic and sentimental songs, jokes, and ballads were offered. The audience,
entirely male, drifted in until at the close of the first curtain
the house was pretty well filled, remaining so, at the popular
places, until early in the morning, newcomers and late roister-
ers taking the places of those who left.

A standard bill opened with a sketch. This was followed by a
single—a song and dance man or woman, or instrumentalist—
any act that could be done in one to give the stagehands opportunity to reset. The next act, in full stage, was usually an
alley oop. Then back to a single, say a seriocomic in one, which
was followed by another sketch, generally a blackface comedy
in full stage. For the rest of the show an average bill would run
like this: a female song and dance single in one; a double
specialty, usually a musical, in full stage; a pedestal or straight
clog, or sand jig in one; a blackface song and dance team, full
stage; a protean man or woman or costume change act in one;
a juggler, full stage (the eighties audiences took their juggling
seriously); then an afterpiece, musical extravaganza, or drama,
with full company.

Even when the bill seemed interminable, asking a performer
to cut his act was a bid for mayhem; the drama that closed the
show had to take the beating. These dramas were mainly
standard plays—frequently lurid things of red fire and murder
or thwarted villainy in unhand-me-sir dialogue—hacked for
hour-or-less performance. Some of the plays reduced in
variety's crucible were "The Octaroon," "Streets of New
York," "The Avenger's Oath," and "The Cuban Spy,"
which had nothing to do with the Spanish-American War.
They were mostly produced by legit actors who never let their
disdain for vaudeville troupers interfere with the lucrative

business of variety production. Still, it was a good deal of a headache, for the producers had to depend on the variety performers for their casts—fine experience for the troupers, but not so good for the show.

The variety actors got nothing extra for their work in the dramas, but they were glad to play in them because they got "preference." As the legit producer traveled the country, playing halls anywhere, he was frequently consulted by managers with regard to their bills. In thumbing over an applicant's note he might remember that the man had given a good performance in "The Lights of London" in Ferranti's Theatre in New Orleans a month ago and recommend that he be booked. This is what the troupers meant by "preference." A number of the performers did play the dramatic roles quite acceptably and some of them went on to the legit stage where they became pronounced favorites, among them Tony Farrell, Pete Baker, and Gus Williams.

Song and dance acts predominated on the bills but there was such variety they hardly conflicted with one another. There were Dutch, Irish, blackface, whiteface, neat, rough, plantation, acrobatic, and "rival" song and dance teams and acts, all with varying technique and effectiveness according to the ability and personality of the actors.

"Sir! Explain Your Presence."

The "rival" song and dance acts are interesting because they were of a pattern, highly stylized, and depended upon clever lines and the ability of the performers. The "rival" act was a male team, usually working full stage with a set showing a cottage entrance, door, windows, et cetera. One of the team enters, and with jaunty step goes into his song and dance:

I just strolled out of town this summer's morning,
To see a darling who lives just over there (*pointing to cottage*).
She is a little fairy, blithe and airy,
With pearly teeth and sunny, golden hair. . . .

At finish of chorus, one dance step, break (a "break" is four bars of music at the end of a step and done in the same time as the song; the music and dance continue, but the singer does not sing), walks to the cottage door, raps, and exits through door as partner (rival) appears from opposite stage entrance.

Rival (*same business*) sings:

> I wonder who that fellow was I saw here,
> No sooner had I seen him he was gone.
> He comes to court my darling little Vivian,
> And sneaks about so early in the morn. . . .

Then one step, break. After the break the rival proceeds to the cottage, enters, and crash, pistol shot, general commotion offstage. Directly after, one man comes hurtling through the cottage door, the other dives through the breakaway window. They face each other, and one says, "I thought you were her father." The other replies, "Why, I thought you were." Then:

FIRST RIVAL: Then since you're not her father I'll forgive you,
                If your presence here and conduct you'll explain.

SECOND RIVAL: I came to court my darling little Vivian,
                She's the prettiest little darling of the name.

BOTH: Then since our hopes seem now to have been
                    blighted,
                Let us take each other by the hand.
                Nevermore again let us quarrel,
                But we'll give the girl the shake, you understand.

Chorus, then four to five steps together, then dance off. Among the superlative performers of "rival" acts were Mackin and Wilson (Francis Wilson who became a legitimate comic star), and Welsh and Rice.

There were also grotesque song and dance acts—umbrella stunts, fan stuff (no infringement on Sally Rand's). All were different, and that of Charlie Dimond, a soft-shoe while playing the harp, was not only the first of its kind, but outstanding. Dimond danced to his own music which he played on a harp slung over his shoulder. The harp was a small instrument known as a "C harp" and without pedals.

The Banjo Players.

No bill of the seventies and eighties or, for that matter, well on into the nineties, was standard without a banjo player. The banjo's brilliant staccato note was superbly adapted to lively tunes for jigs, clogs, solo, and general dancing; it was an excellent prop for comics, and as a portable instrument convenient for use anywhere—in specialties, interludes, or afterpieces—it was unsurpassed.

Although research into the origin of the banjo is not complete, it is reasonably established that its beginnings were not African, as many suppose. Instruments consisting of a frame or gourd or wooden bowl, over which were stretched goat, sheep, calf, or snake skins or bull hide, spanned by strings of fiber or intestines, have been found among relics of savage tribes in every continent. A man named Sweeney, a native of Virginia, is generally credited with developing the instrument to its style and range as variety knew it. His claim is pretty well substantiated by old-timers who have heard his name bandied about the halls for years.

It was Sweeney who added the fifth, or thumb, string. In our time this feature has been junked by the jazz players, but the early variety instrumentalists used it effectively until the banjo was almost completely revamped by experimenting manufacturers who thought of frets for the neck and a gadget for keeping the headskin tight. Thinner strings also were introduced. The improvements bothered the old-timers no end. But enterprising performers, realizing the potentialities of the new instrument, mastered its technique and began playing standard music in accomplished renditions in what became known as "guitar," or "operatic," style. One of the first—and finest—performers on the "new" banjo was E. M. Hall, a favorite for years in variety theaters, whose tragic death in the Chicago

Iroquois Theater fire was deeply mourned. Earlier players with pronounced followings were the Bohee Brothers, Horace Weston, Jack Keating, and Harry Van Fossen, all straight soloists who left comedy to the comedians. But there were a number of good players who varied their strumming with comedy (mostly joke telling) and some of these were Sam Devere, Lew Brimmer, John Carl, and Billy Carter who was perhaps the best of the comedy-banjoists. Billy, who played the halls for half a century, was adept at the topical gag and enjoyed ribbing drunks and politicians in a manner unusual in the seventies.

Many today will recall Sam Devere but not, it is an even wager, as a vaudeville soloist. Somehow variety always seemed to irk Sam and he soon quit to enter burlesque. His billing, "Sam Devere's Own Show," topping a bevy of ham-buttocked blondes, is a rose-colored flashback over the years.

John Carl was a curious performer. After a few bars of banjo music he would stop suddenly and recite, of all things, passages from Shakespeare. Then he would go into a song, cease again, and deliver more Shakespeare. He never explained this juxtaposition but veterans say his recitations were splendid. Throughout his playing time he was identified with a silly song, "The Lively Flea." Its chorus:

> Feeding where no life may be,
> A dainty old chap is the lively flea.
> Feeding where no life may be,
> A dainty old chap is the lively flea.

It was constantly demanded by audiences. Carl always obliged —and concluded with Shakespeare.

Threnody with Red Fire.

One of the cleverest of the banjo entertainers was Ned Oliver. He wrote most of his own songs and played accompaniments for them. Like most of the others, he was self-taught. There was virtually no instruction to be had from either books or teachers and performers learned from each other or practiced things out by themselves. Oliver drifted into the medicine show business and became manager of one of the largest and best shows of its kind. He was billed as "Nevada Ned, the King of Gold."

In 1878 Rollin Howard, an old-time variety female impersonator, managed the Melodion Novelty Theatre in Philadelphia. Oliver, a young performer then, frequently played the house in the closing dramas and Howard, liking the young chap, wrote a sketch in which they were to appear together. Now, the Melodion had been an old dyeworks that was converted into a theater as cheaply as possible and most of its appointments were primitive even for those days. A door in the rear wall of the stage opened on the toilet, a wooden affair with two-customer capacity. The door was utilized in many ways. If a garden scene was set, a house was painted around the door, which served as an entrance to the cottage, mansion, cabin, whatever. The meanest feature of the contraption was that if an actor had to make his entrance from, say, the plantation owner's mansion, he had to remain in the toilet until his cue. An automatic closing arrangement for the door was fashioned of a rope over a pulley with a brickbat tied to the end of the rope. This was the setup for the sketch Howard wrote for himself and Oliver which he called, "The South Carolina Home." Oliver played the old slave returning to his former master, with Howard, the plantation owner, awaiting his cue in the toilet. To slow music, Oliver, as an old, rheumatic darky, limps on:

OLIVER: There's the ol' mansion, jest the same as wen I lef' it twenty-two years ago. Didn't think Ah'd evah live to see mah ol' home agin. 'Spose all the chillen is married an' grown up—some gone to see their Maker where Ah's goin' mahself befoh long. These ol' bones won't support me much longer, Ah know. (*His foot touches something and he looks down to see what it is*) Goodness me! There's a banjo a layin' on the grass. Looks lak one I used to own long befoh Ah lef' the old plantation. (*Picks up banjo and examines*

it) Why, it's mah ol' banjo been lyin' there evah since Ah lef'
(*This banjo's been lying in the grass for twenty-two years, but when he
picks it up it's in perfect tune. He sits in chair and plays and sings an
interminable piece of doggerel the chorus of which went*):

> Don't talk of 'mancipation proclamation unto me.
> Ah was happier in slavery than Ah been since
> Ah been free.
> The slavery days the happiest days of any unto me,
> In mah good old cabin home in South Ca'lina.

(*After the song Oliver feels a fainting spell coming on. He gets up from
chair, staggers a few steps toward right first entrance, and speaks*)

OLIVER: I feel mighty queer. Legs gittin' mighty weak. Kinda
can't see good wiv mah eyes. Maybe mah time is a-comin'. But
I hope Ah don' go till Ah see ol' massa once more. (*Lies down on
grass near right first entrance*)

HOWARD (*entering from toilet*): I thought I heard some one walking
in my garden. I see no one here. (*Looks round stage, sees Oliver*)
Why, it's an old darky. (*Bends over Oliver*) Why, as I live it's my
old slave Pete. (*Kneels and raises old Pete's head*)

OLIVER: Yes, massa. Ah's yo' ol' slave Pete, come home to die.

HOWARD: Oh, Pete, Pete. Try and rally. Look at me. Look at me,
Pete. (*Pete sinks back*) He's gone! Gone beyond those beautiful
gates ajar. (*Pointing rear and upward*)

Now, this should have been the cue for the song and dance
men, the seriocomics, jugglers, acrobats, or whoever happened
to be standing in the wings, to oblige, offstage, with "Sweet
Bye and Bye." Instead, the door of the toilet swung open
giving a full view of the interior. At this point the property
man held up a huge shovelful of red fire in the wings. (Red
fire was used in those days for the climax of almost anything.)
It lit up the toilet so that it became the brightest spot on the
stage, and a man in the audience, carried away by the stark
realism, yelled, "Jesus! The privy's on fire!"

The curtain rolled slowly down. Howard sprang up in a
frenzy. "Who took the brick off that privy?" he shouted. "I'll
fire him this minute, I don't care a damn who he is. Here Mr.

Oliver and myself have labored to make a perfect production, and now the illusion is dispelled because some dirty bum took the brick off that privy." As a matter of fact, it was an accident. The old rope had gradually separated strand by strand. It was just unfortunate that the last strand gave way in the death scene.

Al Reeves, who enjoyed an immense following, was poison to the other banjoists who regarded with suspicion the medals he displayed for excellency in playing. He always billed himself as the world's greatest banjoist and used an instrument that would have adorned the Taj Mahal—it was of gold and set with precious stones. No one ever disputed his title as world's champion—maybe he was. His technique when playing with orchestra, as analyzed by an old-time player (and possibly biased), was to obtain a fine, full orchestral arrangement of a popular march, then thump along bravely, allowing the orchestra to carry the load while he banged a series of loud chords. But he was right up there with the thimble for a noisy finale.

As the banjo grew in popularity a number of performers took it up seriously and some fine artists developed. Some of the early straight players were Tommy Glenn, the Kine Brothers, and Jack Keating. In turn, these gave way to Polk and Collins, the Howard Brothers, Claudius and Scarlet, the Carmen Sisters, and the Tobin Sisters. One of the greatest players was Ernie Forrest, who, about 1900 as a boy prodigy, gave such selections as "The Gypsy Rondo" and "Poet and Peasant" while blindfolded—in a manner to start the audience dancing.

A favorite for years, the banjo as the old-timers knew it never became practical in orchestras. With the tuning in thirds it was difficult to play. This led, some twenty years ago or about the beginning of jazz, to tuning in fifths. Soon wire strings were substituted for the old gut strings because wire could stand better the wear and tear of the pick or plectrum which the jazz boys brought into use. They also shortened the neck and did away with the fifth, or thumb, string. This made the fingering like that of a cello and the instrument was ready for regularly written orchestral parts. Developments proceeded, and today we have the banjo mandolin, the banjorine, the banjo guitar, the tenor banjo, in all sizes and shapes. They sound all right, but modernization for a strident age has robbed the banjo of much of its character.

Afterpieces—and Other
Lost Acts

THE twenty years say from 1870 to 1890 were the heydays of the afterpieces, those interludes, "stalls in one" (to give time to reset the stage), or closing comedies in which all the performers in the olio appeared.

Necessarily simple, the afterpieces were fashioned about stock situations, invariably ad-libbed or improvised and exist now only as vague and scattered dialogue in the minds of the oldest troupers. One of the most popular was "Sim Dimpsey." It was not strictly an afterpiece but a "stall." Yet it followed the afterpiece formula nearly enough and could run, according to the ad-libbing abilities of the performers, as long as fifteen minutes.

An excellent illustration of the tendency of the eighties toward ridiculous plays upon words and phrases and the exaction of comedy from absurd misconstructions is shown in "Three O'Clock Train." This was a standard blackface afterpiece and it embodies better than any other old-timers can remember the comedy incidental to the then prevailing notion that ghosts were also an essence of humor.

THE THREE O'CLOCK TRAIN

The interior a wretched set; two chairs and an old banjo are the only props in a bare and dingy room, which appears in half-light

47

and is sinisterly suggestive. The two characters are a straight man and an eccentric comic—long coat, umbrella, absurd little hat, and fright wig. At rise straight man enters, seats himself and dejectedly scans letters he carries in hand.

STRAIGHT MAN: If I didn't have this hang-out here I don't know what I'd do. I get the place rent free because the landlord thinks it is haunted. (*Inevitable knock*) Come in. (*Enter comic*)

COMIC (*exaggerated Negro dialect*): Good mawnin'. I just stopped in for some information.

STRAIGHT: I'll try to accommodate you. What is it?

COMIC: What time does the three o'clock train go out?

STRAIGHT: The three o'clock train? Why, it goes out exactly sixty minutes past two o'clock.

COMIC: That's funny. The man at the station told me it went out exactly sixty minutes before four o'clock.

STRAIGHT: Well, you won't miss your train, anyway.

COMIC: No, well, I'm much obliged. (*Exits*)

STRAIGHT: Curious sort of chap. (*Picks up banjo and strums quietly as comic reenters*)

COMIC: Excuse me, which is the other side of the street?

STRAIGHT: Why, the other side of the street is just across the way.

COMIC: That's funny. I asked the fellow across the street and he said it was over here.

STRAIGHT: Well, you can't depend on everything you hear.

COMIC: No, that's so.

STRAIGHT: Well, you've got plenty of time to make your train. Sit down a while.

COMIC (*seating himself, and scanning the wretched room*): Nice place you have here. Nice comfortable place.

STRAIGHT: Yes, I get the place for a very reasonable rent. Know why I get it so cheaply?

COMIC: You don't pay the rent.

STRAIGHT: No, no. It's because the place is haunted. (*Comic looks round uneasily*)

STRAIGHT: But you're not afraid of ghosts?

COMIC: Oh, no. I'm not afraid of ghosts. My grandmother used to keep a ghost boardinghouse. Some of my best friends are ghosts. (*Looks nervously around*)

STRAIGHT: Well, I'm glad to hear that because this house is full of ghosts.

COMIC: When do the, that is, when, er, where are they, these, er . . . ?

STRAIGHT: Oh, they're liable to come in any time.

COMIC (*shuddering*): Right in here?

STRAIGHT: Oh, yes, right in here. They just waft in and waft right out again.

COMIC: They, they waft, do they? (*Looks round uneasily*)

STRAIGHT: What's the matter?

COMIC: I thought something was wafting.

STRAIGHT: Well, you wouldn't care, would you?

COMIC (*with exaggeration*): Oh, no. I wouldn't care.

STRAIGHT: Like to hear a good song?

COMIC: Yes, I always liked music. Something lively.

STRAIGHT: All right, I'll sing you a good lively song.

COMIC: Something to cheer us up?

STRAIGHT: Oh, yes. Something very cheerful. (*Sings, in dismal wail*)

> The old jaw bone on the alm's house wall.
> It hung fifty years on that whitewashed wall.
> It was grimy and gray, and covered with gore,
> Like the souls of the sinners who'd passed there before.

> CHORUS: Oh, the old jaw bone, the old jaw bone, etc.

(*Chains rattle and weird noises are heard backstage as stage lights dim. Comic shivers in terror*)

STRAIGHT: What's the matter with you?

COMIC: Oh, nothing. Nothing at all. I'm just enjoying the music. That's a nice lively song.

STRAIGHT: Oh, wait till you hear the second verse. (*Sings, still in dismal wail*)

> At twelve o'clock near the hour of one,
> A figure appears that will strike you dumb.
> He grabs you by the hair of the head,
> And he grabs you about until you are dead.

(*Off-stage noises and wails. Straight Man rises and ghost enters and Straight Man exits, singing*)

> Oh, the old jaw bone . . .

(Ghost slithers to chair vacated by Straight Man and sits beside Comic unknown to him because he has not seen the entrance)

COMIC *(still unaware of ghost):* Why not sing something we both know? We'll sing it together. Yours is a good song but I don't like the way it ends. *(Ghost nudges Comic)*

COMIC: I wasn't asleep. I was just listening to the music. Is it most time for them ghosts to waft? *(He looks casually to one side and sees part of white sheet. He follows his glance, takes in ghost completely, and rises, horrified, as ghost rises with him. He pulls the string of his fright wig and hair stands straight up. Recovering somewhat, Comic edges away and then dashes round stage and ghost, his finger pointing at Comic, pursues. As ghost gradually gains on Comic, Comic exits, diving through breakaway window)*

CURTAIN

The afterpiece seems at best to have been a makeshift for resetting the stage or for gathering all the performers on full stage, a bit of theater technique that endures today in the ensemble finales of our musicals, for example. The development of vaudeville into a specific form of entertainment naturally accented the clever performer, the artist, who rebelled against a recall that would link him with the lesser members of the cast; and when the headline and feature acts became definite in the billing, as they did in the nineties, the afterpiece declined rapidly, soon dropped out altogether, and shows closed with an alley oop or dumb act or a Biograph short.

Exit—Smiling.

Along with the afterpieces, other novelty acts popular in the seventies and nineties fell by the wayside and are lost now except as sealed in the memories of the oldest troupers. The disappearance of some is inexplicable, for, according to firsthand descriptions, some of them were remarkable. The legmania act, for example, of the The Majiltons. (Legmania is a precise form of eccentric dancing emphasizing high kicking.) This, probably the first act of its kind in America, comprised

two men and one woman and was called "A Study in Points."
The eyebrows of the men were pointed, their wigs were pointed
three ways, the lobes of their ears were artificially pointed, as
were their artificial noses, mustaches, and goatees. Their
high-standing collars had long points, the lapels and tails of
their cutaway coats were pointed, and so were their vests.
They wore black tights and long pointed dancing shoes. It was
a spectacular act requiring a full stage set with a grand staircase. At rise they made their entrance down the staircase, the
woman between the men, descending a step at a time, the men
nonchalantly lifting their legs over the head of the woman in
rhythm to the music. Their splits and high kicks were effortless; in fact, their movement was more a loft than a kick. At
stage they went into a sort of three-hand reel—a grotesque
performance.

A standard act, forgotten by the 1900's, was "the flying
perch," a difficult trapeze act that differed from the "balancing perch" in that the flying perch was suspended in front of
the proscenium arch and not over the stage. It was risky
because it endangered not only the performer but a person or
persons in the audience or the orchestra. Probably the most
noted of the flying perch performers was Charles Lane, billed
as M. Charles, who ascended to the perch by means of a rope.
There he would accomplish all the posings, gyrations, and
hazardous positions, frequently sliding to and fro from the
extreme edges of the trapeze, effecting a balance which, if
lost, would have landed him on the orchestra leader.

A double aerial parallel bars act, "l'Eschelle," was also
comparatively short-lived. It was a breath-taking novelty, and
since when have breath-taking novelties failed in interest?
This act should not be confused with horizontal bars. In
l'Eschelle the bars were suspended high over the proscenium arch and the performers (usually two) dropped from the
upper to the lower bars, swung from their hocks, caught each
other on the swing, performed handstands, shoulder rolls, and
spine-chilling drops. A popular l'Eschelle act that played all

the variety halls in the seventies and eighties was the Costello Brothers. They made up as demons and worked with lightning rapidity.

A score of unusual dances were prominent in the seventies, among them egg dance acts, the spade dance, and the transformation dance. The transformation dance was especially popular and variations of it continued well into the present century, but the original was never resumed. It was invariably performed by a woman in layers of costumes manipulated by "strip" strings reaching into the wings and worked from backstage. Its customary routine required the woman to appear first in military uniform. She did a drill with a gun, marching about the stage, and at a signal the handler pulled the strip string. This released the costume, revealing her before the astonished audience before whom she would appear as a washerwoman performing an Irish jig. Another pull on the strip string—presto!—short skirts and a skipping-rope dance. Another jerk and she was a policeman strutting about the stage, singing a song. In the later eighties and nineties this act, with variations, was developed into a routine by male performers. Robert Fulgora, billed as "Trebor, the Man of Mystic Changes," improved it considerably, and years later, in fact, well into our time, the Great Lafayette adapted it for his full troupe.

The sand jig routine hasn't been done for thirty years. During the introduction by the orchestra the performer entered, right or left, carrying a metal or cardboard cornucopia holding about a pint of fine sand. After the sand was sprinkled about the front of the stage the container was thrown off in the entrance. The music was in 4-4 time, accented like a ballroom schottische. The dancing, all on the balls of the feet, was done in shuffles and slides instead of taps. The soles of the shoes were thin and hard, and the dancer, shifting and digging in the sand, produced a sharp, staccato sound which could be doubled and tripled at will. Like all seemingly effortless presentations, it was difficult. Probably the greatest sand jigger of vaudeville was Kitty O'Neill, who flourished in the beer halls during the seventies and eighties.

Sand Jig:

As used by Kitty O'Neill, Jerry Crotty, and other artists.

The egg dance was a fill-in turn, usually performed by a woman. The dancer entered and placed some twenty eggs, grouped rather closely, about the stage. She then dipped and hopped and pirouetted among them, bowed winsomely, and exited. At the applause she would return and purposely break a couple to show that they were real.

The spade dance was performed with a prop of hard wood fashioned like a spade. The dancer grasped the handle with both hands, stood on the spade portion, or blade, and hopped about on it to lively strains from the orchestra and in strict rhythm. Its method of use was similar to that of a pogo stick. The routine was completed by hopping over various objects— a row of bottles or improvised hurdles, sometimes over tall lighted candles.

An early tank act that beguiled the variety audiences of the seventies anticipated Annette Kellerman by some thirty-five years. Its exponent was a man named Blatz who billed himself as "The Human Fish." Completely submerged, he would eat a banana, play the slide trombone, apparently go to sleep after reading a newspaper, and remain under water a remarkable length of time. The trombone bell extended out of the water but the slide was not affected because it was airtight (as it must be in this instrument), and consequently watertight. Veteran performers insist that the act was genuine.

Gone—and Forgotten.

A fine bill could be assembled from the acts that lasted but ten or a dozen years and then dropped out, for apparently no reason. Some of them were funny, a few were grotesque, all were novelties. It is possible their novelty grew threadbare, but the larrikin audiences of the seventies and eighties were far from fussy.

Hernandez, for example. He was a guitar player, really sensational. He made up in black tights, blackface, and wore a curious wig that ran to a point. While playing the most difficult numbers, he performed all sorts of contortions, and as he executed a chromatic run he'd extend his neck nearly a foot and then let his head sink down slowly into his shoulders. He also played a fiddle made of a tomato can and a long broom handle, a comic routine in which he tangled his legs with the broom handle, tripping himself to the floor of the stage, then doing a neat nip-up, without losing the tune.

The bounding rope act was always sure-fire. It was sometimes called the tight rope—an error. The bounding rope was a two-inch cable supported by jacks at either extremity and drawn to the proper tautness with a ratchet. The performer danced on the rope, using a balance pole to maintain equilibrium, executed somersaults, half turns, bounds into the air, turns over the balance pole, then flopped on his buttocks, rebounded to a standing posture, never losing equilibrium. For some reason it was usually done in jockey costume, but the outstanding performer, Juan Caicedo, a squat Mexican, worked in native costume, plus spurs. The spurs were supposed to make his act more difficult; in reality they made it easier. If he felt himself off center he had only to hook a spur on to the rope—just the slightest touch, but it steadied him.

Hat spinners were favorites. They usually worked in pairs in clown make-up. They spun hats rapidly by beating the edges with a long, slender stick and managed to keep them in air, tossing them back and forth, while they themselves went through all kinds of difficult contortions, such as standing on the backs of chairs and tipping them so as to balance on the two hind legs.

The Civil War was just behind and military acts were popular. One of these was a spinning act, though not comparable with that of the hat spinners. Captain McCrosson, the gun spinner, had been a Zouave in the Civil War and always appeared in a Zouave uniform. His was a wild, exuberant act, a good deal on the nut side. He began with a lightning drill in the manual of arms, then went into the bayonet drill— right, left, in the rear, defense against infantry, defense against cavalry. Then he tossed the gun into the air, whirling and spinning it like a drum major's baton. He balanced it on his chin with the bayonet down; spun it, point down, on the palm of his hand; and finished with a volley of shots and a whirl of the gun over his head and around his body.

Other novelties that passed were bone solo acts, "Masks and Faces" and "Talking Hand" acts. Bone solos were skilled manipulation of four pieces of bone, two in each hand. The best were not really bone but lignum vitae which was clear and loud in tone—or perhaps sound is the word. The premier performer was Oliver Wingate. Clinking his bones in either hand he would follow the orchestra with all kinds of obligatos, rolls, and taps and then give imitations of a man sawing wood, a bootblack shining shoes, a cobbler hammering soles and drawing waxed threads as he sewed. He could tone them to a whisper, then bring them up fortissimo. A favorite imitation that he did superbly was of the race between Goldsmith Maid and Dexter, famous trotters of the period. Dexter's time was 2.40 and the Maid was right up there. After a hush, Wingate would proceed to the footlights and announce, "Gents, my right hand is Goldsmith Maid and my left is Dexter. They're off!" After the start he would increase the speed and cry out, "the quarter," then "the half," and "the stretch—Dexter wins." A fortissimo chord from the orchestra, bow, and get off.

"Masks and Faces" was an act in which oil paintings from which the faces had been cut out were used. They were of historical figures and the performer, in proper make-up, would stick his face in the hole where the features had been and assume the character of the portrait. These were always cued by the orchestra. Among the characters portrayed were Daniel O'Connell, Lincoln, and Grant. The inevitable closing was Washington to the tune of "The Star-Spangled Banner."

The "Talking Hand" was one of the craziest of the novelties. An expert performer was a motto singer named Jesse D. Silva who, when playing a Philadelphia free-and-easy managed by Arthur Chambers, an English lightweight pugilist, used it as an effective encore. It was done with a hood and dress, or costume, or bandanna, draped over the hand which was painted to resemble a face. Eyes were painted above the knuckles of two fingers and the thumb served as the lower part of the mouth into which a pipe, if the "impersonation" was of a man, could be thrust. To heighten the effect the pipe was lighted and kept smoking by pressure on a bulb concealed by the performer.

The popular sketch pantomimes of the seventies faded, too, as diapered variety donned the pants of "polite" vaudeville. They were spectacular, required a full stage, and for those days were scenically splendiferous.

As done in American halls they were a bastard adaptation of the French Harlequin and Columbine pantomime; indeed, used those two characters with Clown, Pantaloon, and sometimes Dame Trot, an old woman; or a sailor boy for a sweetheart. One form of this sketch showed a village street, the back set with a bank which bordered a river curtain. On one side of the stage was a cobbler at work, on the other an undertaker. A tailorshop and a fruit stand were in rear, a spinning wheel upstage. Clown and Pantaloon enter and steal fruit from the stand. Then they go into the tailorshop but the tailor chases them, brandishing a hot (tailor's) goose. Harlequin and Columbine enter and Columbine goes into a dance. Both exit and reappear in a boat which seemingly floats down-river in rear upstage. Clown and Pantaloon reenter. Pantaloon indicates he has an idea and they tiptoe to the undertaker's shop and steal a coffin which they place in the "water." They pull the wheel from the spinning wheel and split it in two, making two wheels which they attach to each side of the coffin. They take a keg from the fruit stand and lay it in the middle for a boiler and on top affix a length of stovepipe. Breaking up the rest of the spinning wheel for wood, they toss the wreckage under the keg and presently smoke issues from the stove pipe. Clown and Pantaloon get into the coffin-boat. The wheels revolve, and off they go in the direction of Harlequin and Columbine. The act ran about twenty minutes and was full of action.

One of the great scenery-chewers of the seventies was "The London Ghost Show"; this survived in later vaudeville (burlesque too) in a derivation called "Living Pictures." It was done in the seventies with a large plate glass which leaned at a 45-degree angle over a pit lined with black velvet. One or more characters worked on the stage, the others in the pit. Because of the reflection in the glass (it was not a mirror), those in the pit were seemingly performing at stage level. By clever manipulation of lights—extraordinary if you recall the crude gaslights of the period—the figures in the pit could be made to appear, disappear, fade, or float away during the performance. It was generally dramatic, full of fur-collar lines. Usually at rise it revealed a middle-aged man who apparently had been a wastrel. "Ah, me, another day of toil is o'er. In the east the struggling vapors bid me to hie home. Ah, home, did I say? 'Tis but a rude hut by the mountainside, where the winds and the rains find entrance at every crevice.

Why am I doomed to this lonely life? Why did I forsake my mother? In the lone watches of the night I fancy I see her before me—calling, calling me by name. 'Ah! My dear boy!' " (Mother appears and talks back to him.) "Mother!" he yells. Then a sister appears, chiding; or maybe the wife he has wronged. He rushes to clasp his mother. She fades and he rants all over the stage. "'Tis nothing but a dream. Am I losing my mind?" Thunder sheet sounds. Red fire and lightning flash. He defies the storm, is struck by lightning. Dies. Curtain.

A performer whose name nobody can recall had an act called "The Cat Piano." It comprised a number of live cats confined in narrow boxes with wire netting on the front ends. Artificial tails extended from the rear. This performer was a marvelous cat imitator and miaowed the "Miserere" by pulling the cats' tails. Spits, snarls, and plaintive mews added to the effect of the back-fence serenade.

Last of the "Lost" Acts.

Fleury was an old English character actor who finished his act with a dance in Turkish costume. Across his shoulders he wore a long cape and at the climax of his dance he tossed it up so that it would settle upon his head in the form of a huge turban, exposing his bare chest and stomach. The nipples on his breast were painted to resemble large eyes. A nose was painted below them and his navel represented a puckered mouth. Fleury would conclude his dance, working his stomach and chest muscles to achieve effects amazing in their bizarre grimaces.

This act, or rather the chest and stomach part of it, was revived in our time by Frank Tinney in a number called "Whistling Sam" which he performed in one of Earl Carroll's "Vanities." Tinney made his navel whistle. At one performance Leslie Howard was his unwitting stooge, it being part of Tinney's technique to rib his audience, and the bigger they came the better he liked it. And wouldn't Howard ball up the act with characteristic British naïveté! "Now you ask me," said Tinney to Howard who was sitting in a stage box, "why is an old maid like a green tomater?" And the affable Howard repeated, "Why is an old maid like a green tomahto?" The gag of course was muffed, Tinney's comeback line being, "Because it's hard to mate her."

Well, exhibitionism is no one decade's vice, and it is interesting in retrospect—and somewhat chastening?—to consider with what fine vigor the seventies and eighties tilted a putty nose and cocked a thumb to it. Any Hollywood yes man in a midtown New York restaurant can shade the antics of Fleury with a portable hand-set telephone. Yet not in Hollywood have we anything to compare with the cluster of nut Hamlets that beguiled the honky-tonk variety halls of the seventies. The troupers called them "bughouse Hamlets." Two prime Bellevue exponents of the Bard's melancholy baby were Count Johannes and James Owen O'Connor. Little is known of this pair except that they were pretty awful. But, thank God, there is a fat paragraph about Dr. Landis.

Landis's origin is obscure, and the "Dr." doubtless self-bestowed. He imagined he was the greatest Hamlet that ever lived and so billed himself when he hired a hall and produced the play at his own expense. It was wonderful. He looked like one of the Smith Brothers, playing the youthful prince in a full beard and black tights. The performance (it was in Philadelphia in the early seventies) achieved wide notoriety and the manager of Enoch's Varieties, fully alive to its possibilities, propositioned Landis for a week's engagement. The doc agreed, but seems not to have been able to recruit his original cast, who were probably amateurs anyway. So, abetted by the manager, he assembled a cast from the variety bill at Enoch's and what followed must be the most outstanding performance the Bard ever obtained, and he has had some wonders. A Dutch comic by the name of Larry Tooley played the first gravedigger, reciting his lines in dialect and shoveling up in his big scene a lot of tin cans and beer bottles. Alas, indeed, poor Yorick! Jack Murphy played the ghost in a soldier's coat and a brass-band helmet. One of the wine-room girls played Ophelia. It was a riot and Landis became as notorious as the Cherry Sisters in later years. Toward the end of his career, which was too, too brief, a net was placed in front of the performers, to shield them, as Mark Twain once said, from an outraged audience.

Racial Comics of the Eighties

THE melting pot in America has almost finished its alloy and racial-type comedy is rapidly passing. In pictures Chico Marx's Italian clowning is current and Herman Bing chokes his dialect in the bits to which Hollywood assigns him. On the radio Jack Pearl enjoyed a profitable semester with his "Vass you dere, Sharlie?" and even Weber and Fields were taken on to broadcast a thirteen weeks' revival of Mike and Meyer, which was subsequently albumed by the nostalgic screen. But on the whole our present tendency has been to resist racial characterization. There are few character parts left—almost none in the legitimate theater where comedy is now given mostly to name players for the exploitation of their personal humors; the burlesque of contemporary types; situation laughter; topical razzes and smutty or sophisticated gags.

It was different in the eighties. Most of the comedy of the early variety theater was racial. What we are pleased to call American stock predominated, and to rib the Irish, the German, or the Negro was but to thrust at a minority which generally took the jibes good-naturedly. To be sure, the Russell Brothers, whose Irish servant girls were a famous rough act, were occasionally egged by their enthusiastic cousins (as was Synge's beautiful play of Irish peasantry, "The Playboy of the Western World"), but these instances were rare.

Irish acts predominated, blackface ran a close second, and Dutch, or German, dialect made an important third. For a robust age, robust comedy, and the sons of Erin, as naturals or in character, threw it at our grandfathers with slapstick, bladder, and fist. Moreover, their songs were the most puissant in theatrical history and may well have been the handiwork of some backroom bard inshpired be a dhrap wi' th' bhoys. As topical as they were belligerent, they offer one of the most delightful footnotes in the minnesinging annals of America. Although in essence as Irish as Shannon, here they were written, here they were acclaimed. Whoever the minstrels, they wasted no substance on June-moon rhymes. It is an interesting fact, revealing, too, in characterizing the audiences, that the early variety Irish songs are almost devoid of romantic reference. On their vigor and thrust, Eire's native melodies, for the most part maudlin sentimentalities, are impaled.

Dinegals and Galway Sluggers.

Perhaps the toughest, and accordingly one of the most popular, of the early Irish teams was Needham and Kelly who did a wooden-shoe song and dance act. They made up in Prince Albert coats, pants of different colors, weather-beaten plug hats, and short side whiskers known as "Dinegals." One of their songs, "The Gas House Tarriers," should convey an idea of their act: a magnificent fugue for a Saturday night brawl. But the favorite with the seventies and eighties stag audiences was "The Roving Irish Gents":

Oh we are two rollicking roving Irish gentlemen,
In the Pennsylvania quarries we belong.
For a month or so we're working out in Idaho,
For a month or so we're strikin' rather strong.
Oh, we helped to build the elevated railway,
On the steamboats we ran for many a day.
And it's divvil a hair we care the kind of work we do,
If every Saturday night we get our pay. Right there. (*Hands out*)

Chorus: We can dig a sewer, lay a pipe or carry the hod.
In the western states our principles are strong,
We're the advocates of all hard workin' men,
And if that's the case you cannot say we're wrong.
Are we right?
(*Walk around and repeat chorus, then into a dance*)

Roving Irish Gentlemen

Needham and Kelly usually followed this with a waltz clog
or a burlesque sparring match. "Burlesque" is scarcely the

word. It would make some of New York's Madison Square Garden bouts look like (what they sometimes are) a ballet.

Another rough Irish song and dance act were the two lads, Kelly and Ryan, who, made up as coal heavers carrying scoop shovels, billed themselves as "The Bards of Tara." In those days (maybe today in the mining sections) a coal heaver was called a "spooner," probably because of the type of shovel he used. Thus the featured song of Kelly and Ryan was called "The Lackawanna Spooners":

> Here we are, two Lackawanna spooners,
> While we're here just cast your eyes upon us.
> We unload coal boats from Towanda to Gowanus,
> We're the two selected spooners of the gang.
> When we go home our families we embrace,
> We eat our meals with elegance and grace,
> With opposition shovellers we long to have a race—
> We're the two selected spooners of the gang.

(*Two steps of an Irish reel done in heavy clogs, then eight bars walk around and second verse*)

The Lackawanna Spooners

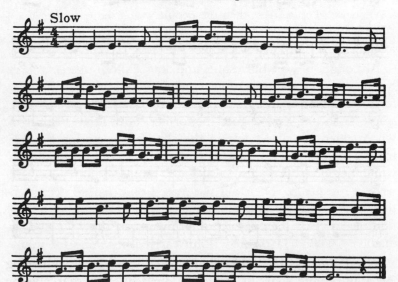

A popular Irish act of the period was Bradford and Delaney's, who varied their routine with costume changes that in those days, for that type of act, were novel. They opened as two old women selling apples and went into a bit of patter of the tongue-twisting kind—"of all the pears that ever I pared I never saw a pear to compare with the pair of pears I just pared." Then into an Irish jig, dancing so briskly the apples bounced out of their baskets. Dance off, quick change into hod carriers, and enter, singing:

Our family name is Carey, so happy light and airy,
We came from Tipperary so far across the sea, my boys.
We've struck a job so handy, with the shovel we're the dandies;
We are true sons of Erin's Isle. (*Break*)

Six weeks ago we struck this country;
Now we have an easy job.
For the man up top does all the labor,
And we do nothing but carry up the hod.

We're two Irish Knights of Labor,
And we're members of the order called the Sons of Toil.
When we're on a strike then the people watch the ruction,
For it's then we give them a sample of our style.
(Heavy reel and dance off)

Although it was burlesque and knockabout, these rough humors and characterizations conveyed nation-wide the misfortunes of the scullery side of metropolitan living. Another single Irish act, and a good performer, was Tony Farrell to whom reference was made in the chapter on closing dramas from which Farrell graduated to the legitimate stage, and on which he played romantic Irish leads. John and Harry Kernell were a fine team. Their act was based on crossfire conversation, ludicrous misunderstandings, and arguments. For a number of years they put out their own road show which was dissolved when Harry died. John carried on alone for many years as a single in variety with jokes, satire, and comic epitaphs. He died suddenly in Detroit at the close of the war.

Rooney and Rogers.

There were two outstanding Irish singles who relied more on jauntincss, originality, and charm. They were Pat Rooney (father of Pat Rooney II and grandfather of Pat Rooney III) and Tim Rogers. In his first routine Rooney appeared in cutaway coat with tight sleeves, fancy waistcoat, pants with large plaid checks, a plug hat of quaint model, and all-round whiskers called "Galway sluggers." In this costume he sang "Owen Riley," "The Day I Played Baseball," "The Sound Democrat," and the highly popular "Biddy the Ballet Girl":

> I am a day laboring man,
> I have a beautiful daughter.
> She never cared much for to work,
> 'Twas her mother's own wish that she'd oughter.
> Somehow she took to the stage,
> So I granted my daughter's request,
> And now she's a great ballet dancer,
> And dances along with the rest.

> CHORUS: On the stage she is Mamselle La Shorty,
> Her right name is Bridget McCarthy.
> She comes at night and from matinees,
> With baskets of flowers and little bouquets . . .
> She's me only daughter,
> And I am the man that taught her,
> To wear spangled clothes
> And flip 'round on her toes,
> Oh, the pride of the ballet is Biddy.
> (*Sixteen bars waltz clog done in ballet style*)

> Last Saturday night I got paid,
> I thought I'd go to the theayter,
> And take the old woman along,
> In the parquette in front I did sate her.
> When Biddy came out on the stage,
> My son Terrence was up in the tier.
> He cried—sister Biddy, go in—but
> They waltzed Terry out on his ear.
> (*Several steps waltz clog ballet style and dance off*)

Biddy the Ballet Girl

As sung by Pat Rooney 1st

Then Rooney would change to knee pants, sack coat, ballet shirt, flowing tie, soft hat and go into a deft song and dance such as "Pretty Peggy" or "Katy Ryan," both of which are still used as instrumental numbers.

Incidentally, during the World War a controversy raged over the origin of the song, "Is That Mr. Riley?" A number of people in America, and even in Europe, claimed authorship. Letters poured into *Variety* about it, but all that was recalled was the chorus. 'Tis Rooney could have settled its origin had he lived, for it was sung by him in the early eighties, some thirty-odd years before the war. And it was published in sheet music form with Rooney's portrait on the title page. Here are the original words:

Is That Mr. Riley?

I'm Terrence O'Riley, a man of renown,
I'm a thoroughbred to the backbone.
I'm related to O'Connell, my mother was Queen
Of China, ten miles from Athlone.
Now if they'd let me be, I'd set Ireland free;
On the railroad you'd never pay fare.
I'd have the United States under my thumb,
And sleep in the President's chair.

Chorus: Is that Mr. Riley, can any one tell?
Is that Mr. Riley, that keeps the hotel?
Is that Mr. Riley they speak of so highly?
Upon me soul, Riley, you're doin' quite well.

I'd have nothing but Irishmen on the police.
Patrick's day would be Fourth of July.
I'd get me a thousand infernal machines
To teach the Chinese how to die.
Help the working man's cause, manufacture the laws;
New York would be swimming in wine.
A hundred a day would be very small pay,
If the White House and Capital were mine.

Is that Mr. Riley

As sung by Pat Rooney 1st

The line—"Help the working man's cause, manufacture the laws"—is significant. Almost every ballad sung in the early variety theater, except the love ditties (and there were few of those), carried some reference to labor, sometimes anticipating strife between employer and worker, and hope for settlement.

Rooney's graceful performance and attractive personality were an important influence in changing (but not too fast) the early Irish kick-in-the-bowels comedy to something more genteel—if that is the word. Anyway, it was softer, decenter, and required more talent. A change that aided Rooney was that he came into the variety picture about the time Pastor was developing the double audience of men and women—a chromo into which the diminutive and rhythmic performer fitted perfectly. It is doubtful if he would have achieved the measure of success that was justly his had he been forced to play the free-and-easies with their raggle-taggle audiences.

Tim Rogers, although no dancer, was of the Rooney stripe in that he gave his songs a kind of Hibernian-Chevalier twist. He made up in a plug hat and Prince Albert and put over his ditties with quiet and infectious humor. One of them was:

I'VE GOT A DONKEY

I've got a donkey, he stands six feet high,
I'll sell to the man who wishes to buy.
He drinks seltzer water whenever he's dry;
In a run on the turf, sure he'll never prove shy.
He makes good time—about one mile a day.
I'll match him against any stallion or bay
He's fought for his country, been all through the war,
And I feed him on red herring, hay, rope, and tar.

> CHORUS: I've got a donkey,
> He's not very chunky.
> I'll trade him for a monkey
> With any old flunkey.
> Arah, wouldn't that be hunky?

> If he had my donkey,
> And I had his monkey and donkey also.

These were the roaring eighties, and more of the lads who kept them roaring were the Irish four-acts. Two, famous for their knock-down and drag-out comedy, were "The Four Shamrocks" and "The Four Emeralds."

The Four Shamrocks were Webster Brothers, Conroy, and Thompson, and each was a broth of a bhoy. They worked in an exterior setting with a practical scaffold, ladders, mortar box, hods, and other implements. One occasionally reads some of their dialogue in the joke columns today:

BOSS: Are ye all sober this mornin'?
ALL: What else?
BOSS: Who's the first one up the ladder this mornin'? (*No answer*) Who was the first one down last night?
WEBSTER: Casey was the first one down.
CASEY: I fell down.
BOSS: You fell down on purpose.
CASEY: No, I had to come down for nails.
BOSS (*calling up above*): How many of ye are up there now?
VOICE (*from above*): Three.
BOSS: Well, half of yez come down. Riley, what are you doin' over there?
RILEY: I'm oilin' the wheelbarrow.
BOSS: Let it alone! What the hell do you know about machinery?

The Four Shamrocks was a brawling act. Instead of pummeling each other they tossed bricks. They fell down ladders and tumbled into the mortar box. After the hostilities they went into a song and dance finish.

The Four Emeralds' routine was similar, but the Emeralds had better songs. At one time this act comprised Kennedy, Magee, Russell, and Gibson. Ancients can give you twenty names of Irish comics who at one time or another were members of this famous four. Accident, temperament—and the bottle—constantly disrupted their personnel. But they did a splendid act, were always featured. And the songs they sang! For instance:

DRILL, YE TARRIERS

Oh, it's every morn at seven o'clock,
There are twenty tarriers a drillin' on a rock.
When the boss comes around he says keep still,
And put all your powers in the cast steel drill.

CHORUS: Then it's drill, ye tarriers, drill.
Drill, ye red micks, drill.
An' it's work all day, without sugar in your tay,
When you're working beyant on the big railway . . .
Drill, ye tarriers, drill—and work—and sweat—and drill.

The boardin' boss went to town one day,
To get some sugar for to sweetin' our tay.
He found that sugar had gone up of late,
And forever after that we took our tea straight.

The boss was a good man all around,
'Till he married a great big fat far down.
She baked all our bread and she baked right well,
But she baked it as hard as the hobs of hell.

Of Ike and Moe.

Jewish comics did not become dominant in vaudeville until after Frank Bush in his inimitable monologues captivated everybody with his characterization of Hebrew types in the early nineties. His humor and pathos (so cunningly allied) would have been lost in America's provinces in the seventies. But Bush, though one of the greatest of the Jewish comedians, and himself an early starter, was not the first. That distinction belongs to the team of Burt and Leon which played the Eastern variety halls as early as 1878. And they were riotous.

Burt had been a street faker and Leon at one time had a clothing shop in South Philadelphia. They worked in a street in one, showing a store front before which clothing dummies were placed. They used a line of crossfire gags (the one-legged man and the plum-colored pants) which were new then, mounted to a high pitch of gesticulation and argument, and finished with an excellent parody on a popular Irish song of the period, "The Widow Dunn," which they retitled "The Widow Rosenbaum."

>Her father keeps a hock shop
>With three balls on the door,
>Where the Sheeny politicians can be found.
>Her husband was a soldier
>But he got killed in the war,
>And his money went to Widow Rosenbaum.
>About three thousand mashers
>They hang around the place,
>But she's got her money buried in the ground.
>You can bet your bloody life,
>You can't get her for a wife,
>She would rather be the Widow Rosenbaum.

>CHORUS: Was hast gesachta? Zu klein gemachta,
>A gang of suckers, around the town.
>The kleine kinder, looks in the winder. . . .
>Dot was sung by the Widow Rosenbaum.

Nearly all of the eighties racial comics were extraordinarily faithful in the burlesque of their types. The Yiddish in Burt and Leon's parody is a sturdy indication of this, and it was carried out by the Dutch comedians who followed them in the next decade. One team—Moore and Lessinger—invariably concluded their crossfire and argumentative routine with a burlesque German drama in the language. It was silly; but it was not dialect.

MOORE: Gut morgen, wei heist du?
LESS: Ich bin zu kald Ich Schwits.
MOORE: Gehen sie nach fert?
LESS: Ich bin gans allein in der welt.

MOORE: Hast du kein gelt?

LESS: Hat Ich ein thaler Ich bin kartoffel salad essen. Hat Ich ein
thousand thaler Ich bin ice cream feressen till bauer fa blatz.
Ich bin soltard! Ich bin soltard! Und der good soltard feressen
kartoffel salad.

MOORE: Kommen sie hier, mein freund.

(Bugle call—tarantara)

LESS: Aus mittem sabreur! Aus mittem sabreur!

(Stabs himself, and falls)

MOORE: Ach, dead!

(Music cue and back to chorus of opening song and dance off)

Moore and Lessinger billed themselves as "The Colawacka
Twins" and opened with a song of the same name which was
sung straight, without dialect, a violation of the comic custom:

> Good evening one and all, we came out to make a call,
> Your attention we would ask you for a year.
> You see he is too fat for to do a somerset,
> And he's too lazy for to walk off on his ear.
> If you give us a chance we will do a song and dance,
> Dance when the music it begins.
> And almost every day you can hear the people say,
> We're the happy German Colawacka Twins.
>
> *(Heavy dance)*

Mit Hans und Fritz.

Watson and Ellis were a standard Dutch act. Watson
appeared in the usual make-up of the eighties Dutch comics—
peaked cap, short coat with full skirts, padded stomach, long
vest, pants above the shoetops, the shoes being the large
wooden type called "dugouts." Ellis made up as a neat
German blonde in cap, short skirts, and apron. They opened
in an interior with a song and dance and then led into a
routine that developed Watson as a butler. His comedy
derived from awkward attempts to carve a turkey and to pour
water into inverted goblets. They finished with a song and
German waltz which carried them all over the stage until exit.

Frank Harrington in the mid-eighties developed a novel German character act. Like Johnny Wild who citified his darky, Harrington Americanized his German; dressed in American-style clothes, somewhat exaggerated, and wore a Tyrolean hat. He did a song and dance, yodeled, used a light accent in his monologue, and danced an effective waltz clog.

Will D. Saphar, who, like Harrington, was a single, used a broad dialect and often incorporated German words in his monologue and songs. He appeared first as a heavy German woman of peasant type—red face, large white cap, fancy shawl, high stomach, large apron, full skirts, woolen stockings, wooden shoes. His act was topical and his routine distinctly New York. His opening song:

> De sveetest ting in life, vat odder peoples say,
> Iss Samstag afternoon, a-walkin' down Broadway.
> Mein schwester in der lager beer saloon vill stay.
> But I should alvays make a valk
> Right down dot pretty Broadway.
>
> CHORUS: I valk dot Broadway down,
> I valk dot Broadway down.
> Der nicest thing as neffer vas
> Iss valk dot Broadway down.
> Der fellers vink der eyes,
> Und ven I look around,
> There ain't no harm I take his arm
> Und valk dot Broadway down.

Saphar followed with a quick change to male attire of the newly arrived German immigrant type. Ambling on with a funny-looking valise, he did a short monologue and finished, sitting on his satchel, with a harmonica solo. No dancing.

Jim Davis was another Dutch single (there were a surprising number of Dutch single acts in the eighties) who did a "hurrah" turn, noisy, vigorous in song and dance, and quite funny and unusual. He always closed with an imitation of a Scot doing a Highland fling, ludicrous in his Dutch costume.

Frank Kennedy, another single, followed Harrington's type
of act in that he Americanized his German. The reader is not
to infer that Kennedy lifted any part of Harrington's routine.
He didn't have to. Kennedy was a clever performer, wrote his
own patter and songs. He was a good dancer and singer and
his parodies were excellent. One of his most popular songs was:

DON'T GIVE TO THIS NAME A BAD PLACE

I keep a saloon in the city,
I sell weiss beer und odder drinks, too.
Und also I keep a lunch counter,
Two tables und chairs dey vas new.
But a lot of dose loafers come in der,
Und try for to knock me about.
But I told you dey can't fool dis Dutchman,
For so quickly I throw dem right out.
(*Kennedy interrupted with a short spiel*)

De odder day dere was a couple of rowdy fellas come in my place.
Dey get a couple of beers und some lunch und vas valkin out ven
I says—'who pays for dese drinks vot you haf got?' One fella says
I should write it down on de ice, und de odder fella says 'you
should keep it in your head till tomorrow und I vill come around
und kick it out.' Py chimminy I vas mad. I reach for der bung-
starter und I vas going to make a fight mit dose loafer fellas ven
my vife comes in und she says—'Charlie,' . . .

> CHORUS: Don't give to this name a bad place.
> She looks at me right in the face.
> The polices will quickly arrest you,
> If you give to this name a bad place.

Clooney, of Clooney and Ryan, and the smaller of the team,
opened with a neat song and dance. Ryan, playing dumb and
foolish, ambled slowly on and proceeded to mess things up.
One of their routines was the rehearsal of a play, but their
operatic routine was the best of their comedy. Clooney sang
an aria in dialect, Ryan accompanying him on the clarinet.
Ryan would gawk around, mugging and clowning at the

audience, and then push the clarinet a foot away from his face, but it kept playing because he cleverly imitated the sound in his throat, keeping his parted lips still as he did so. When Clooney discovered the deception he grabbed the instrument. There was a fight in which the clarinet was broken, its parts spilling beans over the stage. Exit, arguing, with Ryan making discordant clarinet runs.

Murphy and Shannon, a favorite Dutch act in the eighties (and note the number of Irish performers who excelled as Dutch comics), used the customary routine comedy of argument, explanation, and misunderstanding, but they were good performers whose dialect was admirable. The high spot of their act was Murphy's explanation to Shannon of the principles of harmony, using the sentimental ballad "Lottie Lee" for demonstration.

They were an excellent team and it was a bit unfair to liken their fine characterizations to those of Weber and Fields. There was a sadistic quality about the comedy of Weber and Fields that did not appear in Murphy and Shannon. It is not within our meaning to imply that the sadistic element was purposeful or predominant in the work of the illustrious W. and F. As a matter of fact, there is a note of sadism in nearly all comedy. The plight of the harassed moron in any sketch is always justified by an audience, however sympathetic, as deserving—a point excellently illustrated in Weber and Fields's own skit, the famous pool-table episode, which the team originated in vaudeville and played many years before their tremendous success in their Broadway Music Hall. "All the public wanted to see was Fields knock the hell out of me," Weber once told the writer. And Fields added, "I don't know why it was, but the audiences always seemed to have a grudge against him."

Their pool-table skit—Lew Fields, the shark and slicker, triumphing over Joe Weber the dumb, Dutch tyro—is so familiar that its inclusion here is unnecessary. But it is important as a broad brush stroke, a cartoon of New York's meaner streets—indeed, had its origin in the neighborhood of their youth. Both Joe and Lew were East Side urchins, born in an Essex Street house that harbored a saloon, and much of their stuff was comic exaggeration of actual experience. Theirs was an inherent aptness for the ridiculousness of pseudo pomp and they laid bare many a fool in their latter-day clowning. Their burlesques in the heydays of their Music Hall were mainly plotted from contemporary and serious drama, and they kept their public howling at the proper mental barometric level— the critical intent of all burlesques and satires. If a dramatic actress rose too high in footlight fancy—Phooey!—Weber and Fields deloused her in a skit, and she could walk again among understanding people. Here was salutary criticism—for those bludgeoned and for the public which had lost all sense of proportion in their adoration. Many of their gags were topical allusions to the day's catch phrases and slang.

Occasionally they did an encore in one, funny but mostly business, the clowning of which might well have derived from the beer halls and orchestra pits off the sidewalks of New York. Returning before the drop, Fields would inquire of the violinist about his instrument. Oh, it was a violin, eh? And expensive? Uh, huh. Could he see it? No, no! It was a valuable instrument, worth thousands of dollars. But they would be so careful. Couldn't they just see it, in their own hands, for a moment? The violinist finally yields, handing along the bow too. Whereupon the comedians handle it roughly, snatching it from each other; attempt to tune it and break the strings; get into preposterous arguments as to how it was made and how to play it, the while making absurd comments about violins. As the quarreling becomes more heated Fields snatches the instrument from Weber's hands and smashes it over his head. Then, aghast at what they have done, they sneak out, and Weber, still holding the bow, runs hurriedly to the enraged violinist, hands it to him quickly and races off.

It will probably surprise some that Weber and Fields began as blackface comics until it is realized that the majority of comedy acts in vaudeville were blackface in the eighties. And as a matter of fact, so stylized and stereotyped was the comedy of the period, about the only changes in the W. and F. routine when they went on as Dutch comedians at the old Globe Theatre were the chin whiskers, German accent, and pale faces.

Burnt Cork.

The appeal of the Irish and Dutch acts was indicative of the huge immigration of those nationals in the days when Liberty beckoned them up the bay in boatloads. The appeal of the blackface acts was even more immediately social in its significance. To many in the eighties the Civil War was a vivid recollection and in every Northern town and hamlet there was sympathy for the Negro and gentle tolerance for his foibles. These—his supposed shiftlessness, his easy acceptance, his abandon, and general disregard of responsibility—many performers built into characterizations that were sometimes artistic. And to harmonize with the types they portrayed, many of their songs contained references to slavery days and were often semireligious; suggestive of spirituals.

A surprising number of singles were adepts in blackface. Among top performers of this type of act were J. W. Mc-Andrews, "The Watermelon Man," and Frank Bell. Outstanding four acts in blackface were rare, probably because the technique of the act was usually a rapid give-and-take that could be tossed quicker between two than among four. But there were a number of excellent blackface teams: Schoolcraft and Coes, Goss and Fox, Johnson and Bruno, and the half-century favorites, McIntyre and Heath. For a clarifying aside which may possibly stifle impending argument in the reader, it should be noted that not all the blackface acts were Negro comics or impersonators. Those we have cited were exactly that. But many entertainers in the eighties, and long after, appeared in blackface with no attempt at dialect or impersonation. Some of these were Lew Dockstader, Leopold and

Bunnell, Frazer and Allen, Carroll and Nealey, Keating and Sands, Smith and Byrne, and Bryant and Saville. They did monologues or other specialties, jig, clog, and so on, and used blackface make-up. But they were not Negro impersonators; they were blackface entertainers.

J. W. McAndrews characterized the old, Southern type of darky—slow, shuffling, carefree, and wheedling. In his act he wore a hickory shirt, shapeless pants, a battered piece of gray felt that might once have been a hat, and carried in his hands a mule whip which he cracked frequently while talking to an imaginary mule off stage:

Whoa, January, whoa, A wow oo! Doan you back up agin dat lamp post and upset dat load o'melons! (*Effect of mule kicking and braying off stage*) Dat's January. I calls him January 'cause he's slower than molasses. He's a mighty playful mule. He can kick a fly off your nose and never loosen a shoe. Any you folks want to buy a watermelon? Nice and sweet. Only a dime. If you takes two I sells 'em for ten cents a piece. Two for a dime a piece. I sings you a little song and mebbe you wants a melon. . . .

> My ol' missus promise me,
> Gwine to git a home by 'm by.
> When she died she set me free,
> Gwine to git a home by 'm by.
> She did live till she was bald,
> Gwine to git a home by 'm by.
> An' she never died at all,
> Gwine to git a home by 'm by.

> CHORUS: Oh, dat watermelon,
> Land of goodness you must die.
> I'se gwine jine de contraband chillum,
> Gwine to git a home by 'm by.

McAndrews, after further attempts to "sell" watermelons to his audience, usually exited to a "juba," a shuffling dance in 4-4 time. It was like a sand jig sans sand.

Novel Darky Acts.

Frank Bell's comedy was unusual in the eighties and, except for its juvenility (which never alienated his audience), was of a piece with the later, and more pertinent, patter of Lew Dockstader. Bell's was a stump-speech specialty. He stood behind a table and with a battered old umbrella thumped out his points in a discourse on women's rights, political and scientific subjects. He relied mostly on misuse of polysyllabics and absurd similes for his humor. But his characterization was genuine and his act well received. Some of his monologue:

Ladies and gentlemen—and others. It is with feelings of delight, deliciousness and infelicitousness that I appear before you for the purpose of undressing each and every one of you on this suspicious occasion. And the topic I propose to disgust is one of the greatest import and export to all within the reach of my voice at this most monotonous meeting. . . . And there is not a man, woman or child who has passed the age of fifty years who has not known about this for centuries. . . . Why do we hesitate? Why do we vacillate? Why do we wobble like a bobtailed pullet on a rickety hen roost? Must we take one side, or must we take the other side? Let me answer you in clarion tones, that I may be heard from the topmost tip of the flagpole of freedom to the lowest cellar in Canal [or Arch, or Market or High or Main] Street. Let us take both sides! Let us take anything we can get! Let us help ourselves with pernicious plenti-tudinality so that we may all perambulate the pellucid and laby-rinthine paths of our own viscosity. . . .

With a wild swing of his umbrella, Bell would then throw himself under the table. Curtain. When Rube types came in in the nineties, Bell abandoned blackface for the straw-chewing hayseed comic, a change that took him out of vaudeville for some time. Cast as the sheriff in "Way Down East," he was so successful he appeared in that play for years after.

Schoolcraft and Coes's act is difficult to outline because it was 90 per cent personality. In its day their skit, "Miss Dittimus's Party," was accepted as funny. But the dialogue was gagless and there is almost no word play—dull to read. Schoolcraft played a slow, stupid, and tactless darky; Coes was the straight man and banjo player. The inherent humor in the types portrayed accounted for the act's success. In one of his last interviews reviewing his own long career, Jim McIntyre of McIntyre and Heath, called Luke Schoolcraft the greatest Negro impersonator of the American stage.

The act of Goss and Fox was almost entirely plantation and camp-meeting songs. Their voices were good, they harmonized well, and their ditties were quaint:

> Baptist, Baptist is my belief,
> I'm Baptist till I die.
> I'm baptized in the Baptist faith
> And I live on the Baptist side.

But with chameleon adjustment they could shift to meet any town's Protestantism:

> Oh, little chillum I believe,
> Oh, little chillum I believe,
> Oh, little chillum I believe,
> I'm Methodist till I die.
> Methodist, Methodist is my belief,
> I'm Methodist till I die.
> With the butter on a board,
> The sugar in a gourd,
> And a great big Methodist pie.

Johnson and Bruno did what was called (after countless imitations) a "happy Hottentot" act. It was novel in the eighties. In black tights and white breechcloth they worked in a jungle set with a couple of reed huts. Crawling out of these huts for an entrance to sneaky music, a drum crash or horn blast would send them scurrying back. Thereafter they would peer out cautiously from time to time. Eventually on stage, they went into a grotesque song and dance, mostly leg work and slaps, while they mouthed gibberish that occasionally had an English word in it to make a vague point. They were one of the first acts to rib the audience, commenting excitedly on bald heads, big noses, or noisy clothes and expressing great curiosity over the orchestral instruments.

Hennery and Alexander.

McIntyre and Heath made one of the really great blackface acts. Their tenure, and it was mostly vaudeville, was astonishing. Their skit was "The Ham Tree," and in one form or another (once as a full-time musical) the team played it across America's stages fifty years. In their heyday, especially in the provinces, Tom Heath's line: "Alexander, you smell jes like a livery stable . . . " was a big guffaw in street, store, and pub. There was no answer to the gag in their act, or if there was it was lost in the laugh; performers never "walked" on laughs in those days.

Some years ago in Florida, Jim McIntyre told Will B. Johnstone, the cartoonist, that when radio first came in they were asked to adapt their act for broadcasting but turned down the offer because they were making so much "dishonest dough" playing "The Ham Tree" in the sticks. McIntyre said their earnings averaged, even in those late days, $70,000 a year. Had they yielded they might well have become Amos 'n' Andy and doubled those figures.

McIntyre and Heath were a prime example of the age-old vaudeville controversy over act-changing almost as good as Victor Moore and his wife, Emma Littlefield, who for thirty years, off and on, played a skit called "Change Your Act, or Back to the Woods." It is a contention that one of the complications that led to the death of vaudeville was the failure of performers to develop new gags and routines. It was not wholly the performers' fault. Managers were loath to tamper with a successful act. Victor Moore changed his twice. And after trying out the new acts in split-week theaters, was told by the managers to go back to his old one. McIntyre and Heath never did change except in minor bits of dialogue.

They varied the usual blackface acts of their time with the introduction of gags and more pertinent use of stock situation. Moreover, their characters were new for those days. Tom Heath, in pillowed belly, dressed rather shabby-genteel, played Hennery, a big-mouth know-it-all, but not so dumb as radio Andy. Jim McIntyre played Alexander, a hostler in a livery stable from which Hennery lured him to join a fly-by-night minstrel troupe. Alexander was soft, credulous, thin, with a whiny, piping voice, but the character was dejected, not meek. Nor was he that period's Negro Boy Scout, like radio Amos. Heath, save for his shiny clothes and portliness, approached in demeanor the novel "coon dandy" of Johnny Wild; while McIntyre, never servile, carried no suggestion of slavery days, as did so many of their contemporaries. Here is some of their dialogue:

(*As Alexander enters Hennery stops him by taking hold of one of his arms, both of which are outstretched*)

ALEXANDER (*irate*): I had the measure for a pane of glass, you broke the measure. (*Then, observing Hennery's huge brass horse charm dangling from a watch chain the size of a cable*) You want to put that horse in the stable?

HENNERY: No, I just got it out.

(Later, a lugubrious pair, stranded, starved, they sit bemoaning their plight at a railway siding.)

HENNERY: Well, didn't that train stop?

ALEXANDER: No, it didn't stop. It didn't even hesitate.

HENNERY: Alexander, you got egg on your chin.

ALEXANDER: Thas jes clay from the ditch where I slep' last night.

HENNERY: Well, didn't that woman at the house where I sent you up give you something to eat?

ALEXANDER: No, she didn't. I saw she looked kinda hard and I thought of the old minstrel joke so I got down and started to eat the grass thinkin' that might touch her. An' she said to me—'you poor man, you must be starvin', come around to the back yard an' I'll show you where the grass is longer.'

Although they were considered inseparable, like other team acts in vaudeville, Montgomery and Stone, for example, they did not speak off stage for years, probably because Jim McIntyre was fractious and a bottle-tilter of ability. In the nineties the team carried an understudy for McIntyre, who, when Jim was able to go on, sold songbooks in the audience. But he was often called upon to sub, and many an audience unwittingly chortled at the understudy instead of the re-nowned comic he impersonated. McIntyre's thin voice, slouch, and naïve eagerness were easily assumed by a good man, and the blackface offered a disguise virtually impossible to detect. Incidentally, Tom Heath was no teetotaler. Champagne was his tipple, but he usually saved his drinking until after the show.

McIntyre and Heath first teamed in 1874 after an unusual incident. One Butler had been McIntyre's first partner. When they were playing in San Antonio, Tex., in a comedy dance act, Butler, a "sport," donned a top hat to attend a party. The astonished rangers promptly shot it from his head and Butler found a new way out of town. McIntyre then joined with Heath who was playing on the same bill. From this happenstance both made fortunes. And they died, both in their Long Island homes, within a year of each other almost to the day: McIntyre, August 18, 1937; Heath, August 19, 1938. Blackface caricature went with them. Today the Negro comic (what few there are) is himself.

The In-and-outers

ALTHOUGH spawned in vaudeville and illustrious on the circuits, Weber and Fields, like so many distinguished performers, used it merely as a springboard for the legitimate stage. Among others of their period—the eighties—whom variety weaned for the legitimate theater were Sam Bernard, Nat C. Goodwin, Lillian Russell, Evans and Hoey, May Irwin, and Francis Wilson. Each of these occasionally reforaged, as their purses required, in the lush box-office fields of vaudeville; but their careers were mainly identified with the theater at large.

Like Weber and Fields, with whom he had later a long and profitable association as a leading comic at their Music Hall (as did Lillian Russell), Bernard although born in Birmingham, England, was an East Side boy. He lived in Bayard Street, once a lane of secondhand clothing shops with their pullers-in and barkers, and his home was not far from the Grand Duke Theatre, a Bowery dump. Born Barnett, the lad, with his brother, asked leave to go on one night and, to his stammering surprise, was permitted—and, to his speechless astonishment, was retained. A shy boy, he could scarcely pronounce his name when asked for program inscription and Dave Conroy, the manager, thinking he said, "Bernard," so printed it. The type was small enough not to make much difference, but Sam, screwing up his courage, spoke of the error. "You started with the name, and maybe a few people know it already," said Conroy. "Why don't you keep on with it?" Bernard, like Weber and Fields, played the other dumps and slabs in the Eastern cities as a monologist and once worked for George C. Tilyou's father, whose son built Coney Island's Steeplechase, a fantastic catch-all of fun for New York's less fortunate but happy hordes who each Saturday night and Sunday emerge from their warrens and storm it for summer's escape. Tilyou *père* ran a Coney Island basket lunch joint, where Bernard often played. At that he could, as he would often jest, "high-hat" Weber and Fields who were occasionally a rival attraction at Duffy's Pavilion off Coney's Bowery. Tilyou charged a dime admission, but at Duffy's you could see the show for a round of beers.

Of the much-married Nat Goodwin it has been frequently said that he was the No. 1 comedian of his day, an acting period that began with his variety appearances (as a boy orator!) in the middle seventies and ended at the close of the first decade of the twentieth century as a star of the legitimate stage. Old-timers still subscribe to his acclaim. Yet a review of his career does not entirely support this. He received his share of adverse criticism. Of his acting in the political play "Ambition," the New York *Sun* in 1895 reported: "He is distinctly a comedian. It is impossible to take him seriously." Again of his Shylock, which he played to his then wife's (Maxine Elliott) Portia, a Philadelphia reviewer tarred him in the manner the latter-day New York critics bedaubed Leslie Howard's Hamlet in 1936. "His disclosure of Shylock," wrote an unnamed reviewer, "was more like a recitation than a performance."

But we are trespassing with asides. The bibliography of Goodwin's career in the theater is available. Our interest need not stray beyond his vaudeville days. He began his youthful orations, probably upon the unwise advice of his elecutionary tutor, Wyzeman Marshall, in Providence, R. I., about 1875.

They were a dismal failure, and young Nat fled to Boston for the safer, if less glamorous, role of dry-goods salesman. In Boston, his birthplace, by the way, he met Stuart Robson, an actor of parts and no pun intended. It seems to have been at a social gathering where Nat, with youth's precocity, obliged with imitations of Robson and other well-known players. Robson was delighted. He hired him for the role of a newsboy in a play he was presenting called "The Law of New York," and paid him $5 a week. Although scarcely more than a walk-on, Goodwin demonstrated his ability, but it was of no immediate value. Jobless when the play closed, he persuaded his father to advance him a small sum for costumes and the cost of a vaudeville sketch, written by one Bradford. Nat paid the author $65 for its outright use. It was called "His First Rehearsal" and it ran the gamut of song, imitation, farce, and broad burlesque for a small cast.

Nat took his company to John Stetson, manager of the Howard Athenaeum (one of the early great variety houses) and pestered him until Stetson agreed to try it out. This was the season of 1875–1876. On the bill were Gus Williams, Denman Thompson, Sol Smith Russell, and Pat Rooney I— all wheel horses of the variety stage. Against their performances Nat's offering seemed puny. It could not have been too bad, though, for Tony Pastor, who saw it, offered him $50 to play his New York house, then at 585 Broadway, as a single. Goodwin came on to New York where he was terrified to see his billing as "actor, author, and mimic." But he went over. In later years he declared that several weeks after his opening Pastor paid $500 a week for his act. Maybe, but it does not make sense. Pastor did not pay that kind of money—then— and to unknowns.

But Goodwin's ambitions were higher than variety, and when Matt Morgan, manager of the Fourteenth Street Theatre (not to be confused with Pastor's later house in Tammany Hall), offered him the part of Captain Crosstree in a burlesque called "Black Eyed Susan," he quit vaudeville

—for the moment. And the $500 a week? It is confusing. And so was his next step—and statement—for Goodwin could toss more money into a conversation than a mental-betting horse player. "Susan" was a flop, and Goodwin went back to Boston to team up in a variety act with Minnie Palmer; they opened at the Howard Athenaeum, "at a salary," said Goodwin, reminiscing about it in after years, "of $750 a week. I was very proud of this as I had previously left that theater, not particularly successful, at a salary of only $15 a week." Confusion again. The complete pay roll of the Howard Athenaeum bills in the late seventies never approached $750 a week.

When this engagement terminated, Goodwin again deserted variety for the legitimate stage, this time to remain away more than twenty years. But in 1909, when he was having trouble in obtaining suitable plays, Percy G. Williams induced him to play his vaudeville chain in a sketch called "Lend Me Five Shillings." It was successful, but Goodwin, chafing at the two-a-day (as it had become), fled back to his three- and four-acters. He made one last appearance in vaudeville, headlining as a single at the Palace in 1916. He told stories. "The audience seemed to enjoy his quiet humor," wrote a reviewer.

The Confectionery Lillian.

So far as vaudeville is concerned, all one can say about Lillian Russell is that she sang all right and looked nice. Later, in musicals and with Weber and Fields, she learned to clown, but her influence in the variety of her time was negligible. No fault of her own; it was not her sphere. She soon found it in the ruffled furbelows of the Casino's coy operettas; in the very life and expression of the dandy nineties. Lillian Russell was a silken epitome of the period; a ten-carat luster in its diamond horseshoe. She regarded life as a confection, and in the manner of Heine's quip, life made haste to return the compliment. In her early days they dubbed her "airy, fairy"; and she *was* a china doll of teacup grace. Astonishing woman! Her slide-rule features, regular as a movie cutie's, yet had character.

She was born Helen Leonard in Clinton, Iowa, in 1861. When she was three, her parents moved to Chicago, where, at seven, she entered the Convent of the Sacred Heart. The nuns

LILLIAN RUSSELL
(Circa 1885)
As a flower for street wear and (opposite page) a sailor lass for Tony Pastor.

had her eight years, and, bless their souls, inadvertently grooved her career—encouraged her tambourine playing, excused her girlish tripping, and applauded her aptitude for their theatricals. She studied music under a Mme. Scheremburg, and after fifty-odd Sundays in the choir lofts of churches,

made her first public appearance in an amateur production of "Time Tries All," December, 1877, in Chickering Hall. Two years later she and her mother came to live in New York and there she became engaged to Walter Sinn, the son of Colonel William E. Sinn, owner of the Park Theatre in Brooklyn.

Poor Sinn *fils*. Lillian was eighteen, her opening petals an ever-unfurling appeal for Hymen's thrust. The colonel, an important figure in Brooklyn's theatrical life and afterward owner of its leading house, the Montauk, gave a party for her. Couldn't she, asked Helen of the colonel, appear with the chorus just a few nights at the Park Theatre? But of course . . . a lark for you, my dear. She did. And why shouldn't she be singled out? She was. And jilted young Walter to join Rice's "Surprise Party," then making ridiculous money with a shocking burlesque of "Evangeline." It was in this that Tony Pastor saw her, and hired her (he was at 585 Broadway) as a seriocomic at $40 a week, billing her as Lillian Russell; he liked its euphemism. But she was just another singing single, and when her engagement terminated discontentedly entered the chorus of "H.M.S. Pinafore." She soon found solace in the attentions of Harry Braham, musical director of the company. She quit the stage and married him—through, she thought, with a professional career. A year later she was back with Pastor, opening his new Fourteenth Street house in 1881 in her first name part—Mabel—in a burlesque of "The Pirates of Penzance."

These appearances, and a few others in later years, constituted her vaudeville fling. But scrutiny of her career discloses her more as first a public playgirl, and latterly a public figure, than an actress. The general association of her name in the people's minds was as something expensively beautiful—an adornment, a personality, a boutonniere for wealthy swaggerers. Lucky Braham, Number 1, wore her no less as a flower than Diamond Jim Brady or Alexander P. Moore, her last husband. She died a child, her life an amazing contrast to that of her militant mother, Cynthia, one of the first of the pants wearers in the cause of women's rights. Cynthia Leonard ran for mayor of the City of New York in 1888. Five years later Lillian was piping to an eager press:

"I don't believe in the kind of women's rights that will ever lead women to go through a crowd of staring men to vote in one of those little pens that they build up in the street. Still, they might not be so bad if women were admitted just to keep men on their good behavior. But I do believe that a woman that owns property and pays taxes on it ought to have her say about municipal things. Why don't they hold their elections in some school building or public place where a woman can drive up in her carriage like a lady and vote?"

She could be even more naïve. When a cigar manufacturer asked the use of her name for one of his Havana fillers she wrote:

Your letter of the 23rd [June, 1891], requesting permission to use my picture and name on a new brand of cigars was received by me and I grant you the exclusive right to same with much pleasure, being confident that the cigar will be of so good a quality as to keep its namesake in pleasant remembrance.

Maybe she was paid for this, but it is doubtful. At any rate, she didn't say she smoked them.

As Lillian became the courted favorite the theater became more irksome to her. "The stage is so exacting," she said at this time. "It demands your whole life. There is no pleasure in it."

But as Time drew the ermine from about her lovely shoulders and replaced it with the mantle of experience she took on a tragic quality of awareness and sought to translate her natural hoydenism into a pseudo sedateness. We find her saying maudlin things to soldiers and recruits in 1917. And only the year before she put forth a pathetic bid in the candidacy for the mayorality of Pittsburgh. Gone was the Pompadour's fan.

It is too easy to discount the vaudeville careers of Charlie Evans and Bill Hoey. Those familiar with their work may say that their tour de force was "A Parlor Match," a full-length show and beyond variety's boundaries. This is true, but it has already been mentioned that the "Match" was derived from Frank Dumont's smutty afterpiece, "The Book Agent," which slopped around the dumps and slabs like stale beer until Charles Hoyt freshened it into wholesome entertainment. This was in the late eighties when variety began its own cleanup, a laundering process in which Evans and Hoey and Hoyt were factors.

But even before the "Agent," Charlie Evans, alive at this writing, aged eighty-three, and chipper enough for a buck and wing at the Uplifter's Club in Los Angeles, was a standard act in variety, a versatile performer running the comic's gamut in Dutch, Irish, blackface, song and dance turns, and afterpiece roles. His first partner was James Niles with whom he broke in a new act, "Riding in a Street Car," at Pastor's about 1874 when Tony was at 201 Bowery. It was a nimble turn, a "big and little"—Niles tall and slender, Evans short and slight.

Previously they had played in "Muldoon's Picnic" with two other lads named Bryant and Hoey. When the latter closed their season Evans and Niles teamed up with them. The company included Minnie French and her sister Helen, two girls who danced divinely in the filthy "Book Agent," which Dumont sent them. It was presented, apparently for the first time, in Rochester, N.Y., August, 1882. Hoey played Old Hoss, the tramp; Evans, I. McCorker, the book agent. Evans married Minnie French during the run and soon afterward Hoey married Helen. Meanwhile Charles Hoyt had produced a highly successful farce called "A Bunch of Keys," and Evans considered having him make their "Agent" afterpiece into a three-acter. Hoyt agreed, and done and done. "Match" was a gold mine, one of the most popular farces ever produced in America. Evans once admitted they cleared close to $400,000 on the show in which, by the way, he played I. McCorker 3,500 times without missing a performance.

May Irwin—"Madame Laughter."

The forthright humor of May Irwin was so pat, not only to the eighties' variety but to vaudeville's lifelong expression, it is surprising that this fine artist played the halls but six years. Played but two halls, in fact, and those for one man—Tony Pastor. An astute businesswoman, who some years before her death in January, 1939, sold her block of New York City property on Lexington Avenue from 54th to 55th Street for $1,000,000, perhaps she realized that only the managers were taking the important money out of vaudeville. She may also have felt that the legitimate stage was her forte, but whatever she was doing, in character and style she was of the tribe of vaude. President Wilson, one of vaudeville's most ardent devotees, once offered her "the portfolio of Secretary of Laughter."

In all the exhumations incidental to this book, with the cross-current comment, the sometimes laughable displays of temperament, the almost inevitable disparagement of one actor for another—this writer not once read or heard one word against May Irwin, as a person or as a performer. Years after she retired Eddie Darling sought her for one of his old-timers' bills at the New York Palace. A wealthy woman, she said no, but for another reason. "Heavens," she said, "I wouldn't make any business for you. They don't want old people." Within a year Darling succeeded in booking Emma Calvé. It was pure business. Calvé fitted into vaudeville not quite so well as the Avon Comedy Four would fit into "Carmen." But she was the greatest Carmen of her day, some say any day; a world-known artist of the highest rank. And her proposed debut in the two-a-day was attended by all the ballyhoo and condescension invariably fastened upon such interlopers by the otherwise decent and scholarly Walter Kingsley, the Palace's principal drumbeater.

This time he overdid it. The tons of warmed-over tripe that heralded Calvé's "descent" succeeded even in making *her*

sick. At noon before the Monday matinee she was to open (it
was Washington's Birthday, 1920), her manager phoned
Darling she had lost her voice due to nervousness and would
be unable to appear. In about twenty minutes Darling revived
sufficiently to make frantic, and futile, phone calls to "resting"
performers. As a last gasp he phoned May Irwin, then nearly
seventy. "What do you want me to do?" she asked. "Hang
up the phone and come down," he said. "All right,"
said May. "I don't know what I'll do but I'll be there."
This was about one o'clock and she was scheduled to go on
at three.

And on she walked, with that great, beaming smile, that
infectious personality, an American come-all-ye, and she
said, "I'm here as a fill-in. I haven't one thing I can do. So
I'll just tell you three whoppers. They're not mine; I heard
them at Lulu McConnell's yesterday . . . " It is unfortunate
the stories are not remembered. But she was an excellent
raconteur, and they went over big. And then she said, "I
could tell you I'd sing my old song 'The Bully' but that I
haven't got the music. But that would be a stall. I have got it,
and it's right down there (the orchestra pit), and I am going
to sing it."

She was a week's riot. About Thursday Darling said to her,
"You've been marvelous; business hasn't slackened a penny.
I am going to give you Calvé's salary"—$4,000. She would
not take a cent; said she'd done it as a favor for a friend.

This one appearance encouraged Darling to remember her
for his next old-timers' bill. He assembled his acts, Fritzi
Scheff, Blanche Ring, Marie Dressler, with Taylor Holmes as
master of ceremonies, and May agreed to appear. "I think I'd
love it," she said, "going on once more with those old pals.
I'm the oldest one of the lot, I might as well tell you—before
they do."

Then the dressing-room headache recurred. "Why, I never
had a dressing room in my life," answered May. "I'll dress at
home, I'm going on straight." Followed the finest testimonial

a performer can ever hope for. Hearing of the difficulty, Marie Dressler went to Darling and said, "I want to give my room to dear May; there is a couch in it too." May refused it: "These legs are as good as ever. I'll stand in the wings and watch the acts. Maybe I can steal a few gags."

She loathed animal acts because of their cruelty. (So did a number of other performers. Elsie Janis and Sarah Bernhardt had specific clauses written into their contracts barring animal acts on their bills. And for the record—not all animal acts were cruel. Al Rayno loved his two performing bulldogs and they loved him. He bought a place in Connecticut for them to romp. And Mr. and Mrs. Harry Howard carried their clever troupe of fox terriers with them when they retired to Hollywood and still have, at this writing, most of them. One is blind. Each night after a show they would take two of the dogs home with them, in rotation, and the dogs always knew which pair, which night.) But an offender was Galeman whose splendid act of cats, dogs, and a red fox was marred by his merciless cruelty to the fox. It was a tough spot for Darling. After all, he had booked the act and it drew well. Knowing how May Irwin would feel, he invited her to attend a bill at the Hamilton in New York where Galeman was playing and put her in a stage box so she could see his vicious whipping of the fox before it went on. She notified the S.P.C.A. at once. An inspector warned the performer and stood guard over the animal for five weeks during which Galeman behaved himself. But on tour at Erie, Pa., he resumed his cruelty and the Albee office finally got him out of the country. About 1935 Galeman wrote, accusing Darling of "keeping me from my bread and butter." Darling replied, "You are the cruelest man I have ever known. I did not make the trouble for you but I know who did and if you return she will prosecute you." It developed that the action had been taken on the demand of May Irwin who had continued her watch of the act even out of town.

May Irwin was born in Whitby, Ontario, and began her career in Buffalo in 1876 in a straight show under the management of Daniel Shelby. A year later she teamed with her sister Flora in a song and dance act called the Irwin Sisters. Pastor caught them the same year and signed them for 585 Broadway. They enlarged their act for him, incorporating comedy skits. But in 1883, Augustin Daly, convinced he had a find, signed May and broke up the team. Daly was right. In her first Daly show, as Susan in "A Night Off," she took the town by the ears, and repeated her success a year later playing Betsy in a show called "Nancy & Co." These established her solidly and she went over to Charles Frohman, trouping constantly until she retired. Before she quit the legitimate stage she made one earlier excursion into vaudeville in a sketch called "Mrs. Peckham's Carouse." It drew well and Darling would have booked her constantly. But she spurned all vaudeville wooing. It is curious. After she became a legitimate star she always admitted that her early training in vaudeville was her greatest asset. She said Pastor made her aware of her perception of comedy, and that Daly developed it, but that the old tricks, the technique, the ramming home of a gag, or the specific timing of belly-laugh business was essentially variety's masonry.

And although Francis Wilson, one of the really great comics who leaped from the beer halls to the legitimate theater does not stress this in his own career it is the fact with him too. A faded clip from his "Erminie" days gives the reactions of a contemporary: "It was in this line of work [Wilson's blackface variety act] that Wilson gained so many of the quaint movements and comical intonations of voice that made him so popular in comic opera."

Strictly Box Office.

Wilson was born in Philadelphia in 1854 the son of Quaker parents in whose faith he was raised and his deviation from so strict a sect to enter the theater—the variety beer halls, at that—is a quirk that Wilson himself could only interpret in confusing terms, almost Freudian.

"I can explain it only on the theory that it was an overdue protest against the solemn repression suffered by generations of ancestors." Thus he set it down in his charming autobiography. The book is comparatively recent and makes additional comment here unwarranted. And in truth, his variety tenure was short. He teamed with John B. Mackin in a blackface song and dance, and later they did a "rival" act. Wilson does not seem to have enjoyed the association, and the story is that he took boxing lessons solely to become proficient enough to beat up Mackin who was rough with him in their knockabout business. He never forgot the dumps and slabs he played and the managerial gyppings and snubs he suffered. He was one of the most militant leaders in the Equity strike of 1919 and became Equity's first president.

We brought in the name of Emma Calvé. And since this has to do with the in-and-outers it is not inapposite to conclude with Mrs. Patrick Campbell. Her introduction here is not to be construed as a comparison with those great artists mentioned. She was, however, one of vaudeville's box-office bids like Calvé, and it is well to do her now and have done with her.

Since 1902, when she played the "Sorceress" at the New Amsterdam Theatre, Mrs. Campbell had enjoyed the gods' grace of acclaim here. In 1908 Albee asked her if she would like to appear in vaudeville. She didn't know. And what was vaudeville? And anyway she would come in and talk to responsible people about it. Albee saw her. "Will there be other people on the program with me?" she asked. "Of course," he answered. And she said, "Wouldn't it be awful to meet them?" Conferences proceeded. She had the contract read and reread, written and rewritten. She insisted she could not play on the Lord's Day, and Albee said that was too bad, everybody else did. (They did not. Albert Chevalier and Vesta Tilley were by contract absolved from Sunday performances. Tilley's insistence was not based on religious feeling; she wanted a day of rest. Nor did the ruling apply in the Keith theaters. Keith, at the direction of his wife, a devout Catholic, kept his theaters dark on Sunday.) "We are paying you $2,500 weekly and it is for seven days," Albee said. "Take it or leave it." Mrs. Pat screamed and asked for the phone. Albee listened intently. She called a Plaza number and cooed: "My little darling. I am making apologies for being late. I am with these horrible men in this vaudeville business . . . " She was talking to Pinky Panky Pou, her peke.

Still conferences proceeded and arguments continued ("If only you could give me a little more, the price of butter is so high") but she signed for Albee's figure, $2,500, and a hundred and forty-six Tanguays couldn't tie her for temperament. She complained about everything and never spoke to anyone on the bill. In Philadelphia she was invited to a luncheon somewhere along the Main Line. About 2:30 in the afternoon when she should have been in the theater she phoned the manager that she could not possibly go on, she was having such a delightful time. She never showed up. Came Saturday and the manager deducted her lost day. Thereupon she flounced out and said she would quit the tour. The manager paid her.

All these people, with the exception of Evans and Hoey and May Irwin, were not vaudeville people. Vaudeville people were a distinct, now an extinct, breed. These people— the legit stars—were all right in their own way. They were just unfortunate—born to the buskin, not to the motley. We can be more generous. They were far better than the broken-down opera sopranos, hack concert fiddlers, and pianists of the Liszt school banging out digital études for the left hand alone. They were no good at all.

BOOK II
Pastor and Petticoats

Tony, the Puritan

To Pastor go the honors for tossing variety's denimed frowsiness into the ash can and bringing out My Lady Vaudeville in starched organdy—a shining child, washed behind the ears, ready to meet its elders on something more than a gamin basis.

Tony (Antonio) Pastor was born in Greenwich Village in Manhattan. A date—May 28, 1837—appears in some of the data about him, but he was sensitive about his age and forebears and would never verify it. It is recorded that his father was a musician in Barnum's band, but there are other reports that he sold perfume.

If 1837 is the year of Tony's birth he made his first public appearance in the old Dey Street Church in New York at the age of six, singing duets with one Christian B. Woodruff, a New York State senator, at meetings of the Hand-in-Hand Temperance Society. Apparently the boy's talent was marked even then, for his father, suspecting leanings toward a stage career and disapproving, shipped him upstate as apprentice to a farmer who promptly returned him because his clowning disrupted the hired help. At this point his father gave up and Tony went on at Barnum's Museum in New York City as a child prodigy. There is nothing to indicate that he ever saw his father again.

Civic consciousness had not become parentally minded, and the boy was allowed to roam at will, a juvenile sword for any scabbard. This was not unusual. Lads often accompanied strolling players, and E. S. Washburn ("Washburn's Sensations") arranged that his young charges be tutored. When he was ten Tony joined Raymond and Waring's Menagerie

The spangled Tony Pastor as a circus performer (1856).

doing a blackface song and dance and doubling on the tambourine end of the minstrel show (the minstrel show being a part of nearly every caravan troupe even in the late eighties). The same year, 1847, he played juvenile roles and did an acrobatic specialty at Welch's National Amphitheatre in Philadelphia. The following summer he took to the road when Welch joined Delevan and Nathan's circus.

Distinctly a singer in later life when he ran his own theaters (and regarded as a bit on the ham side by the actors on his

Tony Pastor, headliner at the Howard (Boston) Athenaeum.

707 BROADWAY, N. Y.

Tony Pastor, the top-hatted Lord of Fourteenth Street in the eighties.

bills), he seems to have been versatile in boyhood, though his many-sided stunts may have been nothing more than adolescent showoff. His precocity amazed—and dismayed—his employers. While he was with Delevan and Nathan, Tony rigged up a stage inside the tent, roped off a portion for intimate seating, and organized night song and dance shows, a form of entertainment unheard of in circuses of those days because of the inadequate lighting. When the manager began to suspect that the boy's novelty was taking the larger share of the box office, he stopped it. A courageous lad, Tony quit.

Jobless, the incredible boy retained self-confidence and was almost immediately reemployed by another circus. When the ringmaster of this show fell dead, Tony, at fourteen, assumed his duties, doubtless the youngest ringmaster under canvas. It was more of a job in those days. The duties included singing, dancing, and taking part in the afterpieces, but Tony did well, playing various circuses as ringmaster and general performer until 1861 when the Civil War broke out.

Winding up his circus clowning at North's Amphitheatre in Chicago, he came back to New York and at the age of twenty-four opened his first theater, at 444 Broadway. It was a dive. The bar flies dubbed it "444"; it had no other name. There is no evidence that it was a rendezvous for bawds, though how it could have escaped cannot be deduced from the record. These were war years; the issue of the Union was paramount and laxity was tolerated. Billy Pastor, Tony's brother, whose name appears nowhere else, was lessee. Here Tony starred as a singer, and with true showman's instinct opened all his patriotic stops to the tramp, tramp of the volunteers marching south.

He gave the same topical slant to his songs that Harrigan and Hart gave to their burlesques, and his judgment of mob appeal was as unerring as theirs, if less brilliant. The workingman, the plight of labor, which after the war became a stirring issue, the current styles of women, the foibles of the day—all were grist for Pastor's musical mill. One of his songs, a lugubrious ditty begging cheap sentiment for the miner (Tony seems first to have sung it about 1869) became a barroom ballad that has been exceeded as a dirge for drunks only by "Sweet Adeline." It was "Down in a Coal Mine."

For years this maudlin ditty was a parlor chant in thousands of homes. The Republican party used it as a marching song against Cleveland in 1888.

Bowery Nights.

Pastor's reluctance to discuss "444," his first independent venture, suggests that he was not proud of the place. He may have spoken of the moral (or immoral) phase of his business to his friend, Sam Sharpley, an old minstrel singer for whom he probably once worked. At any rate, in 1865, carrying Sharpley with him, he took over the old Volk's Garden at 201 Bowery, another unsavory rendezvous for the bibulous. Rechristening it Pastor's Opera House and remodeling it to anticipate the beer halls of the eighties, he built up a pretentious show around such top entertainers as Billy Emerson and John Thompson.

Thompson was a protean artist, the first to present a sawmill drama, a condensed play called "On Hand." Thompson appeared in many guises during the course of the play, always in time to prevent the villain from sawing the heroine into large gory slabs. Contrary to prevailing opinion, the saw was vertical; later, rivals introduced the circular or buzz type as dramatic improvements. Variety audiences loved the bathetic terrors of the play, and some years later the idea was expanded to meller size and redressed for the ten-twent'-thirt' houses.

Pastor contended he paid Thompson $150 a week in 1867— motion-picture money for those days. It may be true, but it doesn't sound like Pastor. He was a soft touch in show business, but he was also a parsimonious employer. His greatest boast, and he was by no means retiring, was that to Sheridan and Mack, an outstanding post-Civil War team who often headed his bills, he paid a weekly salary of $12.50. And in addition to their own acts these performers appeared in the afterpieces and stock dramas. He once exclaimed that his 1865 shows at Volk's Garden cost but $250 a week, while the weekly average at Fourteenth Street in 1903 (one of the pin-

His second theater, opened July 31, 1865. It had been the un-savory Volk's Garden of the Lillian McTwobucks' yarn.

nacle years) was $2,500. Asked in 1904 what was the greatest change that had come over vaudeville, he said, "Salaries."

Pastor continued to stress the wine room and bar in Volk's Garden, but he gave select bills. The nucleus of his company included top-flight performers like Johnny Wild, a blackface comic, the first to present the "coon dandy," and his wife, Mlle. Bertha, who, as members of the Harrigan and Hart company, were known to entertainment seekers throughout New York City. Others were the aforementioned Johnny Thompson, and Billy Barry and Hugh Fay, a remarkable team. Barry was one of the greatest of the blackface comics.

During his partnership with Sharpley Pastor conceived the idea of a touring variety company. This was presumably in the early seventies. It was not precisely a pioneer venture, but his troupers were a compact unit offering specific entertainment with the accent on comedy, dancing, songs, and sketches. More nearly than any that preceded it, the show approached vaudeville as we were later to know it. To the "headliners" (not so billed at that time) mentioned in the preceding paragraph he added Thomas G. Riggs and George Edison and his wife, forgotten performers whose "specialties" are not recalled. An orchestra of five musicians traveled with the company.

Their first stop seems to have been Paterson, N.J., but the place cannot be fixed. Wherever it was, their success led Pastor to continue across country the tour which was to become his annual feature for twenty years. During the initial venture he visited not only the key cities but such lesser theater points as Scranton and Hartford in the East, and similar thriving communities through the Midwest and to the coast— introducing to America a managed and closely knit, if dappled, vaudeville show.

Returning to New York elated at his good fortune on the road, Pastor reinstalled his show at Volk's Garden, supplementing it from time to time with untried performers who were to become nationally famous. These included Nat C. Goodwin, Weber and Fields, Jefferson De Angelis, Niles and Evans, Sam and Kitty Morton, Gus Williams, a German comic, and Georgina Smithson, who as "The Gainsborough Girl" then was the vicarious love of the land.

Pastor remained at Volk's until 1875. During this time he quit Sharpley, why or when is not known. Apparently it was a pleasant association and, since Pastor prospered in his Bowery theater, it is reasonable to suppose that Sharpley may have

contributed something to the partnership. Certainly when
Pastor moved up to 585 Broadway on his own he was not so
successful. He may have blindly been following the uptown
theatrical trend, but it was not the part of wisdom to plant
himself in immediate opposition to Harrigan and Hart. Later
in Fourteenth Street he learned not to challenge this entrenched pair with analogous, though not comparable,
musicals.

Harrigan and Hart offered superb entertainment. Although
they adopted the form of variety in their olios and employed
many variety troupers in their casts, their show was as superior
to that of the general run of beer halls and "drop-in" joints as
Gilbert and Sullivan was to that of the provincial English
music hall. Ned Harrigan, the brains of the team, was an
exceptional fellow of talent and wit, and his pieces—"The
Mulligan Guards," "McSorley's Inflation," "Cordelia's
Aspirations," "Squatter Sovereignty," and "The Major"—
were musical satires and burlesques that "catch the living
manners as they rise." He was not afraid to surround himself
with players as good as he, or even better. Annie Yeamans
played for him, and so did Nat Goodwin and Johnny Wild.

It is nice to record that the fever of acclaim was visited
upon the team for a decade. The "Mulligan Guards" series
played that length of time—a healthy run. But when Harrigan
forsook his lower Broadway house for a 35th Street theater he
declined in favor, and ability too. Possibly he was saddened by
Hart's wayward and disorganized life. Harrigan died in 1911,
an embittered man. Three years earlier, in an interview with
Frank C. Drake of the New York *World*, he said:

" . . . there's been a great change in the sense of humor
in New York. I tell you it's the Irish and Anglo-Germanic
people that know how to laugh. The great influx of the Latins
and Slavs—who always want to laugh not with you but at
you—has brought about a different kind of humor. It isn't
native, it isn't New York. It's Paris, or Vienna, or someplace.
Lord love ye, I got my fun here, firsthand, from the shipyard

where I used to work along the docks—down MacDougal Street and in the Ninth Ward where I lived. But now we mustn't be reminded of the old-fashioned, hard-working New York that we sprung from. That's too vulgar for us. Now we must have our Salomes, and our dance poems, and our what I call four-cornered plays—you know, a husband and a wife, and a mistress and a lover."

A short time after he took over 585 Broadway Pastor unconsciously introduced a custom that is still a nuisance in the theater. John Loeffler, later a successful Broadway manager but then a precocious lad of eight, introduced himself to Tony as the son of the man from whom Pastor bought his liquor and asked him for a job. "We pay program boys $1 a week," said Pastor, and John accepted. One rainy night patrons besieged him to care for their wet coats, umbrellas, and rubbers. John stored them away, Later, when the owners were sorting out their belongings, an old chap complained that the boy should have given them some means of identifying their property. Next day John's father had 100 brass checks made and affixed to straps, and that night John set up the first theater checkroom, bringing home $7 in tips. His mother said it was dishonest money, but his father approved and his mother withdrew her objections.

Despite his failure to thin the box-office lines at Harrigan and Hart's, Pastor distinguished his six-year stay at 585 by encouraging talented youngsters, but one may be skeptical of his contributions to the technique and artistry of the performers who got their chance with him, worked for a pittance, and subsequently became great under other banners. Let us not belittle the gentle Pastor. He may not have been a great teacher, but he was an inspired consoler. He may not have improved a performer's talent, but he knew when there was talent and would nurse it with consideration and courtesy. He gave every possible chance to acts he thought deserving. His greeting to new performers, in from the West or wherever who had never before played New York, was invariably: "Now, folks, don't be nervous about the place and don't overwork. Why, jiminetty [a favorite expletive and the height of his profanity, which occasionally included 'so help me Bob!'], the audience out there are just people same as anyplace else. I know you're all right and I'm glad to have you here." He was never known to close an act, an epitaph for any showman.

On February 8, 1881, Pastor moved up from 585 to what he called, with characteristic euphemism, "Tony Pastor's New Fourteenth Street Theatre." A bandbox hewn out of Tammany Hall, which then adjoined the Academy of Music at the corner of Irving Place, it was not new nor much of a theater. It was built in 1868 to provide additional revenue for the Wigwam, and Dan Bryant's Minstrels opened the house. Its capacity was but a few hundred seats and before Pastor refurnished it a German theatrical troupe sputtered gutturals across its gas footlights.

Pastor's first show in his "new" theater was the "Pie-Rats of Pen-Yan," a razz of the Gilbert and Sullivan "Pirates of Penzance," an imitation of the musical burlesques and topical satires of the more gifted Harrigan and Hart whose Theatre Comique at 514 Broadway was Pastor's severest competitor. Ned Harrigan paid little attention to Pastor's new enterprise, and still less to his new soubrette, Lillian Russell, who sang the part of Mabel in the "Pie-Rats."

The play was an acute pain, a record for lily painting. Pastor, as in his previous houses, interspersed the "Pie-Rats" with song and dance and funny-saying *entremets*, but the public remained apathetic and the showman sulked. He was a showman, however, and soon realized the stupidity of trying to do something Harrigan and Hart could do better. He junked his musicals, and on October 24, 1881, opened with an innovation: a straight, clean variety show, the first—as such—ever given in this country. It was a daring venture. Only gals on the trampish side attended variety in the eighties. Pastor's move was mainly (and frankly) for profit, a definite and canny bid to double the audience by attracting respectable women—wives, sisters, sweethearts. In boldface type in advertisements and on his programs Pastor announced his pride in offering unblushing entertainment. This gesture was not phony. Pastor was a decent man.

His Bill for the Ladies.

The opening night—a miserable night of rain, whipped by a marrow-chilling wind—seemed inauspicious. The newspapers paid little attention to the event, Pastor being a perennial feature. And Harrigan and Hart, only a few blocks away, had chosen that same Monday evening to present their latest take-off, "The Major." Harrigan had given no thought to the "Pie-Rats," but he had reason to believe that Pastor's new challenge was formidable. He was right. For in spite of the nice things William Dean Howells had written about the "Mulligan Guards" series, "The Major" failed to draw and the première was virtually played to the ushers. But, in truth, the wretched weather cut the box-office take at every house in town—except Pastor's.

To his delight a mixed audience of "ladies and gents" attended; these were to be his characteristic patrons. It was an important night. Pastor gave good entertainment, pat to the response of a day that reveled in ribald gibes, knockabout comedy, and bare-knuckle thrusts. Only this time there was no "blue" stuff. Included on the bill were:

> Frank McNish
> Ferguson and Mack
> The Leland Sisters
> Lester and Allen
> The French Twin Sisters
> Lillie Western
> Ella Wesner
> Dan Collyer

Frank McNish was the originator of an act called "Silence and Fun," which held the precisely correct blood count for

that day's vaudeville—low comedy not yet touched by
Keith's anemia. He came on to an orchestration of old tunes
called an "essence," that is, any medley adjusted as incidental
music to fit a type or style of act. His stage setting was a
kitchen interior, an appreciative touch—in the eighties the
kitchen was half living room. Two barrels, a chair, a table,
and a broom were his props. He stepped from the floor to the
table then to the top of the barrels, light, deft, graceful. It
was what performers called a "dumb" act, no spoken lines.
After various roll-overs, nip-ups, and splits, he placed the two
barrels on top of the table, the chair on top of the barrels,
leaped to the chair from the stage, stepped down in two steps,
did a roll-over and a nip-up, and landed in front of the footlights. It may not read like much but it was a wonderful act
because McNish had a gracious personality as well as acrobatic skill.

Ferguson and Mack did a "rough" Irish act, so rough that
it resulted, after twenty years of slapping around, in a near
tragedy for Barney Ferguson, the little fellow who took the
belting. Their act (song, dance, and character stuff) was a
feeder for their feature known as the "bumps," or hard falls
on neck, shoulders, and head. They finished with Mack
sinking a hatchet in Ferguson's skull; it stuck there as they
made their exit, Ferguson wearing a trick wig to accommodate
the blow.

Poor Ferguson in after years became totally deaf from so
much head-bashing and was forced to work honky-tonks on
the small time. In 1912 or 1913 he came to Chicago in search
of booking and applied to an agent named Doyle. "I can
send you up to Cedar Rapids, Barney," said Doyle, "but all
I can offer you is $60." "Well," said Barney, "$50 is better
than nothing." And he went out for $50. This unfortunate
performer, who had won the clog-dance championship in New
Orleans in 1868, and who chose so hard a way to earn a
living, suffered grievance upon grievance. Twice he was
sandbagged and robbed while on tour, sandbagging being

then a favorite weapon of thuggery. One night after a performance in New York he was hurrying home to his hotel room when, passing through Times Square, a friend caught up with him and slapped him on the back. "All right," said Barney, throwing up his hands, "but don't hit me."

The Leland Sisters did a song and dance act. It was not novel, but their demureness and charm and their dainty costume changes made them an excellent No. 2 act, or second on the bill. The No. 2 act was usually "done in one," or in front of the first drop, to permit a return to the full stage set, known as the "center door fancy," with which most variety shows of the day opened. (For a 50-cent tip to props a performer could have palms on both sides of his "center door.")

Lester and Allen were eccentric blackface comics combining song and dance with crossfire or question-and-answer dialogue. They opened with a song and dance called "Sally Horner:"

> I once knew a gal and her name was Sally Horner,
> Hi, ho, how I love my gal.
> Her father kept a barber shop just around the corner,
> Oh, my, her maiden name was Sal.
> Early in the fall
> I took her to a ball.
> Never shall forget, she lost her waterfall.
> Danced so hard she busted up the ball. . . .
> Oh, my, she couldn't dance at all.

Then into their dance, and as Allen eased off for a costume change Lester kept going. Reënter Allen wearing an immense fur overcoat dyed a luminous yellow.

LESTER: What do you call that?
ALLEN: I don't call it. I whistle and it comes to me.
LESTER: Is that the way you got it?
ALLEN: No, it was given to me. Everybody likes to give things to me.
  I once got $35,000 for a kiss.

LESTER: WHAT!
ALLEN: Well, it wasn't exactly the kiss itself; it was what it led up to.

They developed this into a terrific argument and decide to settle with boxing gloves. At this the property man brought on four inflated bladders with which they slapped each other viciously while props, who acted as referee, tried to separate them. For a climax they beat him off the stage.

The French Twin Sisters were known as a "class" act. They dressed alike and made interesting costume changes. They differed from the Leland Sisters in that one of the girls sang alto to her sister's soprano. We have met them as the wives of Evans and Hoey.

Clever, diminutive Lillie Western was a stanch performer, well regarded by managers as well as audiences. Hers was a musical act. Although she appeared in boy's costume, she was not a male impersonator. She featured her act with the playing of Matt O'Riordan's "Wedding Bells," a tricky instrumental piece she made trickier with her expert playing on an English concertina. She also played banjo and xylophone. Brisk and efficient, she worked rapidly and jumped from one instrument to another and in her staccato presentation anticipated the middle 1900's performer who had no time "to catch 'em in the bedroom scene," as the legitimate actors used to say when a first act went dully, but had to "toss 'em in the aisle" at the start. Few acts, even in the eighties, save for the afterpieces and drama closings, lasted longer than twenty minutes and a performer was made or murdered by his opening.

Ella Wesner headed Pastor's first bill. She was a male impersonator and, though not quite achieving the artistry of Vesta Tilley, whom Pastor subsequently booked, was a good performer, esteemed for her character as well as her art. Her specialty was songs, mostly English music-hall ditties, which she paced with a monologue for relief. One of her best bits of impersonation was that of a tipsy dandy in a barbershop, continually falling asleep in the chair. The lines were period

British and none too good. One gag: "If you don't keep awake
I can't shave you," says the barber. "Then cut my hair,"
replied the dandy. Haw. But there was nothing wrong with
her characterization.

In military costume Miss Wesner made a supreme favorite
of her song, "Captain Cuff," the chorus of which went:

> Captain Cuff, Captain Cuff,
> You can tell me by my collar.
> Captain Cuff, Captain Cuff,
> Not worth half a dollar.
> With my military style,
> My cigaret I puff,
> While they all cry clear the way,
> Here comes Captain Cuff.

Dan Collyer for years had been one of Harrigan and Hart's
leading character comedians and when Pastor learned he had
off time immediately signed him for his Fourteenth Street
opening—a wise choice. A smart comic, Collyer spurned the
maudlin songs of the day. He chose mostly English melodies
and lyrics and, as one of the first to do "patter" stuff, was a
forerunner in developing a response to that type of higher
musical nonsense. One of his best liked songs was a Cockney
ditty called "Tommy, Don't Wriggle the Baby." A verse and
chorus:

Now I am the oldest one of a family numbering twenty.
At the tender age of one begun my troubles of which I had plenty.
The children I had to nurse, with an infant's nursery bottle.
And when they were twins, upon my pins!—the infants I'd like to
    throttle!

> CHORUS: Tommy don't wriggle the baby.
> Please don't tickle the baby.
> Be pertickeler, perpendickeler
> Always carry the child.

Tony himself was a conspicuous number on his own bill,
responding with a medley of old-timers his male audiences

An early bill of Tony's. You have met some of the performers: Kitty O'Neill, the sand jigger, Henshaw and Ten Broeck. The Irwin sisters were May and Flora.

knew and loved: "The Strawberry Blonde," "Lula, the Beautiful Hebrew Girl," "I'll Give You a Pointer on That," and "Yum, Yum, Yum." "The Strawberry Blonde" was published as "The Band Played On." The chorus:

> Then Casey would waltz with the strawberry blonde
> While the band played on.
> He'd waltz 'round the floor with the girl he adored
> While the band played on.
> His brain was so loaded it nearly exploded,
> The poor girl would shake with alarm.
> He married the girl with the strawberry curl
> While the band played on.

It is an interesting sample of the love lyrics of the time, which, without wasted intervals, invariably carried the romantic pair to the marriage bed (a nice preciseness of moral intent) instead of leaving them June-mooning for next morning's radio serial. "Lula, the Beautiful Hebrew Girl" is puzzling. No one seems to recall it, and, indeed, it is an unusual song for the period when humors and sentiment were mainly Irish, Dutch, and Negro. Even the rube type was not yet prevalent.

His Clean Shows Pay.

Aside from its general excellence, Pastor's opening bill is significant because it destroyed the notion that variety was a series of unfunny prat falls and vulgar noises. And for the first time, it delivered this important message to a mixed audience. The mothers and wives and sweethearts kept coming. Sometimes Pastor resorted to tricks to lure them in—gifts of hats, dress patterns, and other feminine gewgaws (forerunners of our bank and bingo nights). The *haut monde* seldom slummed at Pastor's. They did once when Tony booked a Western waitress who had become the bride of Lord Sholto Douglas. She did a song and dance and, to judge from contemporary prints, was terrible.

Not too speedily other managers (though mainly out of town) followed Pastor with "clean" shows, and scattered throughout the pages of theatrical papers of the middle eighties are occasional advertisements of theaters with "no wine room." In the second half of the decade the wine room gradually passed out (one of the last to go was the old Coeur d'Alene in Spokane, Wash.). New theaters were being built, acts were being scrubbed to meet the mixed audience (laudable, perhaps, yet making drab the color of the old expression). Variety was approaching the financially stable enterprise known as vaudeville, its bookings secure, its salaries definite and sizable. Vaudeville moved into the nineties as a distinct expression, its showmen and performers aware of their gold mine and alert to exploit it. Pastor lasted well into the new era, but he belongs to "variety" days.

Pastor regarded himself as a trouper rather than a manager; and, in spite of his fondness for euphemism, always mistrusted his high-sounding sobriquet, "The Impresario of Fourteenth Street." An indefatigable worker, he learned upward of 1,500 songs, possibly the greatest repertory of any performer— learned them laboriously, a phrase at a time, in the little greenroom he set up in his theater, and nearly drove his pianists mad with insistent repetitions.

His "Sarah's Young Man" was worth this sweat and toil.

> My first love was Sarah,
> Oh, none could be fairer,
> The fact is indeed
> I've ne'er seen one so fair.
> On her I grew love sick,
> She was a domestic
> And lived in a mansion
> On Washington Square.
>
> I ne'er shall forget her,
> The first time I met her
> She out of the house

For the dinner beer ran.
It was love at first sight
For the very next night
I with joy was accepted
As Sarah's young man.

This type of song was Pastor's forte. Pork-fat and genial as a barber, Pastor's was a jaunty step across the stages of New York which he trod more as friend than with the distinction of an artist. His was strictly a personal appeal. His idiosyncrasies of dress, his mincing, awkward, sometimes pathetic attempts to dance in his silly patent leather boots that laced nearly to his knees, his fake swagger in closing and snapping his opera hat, his twirl of the handle-bar mustachios, aroused by their novelty—an unthinking reaction. "What a fantastic costume!" exclaimed the admiring female novitiates in his audience, forgetting that it was a hang-over from Pastor's ringmaster days. He needed only his whip, and perhaps fooled with the opera hat in lieu of it—a nostalgic gesture. He could never remember his lines in later years and the actors said the fumble with his hat was a stall to cover a fading memory. But it was the best part of his act to Fourteenth Street patrons for whom the prop opera hat was an anomaly, an exotic delight.

Himself of Italian extraction and a devout Roman Catholic, Pastor had a tolerance for other races and faiths that haled him into court with other managers on a conspiracy charge brought by the late James S. Metcalfe, at that time dramatic critic for *Life*. Metcalfe was charged by the Theatre Managers Association, of which Pastor was a member, with writing articles insulting to those of the Jewish faith. Pastor and his associates immediately barred him from the forty-seven theaters they controlled, but when the case came before Magistrate Pool the court decided, in a ruling that has since held, the managers had no right to do so because theaters are quasi-public places.

Pastor put a poor box in his theater and installed a shrine

backstage to which he would repair (after checking up on the box office). Once a woman tripped on the steps of the Academy of Music, injuring herself fatally. Thereafter when Pastor went by the Academy, as he had to daily to get to his theater, he would pause, raise his hat, and bow, a curious genuflection he never explained.

"Bring in Your Trunks."

There was a curious flaw in his magnanimity. That he was able to continue so long in his Tammany Hall cubicle was because actors paid his way by accepting low salaries. But as the locust years descended, his booking became sporadic and he was obliged to lower his standards. Larger theaters opened by the plutocratic managers enabled them to cut prices. Good seats in vaudeville houses from 1900 to 1910 could be had for 50 cents. Pastor charged $1, but his box office in his little theater was not enough to pay stars' salaries even at S.R.O. His sympathy, too, got into the way of his business management, driving to madness his astute associate, Bert Sanderson, whom he had brought from 585 Broadway. Cracked-voiced tenors and fumbling banjoists were continued on the bill, largely because Pastor knew them when. Altruism is no asset in the theater.

Yet Pastor indulged in a practice completely at variance with this charitable attitude. Finding out what dates an act had open, he would wire it for this information, and, arranging his bill accordingly, would telegraph, "Bring in your trunks" and book them for this open time at a meager salary. Actors were always glad to capitalize a nonpaying period if only for coffee and crullers. Moreover, in later years Pastor's audience was largely professional. Actors like that. Some of the finest performances today in the Broadway theaters are at Sunday benefits for the Stage Relief Fund or at the matinees for the Actors Fund, where the house is preponderantly professional. Before another actor an actor preens.

To forestall his decline Pastor high-lighted ordinary (sometimes mediocre) bills by reviving festivals, anniversaries, and birthdays, including that of his wife who had been Josephine M. Foley. These derived from his earlier and more legitimate Christmas celebrations for children which, in the late nineties and early 1900's, kindled the interest of many notable subscribers, among them the elder J. P. Morgan, Mrs. Cornelius Vanderbilt, and Elbridge T. Gerry.

Pastor literally ran his affairs in his hat. He had vision but he never capitalized it on a nation-wide scale as did his competitors who were to engulf him. Yet he understood vaudeville, had a deeper feeling for it than any of the aggrandizers except Percy Williams. He saw Keith, Albee, Williams, Proctor, Poli, Beck, and Murdock increasing their chains and their fortunes—sometimes unethically, sometimes, the White Rats, vaudeville's abortive union of actors, charged, dishonestly. Proof of Pastor's awakening is poignantly indicated in one of his last statements.

"I owe my good health and good spirits to the fact that I am not worried by ambition," he said. "I frequently have been asked why I did not move up on Broadway. Once I listened to these suggestions and actually commenced negotiations with the Sires. [Times Square theater operators.] Then something or other went wrong and I never made another attempt. I look with amazement and respect at the men who can run three or four playhouses and apparently enjoy it. This one [his Fourteenth Street house] is work enough for me, but it is congenial work after all. I come down every day and attend to the booking, et cetera, and when that is over I am free."

Since Pastor was largely, if indirectly, responsible for the success of the big-time operators, this is more in the spirit of resignation than lament.

That Keith first took vaudeville out of the beer halls and wine rooms, bathed it in purity, and adorned it with silks, is a press agent's lie. Unwittingly, or by design, he but followed the lead of Pastor. Pastor's "clean" vaudeville at Fourteenth Street came two years before Keith even entered vaudeville.

Keith's beginning was humble—a "store" show, half museum, half theater, in Boston. True, it had no bar and no wine room, no drink-percentage girl performers, and no prostitutes; but neither did Pastor's Fourteenth Street Theatre. Pastor left camp followers and dramming when he quit 585 Broadway. And the idea of the double audience—women and men—was his. It was the reformation, and it was Pastor's. He, not Keith, was the Savonarola of variety.

Financially Pastor met the reformer's fate. It was his own fault; he lacked the drive. He was good-natured, friendly. In 1893, some twelve years after his opening, bewildered and downcast, he watched first Keith and then Proctor (not yet partnered) pick up the handkerchief of his "polite" vaudeville and exploit it for the millions he never made. He died, August 26, 1908, of a paralytic stroke, and cut up for $6,153.

Post-Pastor Influences

OTHERS shared with Pastor credit for the development of the new vaudeville. In the East, as early as the late eighties, variety was toning down its slapstick for comic lines, well-thought-out business, and clever characterizations. It was not general, but it was there, and the vaudeville that was to come owed Pastor and his followers a laurel for their boldness. Among the acts that assumed that some of their audiences could read and write and knew what time it was were Henshaw and Ten Broeck, Delehanty and Hengler, the Four Mortons, Ward and Vokes, Eddie Girard, the legmania artist, and McAvoy and May, a superb nut act.

John Henshaw was a sprightly chap, naturally witty, with a fine talent for flinging quips across the gaslights. His partner, May Ten Broeck, long since dead (as is now John), was a lovely lass with a pleasing voice and come-hither manner. The pair were a top team, capable of lifting ordinary stuff to something more than passable. Henshaw, a precocious lad, began his career as "Master Henshaw" with Charles Pettingill's Minstrels. He stayed in minstrelsy twelve years and then, cooking up an act with May, entered variety, and played virtually every house from coast to coast for many years.

The Henshaw-Ten Broeck act was a sidewalk conversation piece called "Deception," and here is some of it. They used a full set and at rise Miss Ten Broeck was discovered reading a letter.

MAY (*with wild delight*): Good heavens! The Count de Suckaire is calling on me! (*Runs off, and enter Henshaw: moth-eaten fur-collared coat, greasy vest, fading shiny clothing—an actor on the lam. The old mistaken identity. Reenter May and they go into a song and at finish terrific crash backstage*)

MAY (*reassuring audience*): Nothing but a house fell in. (*Exit May, and Henshaw turns on monologue*)

HENSHAW (*confidentially*): I am an actor. (*Crash*) I have just concluded my engagement with the Hardly Able Dramatic Alliance —hardly able to get from town to town. Last night I appeared in Sing Sing. Not having the necessary funds to liquidate my expenses I have made my escape and wandered here. If I can stay here until the sheriff gets by I'll be all right. In the meantime I'll go in search of food. People imagine that actors never eat. Actors do eat—occasionally. I had a meal last fall.

Delehanty and Hengler were a versatile song and dance team in both white- and blackface. They had an immense repertoire—neat song and dance, buck and wench, old men, young sports, banjo duets, bone solos and duets, and innumerable character impersonations. Hengler was admirable at this and his characterization of an English fop who is desperately trying to make conversation with an imaginary lady is still remembered by old-timers as of the tribe of Chevalier (Albert). After a number of inane remarks and answers to imaginary questions he finished:

I say—ah—are you fond of cheese? Aw—how extraordinary. . . . I take it you don't care for cheese? What a pity! . . . No, no . . . I mean . . . sorry . . . my fault, I assure you. . . . Does . . . ah . . . Does your brother like cheese? . . . You don't know? . . . No! . . . My word! . . . Oh, you have no brother? . . . Quite unfortunate. . . . Well, if you had a brother, would he

like cheese? . . . You don't know? . . . Aw, quite so . . . quite.
. . . Ha, ha . . . Ha, ha.

In the later eighties Delehanty and Hengler went to England and remained there. In the late nineties the Hengler sisters, daughters of Hengler, came to America with their mother and played variety houses here for a season's tour. They were so pretty, and did a neat, high-class, somewhat mild singing and dancing specialty.

The Four Mortons, a famous act, were Sam and Kitty, their daughter Clara, and their son Paul. Sam and Kitty appeared as an elderly Irish couple with Paul and Clara representing the younger generation. A good deal of the act was based on humorous family arguments. Paul was an excellent dancer, modern style, and Clara played the piano and flute, and danced beautifully. Sam did some Irish-reel steps, and Kitty, well on in weight and years, lifted her voluminous skirts and went into a lively Irish jig which always got over big. The whole act was pure personality. Sam was funny if he didn't do anything. When he peered out across the lights his facial expressions alone rocked the house. They usually finished with a dance ensemble that drew a big hand.

Hap Ward and Harry Vokes did a tramp act called "Harold and Percy." They first put it on at Pastor's in 1887. Pastor had never heard of them but, with characteristic generosity, gave them a chance. They wore tramp costumes, baggy patched pants, heavy stubble beards, buckteeth, and barberless hair. Hap entered first, looked round casually, and observed:

"It's no use talking, that Harold Weathersby plays a wonderful game of tennis. He beat me 40-love to my nothing today and Pa laughed right in front of the boys and I was so mad I could have taken his watch and chain." Nat Goodwin and Jim Corbett (they were friends) were out front and Nat laughed his fool head off. Hap has always maintained he never intended the lines to be funny. But no one who has seen the act will ever forget Hap's gag:

PERCY (*casually inspecting the room, and, upon opening door*): Harold, have you taken a bath?

HAROLD (*surprised*): No, is there one missing? (*Exit Harold*)

A stagehand, who served as a butler, latterly entered with a card from Harold Weathersby. "Show him up," directed Hap, and Vokes was promptly wheeled in on an express truck and dumped out on the stage. Hap signed for him. Exit man and truck.

It was unusual comedy for that period and after the show Goodwin and Corbett came backstage to congratulate the team. Hap was delighted with this praise from Sir Hubert, but astonished when Goodwin said, "Order a dress suit and take those patches off your face. You don't need them." Hap didn't believe him, but heeded the advice. And in dress clothes the act went even better. Pastor paid the boys $70 a week—not bad for those times, but Hap was hoping for more, especially when grapevine gossip brought them news that Pastor was pleased with the act. "Ask him for more money," demanded Vokes. "Not now," said Hap. Pastor booked them for another week, and as they were well into the middle of it asked them how they would like to go on the road. Hap lied; said he lived in New York and didn't think he could afford to go unless they got more money. So Pastor agreed to give them $100 a week and they toured with his unit as far as Chicago, playing the H. R. Jacobs chain in that city. Poor Vokes was burned to death in 1922, but the team long before had split. Hap used to say Vokes saved his drinking until before the show.

Trouping—Old Style.

In the middle eighties Eddie Girard was probably the greatest legmania artist in vaudeville, and a headliner in buck and wing, soft shoe, and pointed toe. His story is instructive in its revelation of the early variety period—its theaters, its hardships (the terms were almost synonymous), its costumes, its experiences.

In 1872 Eddie was a trainboy for the Union News Company

on the Erie Railroad run between Jersey City and Port Jervis, N.Y. Agile, touched with inherent grace, Eddie, though he had never seen a professional dancer, ambled into buck and wing and developed steps of his own. He was a favorite with the train crews, especially with the station attendants and hangers-on at Port Jervis. They matched him against another lad, one Willie Mahoney from Lackawaxon, Pa., and Eddie won. Realizing that they had something that could be exploited, the boys used the money they had taken in to send their trunks of candy, magazines, etc., to the Jersey City office, and quit that kind of railroading for good.

Eddie had a routine which he called "The Essence of Old Virginia." It was a slow tempo, made up of old-fashioned darky steps, a kind of bastard clog, danced to Southern tunes. Willie was a good clogger, but lacked comedy. They worked up an act together and danced the saloons in Port Jervis and neighboring points until Hellmer's Sensations, a traveling variety unit, came to town. Hellmer, who lacked a dancer, heard about the boys, went to the town's pub, caught their act, and made them a proposition: $1.50 a week. They accepted.

Since they had no wardrobes, they made their first professional appearance in shirt sleeves and overalls. The orchestra consisted of a pianist, and a cornet player who had been a tailor. Liking the two boys, he agreed to make costumes for them. Garish color combinations were favored by such acts until the late nineties. Girard's breeches were made of bright red opera flannel and his two shirts fitted with ruffles and adorned with large white sailor collars. A red sash was tied about his middle, ending in a double bow at the side. He wore white stockings. Hellmer was so sure of the act he ordered special clog shoes for the boys from the (then) well-known firm of Shannon, Miller, and Crane. These cost $10 a pair. Upon Willie Mahoney, Hellmer bestowed the stage name of Willie Girard on the showman's belief that a brother (or sister) act goes well and is easy to remember.

Board went with the $1.50, and for an additional $1.50 Eddie looked after the kerosene footlights, ran errands, and did odd chores. The boys stayed with Hellmer until the show folded, eighteen months later, in Charleston, Vt.

Stranded in this tiny village, their plight was made worse by an outbreak of smallpox which quarantined them for months. To relieve their boredom, Eddie began working on a new clog to schottische time and practiced sand jigging. One night they sneaked off across the ice of the St. Lawrence and got into Canada where they hoped to pick up with a show. They were unlucky and returned to Ogdensburg, N.Y., where, for a time, their fortunes improved. There was a show in town called Whitmore and Clark's Minstrels. Its headliner was a blackface singer and monologist named Clapp—the same Clapp who later changed his name to Lew Dockstader. The boys played with Lew's show for a couple of weeks, but business was terrible and they were let out. So they trekked on to Scranton, Pa., where Willie's family had moved and where they were sure of a meal and a bed. En route they played all the pubs for throw money.

It was in Scranton that Eddie and his partner first took up with Washburn who considered himself a figure and billed himself as "the new Barnum." A member of the troupe whom the boys had met on their tour introduced them to Washburn who promptly asked them what salary they wanted. "None," said Eddie. And the boys signed up for two years as apprentices—1874–1876. Eddie's juvenile answer turned out lucky. Washburn proved an excellent guardian, had them tutored, supplied good food, slept them in decent hotels, gave them plenty of spending money, and hired halls for them to practice in.

Washburn had a son, Leon, who ran a saloon and dance hall in Rondout, N.Y. In 1877 the boys played there for a season on a bill that was headlined by "Mr. and Mrs. John Ince," a comedy act. They were the parents of Thomas H. Ince, the late Hollywood director. Meantime the boys' dance act had gone over and they began to feel established. Through a friend they obtained booking at Frank Wild's Variety Theatre in Syracuse. Wild not only paid them the unprecedented salary of $40 a week but gave them top billing. Later, when they were playing the Hartford (Conn.) Opera House, one of Pastor's traveling units visited the town, and, as actors do everywhere, came over to have a look at the "Pavilion" show with which the Girards were booked. They told Pastor the Girards were something and Tony sent for them. He watched them go through their act and hired them at $80 a week, and raised it in three years to $150—important money in the late seventies.

At the turn into the eighties some of the acts brought a new stunt into variety halls, induced the audience to sing along with them. This the boys soon exploited to their own advantage with the Girard Song Book which they had hawked in the halls and sold at stores for a dime a copy.

Also at this juncture many of the vaudeville teams were doubling into four-acts, aping the lead of Lester, Allen, Smith, and Waldron, a comedy quartet that had gained a phenomenal response. Lester and Allen (described in the Pastor chapter) had been a great pair, as had Smith and Waldron—united, they doubled their popularity. So the Girard boys linked up with the team of Seamon and Sumers in St. Louis, billing themselves in a minstrel type of sketch called "Children of the South—Song, Dance, Acrobatic, Eccentric Comedy, and Character." They marketed it around, obtaining various salaries, from $700 in Cincinnati and Chicago, which was good, to $350 in the honky-tonks, which was not so good. This was before bookers and agents, and performers took what they could get.

The four-act lasted until the Girards got a flattering offer from Thatcher and Ryman. George Thatcher and Ad Ryman were popular minstrels whose shows invariably made money; to be booked with them meant a corresponding share of success. The Girards joined them at the Arch Street Theatre in Philadelphia and there, with Frank Dumont, a talented and important skit writer, Thatcher and Ryman produced a travesty on "Camille."

William Henry Rice played the name part, Ad Ryman played Armand, and the rest of the cast was made up of such favorite comics as Billy Carroll, later of Harris and Carroll, Chauncey Olcott (yes), and William Haywood, a noted female impersonator. Eddie had a bit part. Well, it was a riot ("Camille," that is). The show was most aptly timed, for the Divine Sarah Bernhardt was playing Philadelphia in a repertoire which included the Dumas play.

But Bernhardt, instead of storming out of town in a burst of temperament, not only took the gag good-naturedly but actually went to see it. She was overcome with delight and amazement. Indeed, she dickered for its presentation in Paris at her own theater. The negotiations fell off when Thatcher and Ryman received an offer to combine with Primrose and West, one of the top minstrel outfits. They regarded the minstrel show as the lesser gamble and accepted.

At this point the Girard boys quit to join Sam Hague's British Minstrels. They spent the following six months in Liverpool and the provinces. Over there a misunderstanding parted them, and when Eddie returned he signed up with the Thatcher, Ryman, Primrose, West show, an engagement that ended in a fist fight with Thatcher in Cincinnati. Thatcher, a great spender, tosspot, and trencherman, set up a champagne party for the troupe in celebration of their opening. The first to pass out, he was the first to recover; and next day, hang-over or no, he rounded up the party and cursed them furiously for taking part in a drinking bout which he himself had promoted. "Then I hit him," said Eddie.

After this Eddie teamed with Charles V. Seamon, a tried trouper and tripper, and the pair went to Chattanooga, beginning a tour which lasted until 1884. Then Eddie formed his own minstrel combination of Billy Arlington, Girard, and Harry Wyatt, and, except for a few excursions to pick up off-season money, was lost to vaudeville.

The team of McAvoy and May concludes this summary of unusual comedy acts of the eighties. Theirs was an outstanding nut act, and like all such, impossible to describe. Even if one had a complete script of a nut act, it would avail nothing, for how could it indicate the falls, mugging, coughs, squeaks, and spontaneous business of those acts which depended solely upon the performers for their appeal? The reviewers had a difficult time with McAvoy and May, invariably using the cliché— "excruciatingly funny, and winning the lion's share of laughter and applause." McAvoy was most fortunate in his partner, for May was young, pretty, and clever, an admirable feeder and excellent support. Their falls were funny and their impersonations of hicks, tough waiters, and other types were a comic-strip history of the times. They usually closed with a burlesque drama that was a bit on the rough side but a belly laugh throughout. In all the years they trouped together they never became stereotyped, always seemed to enjoy their work —the truest test of an artist.

Although a number of these acts postdated Pastor's cleanup drive for mixed audiences (a linen washing that included smartening of performances), they were part of the general movement that was developing variety from a honky-tonk side show to a definite entertainment expression.

The Foreign Invasion

A s VAUDEVILLE approached the twentieth century, not only the types of audiences were changing, but the geographical variation became pronounced. Performers had to extemporize new lines and business according to their booking. Acts as played at Keith's Union Square were no go for Allentown, Pa., and in turn had to be toughened for Carson City, Nev. Roughly, there were two types of audiences: in the cities the alert and critical with no compunction about hissing a luckless performer; in the smaller towns the family type, adult and more kindly, but harder for good acts to play to. Communication of styles, popular songs, and events, political or cultural, was not facilitated by radio, newsreels, or motion pictures. Thus the topical gag of a comic that knocked them in the aisles on Broadway was often incomprehensible in Wichita and points west or south.

Vaudeville, being the most contemporary of theatrical entertainment, accordingly was graded by the performers, an unfortunate necessity because of the uneven presentations that resulted. Against this tendency (and an improving force generally) was the invasion of the foreign artists. They accented satire, sophistication, and characterization, employed the *mot*, were alive to nuances, and played up, seldom down, to their

135

Albert Chevalier in two of his vaudeville characterizations.

audiences. Most of them were superb examples of the universal quality of art.

American audiences were unfamiliar with Albert Chevalier's English types, had small knowledge of Harry Lauder's bonnie Scots, of Yvette Guilbert's French songs. Yet these artists, and many others, achieved remarkable success in the vaudevilles here because their pure art was tied to entrancing personalities; an unassailable combination.

Albert Chevalier is best remembered for his songs, among them: "My Old Dutch," "Mrs. 'Enry 'Awkins," and "Knocked 'Em in the Old Kent Road." One of his best numbers, forgotten by all but the old-timers, was "Wot's the Good of Hanyfink? Why! Nuffink!" It was a perfect illustration of his work in character. The song involves an impersonation of a disgruntled old man. Chevalier presented it in a make-up of unkempt white beard, shabby dark clothes, and a shapeless black hat, giving a complete demonstration of utter futility:

Wot's the good of tryin' to hearn a livin' now-a-days?
Wot's the good of honesty when 'umbug only pays?
Wot's the good o' slavin',
Or a-ravin' about savin'?
Wot's the good of hanyfink? Why! Nuffink!*

From this he would turn to a genial, chronic loafer who accepted life's futility with less pessimism:

Wot's the use of kickin' up a row
If there ain't no work about?
If you can't get a job you can rest in bed
Till the school kids all comes out.
If you can't get work you can't get the sack,
That's a argyment wot's sensible and sound.
Lay your head back on your piller
And read your "Daily Mirrer,"
And wait till the work comes round.

Most of Chevalier's act consisted of song recitals with orchestral accompaniments, but he often adapted his characterizations to monologues, and one of these—"The Ladies' Bazaar"—was a gem. Although its humor was as delicate as it was exotic it was a great favorite in America. In it Chevalier portrayed a drab, humorless vicar, mincing about among the booths of a fair that was being held for the purpose of raising church funds:

Ah, good evening, Mrs. Drableigh . . . Quite a gathering, is it not? . . . It is gratifying to see such a number in attendance, although some of the booths are not patronized as well as one would wish . . . Mrs. Weems's jumble booth is almost deserted. [Jumble: a thin sweet cake] . . . They say her jumbles are most excellent, too . . . Um-m-m, makes them herself, I understand . . . Oh, no, no, I haven't tasted them, I find that I must abstain from sweets most rigidly . . . I see you have made some purchases . . . What is this one? . . . Ah, yes, a pot-lifter! Quite a useful utensil . . . Quite . . . And only two guineas! How remarkably cheap! . . . That is a beautiful slate pencil, too . . . You won it? How extremely

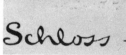

MARIE LLOYD.
FROM THE
JOHN H. JAMES
COLLECTION

54 West 23d St.
New York.

The performer.

ALICE LLOYD
The pretty.

fortunate . . . Only three shillings a chance! . . . [Laughter and
applause off stage] Evidently something of a humorous nature has
transpired . . . They are conducting an auction sale, you say? . . .
Quite a novel idea, it is pleasurable to see that our young people are
taking an interest, although 'twould be more seemly were their
activities conducted with more decorum . . . They are not our
people? . . . Then . . . ah . . . who . . . ? They are artists from
the [music] halls!!! . . . Oh, dear, dear . . . What a sad com-
mentary on the trend of our churches today; our members not only
visit the halls, but they engage artists for our functions . . . An
unwarranted expenditure . . . They are giving their services free?
. . . Um, well, I suppose we must be, ah, lenient, Mrs. Drableigh,
and endeavor to see good in all things . . . Um . . . Um-m-m . . .
There seems to be quite a commotion around Mrs. Shelburne's
booth . . . She is not there! You say she became disheartened and
left? . . . Then who IS in charge? . . . Lottie Foulard! . . .
From the Empire!!! . . . Not the person who appears in such
shocking costumes? . . . Oh, no, no, I have never seen the show,
of course . . . I, ah, . . I, ah . . . chanced upon some of her
revolting photographs . . . What! . . . She sold everything in
the booth, and had to replenish from the other stands? . . . Um-
m-m, perhaps we might do well to investigate and see that there is
nothing, ah, amiss . . . She might be able to dispose of Mrs.
Weems's jumbles . . . Shall I carry the pot-lifter for you? . . .
[*Exit*]

Chevalier was serious to the point of idiosyncrasy in the
theater, but away from it he dismissed the stage from his mind
as one sheds a coat; and though he was a charming fellow and
a grand conversationalist, no one could ever induce him to
talk shop. He was a fanatic on enunciation and part of his
daily routine was the practice of tongue twisters. A favorite,
"The sea ceaseth and sufficeth itself," he maintained was the
most difficult sentence to pronounce in the English language.

Guilbert and Victoria.

The success of Yvette Guilbert was even more astonishing
than Chevalier's. Not only were most of her songs in French,

E. BIEBER   Eigenthum u. Verlag von E. Bieber   BERLIN. W.
K. HOFPHOTOGRAPH.   UND
                                                   HAMBURG.

YVETTE GUILBERT

they were in an idiom only a sophisticated Parisian could understand. It was wholly due to her finesse in putting them over—the expression, mannerisms, and gestures that made the meaning clear—together with a personality unrivaled in the music halls. She made her first American tour in 1897, carrying a concert company of four persons and a pianist. To the chagrin of her intelligent followers, her American manager, Ted Marks, insisted that she add several popular coon songs to her repertoire. She complied, learning "My Gal's a High Born Lady" and "I Want You, My Honey, Yes, I Do." She could have won her house if she had sung in Sanskrit.

But although America feted her with box-office acclaim, she seems not to have become acclimated and in New Orleans was so unhappy she spread misery to her management until restored by a joyous idea of John Loeffler (already noted as Pastor's hat-check boy) who accompanied the tour as a sort of Man Friday to both Marks and Guilbert. Seems she was lonesome for her mother in France. So Loeffler had her record a greeting to her mother on a Columbia phonograph cylinder. The company made similar arrangements for her mother, and after the exchange of records Guilbert's spirits soared. A tall redhead with beckoning features and a stage personality of ineffable resource: La Guilbert—the incomparable.

If she had an English equivalent it could only have been Vesta Victoria who, by the way, permitted Guilbert to use her own song, "Poor John." That and "Waiting at the Church" will be always in the memories of Victoria's vaudeville audiences, but they were not the best illustrations of her talent for commingling satire with broad burlesque, in characterizations worthy of mating with Chevalier's.

One of these was "It's All Right in the Summertime," a song about a husband who was apparently a fifth-rate sign painter with Sargent delusions. He forced her to pose for all her pictures as a side line from the drudgery of housework:

> CHORUS: Oh, it's all right in the summertime,
>   In the summertime it's lovely,

VESTA VICTORIA
"Poor John," indeed!

> While my old man's a-paintin' hard,
> Standin' 'ere a-posin' in the old back yard.
> But, oh, my, in the winter time,
> It's a different thing you know . . .
> With a red, red nose, and very few clothes,
> And the stormy winds do blow.

For this number she wore a costume of pink tights and drapery of a gauzy white material. On her head was a white wreath and she carried a lyre that resembled a cross between a cigar box and a zither, probably the craftsmanship of some gifted stage carpenter. But what always took the house was her extravagant sylphlike exit.

An even older type that she exploited with irresistible humor was "He Calls Me His Own Grace Darling":

> And he calls me 'is own Grace Darling.
> 'E says that I'm 'is pet.
> I've filled each 'plaice' within 'is 'sole'—
> That ain't no 'cod,' you bet.
> When 'e arsks me if I lov'd 'im,
> I said, 'Wot 'O, not 'arf!
> Why I likes you just for your whiskers
> 'Cos they tickle me and make me larf.'

Here is exoticism to the full. America, racing toward the 1900's, recognized no peasant types beyond the genial "rube" or hobo or lackadaisical "coon." Each of these was pictured in foible-forgotten caricature—the rube especially as a straw-chewing hayseed whose table manners and credulity were overshadowed by kindliness and occasional canny reactions. He was kidded, but admitted. With almost unbelievable agility, America fused this genre with Victoria's types in gleeful acceptance—a tribute to her ineffable style. It was Victoria's artistry to blend her Britishers, whether costers or Cockneys, into a common humanity gently critical, wisely tolerant. If this isn't art it is above it.

Not all her songs were of slaveys and navvy types; she was at home as well in the West End. Indeed, one of her best characterizations was the song, "You Can Do a Lot of Things at the Seaside," which Mark Sheridan, an English comic, loaned her with the same kindness she herself shared "Poor John" with Guilbert. (The English music-hall artists owned their songs and never parted with them except as a gracious gesture to a famous artist.)

> CHORUS: You can do a lot of things at the seaside
> That you can't do in town.
> Fancy seeing mother with her legs all bare,
> Paddling in the fountain in Trafalgar Square.
> But bobbing up and down in the ocean,
> With fat, old Dr. Brown. . . .
> You can do a lot of things at the seaside
> That you can't do in town.*

Victoria was never as well received in London as in America which, with comparable contrariness, repeatedly declined to accept the art of Marie Lloyd except in the big-time theaters. Londoners loved Marie. And once the English public fastens to a performer she can do no wrong; it is always her sketch, or the playwright, or the manager, who has done her in. Marie Tempest, regarded with indifference by Broadway, could fill Albert Hall with a "Hesperus" recitation.

At any rate, when Marie Lloyd came over during the period we are discussing, our audiences, unaware of her English reputation (someone bungled her exploitation), saw her only as a fattish, middle-aged woman who sang songs about rather boring characters and uninteresting locations. It was her idiom, and her intense regard for her audiences, that were wrong. She gave them all she had without pulling, always assuming their intelligence. This honesty worked against her: a change of material, simpler and more understandable deliveries, and she might have achieved a more deserved success.

* Copyright 1911 by Francis, Day & Hunter, Ltd. Published by Harms, Inc. Used by permission.

On the other hand, hinterland America always rated Alice Lloyd above Marie although her talent was inferior. Her voice wasn't much, and her songs were innocuous, but she was winsome and pretty and modest with a stage presence enhanced by charming clothes—fairish factors in any theater. Moreover, unlike Marie, she was heavily billed and properly press-agented. And over she went. Vaudeville was full of such unconscious audience malevolence. Happy Fanny Fields, for instance, just another American singing hoofer, went to London and was a headline with a hurrah Dutch song and dance in big wooden shoes; while Daisy Harcourt, a London performer whose English rating corresponded to ours of Fanny, came to America unheralded and was an overnight success. It was Daisy's own fault she didn't last. Much of her material was indigo—no go at the time when Keith and Albee were fire-hosing vaudeville. She refused to tone it down. It was unfortunate, for her mildest song, "Good Old London 'Ria" (Maria), was her best. She faded into burlesque, and faded out with it.

The British Bard; the Cantie Lauder.

Wilkie Bard, a great English music-hall comic, made his debut at Hammerstein's Victoria. His salary was fantastic—$3,500—so was his flop. Despite his failure, Albee brought him over another season and he opened at the New York Palace on a Monday matinee. This was a murderous ordeal. At these performances nearly all of vaudeville's managers, agents, and bookers assembled to determine the appeal of an act. Bard was hissed off. He went to his dressing room, inconsolable, sank to a chair and sobbed audibly, unmindful of his wife's comforting words. Albee came in.

"It'll be all right," said Albee. "I'll put some experts on your act. They'll freshen it up and it'll go over."

"I'm sailing Wednesday," said Bard.

"The hell you are," said Albee. "You've got a twenty-week contract with me and you'll finish it."

He did—with astonishing success. Bard had made the mistake of opening with one of his most exotic characterizations, that of a Welsh miner. He discarded it, and everything was fine. One of his best bits, silly in its routine, was the portrayal of a tipsy London gent in top hat, white tie, and Inverness, carrying a bunch of chrysanthemums and trying to get the key into his doorway keyhole. It was exquisitely done and American audiences loved it.

Bard's genial one-with-the-audience technique was also the forte of Laddie Cliff, a Scotch singing comedian, who, although several rungs below Lauder, played a great deal of American time.

Laddie Cliff never imitated Lauder's style; he got by on his own. As a matter of fact, it would have been suicidal for any performer to try to duplicate Lauder's work. There were, of course, many legitimately stage-announced imitations of Sir Harry singing "She's My Daisy" or "I Love a Lassie." They kindled only warmer affection for the original. Lauder was in a class by himself; the greatest foreign single draw in the history of vaudeville.

As a boy he had been porridge poor, working endless hours in coal mines for a few bob to support his widowed mother. He loved to sing and learned many of the Scottish folk tunes and some of the more modern character songs. These he would try out at impromptu entertainments. They led to an engagement with a small-time concert company. Its bookings were irregular and Lauder scarcely earned more than he had in the mines. But he had faith in himself and soon struck out on his own with his goal the English music halls.

Aware that the burr in his songs was unsuitable for London (whose audiences loath dialect), he wrote some songs in English to sing with a Scottish accent, and Anglicized some of his regular numbers. Then, after a short tour in the provinces, he managed to book one of the lesser London halls. He was a success, and agents assailed him for dates far into the future at about $40 a week. Lauder signed everything—to his bitter regret.

Fourteen Philadelphia lawyers couldn't break an English music-hall contract. If you sign you must play the time. You can set it back, if you get a better offer and you pay the 10 per cent commission on both old and new contracts. But if the artist lives he must play out the old contract sometime—and at the old figure. After his success in America Lauder returned to England heralded like a circus. So the British managers seized upon him, forced him to play out their contracts at the price of a "chorus singer in the front cloth." (English stage jargon for a singer of topical songs, the audience joining in the second chorus; "front cloth"—a drop in one.)

Lauder never changed his style for American audiences. He even followed the English custom of taking his own time for costume changes without regard for the "stage waits." English audiences are accustomed to "stage waits"; in fact, like them. They order drinks, fill pipes and light them, inspect the program or the racing chart, eat a sandwich, hum the chorus of the last song—enjoy themselves. Lauder's procedure, from another, would have driven the average American audience mad. But they took it from Lauder and liked it.

His monologue was no string of gags, no running fire of jokes. He would tell about foolish adventures that befell him in some Scottish village with an unpronounceable name. But in a way that would make one feel he had known since boyhood the characters introduced. He would sing about a nitwit Scottish boy—"The Saftest in the Family"—in a manner that tugged one back to pocketknife-marbles-and-string days. A pretty blonde danced on after his "I Love a Lassie." "That's her," Harry would cry, and off he would whirl with her in a lovelight that would melt the heart of a sadist. His whole act defies the analysis of words, while it perfectly expressed his own saying:

"Ye can sometimes write down what ye think, but ye canna write down what ye feel."

The Lily of Jersey.

Numerous importations, mostly "name" players, flocked to American vaudeville like flies around a honeypot. Some we shall meet again, but those immediately to mind are Bernhardt, Charles Hawtrey, Mrs. Patrick Campbell, Marie Tempest, each of whom succumbed to the sweets of sizable Saturday paychecks. But the cream of the quest was Lily Langtry, the "Jersey Lily." Those who remember her sigh deeply at the recollection—as of a valentine of memories; a long since summer's last rose. She was the most glamorous woman of her time—and its most awful actress. Her appeal was based solely upon her beauty; enough for pictures; a vacuum for art. But what a name! What desire! Oscar Wilde once said: "I would rather have discovered Lily Langtry than America." America discovered her. She made her New York debut in 1882 under Henry E. Abbey. The critics crucified her, and she carried back to England with her £60,000.

Her American vaudeville debut did not occur until 1906 (she was fifty-four and still a flower), and thereafter she dipped often into vaudeville's lush tills, coming over in 1912 (at sixty) and again in 1915 (sixty-three!). Her 1906 offering was a sketch (the word annoyed her; "tabloid tragedy," she called it), "'Twixt the Nightfall and the Light," by Graham Hill. Of it a reviewer on the old *Telegram* wrote, "She is still beautiful." And Alan Dale observed, "While it would be absurd to say that her work was promising, it can be truthfully said that it fulfilled all promises." (In London in the same sketch she was hooted from the stage and police had to escort her to her hotel.)

Yet her American tour was a tremendous financial success. Everyone knew she was Edward VII's crown jewel. That, and her beauty, were all she had to offer. All, indeed! So six years later (it was too long for the voracious managers, but Lily, who had made $1,000,000 in sixteen years selling beauty and ham, could not be bothered), she returned for her 1912 vaudeville tour under the Central Vaudeville Production Co. headed by Martin Beck. She played a sketch called "Helping the Cause," a suffragette theme. It was frightful.

In 1915 she came over with a legit show called "Ashes." It failed to draw, and she folded it immediately in Richmond, Va. Her leading man was Lionel Atwill, to America then unknown. Returning to New York she called Albee. Said she had a good one-acter that could be done cheaply, that it required only one other player and she had him—Atwill. Albee sent Darling to the Ritz-Carlton to talk to her. She turned on the charm, and poor Darling all but dissolved. "What a delightful name," she said, as he introduced himself, and, "Oh, don't sit there; it shows every imperfection in your face." You could have ladled Darling out of the suite. He said afterward he would have given her $2,500 if she'd been a Cherry Sister.

They opened her at Percy Williams's Brooklyn Orpheum, a famous house with marvelous audiences (Brooklyn knew and loved vaudeville), and Monday night after the opening matinee Darling went over to check. "She's wonderful," said the manager, "and the women are crazy about Atwill. The schoolgirls swoon over him." Fine! Darling went backstage to congratulate her. "And your leading man is splendid," he said. And she said, "I've given him the sack. He goes a week Saturday." Darling asked what was wrong. "He's impossible," said Lady de Bathe (which she was then, having acquired the baronet for her last husband). "But, Miss Langtry, you do not understand American audiences; leading men like that mean a lot of business." She was obdurate. "I'm paying him a very large salary, more than he ever got," she snapped. "In England he only got £6, and I'm paying him £70. And he won't look after my luggage." Darling feigned surprise. Perhaps if he spoke to Mr. Atwill? "You can talk to him, but he is an impossible man." Darling set out for Atwill's dressing room and laid down the law. "It isn't nice for a woman of her position to look after her trunk checks and scenery and hire props," he said. "Any man would do that for her." Atwill promised to attend to those details and saved his job.

On her subsequent vaudeville tour Langtry hired Alfred Lunt for her leading man. Lunt admired her for the remarkable woman she was and their relations were always friendly. She often touched on her London associations, royal and otherwise, in acidulous—and libelous—reminiscence.

Then came the story: Her intimacy with Edward VII was an open Continental secret—Edward denied her nowhere; not even kings could do that to Langtry. She related how, as Prince of Wales, he had her presented at court to bow before Victoria. "And I wore for my headdress three large plumes," she told Lunt, "so there could be no doubt about my 'Ich Dien'."

Langtry hated managers generally, especially those in the provinces. She was a constant enigma to them—indeed, many had never heard of her, accepting the Lily only as a flower from Albee's greenhouse but, accordingly, a "must" corsage. A Midwestern manager once asked her, "What do you do?"

"I ride a bicycle on a tight rope," said Lady de Bathe.

"Aren't you afraid?"

"Oh, no. I have fallen so many times."

God rest her.

Managerial Burgeoning and the Critique Caustique

Iмportant in developing vaudeville along the lines Pastor had surveyed in Fourteenth Street were J. Austin Fynes, a Boston newspaperman who in 1893 came to New York to manage Keith's newly opened Union Square Theatre, and Epes W. Sargent who, under the pseudonym "Chicot," became the first critical commentator of vaudeville.

Chicot's advent as a critic was quite by chance. After a short bit covering minor concerts for the *Musical Courier* he drifted to Broadway to work for Leander Richardson's *Dramatic News*. Richardson was a loud-vest sport with a finger in every fly-by-night, and the paper soon folded, mainly because Richardson had sunk most of his money in backing one Santanelli, a hypnotist. Santanelli had been a hit in the sticks, but Broadway knifed him. What money came to the box office Richardson took to the horse park. If he won, the *News* staff was paid—how often you can guess. Chicot once received $2 and a cocktail for a week's work.

After the *News* failed, Richardson induced Blakeley Hall to take him on as editor of the *Metropolitan Magazine* which was then published in connection with the *Daily Mercury*, a racing and theatrical sheet. Richardson carried Chicot with him. At this time—the early nineties—publishers took heed only

152

of vaudeville acts that advertised and reserved their reviews for legit shows. Chicot tried to persuade Richardson to give attention to vaudeville, but Richardson laughed him off, and so did Asa Paine, Hall's chief editor. Still Chicot kept up regular attendance at the variety theaters and wrote caustic reviews which were never published. They just lay around on Hall's desk.

One Sunday when there was the usual shortage of copy (somehow they could never fill their Monday paper) Roland Burke Hennesey, Hall's general manager, scooped up all the loose copy on Hall's desk, including Chicot's reviews, and printed it, Chicot's stuff appearing under the column head, "Chatter of Music Halls." It was unsigned, but later Sargent induced Richardson, who wrote the only signed pieces in the *Mercury*, to allow him the use of a pen name. Sargent, who had been reading Dumas, chose Chicot, "because," he said, "he wasn't as big a fool as he looked."

The column proved to be one of the most provocative departments ever printed in a newspaper, and Chicot's influence on the development of vaudeville can hardly be overestimated. Managers and public accepted his analyses at first skeptically, then with enthusiasm. Both were grateful for guidance, and lazy or indifferent performers, realizing that bad notices might lead to cancellation, sought to better their routines. Chicot became an important figure on Broadway, respected and liked by some, hated, feared, and yet admired by most. But he hit hard and was generally loathed throughout the circuits. Often he was threatened with physical violence. A fighter himself, he responded in person to all letters suggesting he meet the aggrieved performer. None ever showed, but one sent his wife whom Chicot appeased. Only once was he hurt. One day when he was entering George Liman's office, Charles B. Lawler, who wrote "The Sidewalks of New York," swung on him and blacked his eye.

Chicot soon left Hall to cover vaudeville for the *Germanic News*, but in the mid-nineties Hall sent for him again to write for the *Morning Telegraph*, a new paper he was starting. Its genesis is interesting. Tammany Hall, lambasted editorially by every newspaper in New York, bought the *Mercury*, a Sunday publication, to ensure the support of at least one paper; turned it over to Hall and gave him $10,000 to run it with the understanding that he was not to get a nickel more. Hall threw out the *Mercury* title, called the "new" sheet the *Morning Telegraph*, hired Richardson as managing editor, and put it out as a daily sporting and theatrical newspaper. As a side enterprise Hall and Richardson wrote stories of interest to the provinces which they sold to out-of-town papers—inaugurating, probably, the first news syndicate.

The paper prospered for a time under Hall, but eventually the International Paper Co.'s unrelenting "please remit" became so embarrassing he sold it to William C. Whitney, who had been Secretary of the Navy in Cleveland's first Cabinet (1885) and who at the time of his purchase was acquiring his racing stable. This ended the paper's connection with Tammany. Chicot continued with it until it was purchased by E. R. Thomas, another racing man. It is still published as a racing and theatrical paper under the ownership of Moses L. Annenberg. Chicot's writing career terminated on *Variety* (the Broadway weekly he helped Sime Silverman found) with his death in 1938.

Chicot was a born crusader, years ahead of his time. He raged at the hokum and bathos that enraptured the sentimental nineties, and his honest opinions, except for a few spiteful instances (humanly understandable), were influenced only by merit. Throughout his career he was a pain in the neck to the indifferent performer. He sailed into headliners with the vigor he used for the honky-tonk hoofers, and he put the spurs to many a faker and thief. He was in continuous struggle with Albee, Keith, Murdock, Beck, and the meaner bookers and managers.

His disregard of big names is astonishing. He considered Vesta Tilley, an English music-hall artist of considerable draw, an ordinary entertainer and so wrote.

With the worthless freak acts Chicot had no patience whatever and hurled his philippics at them with libelous contempt.
Of the Cherry Sisters, who were an especial loathing, he wrote:

They do not . . . care to be exploited as freaks, and insist on
being treated with due respect. By way of material for press notices
they tell him [the comment refers to a letter they wrote to E. D.
Price, manager of the Pleasure Palace in New York where they were
booked to play the following week] that they were given four golden
horseshoes . . . in Chicago, and presented with a glass cane,
handsomely decorated with ribbons, at St. Louis. If arrangements
could be made I should be glad to present them with a horseshoe
attached to the business end of an able-bodied and hard-working
jackass.

Among the rackets that Chicot exposed was one practiced
by a contemptible European agent for Albee. It was this man's
method to go abroad and book an act on contract for six weeks
in the East at Keith's and six months later for four weeks on
the Orpheum (Western) time, promising to fix up the intermediate dates after his return to New York. But soon after
his return he would write that it was impossible to book the
intermediate time. This left the performer no recourse but to
cancel; he could not afford to come over and play six weeks
Eastern time, return to London, Paris, or Berlin, then come
back in six months to play four weeks' Western time. The
booker knew this, knew also that the contract provided that a
performer who canceled his own act was still liable for the
agent's commission. This the thief invariably collected— until
Chicot stopped him. After the exposé Dan Mills, press agent
for the Keith and Albee interests, told Walter Hunt Turner
of the *Morning Telegraph* that Chicot was costing Albee $20,000
a year and added, "If you don't fire him, Albee will fire me."
Said Turner, "You'd better look for a job."

Chicot combined a natural skepticism with a venomous pen,
a dangerous alliance that sometimes warped his judgment and
carried him headlong. Yet even when he dealt in unwarranted invective or puny cantrips of pique, his comment was
refreshing if only because it was startling in an easy-go, log-

rolling day. At least he did much to break up the winking fraternity of ad rustlers and bilking bums who would sell a lousy act to the public in fulsome texts—blurbs that were often printed in columns adjoining the paid ad of the act. His legit descendant, Alan Dale, often offended with the same personalities that spit a performer for spite. But they made for rousing times and a lively theater, which was justification enough. We have had too little of this in our own day.

Everything but Technicolor.

J. Austin Fynes, manager of Keith's Union Square Theatre, doubled Pastor's clean vaudeville spades with the introduction of legit stars in sketch acts to add dignity and class to his bills. This was in the middle nineties when the Harolds and Arthurs were still pretty snooty about vaudeville. Fynes corrected this attitude with the dangle of big money for less work, and within a season had signed such important fairhairs as Maurice Barrymore, Charles Dickson, a favorite Broadway comedian who teamed with Lillian Burkhardt, Robert Hilliard, John Mason, who paired with Marion Manola (an opera singer whose loss of voice forced her to the acting stage), and Mr. and Mrs. Sidney Drew, the latter having been Gladys Rankin.

Fynes may have borrowed his legit sketch idea from Francesca Redding. Redding had asked herself why a drama couldn't be written to variety size and presented as a definite act on the bill, a unit for booking wherever. The answer was that it could. She did it, and in 1893 she and Hugh Stanton in "A Happy Pair," inaugurated the first sketch team in vaudeville. "A Happy Pair" was a novelty for the time. Its thirty-minute act told a clean domestic story in which no singing, dancing, gagging, or topical allusions occurred. A novelty? It was a feat.

Stanton and Miss Redding had been Pennsylvania stock-company actors in a company of which Stanton was manager as well as leading player. Redding was the dominant partner, but even she had misgivings at her vaudeville opening in

Philadelphia. Under the impression that it was a continuous show lasting twelve hours she appeared for her first bill carrying a dinner pail. She began with $75 a week for the act, but it took hold to such an extent that in less than two months the team (according to her later recollection) was receiving $250 a week. Within four years she had won the title of "evangelist of vaudeville." In fact, she became so entrenched that with other partners (Stanton after several seasons went off on his own) she was booked so solid she scarcely had time to rest. She realized fortune, and in twenty-two years of touring played in only five sketches.

One of Fynes's first recruits for the Union Square was Robert Hilliard. His act was "The Littlest Girl," a dramatization of the Richard Harding Davis yarn and a bit on the dare side since it dealt with divorce. It told of the child who was the pawn in the case—a tear-jerker angle over which the clergy and Puritan picklepusses could cry happily. But it was crude in structure, consisting mostly of two long and two short speeches—by Hilliard, of course.

Redding's sketches were flouncy, but they did tell a story, had real suspense, and introduced occasional bits of satire. (Stanton even bettered this when he quit Redding to put on his own sketch "For Reform." The act was an effective goosing of the clubwoman busybody.) Everyone was familiar with Redding's type of sketch and its success. Why it wasn't immediately copied is just one of those things. A smart new act or brilliant gag or bit of aisle-tossing business in vaudeville usually had its imitators in the next performance. At any rate, Hilliard's name was sufficient draw—and his tag line terrific for those days: "Miss Betty sleeps with her mother at her father's tonight." Curtain.

Whistles and Squeals.

Maurice Barrymore, one of the most popular of the legit sketch players in vaudeville, was never credited by critics and intelligent patrons as a brilliant vaudevillian. He had a large slice of Westphalian and his supporting casts were even hammier because he would never pay decent salaries. Moreover, he was feuding constantly with Albee, the critics, and the newspapers. One night when he got plastered, police picked him up on a Staten Island ferryboat and took a knife away from him. He said he was looking for Albee and our friend Chicot.

Meantime Fynes was doing well with his troupe of legit seals and looking about for other "dignity" acts to top-hat his bills. One woman he signed rates a Hollywood superlative —a Mrs. Alice Shaw. Nobody today seems to remember her, but in 1893 she was a greatly respected and admired performer on the women's club and garden circuits; her carriage trade following almost equal to the Republican vote. But Shaw had an act. Also she had solidity and graciousness and decorum and she laid them right in the lap of the spruced-up vaudeville which was rapidly learning how to sit at table and use a fork. She was a whistler, that's right, she whistled. Rival managers thought Fynes was losing his mind, but there it was, all black on the house statements.

When Edouard Remenyi, noted concert violinist, the Heifetz of his day, was returning from a white-tie-and-tails tour across the country, Fynes again dangled his bait. Would he listen to $750? Mais oui, would he leesen! Remenyi was an extraordinary fellow and a great showman. At his opening bill he laid off Beethoven and gave them "Hearts and Flowers," the "Melody in F" and Mendelssohn's "Spring Song." The audience cheered for more, and Fynes, watching from the top row in the gallery (his custom), gurgled contentedly. The delighted Remenyi (and let us credit him with the beauty of such delicious malicious wit) thereupon strode down to the footlights, and in a wreath of smiles announced, "Now I veel eemitate for you ze peeg under ze gate." And he did, too, before Fynes could fall down two flights of stairs and stop him. It probably released a frustration suffered for twenty years. But Fynes saw to it the "peeg" was out the rest of the engagement.

Fynes's idea was sound. By booking such acts he hoped to lure to vaudeville patrons of the legit who, coming out of curiosity, would be won over for regular customers. They were, too. On this basis Fynes signed Marshall P. Wilder, a hunchback who through sheer nerve and perpetual appeal to his deformity had popularized himself with Chautauqua and Sunday-school audiences.

He clicked heavy in the vaudevilles, but he was the biggest gag thief in the business and was generally disliked by performers. First thing he did before he opened anywhere was to scan the bill so as to omit any gags he had stolen from these acts. His own act over, he hung around the wings cribbing stuff for his next round. He introduced his stolen stuff: "As my old friend, Jim Morton says," or "As that merry wag, Bill Cahill, relates," or "As my old pal, Jim Thornton, says in his inimitable manner." None of the performers hit back because he was a dwarf and a hunchback and the managers didn't care so long as he got away with it. Fynes paid him $600 a week, and he was worth it for he drew well.

In later life Wilder wrote a couple of volumes of memoirs, the first being "On the Sunnyside of the Street." Sometime after it was published he ran into Chicot and observed, "You know, Chicot, you are not in my book because I mention only those who have been nice to me. But [hopefully] I am doing another, and I could get you in that." Chicot said he didn't want to buy anything.

Wilder stuck around on the circuits for several years. Mostly his type of act, the novelty monologue and personality, was good for only once around. But in those days almost any phony could get that first trip. How times do not change.

Standard Acts of the Transition Period

For the most part the transition from variety to "refined" vaudeville was welcomed by the seasoned performer. The new audiences were responsive—indeed, a lot more receptive than the old stag crowds—and performers enjoyed playing to them. Comfortable dressing rooms, bright scenery, box sets, good furniture and props were available, and nobody had to work in the afterpieces, closing dramas, interludes or do fill-in turns, because these were abolished—acts were on their own. The rise in salaries enabled performers to enlarge their territories. This brought in acts from the West, sent there acts from the East, an exchange that was all to the good.

Yet a certain minority was lost in this strange new world. This is not set down in condemnation. Your true buffoon finds for himself as he will where he will. No one puts him in his place. But to your precise variety comic, from slaps to fright wig, the new setting was tinsel and swish—variety had gone pretty-please and there was no longer a chance for "real talent."

Jack Murphy tells of such a team—Basco and Roberts. Tells it sweet, too. Mr. Murphy:

Basco and Roberts did a very rough, almost brutal, burlesque trapeze act. They worked in black face, full black tights, large feet like apes, and frowzy wigs.

160

They jumped on each other's stomachs, kicked each other merrily in the face, fell from the traps with awful thuds that would mean a hospital case for persons less tough and calloused.

In 1893, the year of the World's Fair in Chicago, they were playing the Park Theatre. It was on State Street, near Harrison, and John Long was manager. It was one of the good old kind, and Basco and Roberts were in their element. A spectacular production called "America" was financed as one of the city's attractions and was presented at the Auditorium for the entire period of the fair. One of the producers who was probably slumming drifted into the Park Theatre and the idea occurred to him that Basco and Roberts would fit nicely into a jungle scene where they could scurry around among the tree tops, swing on vines, and otherwise add to the realism. He called on them in their dressing room and asked if they would accept an engagement for the summer.

The promoter was a small, neatly dressed, soft spoken man and did not resemble in the slightest any manager they had ever met, so they concluded that the logical thing to do was "to string the nut along." Basco, who did the talking, said: "Say, party! Them pratt falls we do is worth big coin. There's no bumps like 'em in all show business and if you want us to join your trick it's going to set you back three hundred smackers, get me? We don't do our stuff for pennies, we get the real kale right in the mitt. See?"

The promoter at once agreed that it was a very satisfactory figure and after telling them to call in the morning for their contract he left his card and departed.

Basco and Roberts looked at the card, turned it over, looked at each other and were somewhat stunned. They did not believe it was true, and yet they thought they had better follow it up and find out where the joker came in. Next day they went to the manager's office and got their contract. They came down to the street and thumbed over the document without getting much of its purport. They thought of taking it to a lawyer to see if it was any good, then they thought, "what if the lawyer is no good, either?"

They then decided that the real test would be to make a touch. They went back to the office and drew an advance of $50 with no trouble at all! A miracle like this demanded a celebration of some sort. As neither of them were more than casual drinkers, a round of the saloons did not appeal to them. So they changed most of the money into nickels, and while walking up and down State Street, scattering coins by handfuls, they yelled, "We are the big smokes . . . We never pack no small change . . . " Until the police dispersed the scrambling crowd.

They stayed for the run of the show and bought clothes of appalling patterns, collected some large, murky-looking diamonds, some shrieking neckwear, and established a little aristocracy all their own. On the strength of their Chicago engagement they booked time in the best vaudeville houses with, of course, a much milder act. But the high class continuous they found tame, uneventful and lacking in thrills. They managed to brighten their lives occasionally by battling with stage crews and express men, but they were not really happy and eventually faded out of the picture.

Murphy says this is not an isolated case.

But the different type of performer, the new ones who came in, and the holdovers who found adjustment easy; those who were ambitious and eager to proceed, accepted the new vaude as encouragement to develop new routines. One of the first teams to blossom with a novelty that captivated the late nineties in an act charmingly typifying the change was McCoy (Billy) and McEvoy (Minnie), man and wife. They were exceptional pedestal clog dancers—a routine unique for a woman, for pedestal clog was arduous and difficult.

Pigtails and Pinafores.

McCoy and McEvoy were the parents of Bessie and Nellie McCoy, two of the most delightful children ever cradled in the theater. They were quiet, demure, polite, and observant, and amazing mimics. Billy taught them to dance, and without his knowledge, when they were nine, they routined a little act of their own, charmingly simple. Just ordinary dialogue between two women with market baskets, consisting of neighborhood gossip, delightfully executed and entirely self-taught. One week in the mid-nineties when their parents were playing Pillings's Museum in Boston, the children induced the manager to let them fill in a vacancy. In bonnet and shawl, carrying baskets, they entered on a street in one:

BESSIE: Good mornin', Mrs. Casey.
NELLIE: Oh, 'tis you, Mrs. Doyle, well, and how are you?
BESSIE: It's right well I'm feelin', barrin' the rheumatism in me hip.
NELLIE: That's too bad, now. And can ye do nothin' for it?
BESSIE: The doctor gave me some linnyment for it, and it nearly killed me. I could only take one spoonful. I thought I'd choke.

And so on; no outrageous business; no precocity. And with the touch of the tried performer they led into their "off to Buffalo":

NELLIE: You're as limber as a young girl, Mrs. Doyle.
BESSIE: If it weren't for me rheumatism I'd be as good as the next one.
NELLIE: Well, we're neither of us the women we used to be.
BESSIE: No, and we never were.
NELLIE: We'd better be getting along to the market.
BESSIE: We had that. As long as we're both here we'll go together.

(Music cue and song)

> Then we'll take up our old market baskets,
> And away to the city we'll fly,
> For some pigs' heads and cabbage and turnips
> To make us some fine lemon pie.
> There's corned meat to get from the butcher,
> Some apples so rosy and bright,
> And some candy for Patsy and Nora,
> In the market on Saturday night.

> CHORUS: Now we must be leavin'
> The kids will be grievin'
> To tarry too long is not right.
> The children will be cryin'
> The meat should be fryin'
> For supper on Saturday night.
> *(Waltz clog, and exit)*

Yes, it was Bessie McCoy, she who danced the Yama Yama girl in "The Three Twins" and married Richard Harding Davis.

The McCoy sisters were outstanding in this period when child performers rushed to the vaudevilles as though to anticipate (or provoke) the laws that later clamped down on them.

Some of the pleasanter kid performers (most of them, sordid to relate, parentally prodded for profit) were the Putnam Sisters, Lucie and Vinie Daly, Johnny and Bertha Gleason, the Taylor Twin Sisters, Madeline and Kennedy, and Kitty Bingham.

Johnny and Bertha Gleason were brother and sister, the most noted child wooden-shoe dancers in vaudeville in their or later times. They opened with a double number, faded to singles for exhibition steps, then resumed together for a class finale in waltz clog. The Gleasons grew up with their act and as adults became one of the foremost dancing teams in vaudeville. Their feats in changes of time and steps required such tricky music cues they hired their own pianist with whom they rehearsed constantly. They were the first to correct one of the few bad features of the newly built houses. Most of the new theaters had a "dead stage"; that is, no resilience; taps were muffled. This was because of the double flooring—a hard maple top course over steel joints or cement. In fact, a number of the stages were constructed with a solid cement apron. The Gleasons carried a dancing mat; were the first to use one. Dancing mats are made of hardwood slats, a quarter inch thick, one inch wide, and five or six feet long. The slats are glued side by side on a canvas of any required length and the mat can be rolled up when not in use. It brings out the taps in that sharp, clear staccato so necessary for perfect dancing. The Gleasons quit at their prime, enjoyed the distinction of being "young old-timers," and now operate a dancing school in Trenton, N.J.

The Taylor Twin Sisters were a plain and fancy roller-skating team, a novel act in the early nineties. Their skating has not been equaled to this day. They were perfectly matched twins with likable personalities, true vaudevillians and by no means fastened to their skates. As they grew older, they needled their act with an "umbrella" song and dance. Carrying red umbrellas and moving about in effective positions, they conceived a routine that, in an older team and presented with less finesse, might have been considered risqué. Their umbrella song referred to a chance meeting with two young men whose manners were engaging:

> They tipped their hats politely,
> Those saucy black-eyed fellows . . .
> "Next time, little girls,
> We'll know you by
> Your gay little red um-ber-ellows."

One of the best of the single kids was Kitty Bingham. She was a tiny, bright, blond child, a doll-like Vesta Tilley, the daughter of a ventriloquist. She appeared in male costume, white tie and tails, silk hat and monocle, and was on the precocious side. Her act was a singing specialty and her songs the English music-hall man-about-town things. Best of them was her "Put on Lots of Style":

> If you want to do the 'eavy,
> Like a "mark-ee" or an earl;
> If you want to wed an heiress,
> Or catch a pretty girl—
> Just 'old your eye-glass in your eye,
> And wear a winning smile.
> And don't forget to swagger
> And to put on lots of style.

Gold Leaf and Hollow Humor.

Although brighter scenery and special lighting effects enhanced certain acts of vaudeville, it was of little benefit to the comics. A comedy act is business, lines, personality, and punch, and elaborate sets distract an audience's attention.

Moreover, the comics were lost in the larger houses, and in our time have been completely submerged by amplifiers and microphones. Monroe and Mack, one of the funniest blackface acts of all time, realized this and kept right on working in a dauby, faded street in one and played to belly laughs wherever and never mind the Oriental rugs and *objets d'art*. Mostly, though, the comics suffered from the larger houses. A comic must be close to his audience or the facial expression, eye work, and other subtleties are lost. It is impossible to get over a line effectively in the voice of an auctioneer. The comic who is abused and browbeaten by the straight man can't reply in shouts and yells and still appear intimidated. That is a brawl, not a laugh. The contrast is gone, the illusion dispelled.

On the other hand, neat sketches looked fine in bright, new box sets with modern furniture, and the realistic settings for the dramatic acts were all to the good. Animal acts improved 100 per cent in fresh landscapes or light wood with cut borders. And in harmony, the trainers discarded their undertakerish Prince Alberts or shabby dress clothes for hunting or riding costumes and put snappy uniforms on their assistants.

The mechanical betterments fell like a benison on sight acts and musical and spectacular numbers. Brazil and Alton, for example, a smart, alert aerial team, moved right along with the trend—in fact, a step ahead—in the brilliant setting and presentation of their act. They worked in a beautiful garden set with marble steps leading to a balustraded terrace right and left. Gorgeous fixtures and clusters of lights adorned the newel posts at the foot of the steps; and two life-sized bronze figures stood under the lights in front of them. When Brazil and Alton finished their act and made their exit, the orchestra played the "Stephanie" gavotte and the bronze figures came to life, walked downstage, and went into a marvelous double clog. Howe and Doyle were the statues and they were superb dancers. The act was without dialogue. But how can you imagine a setting like this for the slap-happy comics? For the lads who smashed hats, kicked each other in the belly, and battled their way through twenty minutes of roughhouse, a kitchen interior or street in one was good enough—much better than a palace arch with a fountain and real goldfish. They knew it, too.

The new vaudeville brought in a new type of female impersonator—the sweetheart, the gorgeous hussy, the Mr. Lillian Russell. The women went into ecstasies over Pete Shaw, the prettiest "girl" of the nineties.

Shaw was not so good as a singer, and he was a bit plumpish, but he could dress himself as Mainbocher could you. He had innumerable costumes of Parisian design in exquisite taste; and was probably the first of the direct sex appealers. But there was class to his act, and to his songs too. One of them told of an admiring gentleman friend, a gifted explorer:

> You may look but you mustn't touch,
> You mustn't touch.
> Keep your hands off, you're inclined to be
> A little forward.
> Now please don't intrude . . .
> You may look but you mustn't touch,
> You mustn't touch. . . .

Shaw quit a long while ago and opened a ladies' shop in Philadelphia. Curiously, his rank was assumed by Gilbert Sarony. (Julian Eltinge came later.) Sarony did a scrawny, garrulous old woman. Told about his mother who never allowed "her" out alone and how one day a man sat on "her" lap in a streetcar—"Goodness, girls! was I embarrassed!" and of how "she" once almost lost "her" dress at a party—"I thought I'd die"—and his audience nearly did. Sarony was the funniest of all female impersonators. He used to close with a pathetic little ballad sung in a cracked, gurgling quaver but nobody ever heard it because of the continuous laughter.

James J. Morton, M.C.

The nineties brought other novelties, aside from those inspired by the new sets and lighting. One was the act of James J. Morton and Maude Ravel. Morton was a tall, cadaverous dead-pan comic, a new type of zany; Maude, a plump, blond soubrette with a good voice and vivacious manner. Morton delivered all his material with a perfectly expressionless countenance and the pathetic sincerity of an overgrown boy trying to be good. His routine, new in those days, would be as good in ours. He would make heart-scalding attempts to help Maude with her songs—earnest, futile efforts that never accomplished anything beyond rolling the audiences in the aisles. His songs and parodies, which he wrote himself, were atrocious in rhyme and meter. He would drool along, run into a snag, correct himself, stop in the middle of a song to insert a word from a previous verse, then explain how he happened to forget it. His jokes were always pointless, interminable as a Strauss waltz. When they petered out, he would take refuge in song. To introduce his songs he had an orchestral arrangement made, thunderous, grandiose. It sounded like the prelude of the third act of "Lohengrin" with a Sousa smash that might have hailed the elephants in a circus parade. Then Jim would slouch on to perform on the "acting shelf," as he always called the stage, and announce: "I am going to sing a song; sing a song about a sailor." He did, and it was tripe, but funny the way he put it over.

For an encore, he would return, and:

"When I was out here before on the acting shelf, I left out a couple of lines of the song so I'll sing them now:

She gave him all the jewelry that she had in her trunk,
He got ten cents a pound for them and sold them all for junk.

"They are the lines I left out. You never noticed it but I didn't feel right about it. I didn't know I left them out till my brother told me. My brother is a singer, too, but his voice

SPECIAL NOTICE—The audience is respectfully requested not to encore any of the artists owing to extreme length of bill.

PROGRAMME

Numbers subject to alteration at the discretion of the management.

1 OVERTURE...
PLAYED BY MR. SIDNEY H. HORNER AND HIS ORCHESTRA.

2 MR. JAMES J. MORTON
Master of Ceremonies.

3 MISS MAY WARD

4 MR. CLIFF GORDON

5 MR. PAT ROONEY and MISS MARION BENT

6 THE MR. GEO. BONHAIR-GREGORY TROUPE
The Most Famous in the World.
(By Courtesy of Thompson and Dundy, N.Y. Hippodrome, and F. F. Proctor.)

7 MISS ELSIE JANIS
America's Youngest Star.
(By special permission and courtesy of Geo. C. Tyler.)

8 MR. S. MILLER KENT and
MISS LAURA HOPE CREWS
The First Time on Any Stage of "THE MYSTERY OF PHILLIS."
By Edgar Allen Woolf.
(Courtesy of Messrs. Shuberts and Henry Miller.)

9 MISS ETHEL LEVY
(By Courtesy of Sam Harris)

10 MLLE. DOMINO ROUGE
(By Courtesy of Joe Weber and Leuscher and Werba.)

11 MISS JESSITA'S GYPSY GIRLS ORCHESTRA

12 THE GREAT MR. HENRI FRENCH

13 EMPIRE CITY QUARTETTE
Messrs. COOPER, MAYO, TALLY and COOPER.

14 MR. LIONEL LAWRENCE and
THE RIALTO GIRLS
In "A 10 A.M. REHEARSAL."

15 And a Few Surprises

16 WAIT! WAIT! FOR THE
AMERICAN VITAGRAPH
Showing the Latest European and American Novelties.

MR. S. CLARANCE ENGEL....... } For Ted Marks { .....Business Manager		
MR. ALBERT G. DANZER....... } For Ted Marks { ....Stage Manager		
MR. WM. P SMITH...Treasurer		
MR. WALTER MUNGER.............................Assistant Treasurer		

The first bill introducing James J. Morton as master of ceremonies. It was at a Ted Marks Sunday concert on the roof of the American Music Hall at Eighth Ave. and 42nd. St., New York. The precise date unfortunately is lost but the year was 1906.

isn't as good as mine. When I met him he was coming from the grocery store . . . " And then Morton would go into his "brown sugar" story—confused drivel about his brother's difficulty in getting white sugar from grocer Brown and brown sugar from grocer White. And then he would say, "I feel like singing again. I am going to sing about a poor girl who had a hard time trying to perform on the acting shelf like I do."

Soon after he became established, Morton, for a new stunt, began to comment on the act that preceded him and reveal confidential information about the one that was to follow. He did it so amusingly that it became a feature of this act, and in later years he toured vaudeville introducing and commenting upon the entire bill—the first master of ceremonies. Morton was a great trouper, the essence of vaudeville in vigor, punch, and art.

A number of great acts were developed in the nineties. The headline system of billing had become pronounced, a spur to smartness and snappy routines. And not only did it solace the performer's ego; it paid off in coin. These were vaudeville's halcyon days. Salaries soared. Later the managers got together, said, "Come, come," and began their booking-office racket, but that black chapter lies ahead.

Yet it was the average act that made vaudeville; and by average we do not mean ordinary. We mean the boys and girls who went in there and held the show together, often saving it when the managers Dutched their own books with too much "name" billing. A "name" act was just that—what other appeal had Bernhardt, Calvé, or Mrs. Patrick Campbell in vaudeville? Let us rehearse some of the stand-bys, the "standard" acts that redeemed the name bills.

The Old Reliables.

Golden and Drayton, for example. They did the old-style plantation darky act, but they were not holdovers from the eighties. Their act and manner of presentation were superior to the breakaway-window days. They were fine singers and their dialect was perfect. Golden was the mammy, a kind of Aunt Jemima, whose delivery of "Turkey in the Straw" has never been surpassed. With it he featured what was known as "patting rabbit hash." This meant a brisk recitative accompanied by patting and slapping the hands on knees, hips, elbows, shoulders, and forearms, producing triple time and rolls almost like a snare drum. Drayton played a pathetic, superannuated Negro who sang camp-meeting songs and spirituals.

More in the spirit of the new nineties was the act of Walters and Gray and Louise Llewellyn. They were billed as the "Polka Dot Trio." The act was topical throughout. Walters and Gray impersonated book agents, appearing in eccentric costumes, their collars, shirts, cuffs, vests, and hatbands made of material marked with large round spots, an exaggeration of the fashion of the period which ran to polka dots. Llewellyn had a high soprano voice and featured a song called "Silver Bells" with chime effects by the orchestra. Gray typified a lively, eccentric business Jew; Walters characterized a Swede.

The National Four—Bryan, Moulton, and the Forrester Sisters—was a lively act, characteristic of the vaudeville we all knew. Frank Bryan was the comic and his line was the "butt-in" type—in and out at the wrong time, interruptions, giving the wrong answers, having trouble with furniture, clothing, doors, and windows. He also used mechanical effects for laughs. One was a big guffaw—a fizz bottle and a tall clock which exploded and turned into a skeleton. The girls sang and danced, and Moulton, the straight man, fed Bryan. Bryan wrote his own parodies. One of his best was on the ancient tear-jerker, "Auld Lang Syne":

> A song that always gets my goat . . .
> Though some folks think it's fine
> To get stewed and bust your throat
> While singing "Auld Lang Syne."
> They wore tight pants and homemade shirts
> And went to bed at nine.

And I'm damned glad I never was born
In the days of "Auld Lang Syne."

Nuts, Rubes, Magic, and Marionettes.

The rube acts were introduced in the early nineties and one of the funniest of the knockabout teams in this type of comedy was Sherman and Morrissey. They did a burlesque trapeze in fantastic make-ups—enormous, artificial bare feet adorned with bunions, corns, and warts. The act involved falls and bumps unbelievable to human endurance. As a matter of fact, it was so swift and punitive the performers could stand it only a certain time; the act was one of the shortest in vaudeville for big-time performers—eight minutes. After this they retired to their dressing room to pull splinters out of each other's backsides and apply arnica and plaster so as to be in shape for the next show.

Nuts, novelties, and magicians flourished in the nineties but, with the improved settings, under better auspices. Let us turn to a few—Casman, first. He was an English performer, extraordinarily clever at sleights and quite mystifying with cards. One of his best tricks never has been convincingly explained. Producing a large china plate, he had someone in the audience pound it into fragments with a hammer. The scraps were loaded into a blunderbuss and fired at a screen where the plate appeared, its design intact.

Another popular magician was Weyman, who did sleight of hand, apparatus tricks, and illusion stuff, merging one trick with another into an effective continuity, a sort of magic serial. Best remembered is his crystal-bell trick. He brought out a large glass bell dangling from a standard much like that of a modern bridge lamp and deposited it close to the footlights. With no apparent monkey business the thing would ring in answer to questions from the audience. But a much better stunt was a card trick, admirably executed. He asked someone in the audience to select a card and return it to the pack. Weyman then tossed the pack into the air and, plunging a sword through the flying cards, impaled the chosen one on its point. Weyman himself was a mystery. At the height of his popularity he dropped out and nobody knows what ever became of him.

Yet even more baffling was Ching Ling Foo, the Chinese. His milk-can trick has never been duplicated; or the tub full of ducks, either. There he would stand upon the stage, an inscrutable Buddha. A flirt of his robe, and lo! from its voluminous folds would emerge a container the size and shape of a garbage can filled to the brim with milk which he proceeded to dip out with a ladle. Presto! another flick of the robe, and with annihilating nonchalance he would produce a huge metal tub containing about a dozen live ducks. Out they would scramble to waddle and quack about the stage. He did other stuff with string, candles, and magic fountains. But the milk and duck tricks were his best.

Chasino was a favorite. He did shadowgraphs, animated silhouettes projected on the back of a white screen by skillful contortions of the fingers, hands, and arms, or even, on occasion, the bare feet. He produced birds, animals, flowers, fish— a variety of subjects. He used set pieces cut from cardboard to produce hunting scenes, balconies below which troubadours appeared, sailboats, steamers, cottages from which unneighborly neighbors carried on feuds, etc.

In the later nineties the Biograph flickers closed the show, but before this the most popular—and sensational—show closer was Hassan Ben Ali and his troupe of twelve Arabian acrobats. Their handsprings were never springy, and their tumbling was wild, reckless, effortless. American acrobats could never approach them. At the end of the act Ali held the entire troupe on his head, shoulders, and arms. Then, at curtain, they would take off like pigeons, throwing themselves, so it seemed, out into space. The illusion was perfect. This was the best of the alley oops and no act has beaten it since.

If you didn't skip, you may recall little Kitty Bingham with her top hat and monocle. Well, her pappy was Bingham, the ventriloquist, who used a flock of Charlie McCarthys of both sexes in blackface. A talented man, Bingham. He was an adept at voice throwing and his figures carried on natural conversations among themselves in varying dialects and all manner of inflections. He used an old woman, a country lass, a fresh boy (Mr. Bergen enjoyed a renaissance), an old man, and a colored lad. It was an entertaining ensemble, and cleverly done. He closed with a life-sized walking figure of a colored mammy who strode beside him singing a song. She always finished with a widespread mouth on a high note, bowed, and made her exit with Bingham.

His daughter Kitty, the girl wonder, grew up, got fat. But instead of dieting she went over to character stuff. Married an Italian comic, name of Pisano, and as Pisano and Bingham they put on a funny act in which he appeared as a voluble, excitable barber and she as a phlegmatic Irish girl. They always carried a special set of a tenement house ingeniously contrived; his shop was on the street floor, her flat on the floor above. It was costly; performers had to pay for those things, hoping to cover the expense in salary.

Other interesting novelties of the nineties were the acts of Mr. and Mrs. Stuart Darrow, who made sand pictures; Walter Deaves, who operated a marionette show; Sparrow, a burlesque juggler; and Rudinoff, a bird imitator. Walter Deaves must not be confused with his brother Harry, who also operated a marionette show. Harry's was good, but Walter was a genius. He made his own figures, painted his own scenery, and devised and manufactured all his appliances and effects. His miniature theater was perfect in proportion and color and the action of his puppets was incredibly natural. He had a puppet orchestra and the occupants of the boxes worked in precise relation to his miniature stage performance. He timed his routines to the news of the day and was always introducing public characters, new fashion fads, new dances, and even popular vaudeville performers in their songs and specialties. His puppets performed an exquisite ballet in extravaganza style with silver showers, gauze drops, and lighting effects. There have been some wonderful puppeteers in recent times, Vittorio Podrecca's Teatro dei Piccoli, for example. True, the Piccoli art surpassed Deaves's—but by a string.

Sparrow was by himself. Without doubt his was the sloppiest act ever presented anywhere—a mess from start to finish. Sparrow opened with a couple of melons, or pumpkins, tossed one in the air and looked up to catch it in his face where it burst into slush. Shocked, he crushed the other in his hands. When he attempted to balance a globe of goldfish, it doused him with water and fish; same with eggs and other objects. He used to toss soft oranges to the audience and invite them to throw them back. He intended to catch them upon a fork held in his mouth, but most of the garbage struck him in the face or on the body. Sometimes two or three in the audience, familiar with his act, brought potatoes or turnips to throw at him. These he caught on his fork—had to, they would have knocked him cold. Sparrow carried his own floor cloth and wore a dress suit made of linoleum. His shirt front was rubber.

Rudinoff, a European performer, wore a full beard and mustache, dress coat and vest and black satin knee breeches. Despite his austerity he had a pleasing stage presence and his bird imitations were remarkable. A part of his highly amusing routine was the representation of the flirtation, courtship, quarrel, and reconciliation of two birds. He also made smoke pictures by blackening a large, square, white enamel plate with smoke from a torch. Placing the plate on an easel he made a marine picture by expertly removing the soot in the proper places with a finger. Finished, it resembled a print from a large wood block. Rudinoff remained in America for years, a favorite.

Each of these was a standard act in the nineties vaudeville. They were the stand-bys, the steadies, true troupers year in, year out, not distinguished perhaps as great artists, but pedigreed clowns, all of them, faithful to My Lady Vaudeville as their true consort. Many of the "name" acts regarded her only as a mistress, or, indeed, a courtesan.

Charlie Case.

There is scarcely one name among the really great artists of variety who did not leave her bed and board for musical comedy, legit drama, minstrels, the circus, the movies, or to produce their own shows. That was all right, too. "Don't ee marry for money, but go where money is" runs the old Lancashire proverb. We can recall but two great artists (there must be more) who never divorced vaudeville—Charlie Case and Joe Jackson, the bicycle pantomimist. Jackson is of a later period, but Case flowered in the nineties, although in the late eighties he was noticed. A natural Negro, a gentle neurotic (strange combination!), Case, whose quiet monologue was one of the most entrancing acts in vaudeville, was a product of the beer halls—a curious nursery for his special talent. That he made good before stag audiences, compelling attention through sheer perfection of comedy and personality, is the best tribute that can be paid to his artistry.

Case's act consisted entirely of talk. His material—monologues about his father—was original. He wrote it himself. Many of the monologues have been published; they do not read too well, but when Case delivered them they were superb. A bit:

Father was a peculiar man. Us children didn't understand him. Mother understood him. Mother could always tell when father'd been drinking. We couldn't tell. We used to think he was dead. Father was a great hand for finding things. I remember him coming home one night. He picked up something. He couldn't see just what it was, but he brought it home. When he got to the house he found it was an arm-load of wood. Father didn't mean to take anybody else's wood, of course. We already had a lot of our own just exactly like it . . .

Case was extremely nervous and could not work without a piece of string or rag to twiddle in his fingers. A generous, wholesome fellow, a soft touch and a sucker for a benefit, he once walked out on a benefit because he had forgotten his string and none could be found for him—just quietly took his hat and slipped away. Occasionally a yokel audience would muff his work, usually at matinees in the sticks. When this happened he would not show for the evening performance. The stage manager would generally find him moping in his hotel room, brokenhearted. He was as sensitive as that. Coaxing and cajolery by his friends usually brought him around to finish the week.

He died of tuberculosis at the height of his recognition. It is as well. He would have been about as much at home back of an amplifier or microphone as he would have been in Yankee Stadium. It would have been like Joe Jackson's appearances at Radio City Music Hall—Jackson, one of the greatest of the pantomime tramps, a magnificent intimate act. There he was, the incomparable Jackson—and four thousand people could not see his face, scarcely his bicycle. How great are science and invention to make man puny.

Graduates of the Nineties Class

Among those who won acclaim in vaudeville, then drove on to other thoroughfares (legitimately enough, this is not set down in malice), were John W. Ransone, Lottie Gilson, Al Shean, and George M. Cohan. They were all great performers and probably found the legit stage a necessary expansion for their versatile talents. There were others, but these four developed in the nineties.

Ransone will be recalled by older theatergoers as the German brewer in the Pixley-Luders comic opera, "The Prince of Pilsen"; his line in the part—"Vas you effer in Zinzinatti?" —became a catch phrase of those times. Ransone in the eighties had made money with a "vaudeville" specialty unit (he was, as we have said, the first to use the word "vaudeville") which he assembled and in which he played the part of a Dutch comic. He apparently preferred the legit stage and protean roles, for he scrambled the act and put his earnings into a meller called "Across the Atlantic," perhaps because he wanted the lead in which he could depict the cashier of a steamship line, a Negro valet, a German guide, and an Irish coachman.

Although recognized as a popular dialect comedian, his success in vaudeville was largely as an impersonator of Richard Croker, David B. Hill, Mark Hanna, William H.

178

Taft, and other political celebrities. His "Dick Croker" was tremendously effective; he played the Tammany boss fifty-two consecutive weeks at Koster and Bial's, the undisputed longest run of any single act in vaudeville. Croker had a fondness for noisy apparel and Ransone's appearance in loud checks and pearl buttons invariably brought down the house. He was a favorite with former Governor Alfred E. Smith of New York to whom the writer is indebted for a verse of his song:

> I have to raise the taxes, the taxes, the taxes,
> It's there I come out strong.
> Every loafer in the land
> At politics can take a hand,
> But the king, the king can do no wrong.

Later, Ransone teamed with Charles E. Verner in the latter's sketch, "Happy Dutch, the Burglar," an unusual fade-out for so popular a performer.

Lottie Gilson, "the little magnet," one of the greatest soubrettes in show business, almost ruined her art with an innovation that is still a nuisance in night clubs and on the radio—song plugging. She was the first of the pluggers, singing for an extra fee the most awful junk of the one-finger Tin-Pan Alley boys, a self-depreciation that roused some intelligent patrons to criticism. Aside from the plugs her career as a singer is a treatise on the taste of variety audiences from the eighties to the 1900's. Her early popular songs were the tear-jerkers, "The Old Turnkey," "The Old Sexton," "The White Squall," and "The Little Lost Child," lugubrious keenings that plunged the eighties stag audiences weeping, delightedly, into their beer. For seven years or so she was lost to variety, costarring with J. K. Emmett, Jr., in a long series of "Fritz" comedies made famous by Emmett *père*.

In the middle nineties when she returned to vaudeville better songs, some of them risqué, were at her disposal. To the improved material she reacted like an artist and her deliveries

LOTTIE GILSON
"The Sunshine of Paradise Alley"

of "She's Such a Nice Girl, Too" and "Military Mollie" were excellent. Her greatest song, or rather the one with which she was specifically identified, was "The Sunshine of Paradise Alley." This, although banal, was "cute" and not a sobber, and right up main street for the nineties mixed audiences.

Besides song plugging, she added two other novelties that did her act little good—the singing stooge and the come-on-boys routine. Both were done to death by other performers. In a 1911 *Green Book* interview Lottie told how she first introduced the stooge singer twenty years previous, but failed to give all the facts, or perhaps had forgotten them. Playing at Hyde and Behman's Brooklyn Theatre in Adams Street, she was singing "My Best Girl's a New Yorker," when, at the reprise, a boy in the gallery took up the melody. It stopped the act cold for a big hand and Lottie incorporated it in her performance—although not with the boy who had inspired it. He was Thomas Dimond, father of Eddie Dimond, at this writing stage manager for Maurice Evans's Shakespearean productions. Young Tommy, when thirteen, wanted to join the Gilson act. Mamma said no. The stunt had immediate repercussions, provoking a song called "The Singer in the Gallery" which was featured all over by seriocomics.

Lottie had not the vigor of her contemporary, Maggie Cline, who made "Throw 'Em Down, McCluskey," a hymn of those days, but she was a melodic rabble rouser and more versatile.

Shean—and Mr. Gallagher.

Al Shean ("Oh, Mister Gallagher, Oh, Mister Shean") began in vaudeville with the Manhattan Comedy Four in 1890 and played straight through the decade. Sam Curtis, Arthur Williams, and Ed Mack were the other members of the quartet which was one of the most popular four-acts of the period and one of the first to arise in vaudeville's improved expression which, indeed, they helped develop with advanced songs and smart, if robust, comedy.

They featured Dave Marion's song, "It Isn't What You

Used to Be, It's What You Are Today," which they harmonized into exceptional popularity, and a duet, the name of
which Shean has forgotten. They tossed in a few of the maudlin
old-timers, "Emmett's Lullaby" and "After the Ball," but
mainly a husky, sensible, knockabout realization of life characterized their performance.

In 1900 Shean disbanded the Manhattan Four and teamed
with Charles L. Warren in a ragtag skit called "Crovadus
Upside Down." This lasted Shean another ten years, when the
historic meeting with Ed Gallagher occurred in Chicago, an
association probably more familiar than any other in latter-
day vaudeville. Their first ventures, however were in musical
comedy, chief of which was the "Rose Maid." Then in 1914
something happened, what, Shean won't say and Gallagher is
dead. They did not speak for six years. It was Minnie Marx,
Shean's sister, mother of the Marx brothers, who closed the rift.

Harpo was playing an N.V.A. benefit in New York on the
same bill with Ed Gallagher. To Mrs. Marx, who was present,
Gallagher observed, "Al and I could do a great act together
only he won't talk to me." After a tactful lapse Mrs. Marx
invited Gallagher to dinner at her home on Riverside Drive,
but Gallagher knew Shean lived with her and was loath to
accept. He did, though, and followed through with a phone
call to Shean the next day. Shean promptly seconded the
invitation. They shook hands, and "Mr. Gallagher and Mr.
Shean in Egypt" opened as the team's first vaudeville act in the
Fox Crotona Theatre, Long Island, in April, 1920. Bryan Foy
wrote the lyrics to their famous song and Shean composed the
music, the only song he ever wrote. The song is probably
known to every adult man and woman in America. Shean says
that at the height of its popularity thousands sent in parodies,
among them a professor of languages in the University of
Michigan who sent fifty-six. All were unusable—lacked a
punch line.

Shean played through vaudeville's greatest expansion period
—1890–1910—twenty years of fever, fights, and frolic during

which the avaricious managers ganged up on the actors to curb the soaring pay rolls. At one time, with his partner Gallagher, he strayed off the Albee reservation to line up with Shubert Advanced Vaudeville, but Albee raged and Shean scurried back.

In 1938 Shean starred in "Father Malachy's Miracle," a play about an old priest. The play did not make money, but Shean's performance was praised.

Song and Dance Man.

It is difficult to understand George Cohan's defection from vaudeville until one analyzes his temperament and character. A truer trouper never lived. A precocious lad when he broke in as a child fiddler and bootblack singer, he developed that precocity first to cockiness and then to arrogance, which experience and age have mellowed to an assurance sometimes genial, occasionally provoking.

Cohan is the most individualistic actor in the American theater; a lone wolf all his life. He fought the great strike that was the genesis of Equity in 1919, indeed, organized a union of his own—Actors Fidelity—a dud that sputtered in his hand. He is an actor today by sufferance. He would never join Equity which, with grace, extends him the privilege of playing as a nonunion star. "I am," he once told us, "the only scab on Broadway."

Throughout his long and interesting career he fought with everybody at one time or another, could never take direction either on stage or from the business end. He quit Keith in 1899 after a classic row, and vaudeville in 1901 to write, perform, manage, and produce his own shows. Sam Harris came in later as the masthead for the Cohan colors.

His walkout on Keith ended a long association that had been marked by specific achievements in Keith's career. One was the opening of his first house in New York under the management of J. Austin Fynes. The Four Cohans were headliners on the first bill, which included such standard acts as Daly and

THE FOUR COHANS IN THE NINETIES
Top center is George with his arm about his mother, Helen (Costigan).
His father, Jerry, and sister, Josephine, complete the most famous "four"
act in the American theater.

Devere, Leonard and Moran, Billy Courtright, Gilbert Sarony, and Bryant and Richmond. The Cohans split their act, George and Josephine presenting individual dance turns while Mr. and Mrs. Jerry Cohan played a sketch.

Although the show ran seven weeks it was a flop, largely because of the condensed light opera that formed the main part of the bill. Condensed versions of light opera had long been featured by Pastor and by managers in other cities (Boston and Philadelphia), but they had lost their appeal for New York patrons. New York audiences wanted their light opera straight. They objected to the Keith abbreviations and visited their patronage upon the standard operettas at the Casino and other Broadway houses. Moreover, it was an outrage, even in 1893, to ask a light-opera company to deliver to the accompaniment of a lone pianist.

These were halcyon times for musical comedy, a diversion of gay colors, pretty girls, and lively tunes that was rapidly developing stars in its own right, and right out of vaudeville, too—Francis Wilson, Lillian Russell, Joe Cawthorn, the Rogers Brothers. In that autumn of 1893 Keith had for competition Francis Wilson in "Erminie," Marie Tempest and Adele Ritchie in Reginald De Koven's "Algerians," and a piece at the Casino called "The Rainmakers of Syria," one of those oboe and clarinet things with hip shaking. The cast included Fanny Ward and Harry Davenport, later the handsome lover who sang the absinthe frappé song in Victor Herbert's "It Happened in Nordland."

Keith never caught up with this trend. Fynes did. He spiked his musicals and went in for legit stars and class performers.

Fin de Siècle

At THE close of the nineties there were three theaters in the United States that imported European acts. These were Koster and Bial's in New York, the American Music Hall in Chicago, and the Orpheum in San Francisco. They were exploited as "Continental" and their acts seldom played other American houses, except when the performers fell for Tony Pastor's high-pressure sales talk. Tony made no direct importations, just gathered them in after they had clicked over here. A few he booked for his Fourteenth Street theater were Vesta Victoria, Vesta Tilley, and Marie Loftus, mother of Cissie. Most of the continuous houses could not afford foreign artists, for the majority of the performers, especially the great names, drew important money. The artists themselves, who wished to play here, at first found the situation difficult, for few foreign acts could afford to come to the States and play three houses as widely separated as those aforementioned. Geographical good fortune saved them. Many of the artists were virtually forced by their London agents to accept Australian dates. (And, by the way, vaudeville is still strong down under.) So, to break their long voyage they made it profitable by playing New York, Chicago, and the Coast, then sailing from California to the antipodes.

Miss LOTTIE COLLINS, "Ta-ra-ra-boom-de-ay!"

A popular Koster and Bial's star—and wherever

KOSTER AND BIAL'S

Above is their theater in 23rd St. Below, the 34th St. house at the time of its closing in 1901.

Koster and Bial exploited this feature when booking foreign acts. They paid no attention to Fynes's drift to dignity; but even after they moved up to 34th Street in 1893 continued the women's underwear line which had been on display since their old days in West 23rd Street.

The partners began as brewers with a plant in Chatham Square. When they opened their place in 23rd Street just west of Sixth Avenue, Adam Bial managed the music hall and John Koster looked after the liquor end. It was a drop-in place; you walked out of the dive on your knees—a free-and-easy where companions paused for a few snorts to listen to some barrel-house baritone, or watch Lillian McTwobucks trip a Bowery version of the cancan the while her expansive thighs sought to burst her cotton tights. No bare legs then. Skin in those days was strictly pro.

A seat stub from any other theater was good for admission at Koster and Bial's, for the accent, and the money, was on spirits and wine. It was a ramshackle place with a stage entrance in West 24th Street and built on the lines of an English music hall—a square balcony, all boxes, with chairs and tables on the orchestra floor. As a side line Koster and Bial operated a saloon at Sixth Avenue and 23rd Street, in case any of the music-hall customers had been overlooked.

When the reputation of the hall increased as a dating place for blades (who often brought their soberer friends), Bial, albeit no reformer, toned up his entertainment and piped down his Bowery blues. He introduced operetta afterpieces to close his show, profiting, too, by Fynes's *faux pas*. Bial disdained the foreshortened things of Fynes's, producing broad burlesques of the sedate and mournful classics. Two of Koster and Bial's most popular travesties were Gluck's lovely "Orpheus and Eurydice" and Verdi's "Traviata."

New York's municipal laws at the time forbade the installation of drop curtains in music halls. But as the theaters later evaded the Sunday-closing law with "sacred" concerts, Koster and Bial got around their legal dilemma with a comparable rose— a fan across the footlights that parted in the middle, and, when parted, folded gracefully to each side of the stage—no curtain.

Bial pulled no punches in his burlesques or variety bills. The cops were always cracking down on the partners and the music hall got much publicity. Picklepusses tst-tsted constantly, but Bial laughed. A number of his performers were hauled off to the hoosegow. "An Affair of Honor," in which two women duelists, impersonating a painting, stripped nude to the waist, ended in a police-court brawl expensive and disorderly. Mr. Hearst took credit for that one—the raid, that is: JOURNAL WINS ITS FIGHT FOR DECENCY ON THE STAGE.

This happened in Koster and Bial's 34th Street house which the partners opened, August 28, 1893, as the result of a $500,-000 deal with Oscar Hammerstein. Oscar had just completed his first Manhattan Opera House which was in 34th Street running through to 35th and is now the rear end of Macy's department store. He opened it with, of all things, a non-musical and dramatic version of "Cavalleria Rusticana," with Alexander Salvini, son of the great tragedian, playing the lead. It was an expensive failure. At this time the trend of the theaters was ever north. Fourteenth Street was no longer the gay Rialto it had been in the eighties, and even 23rd Street was, by the mid-nineties, beginning to be downtown as a theater district. Koster and Bial felt this migration in diminishing business and Oscar's flop in his new 34th Street house interested the partners. Well-meaning friends brought them together and a bargain was made that brought Oscar in as a partner with a voice in the management. And what a mistake that was! Oscar would fight with a mirror.

The wise boys, knowing Oscar, were aware the association couldn't last and a number of them said so in printed remarks. But Oscar was all for it, and arm in arm with Koster and Bial started out to lick the entertainment world. Difficulties ensued at once.

Clashing Temperaments.

A familiar character of the time was Carver B. Clive, Koster and Bial's press agent. Affable, something of a wit, and with a pleasing personality, he was popular with decent men and women in and out of the profession. To Clive, Hammerstein was just a cantankerous screwball, ripe for somebody to pin back his ears. A silly dispute involving Clive was the initial row in a series of equally ridiculous episodes that doomed the partnership to failure. The second floor of the 34th Street theater had a two-room suite, large, light, and airy, with quite the authority of detachment a responsible manager would seek for his privacy. Clive set it aside for Hammerstein, but the perverse Oscar insisted on taking the lobby-floor office of only one room, forcing Clive to the better equipped, if inconvenient (for Clive, who had to be about the theater), suite upstairs.

The night the house opened Clive put up a sign in the most prominent part of the lobby:

C.B.C.
Office Upstairs

which the furious Hammerstein immediately tore down. The furious Clive restored it the following night, and again Hammerstein tore it from its fastening and heaved it into 34th Street. Both signs had been of cardboard. The third night Clive put up a tin sign, painting it white, so that from a distance it resembled cardboard. Unaware of the change, Hammerstein again reached for it and in his attempt to rip it from the wall cut a gash in his hand that required medical attention.

Hammerstein dragged along with Bial and Clive until the following spring. At that time Bial brought over from France a Mlle. de Dio. She was an undistinguished seriocomic but Bial was stuck on her and paid her off, at least partly, in exaggerated billing quite beyond her limited stage artistry. Hammerstein resented Bial's unreasonable presentation of so breasty a ham. He waited for her performance one night and at her appearance hissed her. The demonstration of a manager Bronx-cheering his own talent made interesting copy for the theatrical commentators, most of whom were present on Oscar's invitation. Next day when Bial read of Hammerstein's noisy deportment in a series of razzing pieces he confronted his partner. The resultant row crystallized their differences, and Oscar stomped from the theater and began negotiations for the purchase of the carbarn and stables in Seventh Avenue, 44th to 45th Street. Soon after he built thereon his Olympia house.

Bial kept on in 34th Street until his death and then John Koster *fils* took over. It was no go, and John lost the theater to one Najib Hashim who, despite his Mohammedan name, was a Greek. Hashim was one of a long succession of managers for the moribund Koster and Bial's. Among the supervisors in at the lingering death was Alfred E. Aarons. Even this astute showman was unable to recapture the old *élan*. The 34th Street house was too big. And the New York of the day had not yet been educated to the night life that is now so pronounced.

The old 23rd Street place was a clubhouse revel. Its famous "cork room" was a treasure of interest and, by the way, was not removed or its feature continued when Bial moved up to 34th Street with Hammerstein. The cork room was a small room about 15 by 20 feet, to the right of the stage and slightly below it. Only champagne was served there and the room was so styled because after each opened bottle its cork was fixed to the wall so that in time the room's wall decoration consisted only of corks from well-known wine brands of the time. It was a dingy and smelly little keep, but in it one could open a bottle for an actress, a bit of glamour the playboys relished—and paid for. If one ceased buying, one was asked out. When K. and B. closed to move uptown, the corks were placed in tiny coffins and presented to the regulars as souvenirs.

Koster and Bial's folded forever in July, 1901, and Rennold Wolf, Broadway columnist, wrote its epitaph for the *Morning Telegraph* in a piece astonishing for its bad taste. He condemned the house as a den of sin and a sink of iniquity

Schloss —

54 West 23d St.
New York

ANNA HELD

In her Koster and Bial days. The caustic Chicot lampooned her act. Said her greatest
asset was her "most able press agent." He meant Florenz Ziegfeld whom she married.

(favorite clichés of the Parkhurst period) and it came from his pen with ill grace, for Wolf long accepted K. and B.'s hospitality and had seen there some of the greatest vaudeville and music-hall talent the world had known.

Anna Held, Lottie Collins, Marie Lloyd, Otero, Yvette Guilbert, Eugenie Fougère, and Albert Chevalier made their American debuts at Koster and Bial's. With the exception of Otero, whose magnificent torso and tendril legs were her only appeal (indeed!), these were artists of the very first rank.

BOOK III

The Golden Days

"Sixty-cent" Albee and
"Grifter" Keith

IT WAS an interesting setting—socially, politically, industrially —as vaudeville swung into the 1900's. Many of America's great fortunes were on the make or already made, and soon we were to hear the early Roosevelt's cry—"malefactors of great wealth." At the turn of the century the dandies of the nineties became the dudes of the 1900's—"sports" in paddock over-coats, peg-top trousers, wide-flanged buttoned shoes of horrendous yellows, and "iron" collars of the type worn by Dan Frohman. Seasonal hats were a weighty derby or an enormous straw called a "katy," which was battened against the wind by a silken cord affixed to the lapel of the coat; a fastening called a "trolley."

The pompadour of the Gibson girl was a synthetic creation fashioned over a wad of hair or roll of wire called a "rat." The ladies, too, unleashed their bustles of the nineties. In New York, Siegel-Cooper's ("Meet Me at the Fountain") were advertising bargains in corsets "reinforced to prevent bone and steel from cutting." Full bosoms were *de rigueur* . . . "The Bust Beautiful," reads a New York *Herald* personal of the times: "Our method of treatment is rational and healthful. Endorsed by the medical profession."

Widely in many prints "Old Dr. Grindle" and "Old Dr.

ay" extolled their fakery in the treatment of the now mentionable (and happily lessening) diseases of syphilis and gonorrhea—"advice free."

The period was a paradise for con men, quacks, and gold-brick peddlers. Many a sucker let go a dollar for that "steel engraving of George Washington," receiving by return mail a United States postage stamp. Saloons evaded the Sunday-closing statute by implanting upon each table a moldy slab of bologna or ham between two equally moldy slabs of bread. This prop was known as a "Raines Law" sandwich, after the New York legislator who fathered the bill permitting Sunday liquor sales if "food" was served.

The growing pains of our people were fostered by an imperialism deriving from our victory over Spain and the acquisition of the Philippines. It was a great sprawling era, that of the 1900's, geyserish in effort, fulsome in tone, hilarious and jerky; and into this picture vaudeville fitted like the final piece of a jigsaw puzzle—a setup for Edward Franklin Albee and his partner, Benjamin Franklin Keith, who were to become vaudeville's most dominant characters. They made of enter-tainment a specialized, regimented industry; were products of their time—in organization and development for financial gain this pair was to vaudeville what Frick and Carnegie were to steel, the elder Rockefeller to oil, the elder Morgan to banking.

Albee was born in 1857 in Machias, a pinched Maine village, bleak and uncompromising as this native son. After a brief schoolhouse education he went off with a circus. Sup-posedly he was so unpopular the roustabouts forced him to labor with the backbreaking tent-pole crew. He soon became an "outside ticket" or "sixty-cent" man. These set up ticket wagons along the lanes to the main windows and sold seats in excess of established prices. Albee's spiel was something like this:

Don't stand in a long line at the ticket window, folks. Take the ladies and little children out of the hot sun and pass right in to the large cool pavilion . . . Go in at once, without waiting. Give yourself ample time to see the mammoth menagerie where the wild man, eating bumbergiff, is on exhibition . . . No waiting . . . No confusion . . . Don't miss any of this greatest show, this gigantic entertainment, this stupendous spectacle . . . Get your tickets here . . . Thank you, folks . . .

The "sixty-center's" prices were what he could get on a what-have-you principle. Also "mistakes" could be made in change, and the "walkaway" was sometimes large. Succumbing to the sixty-cent man, many a yokel hurried on, fascinated and confused by the blaring bands, the shouts of side-show spielers, or the smell of bumbergiff, leaving the change from maybe as much as $10.

Meanwhile Albee's partner-to-be, Benjamin Franklin Keith, born in Hillsboro Bridge, N.H., in 1846, and likewise to begin his showman's career as a circus man, was monkeying with the notion of opening a theater and museum in Boston. He propositioned his friend, Colonel William Austin, and the colonel agreed to come in with him. Accordingly, the pair opened Keith's first house as a curio museum on Washington Street, Boston, in what later was part of the Adams House.

The original hall was 35 feet long, 15 feet wide in front, and 6 feet wide in the rear. The opening attraction was "Baby Alice," a midget who, at the age of three months, weighed but three and one-half pounds. This was January 8, 1883. By the following May Colonel Austin cried enough and Keith replaced him with George H. Bacheller, a Providence, R.I., showman. Together they cooked up a continuous show of entertainment, freaks, and exhibits which Sam K. Hodgdon was hired to extol as a "lecturer," Bacheller doubling with him as spieler.

One afternoon when the enterprise had been going a few months, a chap walked into Keith's office, said he'd been with a circus, was tired of the life, and asked for a job. "All right," said Keith, "go out in the front of the house and make yourself useful." That afternoon Sam, who was doing the spiel, came back after the show, as Keith always insisted, for a conference checkup.

"How'd it go?" asked Keith.

"Pretty good," said Sam. "In fact, better than usual." Then, after a pause: "Funny thing happened. When I'd stop for a second during my spiel on the exhibits, a chap in the crowd would interpose—'yes, that's all right, that's fair enough. Yes, it sounds reasonable to me. Certainly, I can believe that . . . ' With the result," added Sam, "we did almost twice as much business. I wonder who he was? What a shill!" Keith, who had dismissed from his mind the young chap he'd hired, didn't identify him until Albee came back with additional suggestions.

But despite Albee the museum was not much of a go. Bacheller dropped out, and after a number of huddles Albee induced Keith to chuck it. Over at the Holly Street Theatre a company was cleaning up with "The Mikado." Albee suggested what we should call today a streamlined version of the Gilbert and Sullivan operettas. Keith finally agreed.

The First Link Forged.

Albee started his campaign with a slogan—"Why pay $1.50 when you can see our show for 25 cents?" Of course, they thefted the show, but G. and S. were not copyrighted in America and the pilferers could not be sued. It was all very geisha. Albee decorated the front and lobby of the little theater in the setting of a Japanese garden, hiring Japanese girls to serve tea in kimonos—first evidence of the touch he developed in erecting the cathedrals that later adorned the Keith chain. It was a tremendous success and Keith and Albee immediately formed a road company, in the chorus of which was a hoofer named Raymond Hitchcock.

With the returns from "The Mikado," Keith and Albee, whose fortunes thereafter were inextricably intertwined and severed only by death, opened the Bijou in Boston. There, July 6, 1885, the partners initiated their first continuous vaudeville show. It ran from 10 A.M. to 11 P.M. and as his first bill Keith presented the Durville Family, the Olympian Quintette, the Arctic Moon (a lecture by Sam Hodgdon), Rolla, an illusionist, Marion Fisk, a singer, Murray and Monarch, the Ainsley Brothers, Hughes and West, and John Barker, a bone soloist. Admission was a dime, and for five cents more one could obtain a chair. Later, seats were boosted to 20 cents. This was the first link in the Keith-Albee chain of theaters that in the 1920's were to number more than four hundred houses throughout the East and Midwest.

Since it is virtually impossible to refer to Keith without summoning Albee, or vice versa, it would be well to dispose of Keith's early background up to the time he cast lots with the partner who was to shape his destiny. Keith was shrewd, but he lacked the business touch of Albee, and he allowed himself to be swayed by his first wife, the former Mary Catherine Branley, a Providence, R.I., girl, and a devout Catholic whose church affiliations influenced her husband's theatrical enterprises.

Mr. and Mrs. Keith were a picturesque pair. B. F. invariably carried a hammer in his belt, going about his theater, tinkering here, puttering there, nailing down this, prying loose that, or lining a tiny closet with tin for an improvised smoking room backstage for his actors. Similarly, Mrs. Keith, in apron and bandanna, went through the Bijou like a housekeeper, dusting the chairs, cleaning upholstery and draperies, and sweeping rugs and carpets. To Mrs. Keith was ascribed the impulse that "cleaned" the New England theater, for her influence in vaudeville reached over to the legitimate stage.

She would tolerate no profanity, no suggestive allusions, *double-entendres*, or off-color monkey business. Years after, when the Keith-Albee-Orpheum chain linked every important vaudeville house in America, performers called it the "Sunday-school circuit."

Each theater carried verboten signs nailed to the back stage bulletin board. One:

"Don't say 'slob' or 'son-of-gun' or 'hully gee' on this stage unless you want to be cancelled peremptorily. Do not address any one in the audience in any manner. If you have not the ability to entertain Mr. Keith's audiences without risk of offending them, do the best you can. Lack of talent will be less open to censure than would be an insult to a patron. If you are in doubt as to the character of your act consult the local manager before you go on the stage, for if you are guilty of uttering anything sacrilegious or even suggestive you will be immediately closed and will never again be allowed in a theater where Mr. Keith is in authority."

Keith was thirty-seven years old when he opened his museum show in Boston. All of his previous life he had been involved with circuses in one capacity or another, although never as an official. His greatest success was as a "grifter." There is a fine distinction between a circus "grifter" and a circus "grafter." The "grafters" ran the games: shell, tivoli, monte, eight-die case, hironimus, or spindles. The "grifter" was a "privilege" man who was permitted to sell novel merchandise on the lot.

Keith sold blood testers. These were curiously shaped contrivances of glass; usually in the form of two hollow glass balls connected by a curved or twisted glass tube. One ball was filled with a nice, pink liquid, probably poured from a bottle of hair tonic. The other was empty. If the bulb containing the liquid was held in the hand a few seconds, the liquid would begin to bubble and flow through the tube into the empty bulb. If it flowed quickly, Keith would start a spiel like this:

Your blood is in excellent condition! The best test I have seen in weeks! You are really in wonderful shape, WON-der-ful! BUT— the important thing is to keep that way. By having this perfectly regulated scientific instrument at hand you can tell the minute your blood needs regulating . . . An infallible test . . . The famous Professor Spivins spent forty-two years in perfecting this instrument . . . There is his picture and signature on the box lid . . . And now, without consulting expensive doctors, we can see at once just where we stand . . . The little apparatus tells us. Why, one doctor bill might be ten, twenty, fifty times the cost of this little guardian of your health and home. All expensive fees are saved by Professor Spivins's blood tester which costs you only . . .

The price was whatever could be got.

If the liquid moved slowly Keith had an another spiel:

A slow, even flow of the secret chemical distillation which is hermetically sealed in the specially blown, crystal glass bulb, denotes a perfect blood condition . . . No feverish symptoms . . . No uneven heart action . . . No dieting necessary . . . The most perfectly balanced blood I have tested in weeks! See that tall gentleman standing by the ticket wagon? That is Colonel Koshokus. He just bought one of the testers, and it probably saved his life . . . Why, gentlemen, the liquid fairly raced through the highly sensitized tube . . . Feverish condition . . . Heart palpitation . . . apoplectic symptoms . . . Detected at once by the little apparatus that never fails . . .

If two or more suckers were trying the tester at the same time the grifter cleverly played them against each other. The technique of the grifter was always to inflate the ego of the sucker, to seduce him into buying so that he could show his friends what a hell-roaring, red-blooded he-man he was. The grifters never resorted to loud ballyhoo; they worked quietly, used the "long con," meaning slow, deliberate, expert persuasion. ("Short con" is quick, snappy, aggressive jollying. "Bull con" is rapid-fire insistence accompanied by elbow shoving and intimidation.) The profit on the tester was about 1,000 per cent, but 40 per cent of the day's take had to be turned over each night to the manager of all the privileges. This was the pay-off for the concession, and for transportation in the "privilege car," a sleeper for the special use of grifters, grafters, and "butchers" who were the minor privilege sellers of peanuts, candy, funny noses, squawkers, and balloons.

Keith's entrance into show business seemed to sober him; at any rate, a pronounced change is apparent from his first days with Albee. Throughout his theatrical career there was never a hark back to his circus days. Close, forever pulling a poor mouth, it is doubtful if he would have achieved the financial success that he won had it not been for the more lavish Albee— lavish, that is, in the expenditure of moneys that were sure to bring larger returns.

With the Bijou established, Keith and Albee set out to enlarge their holdings. In 1887 they opened the Gaiety Museum in Providence, and under the noses of competing managers succeeded in acquiring the site of an old church and burying ground in Eighth Street near Race in Philadelphia upon which they erected their Philadelphia Bijou. Since Albee had but $78,000 to spend for the Philadelphia house, he had to bid for property in what was then a disreputable neighborhood.

Women, Children—and Gentlemen.

When the theater opened, Albee hired an officer to pace a beat between the lobby and the corner to give a semblance of law and order, but it failed to restrain some of his more expressive patrons who, in the uninhibited manner of the beer-hall stag audiences, spat tobacco juice from the windows, neatly picking off luckless customers.

To minimize the effect Albee hired another man to mop up the sidewalk with bucket and broom. He was more help than Albee had thought, for, with characteristic display, Albee had attired him in a white suit. This proved a lovely diversion and centered the fire.

Albee had an even tougher time with the gallery boys who came purposely to break up the show. They screamed at acts, shouted obscene epithets at girl performers, and otherwise made life a hell for actors and more orderly patrons. To curb them Albee hired two husky bouncers, strategically placed them in the gallery, and himself lectured the hoodlums during intermissions, giving pep talks in sweetness and light from the stage. His first appearance was greeted with the bird, but he persisted. "Our theaters," he said in effect, "are for women and children and, we had hoped, gentlemen." In a fortnight there was little trouble and gradually none at all. So Albee fired the bouncers and, having his gallery on the run, insisted that hats and caps be removed, forbade smoking, and banned all whistling, stamping, spitting on the floor, and crunching of peanuts.

His policy served him well. Some years later when the partners took over the magnificent new Keith house in Chestnut Street, Philadelphia, they laid out the royal carpet for a Main Line audience and the theater opened with the decorum of the Metropolitan Opera. Some of the city's snootiest families subscribed for weekly locations, among them the Strawbridges. Some time later said Mr. Strawbridge to Mr. Albee: "You know we like to think this house on Chestnut Street belongs to us. We wouldn't give it up without a struggle. But something was said on the stage at the matinee today that greatly embarrassed my daughter who attended with some of her Sunday-school friends. It was a remark that coupled a Scriptural quotation with hash. Don't you think that this might be taken out?" Said Mr. Albee to Mr. Strawbridge: "I heard the line you complain of this afternoon and even before you came to me I had it cut out."

Encouraged by the success of the Philadelphia Bijou, Albee, who, unlike Keith, never forgot his circus days, began to splurge. In September, 1893, the partners opened the first Keith house in New York, the Union Square Theatre, under the management of our friend, Fynes. It was an old house that had been run as a "combination" by Greenwall and Pearson. Albee renovated it, Albee style, and when it blazed before an astonished public that September night a local commentator, one Robert Grau, a booker, called it "the prettiest, coziest, daintiest vaudeville theater in New York." Albee had installed a corps of boy ushers and dressed them in Turkish costumes. Other attachés were garbed in military uniforms and the ladies'-room maids wore lace caps and frilly aprons. The

ensemble looked like a cross between a comic-opera finale and
a Balkan military guard.

It was also in 1893 that Albee opened the Colonial in
Boston with a big-top fanfare more characteristic of the tan-
bark than a vaudeville house. The grandiloquent Albee, "to
clear the air of that tainted variety," as he termed beer-hall
vaudeville, lavished $670,000 on the Colonial's appointments
alone and the theater became, after a sensational opening, not
only the first of the Keith-Albee temples, but to the end the
capital of their empire. Albee invited a celebrity audience to
its dedication, and to his surprise they attended, many pro-
ceeding from New York and Washington by special train. He
may well have been astonished. Neither he nor Keith in the
early nineties was a national figure. What strings he pulled he
never disclosed, but his distinguished guests came in droves,
among them Senator Chauncey M. Depew, Robert Ingersoll,
and Edouard de Reszke, famous Metropolitan basso, who
brought with him his fellow artists Mme. Emma Eames and
Pol Plançon. They came to scoff. Instead, they lapped it up,
with the result that vaudeville, on *that* scale, became the cup
of tea for the swanks as well as the dish for the masses.

Albee never forgot the Colonial opening. Years later John
Royal asked what he regarded as his greatest feat in showmanship. "An $89 carpet," replied Albee. It was laid in the coalbin
in the cellar of the Colonial. Audiences were allowed the
freedom of the front and "the carpet in the coalbin" was
almost as big an attraction as the headliner.

Each of the Keith-Albee houses, as the circuit developed,
was similarly exploited, most interesting and important being
the Cleveland Palace at Euclid Avenue and East Seventeenth
Street which Albee opened in November, 1922. The theater
was housed in a 21-story office building and cost $5,000,000.
It had a seating capacity of 3,680. Its lobby was of marble and
was hung with paintings by Corot, Lely, Bougereau, Van
Marcke, Innes, Henner, and Lillian Genth. The rug (then)
was the largest piece of single weaving in the world. Backstage

the performers checked in as at a hotel. The greenroom was decorated handsomely. An individual dressing table in boudoir style was installed for each chorus girl and there were showers for all, including the porters. Animals were kept in a separate chamber of special design. To his brilliant first audience of national and state officials (a number of New York socialites also attended), Albee declared that he erected the theater as a memorial to his lifelong friend and associate, B. F. Keith. The bones of Keith must have rattled in disapprobation. Any dimwit could have told Albee, as indeed Bill Morris had told him five years earlier, that vaudeville was dying fast and the chances of recovering on the investment were puny. Albee was slipping.

He was smart enough earlier, although never brilliant. His ability lay in his strength: he bulled through, scattering his rivals and opponents by a force that was sometimes cruel. He was a good executive and a shrewd organizer, but he was never the great showman his few friends maintain. He lacked the imagination of Dillingham, the artistic sense of Ziegfeld. But Dillingham died a pauper, and Ziegfeld's funds at his death had vanished with his tinseled sets.

They were an astonishing pair, Albee and Keith. It was virtually impossible to best the partners in their heydays. Ray Burnside, Charles Dillingham's general manager and stage director, once negotiated with them for the Hippodrome in Cleveland. His description of the conference, given later to John Royal, is a neat characterization. "I'll take any one of those birds on alone," said Burnie, "but God deliver me from sitting between them. They act like conjurers. I came out with my eyeteeth. But they got my watch and shirt and pants."

The Court of Managers:
Murdock, Williams, Beck

THE managers who dictated the policy of vaudeville were a motley crowd, some with fantastic backgrounds, some unique as personalities. Only vaudeville could have spawned them. In the late nineties John J. Murdock, a man of Scottish drive and business callosity, made the Masonic Temple Roof in Chicago an outstanding seasonal vaudeville theater. To be booked at Murdock's Roof was equivalent in prestige and salary to booking at the New York Palace in its great days. The talent Murdock corralled cost a fortune. He booked whole bills of headliners; the No. 2 spot of his programs would have carried the show in New York's leading theaters. His Chicago competitors, knowing him for a nickel chaser, thought he had gone off his head.

On one occasion, Murdock for weeks plastered three-sheets all over Chicago announcing "The Girl with the Auburn Hair." No name was mentioned, and all Chicago speculated. So great was the interest and so successful the act it commanded $1,000 a week in a subsequent season. Hating to see all that money go, as the yarn runs, Murdock married the girl. She was Grace Akis. Her turn was a pose with drapes before a group of choir boys who sang carols and semireligious seasonal songs—one of the first of the "Living Picture" acts. It did well for years.

But although Murdock paid top money for his Masonic Roof bills, as a member of the Western Vaudeville Managers Association he was far from profligate. At the meetings where acts were discussed, appraised, and booked (maybe) for the circuit, he stood aloof from the table conferences, stolidly gazing out the window at a brick wall opposite, listening without emotion as the secretary droned off the names: "Smith and Brown, $150 open time week of October 12; John and Lizzie Blick, $200, open time November 15; Blotz and McPack, $75 . . . " And before the secretary could announce the "open time" Murdock would turn: "I'll take them." He was never known to go above $100 a week—except for his Masonic roof, and unless he had to.

Coming east to join Albee, Murdock became almost at once a leavening influence on his more impetuous associate who placed a trust in him that others considered not wholly warranted. Cagey, hesitant, it was almost impossible to get a definite answer from him. Rae Samuels, a fine song and dance comedienne, and later the wife of Marty Forkins, Bill Robinson's manager, describes a characteristic Murdock interview: "He would sit cross-legged and pull out a little desk drawer containing more junk than a schoolboy's pockets—hooks and eyes, films, string—and while you were trying to make your point he'd take up a roll of film, hold it to the light, inspect it, ask your opinion of a shot, and then snip it off with a pair of scissors—all while you were doing the talking."

With Albee, Murdock countenanced the booking of stool-pigeon acts who reported by letter almost daily the backstage conversations and remarks of performers, a practice which led to the blacklisting of a number of them. Once he rebuked Eddie Darling because Eddie had signed up a woman singer of established reputation after dining with her and her husband. "You must not be too friendly with the ladies in the profession," counseled Murdock. Whereupon Darling reminded him that he (Murdock) had married "The Girl with the Auburn Hair."

"Hey! Two Beers!"

The representative of the Orpheum interests in the Keith-Albee-Murdock combine was Martin Beck. There are a hundred stories about Beck, many of them unfavorable, for he was not popular with associates or performers. He is said to have started as a waiter in a Chicago beer joint and to this day old-time actors call him "Two-Beers Beck."

Beck denies his waiter origin. He says he was a German actor in a traveling company and that, upon reading an advertisement in a German paper—of one Ratke who wanted a manager for his North Clark Street Chicago beer garden— he applied and was hired. According to his story, he induced Ratke to add a stage and dressing rooms and put on a vaudeville show; in a fortnight it was functioning successfully. Thereafter Beck says he was introduced to Martin Lehman, associate of Morris Meyerfeld and founder of the Orpheum chain, by Frank Witmark, music publisher. This led to his identification with the Orpheum interests.

The circuit's initial theater was the Orpheum in San Francisco. It was owned by Gustav Walters, a likable but irresponsible and inexperienced manager who failed to make a go of it, despite the beer hall's (it was then) popularity. After Walters ran up a wine and liquor bill of $40,000, Meyerfeld, with his partner, one Mitchell, took over the house. Meyerfeld also was a novice in show business. But he was a man of natural intelligence and, realizing his lack of knowledge, went to Los Angeles and proposed to Martin Lehman, who owned a vaudeville theater in that city, to come in with him on a partnership basis. Lehman refused. Meyerfeld threatened to build an opposition house in Los Angeles and Lehman, who forgot that he could counter with a comparable threat, yielded. The association jelled financially and in the late nineties Lehman proceeded to Chicago to establish an office for booking acts through to their coastal theaters. It was at this point that he hired Beck. Later Charles E. Bray was taken in as secretary. Bray, a suave, handsome chap, was an excellent "front"; when he entered a restaurant the waiters did nip-ups to give him a ringside table.

Working together, the three speedily organized Western houses between California and Chicago. Lehman brought into the circuit, which he called the Orpheum after the San Francisco house, an important theater in Kansas City (Lehman's son still owns the Orpheum there) and several small theaters in Arkansas. These were the forerunners of the chain that was to embrace, in 1905, seventeen houses from Chicago to the Coast. A wise policy guided the operators from the start: the houses they built they conducted through local control and investment. This not only stimulated but maintained concern. Beck, who says that his initial interest in the chain was 10 per cent, was of considerable value to his associates in obtaining property. Somehow, a site he would acquire in an off-the-beat district would suddenly become the center of civic activity and his theater on a new and important thoroughfare.

After the Orpheum chain was established, Beck, Kohl, and Castle booked through the Keith-Albee United Booking Office. About 1906 Beck came on to New York to oversee these interests, establishing offices in the St. James Building, later moving up to the Putnam Building where Keith, Albee, and the U.B.O. were quartered. He fitted in well with his colleagues there, shared their views, their harvests, was stamped with their die. In such company his success was assured and his rise to the head of the Orpheum circuit was no surprise.

James J. Morton, the monologist, playing the Orpheum in San Francisco on a week during Beck's rise to power, idled over to the "Barrel House" after his show. The Barrel House was unique, even in San Francisco. There was no bar, there were no tables or chairs. The furniture consisted of highly polished, fancy-hooped barrels which were set about the floor. Large schooners of steam beer were the specialty. While Morton was sipping his suds, a soldier, home on furlough, approached him. Said he'd seen Morton at the Orpheum,

THE VAUDEVILLE MANAGERS ASSOCIATION

From left, standing: Edward F. Albee, Paul Keith, Lou Eric, Edward Kohl, "Mister" Cronin, Keith's Boston lawyer, J. K. Burke, James Moore, and J. J. Murdock. From left, seated, (as their faces appear), Lou Behman, George Tate, Martin Beck, B. F. Keith, "Pop" Wiggins, John Hopkins, Mike Shea, George Tinker, Max Anderson, and Morris Meyerfeld. Photo was made in 1900 soon after organization of the VMA and is reproduced through the courtesy of Martin Beck.

and how are you? He owned, he said, ten shares of Orpheum stock and if Morton cared to buy the block he would sell for what it had cost him. The price was low and Morton bought, next day having the transfer of ownership recorded on the books of the Orpheum Corporation. Months later, finishing his Orpheum time, he played back to New York and soon after met Beck. "I see you're a stockholder in the Orpheum," said Beck, and offered to buy the shares. Morton said no, and Beck insisted. Morton still said no, and Beck threatened. Morton sold. Thought he might better than never play Orpheum time again. Beck didn't want actors in his organization.

Beck built the New York Palace at Broadway and 47th Street in 1913. It was reported at the time that Willie Hammerstein was legally prepared to hold up its opening with an injunction on the grounds that operation of the Palace violated the zoning agreement of the New York managers. By its terms Oscar Hammerstein had exclusive rights for his Victoria Theater to Keith acts from 34th Street to Columbus Circle. Beck, with a new theater on his hands and nothing to put on its stage, was forced to purchase these rights or make a honky-tonk of his Palace. Accordingly, he bought the rights, paying Oscar $225,000 to raise his curtain. But it lowered Hammerstein's. A year later the Victoria folded.

Palace Memories.

The field clear, the Palace soon became the premier vaudeville house of America: the distinction of playing its bills was coveted by every act of whatever circuit.

Each Wednesday sessions were held at the Palace of utmost importance to the actors—general office meetings at which some twenty-odd Keith managers and bookers went down the list, deciding the performers' fate.

From a pile of memoranda one would draw a slip and call out the name written thereon—"Joe Blotz." "No interest," someone would answer. Two words, and the poor chap was ruined for Keith time. Sometimes the response would be—

"pick up." This meant that, if the actor's agent's sales talk was plausible, maybe they would give him a chance. The great words were "give him a route." This meant from forty to eighty weeks straight time. And the performer was made.

One Wednesday afternoon the name of Bill Robinson was called, and somebody answered, "Pick up." At this, Robert G. Larsen, a shrewd Boston manager and father of Roy E. Larsen, publisher of *Fortune*, *Life*, *Time*, and, when this gets into print, probably of *Universe*, interrupted: "Is that the Robinson of Cooper and Robinson?" he asked. It was. "I'll take him for Boston," said Larsen. Bill stopped the show—as usual. In fact, Bill was a nuisance to the managers. Nobody could go on after him; the reason why he invariably closed the show.

At another Wednesday session the name of Ruth Draper was called. "No interest." A number of the managers had never heard of her. Those who had knew her act as a class-character interpretation, no good, they thought, for vaudeville. She was about to be passed when John Royal said, "I'll take her for Cleveland." They hissed her off the stage. "I suppose I'm through," said Draper. "No, not yet," said Royal. "I think your sketches are too long." So she trimmed them for the night performance, and again was hissed—couldn't finish. Royal went to work on her, and by spotting the climaxes and speeding up her presentation enabled her to continue. At the Wednesday night performance the audience cheered. Incidentally, on the same bill was Mae West, who had second billing. Draper to Mae—that was vaudeville.

The Palace closed as a strictly vaude theater, November 16, 1932, with this bill: Nick Lucas, Hal Le Roy, Sid Marion, Giovanni (a magician), Ross and Edwards, Ola Lilith, and the Honey Family. Thereafter it continued as a presentation house (five-a-day), showing feature pictures. Now it is a grind. A few of its performance records: Ruth Roye held the top as a single woman with six consecutive weeks. The dance-team record was held by Adelaide and Hughes—ten consecutive weeks. The record sister act was the Dolly Sisters—four weeks. And the record bill—nine weeks—was the Cantor-Jessel thing.

Williams, the Actors' Manager.

Best liked and decentest of the metropolitan managers and one of the best showmen in vaudeville was Percy G. Williams whose string of a dozen theaters in Manhattan, Brooklyn, and the Bronx was as profitable as any on the Keith-Orpheum chain. Williams was born in Baltimore in 1859, the son of a physician, Dr. John B. Williams. When he was nineteen he left home and joined a troupe as general utility man and second comic, receiving training from George R. Edeson, father of Robert Edeson. Williams's salary was $6 a week. He thought he was better, gave notice, and assembled a "Tom" show on his own. After a season's tour of the sticks he only broke even. Disgusted, he dismantled the show in Chambersburg, Pa., and went back to acting with Oliver Doud Byron (father of Arthur Byron, distinguished actor and former president of Actors Equity) in Byron *père's* "Across the Atlantic."

But his was the promoter's, not the actor's, instinct, and after a friendly good-by to Oliver, Williams in the early nineties, with J. B. Radcliffe, doctored up a medicine show that sold liver pads—little sacks of herbs originally made by Williams's father. The son marketed them as the "Williams Health Bag," peddling them to music from street stands on which he gave a kind of show. He was so successful he opened a factory to make them faster. Thereafter he engaged halls and gave something like a vaudeville bill, not forgetting during intermissions: "Get the little health bag, folks, the charm for good health; the never-failing remedy for man's internal ills."

At one time in the middle nineties Williams had about forty of these halls scattered about the country and admitted a revenue from his health-bag sales of $25,000 a year. Capital in hand, he began to enlarge his interests and with Thomas

F. Adams, of the chewing gum tribe, bought Bergen Island in Jamaica Bay and converted it into an amusement park called Bergen Beach. In 1895 he purchased the corner on Fulton Street, Brooklyn, where the Orpheum theater stood and five years later, January 1, 1900, opened it as a high-class vaudeville house. This was the first of his chain which ultimately included the Gotham, Novelty, Crescent, Greenpoint, Flatbush, and Prospect in Brooklyn, the Circle, Colonial, and Alhambra in Manhattan, and the Royal in the Bronx. His first house in Manhattan was the Circle, at Broadway and 60th Street. Performers called it the "Arctic" Circle because of the unresponsive audiences.

Williams distrusted Albee and his associates and at first refused to join the Vaudeville Managers Association and their company racket, the United Booking Office. Before he was forced to join (to get talent), he proposed to the Vaudeville Comedy Club, whose membership then (about 1901) comprised some two hundred of the leading circuit comedians, that if they would agree to play his houses twice a season, he would not join the V.M.A. At that time Williams had but four houses, which meant that, if the comics agreed, they could play but eight weeks solid time and wildcat the rest of the season—for they were certain of Albee's black list. Nonetheless, they voted unanimously to go with Williams. But pressure was brought to bear on Williams's stockholders and associates, who forced him to withdraw his proposal, be a good boy, and place his hand in Albee's.

In February, 1903, a month after Williams opened the Circle, Keith trained his guns on him, charging that Williams's entry into Manhattan was an unwarranted invasion of territorial rights and a deliberate violation of the zoning rules of the V.M.A. Williams pointed out that his New York franchise was unbounded and accused the V.M.A. of bad faith since they withheld the "benefits" of the manager-controlled U.B.O.

What Keith was sore about, and it came out in the name-calling, was that Williams paid more for his acts than the

Keith-Albee crowd, thus giving the actors wrong ideas. Marie
Dressler was cited. Williams paid her $1,000 a week—Albee
$650. Keith carried his battle to the V.M.A. and on March
18, 1903, after a violent session, Williams was expelled. He
announced that he would open opposition theaters in Philadelphia and Boston, both Keith strongholds. He did, but the
fight didn't last long and Williams was readmitted to the
managers' trough.

Williams was no prude and never a hypocrite. He kept his
shows clean without yelling to heaven to witness his righteous-
ness as the breast-beating Keith and Albee were forever doing.
He supplied unblushing family entertainment and was
astonished, one morning, to receive a mailed complaint about
one of his Orpheum, Brooklyn, acts from the Reverend Dr.
Lindsay Parker, rector of St. Peter's Episcopal Church in
Brooklyn. The story Dr. Parker complained of was told by
R. G. Knowles, the same single Williams had hired for his
medicine show at $15 a week.

This is it, and remember the humor is circa 1900:

It was decided by a young married couple to have as one of their
Christmas decorations a motto in holly and green, and after much
thought they selected the text: "Unto Us a Son Is Born." The husband started for the florist with the text and the dimensions of the
piece. But on his way downtown he mislaid the memorandum. Not
recalling the text or dimensions he sent this message to his wife:
"Forgot what you told me." The wife replied: "Unto us a son is
born, ten feet, two."

Williams instructed Knowles to cut the story from his
monologue. Knowles refused, and Williams fined him $100.
Knowles used it again and Williams again fined him $100.
Knowles then filed suit, asking $10,000 and an apology. There
is no record of its disposition, but the chances are Knowles
didn't get a dime or an apology.

Williams loved Western mellers and wrote a number of
the 30-cent thrillers, one being "Tracy the Outlaw," inspired
by the escape of Tracy as Williams was making a Western

tour. Williams wrote a blacksmith scene into "Tracy" which was later used for a Vitagraph short—300 or 400 feet. It was called "The Fight in a Blacksmith Shop" and ran as a "chaser" in many vaudeville houses throughout the early 1900's.

Williams retired in 1912 after little more than a decade in vaudeville. With his kindly presence and expert showmanship he enriched the expression far more in his brief tenure than either Keith or Albee did. He paid the best salaries, booked the best acts. His theaters, the Brooklyn Orpheum and the New York Colonial, were rivaled for their bills only by the Palace in later years. Williams died, July 21, 1923, at the age of sixty-four. He left a net estate of $3,354,829 which, with his thirty-acre country home, Pine Acres, in East Islip, Long Island, he willed to aged and indigent performers. It was dedicated as the Percy G. Williams Home on the death of his widow in 1927. A clause in his will is a complete characterization: "I made my money from the actors; I herewith return it to them." In 1900, almost on the very day the Vaudeville Managers Association formed the United Booking Office, Albee said to Chicot: "All my life actors have been gypping [printable translation] me. Now I am going to gyp them." Albee could never understand Williams.

Poli, Pantages, and the Home-town Boys.

Before Albee effected the national consolidation and resultant monopoly that was to wreck vaudeville on the conveyer belt of a standardized industry, he had a quart or two of lesser lights to bottle. They fizzed with as much authority behind their smaller bars, made little effort to stray from their reservations, and in their own rights and purses built up prestige and credit.

Sylvester Z. Poli, who owned a chain of theaters in New England, had been a manufacturer of wax figures for stores and museums. He was closer than an unfrosted chestnut burr and old-timers can still hear him whine. In the late eighties Poli opened a wax exhibit and theater in Troy, N.Y. He then went to Toronto, Ontario, and opened a museum and theater, booking his shows from Robinson's Museum in Buffalo. About the mid-nineties, he turned up in New Haven, Conn., and started an upstairs vaudeville house. It was of fair size, well attended, and Poli made money. Two or three days each week he would come down to New York, hang around Bill Morris's office, and wheedle performers. "It's a small place, my theater, not much business. But you play for Poli now and when he has big place he pay you good salary." Poli ran the New Haven house on a shoestring. A melancholy pianist furnished the music and a surly relative constituted the stage crew. Poli's great pride was that he had been admitted, God knows how, into membership in the Ancient Order of Hibernians, and he featured a shamrock on all appropriate occasions. Poli was a joke to performers, but where was the laugh? Whining to the end, he left holdings that some years ago were appraised at $32,000,000.

In a smaller way Alexander Pantages was a West Coast Poli. During the Klondike gold rush, Pantages was a waiter in a concert hall in Nome. Through his friendship with a burlesque producer, Jack Flynn, who brought up the dance dames, he became interested in show business, and after his return to California opened one vaudeville theater after another until his circuit menaced the longer established Sullivan and Considine time. A bitter war ensued. Each overbid the other in seeking acts; occasionally they shanghaied performers—literally dragging them off railway trains on some such promise as "twelve weeks' time, you can't afford to pass that up." Eventually Pantages's circuit outnumbered that of his rival. By the early 1900's he had not only acquired theatres in every one of the Considine towns, but had opened three additional houses in Leavenworth, Kan., and Pueblo and Trinidad, Colo. The practices in the war between them somewhat lessened the prestige of the Considine circuit, which had been a sizable chain with houses in Butte, Tacoma, Seattle, Vancouver, Victoria, Spokane, Portland, Sacramento, San

Francisco, Oakland, Stockton, Salt Lake, Ogden, and Denver. They paid good salaries and booked good acts and most performers were glad to play for them.

Ackerman and Harris operated a circuit in small towns throughout the Northwest. Performers called it the "death trail." The time was so badly scattered an act lost money making jumps. Much of the booking was made up of three-night stands, and the last half of the week was lost for an act who required the time to make the next date.

Managers operating in the Midwest and the East included Gus Sun, who had a chain of eight theaters chief of which were those in Springfield and Hamilton, both in Ohio; Fred Mozart, a former fire-eater in circuses and museums, who owned a string of houses in Pennsylvania, and Kohl and Castle who owned the Olympic, the Clark Street Museum, and the West Side Museum on West Madison Street, all in Chicago, and museums in Minneapolis and St. Paul.

Mozart opened his first house in Lancaster, Pa., in the early 1900's and it became popular at once because of its handy location in breaking jumps from Philadelphia to the West. For a time he had unusual competition. The late F. W. Woolworth opened one of his first stores in Lancaster, a rather tall building on the roof of which he built a theater and in which he booked the best acts available: an unusual side light on Woolworth; few ever knew the canny five-and-dime merchant had taken a flier in show business.

Old George Castle, father of young George, handled the booking for all five of the Kohl and Castle houses. He made all appointments on the sidewalk in front of the Olympic, had his office in his pocket, listed dates and acts on a Pierce's Purgative Pellets memorandum book, and charged the performers 5 per cent commission. Young George, who took over later, was a brusque, unsmiling, laconic man. He would scarcely speak to performers and his correspondence was the briefest on record. In those days acts wrote for time on elaborate letterheads picturing their act in costume. Across these Castle would scrawl "No," or "Time filled," or "Write later," or "Too much money," or "Week Sept. 17, send billing." These he shoved into envelopes and returned to the writers.

Young Castle always sat in the left first entrance throughout the Monday opening. His face never changed. If an act introduced a bit of business or lines thefted from some other act, Castle admonished the offender at once. "Cut that out," he'd say. "I pay the act it belongs to to do it right. If you want to play here, do your own stuff." Condit and Morey, a dramatic sketch team, once played the Olympic with a playlet called "The Baby's Shoe." It was a pathetic skit and quite effective. Castle sat rapt. At the curtain he went to their dressing room. "Never write in here for that act again," he said. "It's a good act, a fine act. But I don't want my audience to cry, I want them to laugh. The next two acts will be wasted getting the show started again. Get a comedy act as good as this one and I'll book you any time."

His partner, Kohl, was a drab, unhappy man. He scarcely ever was seen about the theaters. One day he told the sign painter who lettered all the lobby work, act cards, and photo mounting to fashion a sign: "Matinee Today." The young chap went at it like a Howard Chandler Christy and came up with a knockout in Old English lettering high-lighted with colored tinsel. "What in the hell did you letter it in Dutch for?" Kohl asked. "Make one in English so people can read it. Make letters like that." And he pointed to a passing coal wagon.

Mike Shea—Suspicious, Honest.

Other managers, small fry in relation to Albee but interesting characters, were Mike Shea of Buffalo, Harry Williams of Pittsburgh, Wilmer and Vincent who began in Utica, N.Y., Hurtig and Seamon of New York City, W. L. Dockstader, Wilmington, Del. (no connection of Lew's), and M. C. Anderson, originally of Wilkes-Barre, Pa.

Mike Shea's first theater was in a cellar. But Mike, a tough but kindly Irishman, not only kept order but booked the best acts obtainable in the eighties. When the place was destroyed by fire, Mike, after a short tenure on a side street, opened his Garden Theater and later a new theater which he ran to the end of his time. Mike disliked exaggerated make-ups and crude caricatures, but, like Pastor, he never turned down an old-timer if he could help it. To youngsters coming in he was as friendly. He'd come back to visit a new song and dance team, hop on a trunk, tilt his cigar, and say: "Know what's the matter with you kids? You ought to get more money." And their envelope the following Saturday would be fattened by $25 or $50 more. Mike, of all the managers, distrusted the Albee Managers Association and was the last to come in. Even after Albee forced his entry he still would not play an act he did not want because it would accommodate someone else. His judgment of talent in relation to public acceptance was generally unerring, and the new acts he booked were assured of other time.

Harry Williams was an excellent appraiser of acts, and his program at the Williams Academy, Pittsburgh, was a model for managers elsewhere. He never haggled over salaries. But if he considered an act overrated he told them off, paid them in full, and dropped them.

Wilmer and Vincent began in the early 1900's with a small upstairs house in Utica, N.Y. Under the careful booking of Walter Vincent it thrived so that soon after its operation the partners acquired a larger house on the street level, the nucleus of the Wilmer and Vincent circuit. Vincent was well liked and not only because he paid good salaries. Courteous and kindly, today (1940) an elderly man, he is always delighted to meet old-timers. Besides supervising his own picture shows and other interests, he is vice-president of the Actors Fund of America.

Hurtig and Seamon operated a music hall in 125th Street, New York. When they could come to terms with the performers they played standard and headline acts. Later they went into burlesque, but when the slump came they were clipped.

Originally a blackface performer (and still not to be confused with Lew), W. L. Dockstader about 1895 remodeled an old carriage works in Wilmington, Del., and opened Dockstader's Theatre. His house did good business, but he could never pay metropolitan salaries. Nonetheless, performers having open time between Philadelphia and New York willingly came down to play a week for peanuts and friendship. Dock spent most of his time perched on a trunk in dressing rooms, sucking an old brier and kidding with his acts. Best of his gestures was his assent to new stuff. It was always O.K. with Dock if performers wished to try out new material.

M. C. Anderson, who had been a fancy glass blower, got the show business yen and opened a museum and theater in Wilkes-Barre, Pa., in the early nineties. It was successful and Anderson reached out as far as Cincinnati where he opened the Columbia Theatre. He paid well, booked the best acts he could, was friendly with the actors. Later he came to New York to manage the Hippodrome, now a parking lot at 43rd Street and Sixth Avenue.

In almost every instance these men were identified with their communities, friendly with the townspeople. This relationship was further enhanced by an independent booking system that gave them the right to say what act would play their houses. The United Booking Office, soon to be set up, took over the smaller manager's function in a blanket, dictatorial arrangement that spread acts hither and yon, regardless of community acceptance. Heaped upon this was the more sinister policy by which the U.B.O. muscled in on the provincial houses. They took, in many instances, a percentage of the theater, and without investment. So you won't book our act? they said, in effect; so you won't get any talent. No one could estimate how much Albee and his confreres benefited by this racket but their yield must have been vast.

Bookers and Agents

IN THE early eighties and even into the middle nineties bookers and agents were not important in vaudeville. Even in the late nineties no one foresaw the boom days when vaudeville was to outbox-office the legitimate stage, and these parasitic posts were neglected. Eventually they assumed due proportion, and when their duties were taken over by the United Booking Office, set up by the managers to increase their unholy yield, they became a major factor in provoking the organization of the performers' union known as the White Rats.

But the rise of the bookers was slow. The first were novices, and performers—gullible enough, God knows—were reluctant to accept them.

First of the bookers may have been James Armstrong. He had an office at 10 Union Square in New York and an entree to the managers of all the leading theaters as well as the big summer parks, important playing time in the eighties. Armstrong was brusque and honest, but he misbooked commanding acts and was soon excelled by George Liman, a prominent agent of the nineties, who increased his business by taking over a number of foreign acts. Liman would book anything from a honky-tonk beer hall to Koster and Bial's.

Contemporaries of Liman were Clint Wilson and Jo Paige Smith whose offices were at Broadway and Fourteenth Street. Smith had an in with Proctor; and Wilson, to some extent, with Keith. Wilson handled the small acts; Jo Paige Smith booked their big time. When the United Booking Office took over in the 1900's the partnership was dissolved. Smith tied with the U.B.O.; but Wilson, a good-natured yokel, was utterly stymied and made frequent trips to the 42nd Street sector to meet Smith, make a touch, and somehow keep going. One Christmas Eve Wilson came uptown and met Jo, who took him to a near-by saloon for some cheer. They had a number of snorts and Jo became seasonally friendly.

"I know things haven't been going well with you, Clint," he said, "but I am going to do something for you. Yes, sir, my boy, I am going to do something big for you." And Clint, beaming, thinking it couldn't be less than $20 or maybe even $50, listened on, enraptured. "Yes, sir, Clint, something big," continued Jo. And then: "Remember all that mazuma you've touched me for in the last year? Well, I'm gonna forget about it." And the spirits of Clint, who had never intended to pay it, sank deeper into his glass.

An early rival of Wilson and Smith was Richard Pitrot, an impersonator who came to America in the late eighties to play Koster and Bial's. He died penniless, but for a time Pitrot was the leading representative of foreign acts whom he protected as the initiator of the movement to stop the gypping of Europeans by unscrupulous agents and bookers. Pitrot was a Union Square character for years, always identifiable by the cane he lugged around until he actually walked lopsided. It was solid silver, weighed twenty-five pounds, and was given him by Willie Zimmerman, a headliner as an impersonator of composers.

Other bookers in the early nineties were Harry Covell and Robert Grau. A little later M. S. ("Commodore") Bentham set up shop. He was well liked and still functions. Covell for years booked the Brockton, Mass., fair, the biggest attraction in the East in the eighties and nineties, but he also supplied acts for the halls. Grau was unimportant, but he was the brother of Maurice Grau, general manager of the Metropolitan Opera, a relationship he exploited unduly.

Vaudeville's top agent was William Morris, a native German, born in Schwarzenau. He began as an advertising solicitor for a fur-trade journal and must have been good, for his earnings averaged $15,000 annually until the journal folded in 1893. Then he took up with George Liman for a comparative pittance, but he learned the business fast and within two years was doing most of the work while Liman sat around.

When Liman died everyone supposed that Morris would carry on for Liman's widow. Instead she gave the job to Harry Brunelle, Proctor's manager, who was universally disliked by the actors. Brunelle was originally a vaudeville performer: did a "cat" act on a set that resembled a Punch and Judy theater. When Proctor made him his chief booker and manager he quit performing.

Brunelle always offered $50 less than he thought an act was worth, and his appointment to take over by the Widow Liman was not only unpopular but unsound. Twenty-four hours after he stepped in as head of the agency, Morris opened an office of his own directly across the street at 102 East Fourteenth Street. Opened with the brass band of his brother-in-law, Berlinghoff's Band. Rapidly Morris pulled away all the important Liman clients—Hammerstein, Poli, Williams, Wilmer and Vincent among others—and in three months the Liman office closed.

Shrewd, intelligent, and a persuasive talker, Morris was largely responsible for Willie Hammerstein's early success. They first met when Willie was booking acts through the Liman office for Oscar's Olympia Theatre, a music hall at Broadway and 45th Street. When the Liman offices closed around 6 P.M., Morris and Willie would go down to the pool parlor in the Dewey Theatre building on Fourteenth

Street near Third Avenue, get a five-cent package of Jack
Rose little cigars (later called "squealers," after the witness
by the same name who informed in the Rosenthal case), shoot
pool, and talk. Willie would tell Morris about an act he'd
booked.

"How much?" Morris would ask.

"$250."

"Too much. I'd give it $150." Then Morris would tell why.
His advice was no end of help to Willie.

Morris induced Patsy Morrison, who ran a beer garden
and restaurant at Rockaway Beach, to toss out his cheap show
and put on headliners, with the result that Patsy did more
business in the evening with the crowds from Arverne and
Far Rockaway than he did through the day with excursions.
On his own end, Morris got his leading acts to play Morrison's
for about half salary. Told them they'd have a good time, that
it was a novelty, and that anyway by taking the 50 per cent
cut they could obtain full price the following week somewhere
else. It was sales talk, but Morris generally made good.

Morris's success naturally made him venom to Albee. Under
the nose of Albee's United Booking Office Morris was able
not only to find talent but to lure it in to his own fold. But
gradually Albee tightened the screws and one by one Morris's
managers—those he'd taken from Liman—abandoned his
ship and signed with U.B.O. Even then Morris hung on for a
time, but when Percy Williams sold out to the Keith-Albee
interests he was nearly broken.

Instead of giving up, the indomitable man went to Boston
and sold a real-estate operator named Allen the idea of putting
a vaude show in a hall that had recently been abandoned by
the Boston Symphony Orchestra. Allen agreed, and it worked
so well the following year he moved down to the Museum and
put on a show almost next door to Keith's house, thus not
only stealing Keith's business but his strategy. The threat to
open opposition houses was invariably the first barrage of
Albee against a recalcitrant manager. Again, on Morris's

advice, Allen installed a full orchestra, and Keith and Albee began to froth. The orchestra was so successful it forced them to put orchestras in nearly every one of their theaters where previously inexpensive piano players had sufficed.

Formation of the U.B.O.

A hundred or so of the early managers and agents took credit for the juicy idea of setting up the United Booking Office, a clearinghouse by which the performer was taken, coming and going. Their claims have no basis: it was the Machiavellian scheme of Pat Shea, a New England manager with a house in Springfield, Mass., and no connection of Buffalo Mike Shea. Incidentally, the business of the United Booking Office referred to throughout this book has no connection with the organization of the same name that operates today.

Coming into New York in the winter of 1900, Shea laid his plan in the laps of Clint Wilson and Jo Paige Smith. Lips smacking, the bookers carted the idea up to Albee who, already dipping his bread in the gravy, called an immediate conference of managers in Boston. Although New York would have been vastly more convenient, Albee deliberately changed the scene to favor Keith. Keith hated Proctor (with whom he was then allied), and by hiding away in Boston, he and Albee could double-cross him with less chance of detection.

Some of the managers objected. F. F. Proctor, in 1900, was important. "And if this [the U.B.O. plan] is to be the strangle you expect it to be," argued the recalcitrants, "where are you going without Proctor?" For two days Keith whined "no" to each suggestion that Proctor be summoned. He was finally won over. Proctor was no fool. Convinced that monkey business was afoot, he replied that New York was his home and if they wanted to confer with him they had better return. They did, and a session was held in the Hoffman House.

The first day Albee and J. Austin Fynes did the talking.

"I thought only those who owned theaters were to be permitted to announce plans," said Proctor. This was a crack at Albee, who held no properties.

"Mr. Albee owns the Providence house," answered Keith. Which was true. Keith had given it to him coming in on the train the night before.

After three days of meetings the managers agreed on all points and the United Booking Office was set up under the V.M.A. management.

Epes W. (Chicot) Sargent knew of the plotting and Keith knew that he knew. Apprehensive that Chicot would break the story in an exposé embarrassing if not ruinous, Keith summoned him to his suite in the Holland House with word that he had "a few more notes." When Chicot applied at the desk to be announced the clerk handed him an envelope, stating that Keith had asked not to be disturbed and that full information would be found in the enclosure. The envelope contained two $50 bills. Chicot opened it—insisted on seeing Keith. After a short delay Keith phoned down to send him up. Immediately upon entering the room Chicot tossed the money back at Keith, and Keith showed him the door. "I never trust a man I can't buy," he said. And the feud went on.

Not all the managers came into the new organization willingly. Poli was one—held out to the last. Indeed, Poli, constantly suspicious of Albee, so regretted his agreement he stopped payment on his initial check. Directly, Keith and Albee sent letters to every bank in the towns in which Poli had a theater stating that they planned to open an opposition house and the banks could extend credit to Poli at their own risk. Poli came back in.

A year later, in April, 1901, Proctor quit or, if one subscribes to the V.M.A. version, was forced to resign. What the row was about has never been divulged, but it is a sound conclusion that Proctor believed he was being taken. As the actors were. He remained out several years but was forced to come back.

Testifying in the 1913 suit brought by H. B. Marinelli against the U.B.O. as violators of the Sherman Antitrust Act, Albee swore that the formation of the booking offices was to protect actor as well as manager. A measure of this "protection" is indicated in the contemporary complaints of the performers.

Agent and booking fees had been a flat 10 per cent. This the U.B.O. took over, charging 5 per cent for its service and paying the agent the remaining five. But the managers association soon reached out for more, upping the actor a $2\frac{1}{2}$ per cent to collect the agent's commission, thus forcing the actor to pay $12\frac{1}{2}$ per cent. Actually because of bonuses, split commissions, fees, etc., the performers paid more. Commissions sometimes reached as high as 15 and 20 per cent. And there were other frame-ups.

"What are you getting?" a gyp agent would ask a performer; "$200? I'll get you $300 for 20 per cent." The performer would gladly assent. And the agent, framing it with the booker, would put the act through for $500, pay the performer $300, and split the difference with the booker.

What further irked the performers were the stupid booking routes, the various other swindling methods of some of the agents, and the inequitable U.B.O. contracts. A clause in all U.B.O. contracts permitted cancellation of the act by the house manager any time during or before the third performance. This meant that an act could be tossed out before the Tuesday night performance, if the house was a two-a-day, or after Monday night if it was continuous or three-a-day. So a forty-week contract could be good only until the Tuesday afternoon of the first appearance. But the actor couldn't cancel the managers. More: The U.B.O. would make a salary proposition based on minimum fares which meant easy jumps—New York to Philadelphia to Baltimore to Washington, for example. Time and again an act so routed would be notified while playing a Philadelphia date to jump to Buffalo and then back to Washington. These were the hardships performers rebelled against and which prompted George Fuller Golden to organize the White Rats.

Cohan Buys a Book.

Golden was a rough, tough pugilist; a lover of poetry, a voracious reader of the classics; a radical idealist. He varied prize fighting with dancing and after a few tours of Michigan, where he was born, and other Midwestern states, meeting all comers for whatever purse could be raised, he teamed up with his lifelong friend, James (Gypsy) Dolan, in a song and double-clog act, later playing big time with Dolan in a sketch called "The High-toned Burglar." When the team split, Golden did a monologue, a series of Casey stories—"Casey at the Wedding," "Casey in Paris," "Casey at the Fair," etc. He always regretted that to make a living he had to be a clown or, as he expressed it, "don the ass's head."

Whatever his shortcomings, Golden was a man whose integrity was never questioned. He wrote a book, "My Lady Vaudeville," a fantastic summary of the White Rats movement, couched in purple passages, a neurotic, florescent, honest outpouring of heart. At the height of his career Golden contracted tuberculosis. To ease his last days and aid his vain fight for life, George M. Cohan, on an afternoon in the Metropole Café, New York, gave him $10,000—for the book. Others helped. Golden had written an act for Al Jolson, who was then coming up. Jolson had agreed to pay $500, depositing $100 on account. When he heard of Golden's illness, Al, probably borrowing the money, wired Golden the balance.

The origin of the White Rats as a vaudeville actors' union stems from a similar organization of London music-hall artists called the Water Rats. In 1899 Golden went to London, played the halls, failed miserably. (It should be noted that six years later he again booked London and was the hit of the season.)

Without funds in the winter of 1900, his wife ill, Golden tried everything, accomplished nothing. The Water Rats heard of his plight. They paid his debts, his room rent, the medical expenses incurred by his wife, advanced him money for food, and when it was apparent the music-hall managers would have none of his act, bought passage back to the United States for himself and his wife. Golden returned to New York in May and, lining up at the bar of the Parker House, told a group of his actor friends of the kindness that had been extended him by the Water Rats. "Why shouldn't we have an organization like that over here?" he asked. "Especially at a time like this when the managers are organizing against us?"

It was agreed and on June 1, 1900, the original seven (exclusive of Golden) met at the Parker House bar on Broadway and officially formed the White Rats. These seven were Dave Montgomery, his partner Fred Stone, Sam Morton, Tom Lewis, Sam J. Ryan, Mark Murphy, and Charles Mason. Gypsy Dolan was on tour at the time, but at the next meeting, which he attended, he was voted one of the "original eight," an earnest if boyish gesture characteristic of the juvenile enthusiasm that made this first American artist-labor movement naïve to the public and, unfortunately, silly to the managers.

Like most talent-member organizations, the first thought of the leaders was to keep their band exclusive, and an initial agreement was made to limit membership to a hundred select artists rated according to character and ability. Although this limitation prevailed no longer than it took the rank and file to sound their who-do-they-think-they-are? protests, it was damaging. It was an error to suppose that a victorious demonstration against the managers could be accomplished in any other way than en masse. It created the suspicion of snobbery, fostering the feeling that only top-billing actors were entitled to economic benefits. All this, allied to the actors' jealousy and greed, prompted the disloyalty that was to make abortive each successive attempt to gain managerial justice. And it provided the setup for Albee's National Vaudeville Artists, which masked as a club but in reality was a company union.

It had been Golden's desire to appropriate the Water Rats' name of the London organization, a title that derived from a race horse of that name. It was a good horse, owned by a group of actors for whom it made much money. Some of the money was disposed for benevolent purposes and out of this grew the idea of a benefit association for performers. Accordingly the horse-owning actors duly incorporated (in the late eighties) their Grand Order of the Water Rats.

But the London order objected to sharing their name and the title "White Rats" was ultimately chosen. Two or three who felt that "rats" was an egregious term were silenced by others who argued that "rats" was the backward spelling of "star," and the name stood. At Golden's suggestion the first tiny quorum adopted, apparently unchallenged, the Water Rats' song, "The Emblem," which had been written by a music-hall performer named Wal Pink. Substituting the term "White" for "Water," here is the chorus:

> And this is the emblem of our society,
> Each member acts with the greatest propriety.
> Jolly old sports, to us they raised their hats!
> A merry lot of fellows are the real White Rats.
> Rats! Rats! Rats! Rats! Rats! Star!

And here is the music:

White Rats Emblem

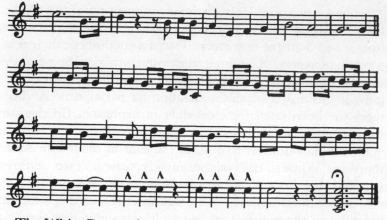

The White Rats order was duly launched, and when sixteen members showed up at an early meeting the following official slate was voted in:

George Fuller Golden, president, or Big Chief; Dave Montgomery, vice-president, or Little Chief; James J. Morton, secretary, or Scrat; Mark Murphy, treasurer, or Treasurrat; and board places were assigned to Sam Morton, Tom Lewis, Fred Stone, James (Gypsy) Dolan, Sam Ryan, and Nat M. Wills. Golden devised a ritual, a combination of Masonic rites and the marriage sacrament of the Roman Catholic Church. A few weeks later, when the ritual had been accepted, Charles T. Aldrich, a respected performer, was inducted as chaplain or, as they styled him, Chap Rat.

But if the ecstatic Golden was a bit balmy in his attempts to make real his poetic fancies, he was very sound on a matter that as early as 1900 was infiltrating vaudeville—the freak, polite, and hammy legit acts that were to make anemic the vigorous, lusty, kick-in-the-belly-and-lima-beans vaudeville which, for all its grossness, was virile and forthright. Against this Golden fought for the rest of his short life.

All Risk—Small Gain.

He fought, with no lessening vigor, for the White Rats on a platform that listed all manner of grievances beyond the thieving commissions. In rally after rally he brought to public attention what the actors already knew: that the theater owners and big-time operators risked nothing except their real property expenses. The actor risked everything. He paid for his sets (if he used scenery), paid for his costumes, for his cast, and for his material unless he originated it himself. The manager contributed the four walls of his house. If an actor devised an act he had to beg, buy, or trick his way into a chance to show it. The tryouts, at the time of the White Rats' inauguration, were held in the Fifth Avenue Theatre Thursday mornings, usually before cynical representatives of the managers. If an act was received with apathy the curtain was rung, a severe humiliation.

If an act had apparent merit it was booked in a Yonkers honky-tonk or sent to, say, Union City, N.J., a small town across the Hudson from New York. These were no audiences to judge new material or pass upon novelties. Assuming the act was moderately successful, it was then booked outside— Scranton, Asbury Park, etc.—in small-time theaters which the managers kept going by these methods. Moreover, the U.B.O., which now controlled many of the theaters and virtually all the talent, slashed salaries so that the return, especially to a new act, was scarcely enough to meet expenses. Nor were these conditions visited solely upon new talent: noted actors with new sketches received the same treatment.

Now if an act, after repeated appearances in the sticks, did go over so that it was finally admitted to big time, how did it fare? None too well. Besides the commission splits and the general system of chiseling—"bits," as the actors termed the constant handouts to the parasites in power and the incessant tips—decreased the performer's purse-load. Everybody had a hand out and an actor who failed to cross each palm was never sure he would be able to go on. The stagehands, electricians, spotlight man, the musicians, especially the transfer men, each must have his gratuity, or sets were improperly hung, lights went haywire, music cues were ignored, and trunks were "lost." Everyone "had a mitt out." And the tips ranged from $2 to $10 a week for each service, according to the standing of the act.

Golden first appealed, then demanded. His only answer was a tightening of the screws. In addition to exacting the unfair commission, the managers put the tap directly on the performers. There were favored bookers and favored acts. And the rumors that such box-office performers as Irene Franklin, Sam Bernard, and Stella Mayhew received scarcely a tithe of their reputed salaries, although constantly denied, were as constantly reiterated.

Against these conditions the White Rats struck.

George M. Cohan's walkout on Keith in 1899 did not precipitate the strike, but it came at a time when there was much unrest and dissatisfaction among performers and Cohan's action was widely hailed in the profession. The Four Cohans had been a headline act for years and the brawl had important repercussions. Here is Cohan's explanation of the incident given to the writer in 1938:

We [the Four Cohans] signed a contract with B. F. Keith to play eight weeks a season during the years 1897, '98 and '99. We had played twenty-two of the twenty-four weeks and had lived up to the contract religiously. In the meantime our outside bookings had been popular and profitable, so much so that when we came into Boston to play the remaining two weeks our salaries had risen to three times that called for in the Keith contract. Well, when we got in I went over to the theatre and took a look at the bill: we were bottomlined. Previously we had been headlined and our contract called for that billing.

I went at once to the house manager, a man named Bryant, and complained, told him it was impossible to play under that billing and he told me to see Keith, which I did. And Keith said, "Well, I'm sorry. It's some mistake, some press agent's or sign painter's mistake, not mine."

COHAN: It isn't mine, either.

KEITH: What are you going to do?

COHAN: What would you do in my position?

KEITH: If I'd been associated with a man as long as you people have with me I'd certainly go through for him.

COHAN: Well, Mr. Keith, I haven't any particularly fond memories of you. The only thing I can recall in the early days of Keith is a lot of hard work, a lot of extra performances, a lot of confinement, six and seven and eight shows a day, running up eighty and ninety steps to dressing rooms, and a million rules and regulations hanging all over the place. Any time you wanted to smoke you had to go into a little tin closet. So the nice little speech you just made to me, inviting me to go through with the broken contractual conditions, doesn't mean much. Besides, Mr. Keith, I remember a little incident in Providence on a Saturday night. You didn't have enough to meet the payroll. And you came back to ask us [the Four Cohans] if we'd mind waiting until the following Tuesday or Wednesday. And my father, Jerry, said, "Why, no, if you're short, and maybe we could lend you a little money and how much do you want?' And you said about $600 and we let you have it.

KEITH: I don't remember it.

COHAN: Another thing; you probably don't stop to realize, Mr. Keith, that we are getting a whole lot more money in outside booking than we did when we signed this contract three years ago.

KEITH: Oh, that's the idea. You want more money.

COHAN: Yes, a whole lot more.

KEITH: I understand now; it's a shakedown.

COHAN: Call it what you like, Mr. Keith, but just because of that crack I'll make you a promise right now—that no member of the Cohan family will ever play for you again as long as you are in the theatrical business.

They never did.

The strike was a sporadic, ineffective move and it is dreadful to have to record that it failed largely because of the disloyalty of the actors. Many, frightened at the U.B.O. black list, took no heed of the call. Others, more faithless, actually accepted time relinquished by striking White Rats. Harassed internally, beaten by the managers, the organization dwindled almost to extinction until rejuvenated by an English performer, Harry Mountford, who came to America in 1907. We shall catch up with Mountford.

The Shuberts vs. Albee.

In 1907 Klaw and Erlanger, then the theater trust, united with the Shuberts to pan some of the gold filtering through the Keith-Albee box offices. On April 28 they incorporated in New Jersey the United States Amusement Co. to produce vaudeville shows: K. and E. to supply the talent, the Shuberts to furnish the houses. Bill Morris was given the contract to book the company's vaudeville theaters. The terms were excellent, involving nearly a million dollars over a five-year period as Morris's fees.

Immediately there was hell to pay. Acts that went over to this so-called Shubert Advanced Vaudeville were blacklisted by Albee's United Booking Office. Performers, therefore, looking to their own interests and well aware of Albee's might, hesitated to join the Shubert forces despite the higher salaries offered. It became increasingly difficult for the Shuberts to obtain talent, and after about three months of costly battling a truce was declared which led to a settlement.

The final agreement was dated November 9, 1907, but its terms were not revealed until seventeen years later in the suit of Max Hart, an agent, against the B. F. Keith Vaudeville Exchange. They came out in a deposition by Marc Klaw, then retired and living on the Riviera. Klaw swore that the Keith interests in 1907 took over from K. and E. performer contracts totaling $1,500,000 and, in addition, paid the Shuberts and Klaw and Erlanger $250,000 to stay out of vaudeville for ten years.

The Hart trial is worth more than passing notice. It tore the roof off vaudeville; exposed it, as operated by Albee, as a practical monopoly. Despite the testimony, Federal Judge Augustus N. Hand dismissed the suit on the grounds that proof of violation of the Sherman act and the interstate commerce laws had not been offered. Hart fought until his final defeat, November 23, 1926, when the United States Supreme Court refused to review.

So secretly was the 1907 settlement carried through, that even Morris's attorney, Jerome Wilzin was unaware an agreement had been reached. Indeed, Wilzin recently declared that no money changed hands—a naïve conclusion when one recalls the two principals: Abe Erlanger and Ed Albee. Wilzin's first hint of it came when Erlanger, czar of America's legitimate theaters, summoned him and Morris to his offices in the New Amsterdam Theatre building. There, to Wilzin's chagrin, Erlanger told of the settlement. Turning to Morris, he said, "But I've taken care of you, Bill." And smiled happily, as though musing over the ease with which he was slipping out of the iron vise of Morris's contract. "I have arranged that you will be given the post of general manager of the United Booking Office at a salary of $35,000 a year." This was the Albee outfit, and Morris declined. Erlanger, no longer smiling, said: "$50,000." Morris said no. Then Erlanger, realizing Morris's stupendous claim against him, yelled murder, called thief. Whereupon Morris took the contract from his pocket, tore it up, and tossed it on Erlanger's desk. Erlanger scrutinized the signatures to see if it was the original instrument. "Bill," he said, "that is the whitest thing you have ever done. If I can ever do anything for you just call on me. I promise to grant any request you make." Morris, who could have sued him to his underwear, never asked him for a match. Incidentally, when Percy Williams sold his chain to the Keith-Albee interests he insisted that Morris be appointed general manager of the U.B.O. Again Morris declined, preferring his independence.

After the settlement Morris went all over the country, opened up leads, developed plans, won support. But as fast as he got something started Albee tried to stymie him.

The Scotch Oath.

Albee stopped at nothing short of mayhem, but with the aid of Harry Lauder, Morris managed to keep going. Although

his box-office reputation was immense, the Keith-Albee interests would have nothing to do with Lauder and Morris was
forced to book him in halls, Masonic auditoriums, tents,
shacks. Lauder never had a contract with Morris, and his
salary range was from $3,500 to a top of $5,500 weekly. They
took a Scotch oath (joining the thumbs of the open right
hand) in a Liverpool saloon in 1908. An Irish bartender was
the only witness. It bound both until Morris's death in November, 1932.

Lauder had first played America in 1907. George Foster, a
London agent, is said to have brought him over as Klaw and
Erlanger's headliner in their advanced vaudeville foray against
Albee and Keith. He was booked at the New York theater
and drew astonishing crowds. Later there were interesting
conflicts. In 1911 Morris booked Lauder into the Manhattan
Opera House for his first appearance in a coast-to-coast tour.
The deal for the theater was made with the Shuberts, and they
promptly demanded 33⅓ per cent of the gross. Morris said
no, and offered 25 per cent, then 27. The Shuberts held out
for their top figure and the deal almost collapsed, but as
Morris was about to walk out they said they would rent him
the house for a flat $4,500 for the week. Morris accepted, not
too eagerly. Lauder grossed $36,000 for the six days and the
Shuberts, contending that in playing an extra show past
Sunday midnight on the last night Lauder had exceeded the
terms of the lease, held out part of the receipts. It was settled.

The opening at the Manhattan was memorable. Lauder was
to arrive the day of the performance. But his ship, the *Saxonia*,
was delayed by storms. A house packed to the fire-law regulations waited and waited. To keep them Morris frantically
tapped every actor he knew; in several dashes up Broadway
from 34th Street, he dragged them out of restaurants, saloons,
and dressing rooms and off the sidewalk, recruiting a bill
worthy of competing against the cantie performer. Among
those who responded were Frank Tinney, Carter De Haven,
the Empire City Quartet, and Billy Gould.

Meanwhile Morris arranged with William Loeb, Jr., collector of customs for the Port of New York (the title then), to transfer Lauder to the *Owlet*, a chartered tug, at Quarantine. This was done, and Lauder was brought to the Battery in make-up and kilts and rushed to the theater. He arrived at 1 A.M., went on at once, and greeted the audience with—"Hae ye nae hames?"

The following year Morris brought Lauder back, and again ran afoul of Albee. Albee's row with Klaw and Erlanger and the Shuberts had been settled and one of the provisions was that they were not to poach on Albee's vaudeville preserve upon penalty of $25,000 for each offense. This agreement had still a number of years to run when Morris booked Lauder for his 1912 opening in the Belasco Theatre, Washington, a legit house. The engagement had been announced for weeks and tickets were being sold openly when the management gratuitously reminded Albee of the invasion clause in the K. & E. settlement. Albee turned on Erlanger, demanding immediate cancellation or forfeiture of $25,000. Erlanger, having no recourse, ordered the cancellation, and Morris, Jerome Winzer, and William Morris, Jr., then a lad in knee pants, hurried to Washington.

The morning of the night Lauder was to appear they saw President Theodore Roosevelt. The President listened patiently, then sympathetically, and then, as Morris explained the ramifications of the operations in which he was caught, with a trust buster's interest. Believing his cause for the theater was doomed, Morris asked that Lauder be permitted to stage his entertainment in the Blue Room of the White House in a private performance for the President and his guests—for free.

"Well, I think that could be arranged," said Teddy, and added (being a smart showman himself), "it would certainly be good publicity for you. But I think you had better count on his appearance in the theater." The President then telephoned the Belasco's manager that unless Lauder's engagement was guaranteed for that evening he would instruct Attorney

General Charles J. Bonaparte to institute an immediate action against the theater trust. Lauder appeared, and Teddy attended the performance. Had a good time, too. Everybody had a good time except Albee. For having to waive the invasion clause he demanded a cut of the box office. Morris laughed. Few men took Albee. One, maybe two, double-crossed him. Morris was the only agent who took him, and Morris fought fair.

Nut Houses—The Boston Colonial and Hammerstein's Victoria

THE essence of American vaudeville was comedy despite Albee's contention that it was women's backsides. About 1905 Annette Kellerman, then unknown to larger America, was appearing in Wonderland, a miniature Coney Island near Boston. One day it was announced she was to swim from a Boston bridge to Charlestown Light. She didn't make it but she drew so much publicity the local Keith manager signed her for two weeks. She almost ruined the bill. As the act was presented, Annette entered first as a toe dancer—no good. Then into a spinning-top routine—worse. Then she went into her diving act—fairish.

Albee saw her opening. At the close of the show he went back. "What are we selling?" he demanded; then answered his own question: "We're selling backsides, aren't we? All right. If one backside is good, a hundred backsides are as many times better. Go down in the cellar and bring up those mirrors Loie Fuller used for her dance." They did, and Albee refashioned her performance against the mirrors in a new routine of diving, swimming, and posing. And the act came to life.

Loie Fuller, by the way, a big dancing draw, was the admiration of many vaude artists: nobody ever knew how she did it, but Loie never paid her bills. There were always

162 sheriffs on her trail. Now Boston, at the time (about 1905), had a frightful debt law. They could seize your right leg for an unpaid newspaper bill. Except Sunday. The accommodating management at Keith's accordingly placed a cot in Loie's dressing room, and she never left the theater. Except Sunday. On the bill this certain week was the Princess Rajah who did a snake act. The sight of the imprisoned Loie avoiding two sheriffs seated just inside the stage door in case Loie forgot and stepped out (they could only seize you on the street) inspired Rajah's sympathy. She said to Loie: "Tonight you are going out."

A few minutes later one sheriff, his voice shaking, said to the other, "Do you see what I see?" He did. And the terrified pair dashed through the stage door and raced up the street. Rajah had released her two pythons to wriggle across the darkened stage. An unset stage in an empty theater, with a dim spot the only light, intensifying the eerie shadows that seemingly beckon the ghosts of actors, is enough of a graveyard—without snakes.

All this at the Boston Colonial, where anything could happen. New York and officials elsewhere on the circuit ribbed its management constantly. One of the biggest laughs was the Colonial's policy of handing a patron enjoying boisterous hilarity a card on a silver tray. It read: "Please do not laugh too loud." This ought to bring us back to our subject of comedy but the Colonial is too good a house to let go.

Mrs. Jack Gardner was a constant violator of the Colonial's rule that women must remove their hats and they had a dreadful time with her about it. One night the manager ejected her, it then being the law that women must take off their bonnets (these were the plume days). She turned up again the following week and again offended. But when the ushers descended upon her she showed them a headdress of ostrich feathers—no hat. It was more bothersome to those behind her than a hat. But it was not a hat. To eject her might have invited suit, and they let her stay.

Another Colonial caper was a lovely "who dunit." We say the Colonial because that is the recollection of many; at any rate, it was at one of Keith's Boston theaters some years ago that a man slumped in his orchestra chair, his head a bloody mess. Ushers reached him as he collapsed with a fractured skull. The man was cared for at a private hospital, and after the show, mechanics and electricians, examining the theater, found a large iron bolt on the floor near his seat. The incident was scarcely forgotten before it happened again—another man terribly hurt in the same manner. Again a bolt was found near the seat of the injured patron.

The bloody incidents kept on for a month at the rate of three or four a week and Keith, Albee, and their entire staff hurried on to Boston, not only alarmed at potential lawsuits, but concerned as well for loss of patronage if news of the accidents leaked out. How they were able to keep the ruinous stories from the newspapers no one ever learned.

Hundreds of private detectives in plain clothes were scattered about the house, hidden back of curtains, behind pillars. Smaller men were concealed in specially built traps under the seats. Thousands of dollars were spent in renovation of the theater, and inspection by carpenters and engineers was continuous.

After a score of persons were injured (none fatally), the culprit was caught. He was a demented house policeman who perpetrated his act while detailed to catch the perpetrator. With a bolt concealed in his hand he would take his station in the balcony. Then, while apparently on the alert for mayhem, he surreptitiously flipped the iron missile over the balcony rail. The man was sent to an insane asylum.

Oscar's Marvelous Idea.

The great nut vaudeville house of New York was Hammerstein's Victoria at Broadway and 42nd Street. Willie Hammerstein ran it for his father, and ran it well—an expert showman. The profits enabled Oscar to keep monkeying with his favorite, and expensive, passion—grand opera. It was this that brought about the one serious rift between father and son. Oscar seldom interfered with Willie, but one day he came into the Victoria and said, "Willie, I've got a marvelous idea. I'm going to build a chain of thirty-five grand opera houses straight across the continent." When Willie recovered he said, "God damn it, you've got four opera houses already that eat up all the profits of the Victoria and now you come in with a scheme to build thirty-five more!" And Willie stalked out of the theater and remained away for months.

When the Victoria was opened in 1904 Willie limited his billing budget to $1,900 a week. Later when the house was an assured success his weekly pay roll averaged $7,500. From then until he quit the management of the Victoria in 1912 its annual earnings averaged $300,000. Albee once tried to hire him for $35,000 a year, but, loyal to his father, Willie declined. Besides, he was doing all right where he was. Oscar paid him $550 a week and, in addition (and unknown to Oscar), Willie split the lobby privilege 50-50 with Morris Gest, then the house speculator.

The price was never printed on the Victoria's tickets, a notable convenience for the box office. Thus for a good bill on rainy days or nights Gest or the box office could virtually name their figures, while on delightful afternoons when patrons were tempted to horse parks or ball games they could dip the price. Some kind of audience was always assembled. Incidentally, "the old man," as everyone called Oscar, had small use for Gest. "Why the hell do you have that fellow hanging around here all the time?" he once asked Willie, not knowing, of course, of the partnership.

The Victoria was strictly a freak house and was so exploited. The aforementioned Princess Rajah was a favorite here. Willie found her in a Coney Island side show. To eliminate her honky-tonk background he secretly booked her in Huber's Fourteenth Street Museum before putting her on for her vaudeville debut at his 42nd Street theater. "Direct from

Huber's to Hammerstein's," her billing read. Willie liked the alliteration. Rajah did an Oriental dance with snakes. At one of her appearances a snake bit her on the face and Jack Johnson, the former heavyweight champion who was playing on the bill, carried her off and sucked the blood from the wound, believing the snake poisonous. It wasn't—it was a python. Rajah's other routine was a dance with a kitchen chair. She would take hold of it with her teeth and, gliding about the stage, sway it forward and backward with arclike movements that finally restored it to the stage on its legs. Willie paid her $300 a week to start, but she drew so well he raised it to $400, to the chagrin of Percy Williams, who had predicted she would flop. Later Williams admitted his mistake and booked her on his own chain. From this she went on to Keith time at $750. On a European tour she married Clifford C. Fischer, a prominent agent who recently operated the French Casino in New York and a 1940 Folies-Bergère razzle-dazzle.

Willie combed the museums and side shows for his freaks. In Philadelphia he found the wonderful Sober Sue. He brought her on in June, 1908, and since the poor girl could do nothing but stand or sit, he used her during intermission as an exhibition stunt in the theater's "miniature farm" to the rear of the roof garden. Willie billed her as "Sober Sue—You Can't Make Her Laugh" and posted a $1,000 reward for anyone who could. A number of the best comics of the period tried— Sam Bernard, Willie Collier, Eddie Leonard, Louis Mann. All failed. But the customers kept coming, not to see Sober Sue, but the comedians who (without salary) were contributing thousands of dollars in prestige and box-office take. Sue ran fourteen weeks at a salary of $25 a week and a couple of $10 dresses. When the engagement terminated it was discovered that her facial muscles were paralyzed and it was physically impossible for her to laugh.

Rajah's European booker, H. B. Marinelli, a former contortionist, watched the London and Continental halls for

Hammerstein. In 1909 he sent over Mme. Polaire, an attractive woman whom Willie immediately billed as "The Ugliest Woman in the World." She had a remarkably small waist and

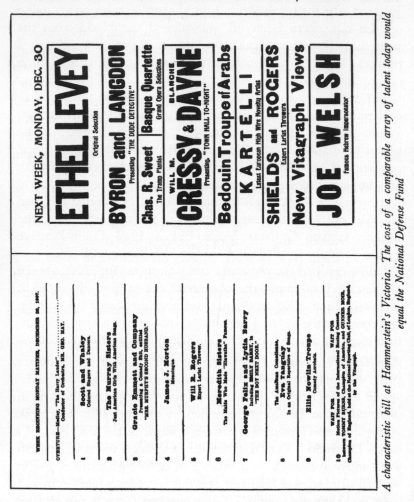

A characteristic bill at Hammerstein's Victoria. The cost of a comparable array of talent today would equal the National Defense Fund

Willie announced prizes for any woman who had a smaller one. The girls laced their corsets to murderous constriction, but none was able to lessen Polaire's measurement of not quite fifteen inches.

Once a nut came to Willie and said, "Mr. Hammerstein, for $2,500 I'll commit suicide on the stage." "What would you do for an encore?" asked Willie. But Willie would have been interested in James Berry, a British hangman who asked $150 a week to deliver what he called "an interesting and instructive lesson on my career, illustrated by the stereopticon, showing pictures of celebrated English hangings and portraits of noted criminals I have executed." This was in the nineties and New York managers turned him down. But he did succeed in selling the English music halls, where he was quite successful.

Willie would have booked him. He booked Conrad and Graham, the two girls who shot W. E. D. Stokes in the Ansonia Hotel. They had no ability and no stage experience, but Willie gave them $300 a week. They squawked, and he raised it to $300 apiece. They were billed as "The Shooting Stars," and the wonder is they weren't shot. For two weeks Loney Haskell, the monologist, rehearsed them, patiently teaching them how to walk on and off and what to do with their hands. It was no use; the girls couldn't go on without him and when they got on they couldn't make sense. So Haskell had to lecture on them as though they were freaks, which, oh, well . . .

Hammerstein's was the most topical theater in America. A headline in the news led directly to a headline at the Victoria. Any outstanding contemporary figure in the public prints could obtain a week's booking. Thus Willie promptly took on Dorando, the Italian runner who won the 1908 Olympics marathon and inspired the song, "Run, Run, You Son of a Gun, Dorando." Dorando could not speak a word of English. He simply appeared, in a misfit suit of foreign clothes, gawky and ill at ease, while Loney Haskell went into his "lecture."

In 1913 when Harry K. Thaw escaped from the institution at Matteawan, Willie got his luckiest break. Evelyn Nesbit, Thaw's wife, for whom he had shot and killed Stanford White, was on Willie's bill at the time with Jack Clifford as her dancing partner. Thaw's escape and the Nesbit and Clifford opening on the Hammerstein bill were so perfectly timed that many newspapers believed Willie had framed it and for weeks he was admired for a piece of publicity with which hc had nothing whatever to do. Willie paid the act $3,000 for the week. It would have been worth $10,000. He tried to book them for ten weeks, but other commitments kept them touring and he had to let them go.

Willie was a great billmaker and a great showman. A few years after the Victoria opened he conceived the idea of putting on New York cartoonists, not because he had any regard for their acts as entertainment, but because he could cash publicity through them. He booked four outstanding men: Winsor McKay, Bud Fisher, Rube Goldberg, and Tad Dorgan. Their patter was terrible and the acts were flops, but Willie got his advertising.

Willie also arranged for the first presentation in New York of "The Great Train Robbery," famous silent movie, first of the three-reel thrillers. With its "daring" portrayal of a holdup à la James boys, it drew audience raves and ran for three weeks.

Willie was a grand fellow, a good deal like Tony Pastor for whom, by the way, he reserved a box every Sunday night. And when Pastor died Willie kept the box inviolate in honor of the great showman. Often Willie played an act without contract. Meeting a performer he would ask if he was working the following week. If the answer was no: "Then you play for me." Willie was a friendly man, with a fine sense of humor and quick wit. He adored his wife and two sons, Oscar II and Reginald, and never played around; shunned Oscar's follies. He died before the Victoria folded, a bit of staging that as a showman he would have timed himself.

Great Comics of the 1900's

SOME pages back we were saying that comedy was the essence of American vaudeville. Witnesses are the great comics who livened the two-a-day in the halcyon (for the audience) times of the 1900's—a lengthy scroll. More important is the fact that vaudeville, being largely topical fun, reflected in its humor almost the entire social setting during its short-lived but superlative period. The lumbering times at the turn of the century when giant America stirred with definite realization of its vastness induced a corresponding vigor in variety-theater comedy. The puissance of the acts was not precisely burlesque; it was rather a combination of outrageous distortion, noisy satire, and mad humor, adding up to an insanely imaginative entertainment—"nut" acts, in the argot of the profession.

As early as 1902 Ed Wynn was razzing our college youth: "Rah, rah, rah. Who pays my bills? Pa and Ma." These were Wynn's opening lines in his first vaudeville sketch with Jack Lewis. It was called "The Freshman and the Sophomore" and gently panned the college sons of rich parents. Wynn wore peg-top trousers and a funny Panama hat; entered with a meerschaum pipe in his mouth and bulldog on leash. He made his hat famous throughout his eleven years in vaudeville. It was a trick hat from the factory of his father, a millinery manufacturer in Philadelphia, and Wynn could make twenty-eight different shapes of it by a touch here, there. In 1913 Ziegfeld said to him, "The only thing you can do is that hat." Said Wynn, "I'll throw it away." He hasn't used it since.

Wynn's parents—name of Leopold—had means and they were pretty sore when, at sixteen, the boy took to the stage, upsetting the old man's intention to make him a businessman. His first appearance was with a New England repertory company (Thurber and Nasher) in Norwich, Conn. The play was "Jim Bledsoe," a meller in which Wynn played a seventy-year-old Methodist minister. It flopped, and things got pretty bad. Wynn rented a $2.50-a-week room in a theatrical boardinghouse in West 44th Street, New York. (Seventeen years later the site became the 44th Street Theatre and Wynn walked through the stage door at a salary of $1,750 a week in "The Gaities of 1919.") One night he went over to Kid McCoy's rathskeller on Broadway and entered the back room the Kid reserved for actors. There he met Jack Lewis and told him of a college act he had written. Wynn had received some publicity on his first theatrical venture—"Millionaire's Son Quits College for Stage"—and it seemed smart to Lewis to cash in on the news stories while they were fresh.

They went through the act and with help from experienced writers fixed it up—lost labor. Agents wouldn't look at it. But some time later a benefit was announced for Ben Sugarman, a cousin of Lew Fields. It was to be held in a theater in West 125th Street and Jim Corbett was to be a headliner and introduce the other acts. Wynn and Lewis offered their act and were tossed out. Wynn was dejected, but Lewis knew Corbett and insisted on seeing him. Finally Corbett told them he'd find a spot for them. It was a rough audience; they even hissed Metropolitan Opera stars off the stage. They only wanted to hear Jim Corbett. Finally the fighter went on with his own act (anecdotes, stories of his exploits), and then: "Now I want you to meet a couple of great guys. Just came from the West. I want you to give them a chance to see that New York is all right," and out walked Wynn and Lewis. They were a riot, and after the performance Joe Shea signed them and booked them the next day on Percy Williams's chain; for ninety-eight weeks thereafter they played without a break—at $200 a week.

In 1904 Wynn broke with Lewis to headline his own name and toured until 1913 in a succession of acts: "The Rah! Rah! Boys," "Daffydills," "The English and American Students," "Upsanddowns," etc., all of which he wrote. It is Wynn's boast today that not a line he has spoken on the stage was ever written by anybody but himself.

Wynn quit vaudeville in 1913, the year the Palace opened, after appearing, as a matter of fact, on the Palace's first bill in a meringue called "The King's Jester." It was a crazy sketch about a surly king who, if he couldn't be made to laugh, had to die. Candidates for the job of tickling the king's unresponsive risibilities met a similar fate if they failed. Wynn came on and told gag after gag; no laugh and he was about to be killed when he went over and whispered in the king's ear. The king grinned, then smiled broadly, then shrieked with merriment. "Why didn't you tell me you wanted to hear that kind of a story?" asked Wynn.

Wynn was one of the first comics to cut out the bladder, slapstick, and slippery stairs. His act was sidewalk conversation; but he eliminated the straight man's crack at the comic with a newspaper after the comedian's joke. His popularity on the radio was an ironic success, an interesting side illustration of the body blow broadcasting dealt vaudeville. "I spent $750,000 publicizing myself as 'The Perfect Fool,'" Ed once moaned, "and almost overnight it is forgotten and I was known only as the 'fire Chief.'"

Pete Dailey, a unique performer, used a technique in utter contrast to Wynn's studied comedy. Dailey being a natural comic, most of his lines and business were impromptu. He never took himself or his work seriously and in all the musicals and farce comedies he played it is doubtful if he ever read a line that was written into the productions. He was apt to

GREAT NAMES OF THE GREAT DAYS

A group of Friars corralled a quarter century ago when that organization vied with the Lambs as a theatrical club. From left, standing: Andrew Mack, Neil O'Brien, James J. Corbett, Harry Kelly, Felix Adler, Harlan Dixon, George Daugherty, Vaughan Comfort, Johnny King, Tom Dingle, Eddie Garvey, Julius Tannen, George Sidney, Tommy Gray, and Bert Levy. Seated, from left: Max Figman, Laddie Cliff, Will Rogers, Sam Harris, Terry Cohan, Louis Mann, Fred Niblo, George M. Cohan, Lew Dockstader, and Frank Tinney walk on in the middle of a scene, carry the leading lady off in his arms, and then return and sing, "Oh, Fireman, Save My Child." His cast had to be certain of their lines to work with him for he paid no attention to cues; nor could they ever be sure what to expect from him—and he seldom repeated. Yet nobody ever became angry with him; he was one of the most beloved characters in show business.

Almost as good a "nut" act was the single of Bert Fitzgibbon. Bert, of a long line of variety comics, began at twelve as one of the Fitzgibbon Family—Father, Mother, Bert, Dave, and two sisters. In the act Dave played piano and Bert did the comedy. His work was entirely extemporaneous and excruciatingly funny, although he was troublesome to Albee because of his tendency to slip into the blue.

Since he had no routine, it is impossible to analyze his act. He would walk on and depend entirely on a cue from the audience whom he used brazenly as stooges; yet so gracious was his demeanor, so kindly his approach, no one ever took offense at his ribbing. He could, and often did, evolve a whole act from someone in the audience with a funny cough, or a woman who laughed loudly in the wrong places. Sometimes he'd carry on a conversation with a little girl in the audience, jump a skipping rope, and invite the child to come up on the stage and play. He'd sing "Ring Around a-Rosy," or some other nursery tune, and the children, who adored him, would correct him if the lines were not as they knew them—always good for a laugh. Later, Fitzgibbon toured England and was wonderfully received. An exercising elbow got him down. He is dead.

One-man Vaudeville.

Biggest of the nut headliners was Joe Cook—happily alive and at the peak of his talent. Joe began in blackface, and at one time appeared with his brother. About twenty years ago in Jim Young's Cozy Bar, No. 1 and No. 2, Dallas, Tex., at a New Year's party given by Joe's friends, Bert Swor's family,

Joe did an imitation of a one-man vaudeville show. It was an ad-lib lark, but it went over big, and Jim Young said, "Better clean that blackface act, Joe." That was the origin of Joe's famous nut act.

His Four Hawaiians bit was another of those things—an impromptu, lengthy gag that was an instantaneous smash. Curiously, Joe never cared much for it, preferring his baseball yarn. At first he used it only occasionally. But on the advice of George McFarland, a baritone playing a Detroit bill with Joe at the time, he kept it in.

Joe depended largely upon ridiculous mechanical contrivances. They were cumbersome props, but he always carried them. His act consisted almost entirely of unrelated business. In one bit, Joe, as the landlord, would approach a miniature cottage to collect the rent. He carried on a preposterous argument with an imaginary tenant who refused to pay. Thereupon Joe walked off with the cottage. He would reappear with three life-size papier-mâché figures of gymnasts standing on each other's shoulders which he in turn supported on his own. He staggered about the stage, apparently balancing them with great difficulty. One of his props was a huge machine that cluttered clear across the stage. At one end of it a man sat sleeping. Joe explained that it was an apparatus for calling the hired man to dinner, described each part and gave a demonstration. When he pulled a lever at one end of the machine, it set in motion a number of crazy-looking gears, cams, and pistons, eventually liberating a slapstick which smacked the sleeping man who woke up and struck a gong with a mallet. This called the hired man to dinner.

For his Hawaiian yarn Joe sat on a chair, center, with a mandolin in his lap:

I will give an imitation of four Hawaiians. This is one (*whistles*); this is another (*tinkles mandolin*); and this is the third (*marks time with foot*). I could imitate four Hawaiians just as easily but I will tell you the reason why I don't do it. You see I bought a horse for $50 and it turned out to be a running horse. I was offered $15,000 for him and I took it. I built a house with the $15,000 and when it was finished a neighbor offered me $100,000 for it. He said my house stood right where he wanted to dig a well. So I took the $100,000 to accommodate him. I invested the $100,000 in peanuts and that year there was a peanut famine, so I sold the peanuts for $350,000. Now why should a man with $350,000 bother to imitate four Hawaiians? (*Joe then picked up the chair, and exit*)

It always drew as big a laugh as the baseball yarn, but as Joe says, the latter was a better bit and he always gave it all he had. Here it is:

As I look around me this evening (*the set was Times Square*) I see very few of the real old-timers. I mean men and women who were in this neighborhood when I first settled here years ago. (*Business of pulling a huge megaphone out of his vest pocket—one of Joe's gadgets—and in stentorian tones he would shout*) Who remembers when on this very site formerly stood the old Polo Grounds? Well, folks, just as I thought, I am the only one who knows that. And I don't mean the old Polo Grounds. I mean the O-O-OLD Polo Grounds.

Well, sir, some seventy-two-odd years ago this coming Wednesday, we played the deciding game of the season. There were only three cities in the league at that time—New York, Philadelphia and San Francisco. We used San Francisco to break our jump between New York and Philadelphia. A million people were at the game that day. I wouldn't be exaggerating if I said there were less than a million.

Just to give you an idea of the size of the grounds: home plate was right here in Times Square, and the center field bleachers, if I am not mistaken, and I probably am mistaken, were over in Jersey City. It was in the ninth inning. The score was tied—five to three—in favor of us. We needed six runs to win. Babe Ruth's grandfather was pitching. I was playing second base and right field, as I was too good for one position. We have four men on base—two men on second, one a little short guy the umpire couldn't see.

My manager says to me—"Mr. Spalding" (I went under the name of Spalding in those days; saved me autographing baseballs), he says, "You're next at bat." So I turned to our bat boy, little Gerry Nugent, and says, "Gerry . . . " He says, "What is it, Mr. Delehanty?" (I went under the name of Delehanty for some time.) I says, "Bring me my bat." So Gerry and three other fellows carried my bat over for me. I used a telegraph pole for my bat in those days. I was very tall at one time but I have been out in the rain.

Well, sir, I crouched down in that well-known pose of mine; the ball comes sailing over the pan. I land into the old apple and she goes sailing out right over center field fence, and at that I topped the ball.

I started for first base. The crowds were hollering: "Hurrah for Weber" (they knew me under the name of Weber). The fans were cheering, bands playing, the King and Queen throwing kisses to me. The railroads started running excursions into the park. The crowd started to throw money at me. I picked up over $9,000 on my way to first base alone and put it in an old steamer trunk I always carried on my back when I ran bases.

I light out for second base—third, fourth, fifth, sixth—this was a double-header we were playing—and just as I am sliding home the umpire, Daniel Boone—Daniel Boone was umpiring—yells out— "Foul Ball!"

Well, sir, you wouldn't give a cent for me at that moment. I rushed up to him, threw off my overcoat—we always played in our overcoats—and there I stood in my bathing suit. I got off my bicycle and says: "Hey! Where do you get off to call that a foul when I hit the ball to center field?" And he says: "Yes, but you hit the ball over the center fielder's head."

Of course, he had me there. I couldn't answer that. This disaster so discouraged me with baseball that I tore down the old park one night, moved it further out of town, and built a saloon. The old Mansfield-Silver-Dollar-Last-Chance-Saloon-Cafe-Cocktail Bar and Grill. You may have heard your fathers speak of it. Six hundred and sixty feet in length, and only ONE bartender. He worked on horseback.

I'll never forget one hot day in July. The place was crowded. He was working at the Eighth Ave. end when two men came in the Sixth Ave. entrance dying of thirst. Digging his spurs deep into the flanks of Man o' War's great grandsire, after a magnificent spurt he reached the two men in time to save their lives—having fixed up two gin rickeys en route. Finally prohibition came along and I had to buy him a motorcycle.

The Legendary D. & S.

When the fabulous "Mr. Duffy and Mr. Sweeney" were moderately sober, theirs was one of the funniest nut acts in vaudeville. Jimmy Duffy started with his father and mother in a three-act called "Duffy, Sawtelle, and Duffy." Jimmy was a smart, good-looking youngster, a good singer and dancer, the outstanding feature of the act. Impatient, restless, and tired of old-time methods as he matured, he dropped away from his parents and went out on his own. He worked as a singing and dancing juvenile comic with the Gertrude Hoffman Revue and at the Winter Garden shows. Everyone recognized his talent, but his penchant for the bottle made him so unreliable managers could not afford to take chances with him. After drifting around for a while he formed a partnership with Fred Sweeney whose interests and tastes, especially in bottled goods, were similar.

They contrived an act which was nut from start to finish. After entering, Mr. Sweeney would begin a pointless story while Mr. Duffy dozed. Waking suddenly, Mr. Duffy, noticing that Mr. Sweeney was still talking, would casually slap him in the face and then bow and apologize profusely. So would Mr. Sweeney bow until no one could tell who was apologizing to whom or for what. When the bowing and handshaking subsided, Mr. Sweeney would say, "Pardon me once more," and cuff Mr. Duffy on the jaw. After more apologies, bows, and appeasements, they took seats beside each other; whereupon Mr. Duffy would push Mr. Sweeney off his chair. Politely helping him up Mr. Duffy would then seek to seat himself in a chair that was not there. Then Mr. Sweeney would help Mr. Duffy to a seat, make him comfortable, and nonchalantly kick him in the face. It may sound awful; but their eye work, facial expressions, and pantomimic byplay drew convulsive laughs.

They were a legendary team; because of their wit, exploits, and general clowning, the most talked-of two-act in the profession. A widely circulated story concerns their appearance in a Memphis theater. Memphis is rated one of the poorest show towns in America, and the boys had just concluded their act before a dead-pan audience. Taking a forced bow, Duffy appeared and said: "And now, ladies and gentlemen, my partner will go through the aisles with a baseball bat and beat the bejesus out of you." For this Albee fired them from the circuit, subsequently reinstating them, however, after Duffy brought his young son into Albee's office and said, "Mr. Albee, you don't want this boy to grow up hating you, do you?"

One time when the team was playing Buffalo a cowboy quartet and a lone cowboy singer were on the bill. By chance they were all assigned to the seventh floor of the Statler Hotel. Pouring in one morning about 2:30, Duffy and Sweeney overheard assorted cries and caterwaulings coming from a certain room. Tracing the noise, they knocked, and were admitted to a room where the cowboy quartet and the cowboy single, all in hilarious mood, were exchanging prairie calls. Entering into the spirit of the contest with characteristic vigor, Duffy and Sweeney obliged with what they called the Canarsie mating call. At this point, his endurance shaken, the sleepless guest in the next room rapped soundly on the wall. Duffy paused and called for silence. "A hell of a time to be hanging pictures," said Duffy.

Some years ago on a Saturday afternoon about half past three, Charles MacArthur, the playwright, and Duffy were walking east on 42nd Street. At the intersection of Fifth Avenue Duffy halted at the curb, took MacArthur's arm and observed, "It only takes 'em forty seconds." Leaving MacArthur, Duffy stepped to the center of the intersection, took pad and pencil from his pocket, wrote, "How do I get to 2678 Grand Concourse?" and handed pad and pencil to the traffic cop. "Well, now," said the cop, having read the query, "you go over here to Grand Central and take a Bronx express and get off . . . " Interrupting, Duffy pantomimed he was both deaf and dumb, and motioned to the cop to employ pad and pencil. Good-naturedly, the cop wrote down precise directions on how to get to 2678 Grand Concourse. Duffy read it, wrote thanks and another question—and handed pad and pencil back to the cop. By this time traffic at this busiest of corners was backing up north and south from 110th Street to Washington Square and east and west to both rivers. After a half dozen questions and answers had been written and the poor cop was deep in fenders, said Duffy, his voice scarcely audible above the bedlam of motor horns, "Thank you very much, officer," and fendered his own way back to MacArthur.

As the pair started back toward Broadway, Duffy said, "Look around." And MacArthur turned to see a furious cop, his fist upraised, pantomiming a vicious "you so-and-so . . . " "See?" said Duffy. "It always takes 'em forty seconds."

Duffy is dead. In the spring of 1939 his body was found at the corner of Eighth Avenue and 47th Street, New York. Deemed a bleary has-been by many, only a few know how untimely was his passing, for but two or three weeks prior to his death he had managed to pull himself together and had been working on a radio act for NBC—a kindly redemption offered by his old friend John F. Royal, Albee's one-time No. 1 manager, currently a vice-president of the National Broadcasting Company.

May his antic soul rest peacefully. Sweeney, incidentally, when last heard of was in Albuquerque, N.M., where it was touch and go with him. So far as one knows he has no knowledge that Duffy is canceled.

Williams, Rockwell, Allen.

Of the many other nut acts, three should be recorded: Herb Williams, Doc Rockwell, and Fred Allen. Williams, who is dead, had the greatest talent. He began as a pianist in one of Gus Sun's Ohio vaudeville houses. In this theater, as with so many others in the nineties and 1900's on the smaller circuits, there were no other musicians in the pit. Williams used to play for the shows alone with, he would say, "my three-piece orchestra—Williams, piano, and stool." He also used to say, "I'll have an act of my own someday that will surprise you chaps." But it was no surprise to the performers when he did break out an act; they were aware of his qualities. An expert pianist, but with a sense of humor, he built up the acts he played for with funny little trill interpolations, cadenzas that pointed gags or the introduction of plaintive themes in timely spots.

When Williams went out for himself he opened with a parody, but soon abandoned it to develop his trick playing, with pantomimic comedy and effects. It became the funniest nut piano act in vaudeville. He had trouble with the piano stool, which kept sinking until he could scarcely reach the keyboard—adjusted, it would raise him almost above the piano. Certain keys produced clacks, gongbeats, and plunks; trying to avoid them got him into more trouble—fearsome faces would arise and objects appear from the piano's insides. At the finish of a long and difficult cadenza, a hand reached out and smacked him on the head. Finishing his piece in spite of handicaps, he drew a glass of beer from a tap on the side of the piano, and went into another number.

Rockwell at one time had a partner. But his act was not doing so well and, happening to be playing Cleveland at the time, he asked John Royal, then manager of the Palace there, if he thought a chiropractor act he was working on would go. Royal told him to try it out at the next advertising club luncheon. As a prop Rockwell required a spinal column. This stumped the property man who did, however, produce a banana stalk. Rockwell thought it would enhance the comedy and when he tried it out at the club luncheon he went over. It made Rockwell a single—and an act, too.

Most successful financially has been Fred Allen, but his money has come out of radio—vaudeville never heard of such sums as radio unfolds from the pockets of old man sponsor— except for name acts like Bernhardt, Tanguay, Bayes, and one or two others. And these worked fourteen shows a week, not from thirty minutes to an hour weekly.

In vaudeville Allen was a carefree, irresponsible performer, a clean nut comic who presented any ridiculous thing that occurred to him. He'd quit off in the middle of a routine, sit flat on the stage almost in the footlights, and read his press notices to the orchestra leader. At one time he used a shapeless and dilapidated ventriloquist's dummy for a purposely atrocious ventriloquial specialty; another time he used a frightful banjo to accompany an equally wretched song. His dead pan was superb, making the foolish things he did get over for riotous laughter.

As great a reflection as the nut acts of the muscle-bulging days of the 1900's were the "rough," or "sight," acts—usually acrobats, straight and comic. America had not yet learned to amuse itself. Sports and exercise were generally taken vicariously and the gymnasts and acrobatic clowns of vaudeville fed this tendency with face-kicking generosity. Usually they worked in teams. Among the most popular at the turn of the century, and beyond (you cannot pin a standard act to a definite year), were Collins and Hart, Hickey and Nelson, Caron and Herbert, and Rice and Prevost.

The Bone Crunchers.

Collins and Hart were the most brutal of the bone-breaking sight acts, and one of the funniest. Their costumes of fake muscles and phony balancing were hilarious burlesques of the all-wool alley-oop acts and their tenure in vaudeville was a continuous scream. Quiet off stage and serious, not given to quips or rendezvous clowning, they drew a well-merited measure of acclaim.

They were a great team, but they got many a break from the press that might well have been reserved for Bill Hickey and Sadie Nelson. Hickey and Nelson's act, to this commentator, was the funniest of all chair, table, and barrel turns. Natural endowment gave Hickey a start; he was a funny-looking guy to begin with. Even in respose, his face resembled an enormous potato, and when he assumed a winsome or appealing expression it was something to see. He wore a misfit coat, knee-length vest, pants that would shield three persons, and oyster-shaped shoes eighteen inches long. Sadie (his wife) was an attractive Danish girl with a pretty singing voice and an adorable musical laugh. She was large; Hickey used to call her the Great Dane.

They opened with a romantic song and dance, "The Wedding of the Lily and the Rose," a startling introduction for the comedy to come. It required some vocal ability and Sadie carried the straight singing neatly. Bill came in with a whisky tenor for attempts at harmony and tremolo that were so funny no one ever heard the complete song. In the dance Hickey, attempting to emulate Sadie's steps, always fell over his own feet and generally managed to kick himself in the face. Then he would try to climb onto the table with a chair under his arm, and after many difficulties would finally succeed. The chair leg got caught in one leg of his pants, and, trying to get it loose, he got both his own legs into one of his pants legs. Discovering the empty pants leg, he looked about everywhere for his missing leg until, peering into the empty pants leg he leaned over too far and fell off the table onto his face.

Taking off his coat for another routine, Hickey noticed a cigarette paper on the floor. He paused, eager and curious, then walked over to pick it up, but every time he stooped his big shoes fanned it out of the way. Then he took off his vest to use for a net. Sneaking up on the paper, he threw himself and the vest at it and fanned the damned thing into the orchestra pit. He crawled to the footlights. Leaning over too far, he lost balance and tumbled headlong into the scrambling musicians, suspending himself from the footlight rail by his feet. Sadie tugged him halfway out, but could hardly pull for laughing and let him slide back again. Finally she got him out, with almost total loss of his pants.

Back on the stage Hickey tried to put his vest on again, but got it wrong a dozen ways. Furious, he tossed it into the air and tried to jump into it, but it twisted around his head like a turban, and even with Sadie's help he had a hard time trying to pry it loose.

After this Sadie demonstrated her high-kicking prowess. Hickey placed a chair on the table and held a plug hat for a target. She did several good kicks. Then, as she was about to do a hitch and a kick, Hickey leaned over to look into the hat; the kick jammed it over his head and face and Hickey fell from the chair, landing on the back of his neck. Unable to see, he scrambled under the table, attempted to rise, and upset chair, table, and himself.

After Sadie pried him out of the hat, he put a barrel on the table, the chair on the barrel, and managed to climb into the chair and hold out the hat. At this point something in the gallery would interest him, he'd lose balance and do a shoulder fall to the stage. Then, deciding to do some kicking himself, he'd get Sadie to hold the hat. With a run, jump, and a kick with both feet he'd turn completely and land in a split on the floor. Intensely angry, he set out to kick the hat to pieces, but Sadie had surreptitiously placed a brick under it. Measuring his distance carefully and making elaborate preparations, Hickey finally kicked the hat. It exploded with a loud report throwing him into the air and landing him in a headspin. Exit.

The foregoing is a description of their act at the height of their careers, and Hickey was by no means young at the time. He came from Seattle originally and worked across country giving one-man shows in cow camps, forts, mining towns, saloons, depot platforms—anywhere interested spectators could be assembled. Somewhere en route he acquired Sadie and the team eventually landed in New York. The bookers were apathetic and the best the pair could get were a few obscure unprofitable engagements. One night as a last resort a frenzied booker rushed them as a stopgap to the New York Theatre Roof. They stopped the gap—they stopped the show or, in vaudeville patois, "ruined the audience" (for the following act). Indeed, it was necessary to put them down to closing spot.

After quite a run at the New York Roof it was easy for them to obtain booking. But although they were a laugh hit everywhere, by some nasty quirk—with one exception—they never got newspaper recognition. The reviewers inevitably wound up with "Hickey and Nelson also did their share to amuse" or, "The antics of Hickey and Nelson were received with hearty laughter."

During a Monday rehearsal at the Orpheum in Minneapolis, the press agent, Earl E. May (known as Early May), asked a performer on the bill who was something of a writer to review the show for him because he was taking a girl friend to a matinee at another house. Aware of Hickey and Nelson's unlucky press breaks and deeming them unwarranted, the performer gave the team about two hundred words.

When Hickey saw the notice he read it (unwittingly, of course) to the performer who wrote it and observed, "That's the first guy to find out we were on the bill. I'm going to stake him to a box of cigars."

He bought a box of the biggest, blackest, most expensive cigars he could find and left them at the box office for May. (Money meant nothing to Hickey; he'd got along without it for years.) May took the box back to the performer who had written the review and said, "Here, grab a handful; you're in on this, too." Later the performer went to Hickey's dressing room and casually handing Hickey one of his own cigars, said, "Have a smoke, Bill?" Hickey took one and lighted up, sniffed its aroma, and asked, "You smoke these all the time?" "Oh, yes," lied the performer, "my favorite brand for years." "Well," said Hickey, "they're better than I can afford."

Hickey and Nelson closed shows and sent audiences out screaming, for years. They had their imitators, but it was a tough act to copy and those that tried it were no good. After Sadie's death Hickey worked with another partner for a time until he retired to a farm in New York State.

Facials and Knockabouts.

The relationship of Caron and Herbert to Rice and Prevost was almost identical with that of Hickey and Nelson to Collins and Hart. Caron and Herbert were a master "sight" act, yet Rice and Prevost led in popularity for years. Rice and Prevost's was a fine, funny act, deservedly popular, but Rice lacked the finesse of Caron who, stemming from a long line of panto-mimists, was a great artist.

There are many types of clowns—acrobatic, singing, panto-mimic, talking, trick, knockabout, dramatic, and facial. Caron was a facial and knockabout. Herbert, playing straight, was a splendid high-somersaulting acrobat. Their act was unrivaled. Caron tried to duplicate Herbert's tumbling, always failing miserably—and ludicrously. The Egyptians, doubtless, had a stock comedy prop equal to our seltzer bottle; yet Caron could get more laughs with that ancient gag than any predecessor. The earnest way in which he tried to unscrew the bottom of the bottle, pull off the top, or suck the seltzer through the nozzle kept the audience in a state of hilarious suspense wondering how the inevitable squirt would happen. Finally Caron tipped the bottle to peer into the nozzle, squeezed it to hold it steady, accidentally pulled the trigger, and was doused.

Herbert then made a series of splendid dives and front hand-springs over a row of chairs, increasing the number one at a time. Taking off from backstage he would soar over the row like a bird, land on his hands, and spring lightly to his feet. On one of his exits, Caron turned the last chair upside down so that Herbert would land on its legs. Then Caron would wait, chuckling in anticipation. No Herbert, and Caron would become anxious, lean forward to see if Herbert was coming. Then he would dodge back suddenly and begin a wait that at first was stolid, then sleepy. At last, as Caron dozed off, Herbert appeared from a different entrance and dropped a beautiful goal with Caron off the seat of Caron's pants. Throughout, Caron's pantomime and expression were remarkable.

After this rousing bit, Caron would look around and again his gaze would fall on the seltzer bottle. He reflected an idea and, in pantomime, explained to Herbert he had something to show him; got him to stand perfectly still, changing his position several times, while gloating over the dousing he was going to give his partner. Then he would take careful aim with the wrong end of the bottle, pull the trigger and soak himself. He gasped, sputtered, but couldn't let go the bottle until it was emptied. Herbert chased him around the stage and the act ended with some brilliantly executed porpoise leaps. Caron died, and Herbert took another partner. The new act got plenty of time, but Caron was irreplaceable.

Rice and Prevost's was the same type of act—a rough, straight, and comedy acrobat. It was a featured act for years until poor Rice became partially deranged. Helpless and unemployed, he wandered aimlessly about New York. Some years ago he was struck by a truck on Eighth Avenue, New York, and killed.

The Comic Character Artists:
Tramp, Blackface, Negro, Jew

The tramp, the legitimate tramp, or hobo, he of the jungle and ennui at even the suggestion of work (not the dime-for-a-cuppa-cawfee moocher) seems to have passed out of our national life, or at any rate has lost his significance. The only tramp cartoon in our times of any worth is Denys Wortman's "Mopey Dick and the Duke." Not only are they superb characterizations, they are most excellent drawings by an admirable artist. In the first decade of the 1900's tramp comics swarmed through vaudeville almost as a national symbol; legit musical stages were heavy with them; and joke magazines and newspaper strips (a few are left) detailed their haphazard lives with jesting abandon. The appeal of the tramp was twofold: he had the quality of pathos and suggested to reader or audience the "there but for the Grace of God . . ." Besides, the human inherently views the underdog with tolerance—when he is amusing.

A countless variety of tramp comics high-lighted vaudeville's great days—melancholy, philosophical, satirical, burglar, juggler. Among the headliners were W. C. Fields, Nat Wills, Paul Barnes, Lew Bloom, Charles R. Sweet, and Harrigan.

Harrigan, like Fields, was a tramp juggler. He was not in a class with Fields, who still is one of America's greatest comics,

W. C. FIELDS
In his vaudeville days as a tramp juggler

but he was standard if not feature. Unlike Fields, who started as a silent single, Harrigan talked constantly. He missed his tricks purposely, then explained why. He used old plug hats, broken cigar boxes, all manner of junk in keeping with his make-up, and he always topped his misses with a perfect trick to the line: "This is the time I never failed to miss."

Charles R. Sweet's tramp burglar was a top act. The patter was funny and the routine versatile. He made his entrance with a dark lantern through a window that gave on to a living room and explained that he was examining the property by night because his business affairs were so engrossing in the daytime. He'd just been looking at another property in the neighborhood; a detached house: the shutters were detached, the chimney was detached, in fact, everything was detached except the mortgage.

Paul Barnes used the standard tramp make-up: red nose, ragged beard, broken derby, and disreputable clothes. He arranged his own material and always used "locals":

I was in Evanston [Canarsie, Brooklyn, Oakland, Camden, Brookline] the other day. I found the people there very friendly. A man who was a perfect stranger to me came along and conversed casually, although we had never been introduced. I think he was a naval officer—no—well, some sort of an officer. He invited me to take a walk with him. I said I didn't care to go. When he asked me the second time I said that I would go. He took me to some kind of clubhouse and introduced me to another officer, I think he was the secretary of the club. He was sitting behind a high desk and had a large account book, pens, ink, everything . . .

Barnes's patter was similar to Sweet's, but who filched from the other no one knows. As a matter of fact, the "officer" lines were used by J. W. Kelly (The Rolling Mill Man) before either Sweet or Barnes was billed anywhere. "Lifted" material was an important side line in vaudeville and here is a suitable place to digress about it.

Performers had no way to protect their gags, business, or

parodies. Nobody paid any attention to the copyright law.
Good gags spread like gossip. If a team at the Palace in New
York introduced a new gag or bit of comedy, it reached San
Francisco the next day via wire, or vice versa. Conners and
Aldert, a young, crossfire, singing, and dancing act, offer an
amusing illustration of the transfer of gags. The team separated, each taking a new partner, but both teams used the
same patter and business. It was the first of a succession of
splitting and joining until there were about eight teams, all
playing the same act.

Probably the greatest sufferer from a thief was Frank
Fogarty, a cadaverous-looking monologist who got himself up
like a small-time undertaker. Frank did a casual routine of
Irish jokes and gags, but he was an accomplished handshaker
and blarney expert and his act, at least in the East, went over
well. Once an amateur asked him for a few gags, said he
wanted them for a Knights of Columbus party, and Frank
said, "Sure. Here's a book of them." The fellow went over at
the party and later managed to get some Gus Sun time in the
Midwest and other sticks booking. After he'd been about a bit,
he was booked into a small theater in Beverly, Mass., the
summer home of President Taft.

Motion pictures had recently been taken of the President's
estate, and Taft asked to see them. The management accordingly put on a special show for him. Our amateur, who by that
time may have been a semipro, was on the bill. He rattled off
a lot of Fogarty's gags and yarns and the President's belly
rolled with guffaws. Smart, the thief then billed himself as
"The Man Who Made President Taft Roar with Laughter."
So he got a route—about forty weeks' time. And year after
year Frank followed him on the route and "died" (stage argot
for a performer who doesn't get over). On a night in Cleveland
Frank finished a show. The audience was downright hostile
and he came off frightfully upset. "What's the matter with
me?" he asked the stage manager, who said, "Frank I'm
surprised at you. You ought to know it's a dirty trick to steal

————'s act. He was through here last week with the original stuff and the people just won't go for your steal, that's all."

Meanest of all were the German thieves. When booked in Germany, performers were required to send photos, billing, and description of act several weeks in advance. The German managers copied the costumes from the photographs and duplicated the act as nearly as possible from the description. They would then book a phony act ahead on the bill, accuse the American act of stealing the German one, and use this as an excuse for cutting the American act's salary. On the last night the American act was invariably required to close the show and a boy would carry their salary to them in small coins. It was always short, but there was no redress.

Bums—Philosophical, Genial.

But we were tramping. Lew Bloom was a famous tramp single. His characterization of a philosophical bum highlighted vaudeville for years. Instead of the exaggerated patches, he wore a simple, shabby suit, and used virtually no make-up. He delivered his monologue with dead-pan seriousness—indeed, sadly:

> But I don't spend all my time in saloons. I can't do it. They have to close up some time. The early closing law is an imposition on people who enjoy club life. The other day I went into a saloon and the bartender must have mistaken me for somebody else. He let me pour my own drink. When I told him I forgot to bring my check book he hit me on the head with a bungstarter. I was awful scared. Thought it was a stomach pump. It was not a gentlemanly trick . . .

A petal from Bloom. No one ever knew what happened to him. Like so many others, he just dropped out.

Everyone is familiar with the work of W. C. Fields but some of his early background is not generally known. His father kept a poolroom in Philadelphia. It was a favorite rendezvous for young Bill who was in no favor at home. One summer's night he went to a lawn party. The yard was full of fruit trees and Bill was surprised, when he snagged a few unripe apples, to see how easy it was for him to juggle them. He went around pestering everybody with exhibitions of his new-found talent. Soon after he rowed with his father and left home, taking up residence in a boiler in a vacant lot. Boys in the neighborhood brought him food. He got hold of some wooden balls, a cane, and a battered plug hat and practiced juggling hours on end. He made himself an Inverness out of an old cape of his mother's, fashioned some whiskers out of bits of fur, pasted them to his face, and booked himself in a couple of Pennsylvania parks.

Later he booked a circuit of parks operated by Grant and Flynn. They were all in New England—Lynn, Lowell, Lawrence—Massachusetts towns. After the park season, Fields went into burlesque and then to vaudeville. All this time he was silent, and all this time he was developing the art that made him a headliner not only in America but in England and on the Continent. (His first speaking part may have been with McIntyre and Heath in "The Ham Tree," the musical the blackface comics expanded from their vaudeville act.)

One of Fields's funniest bits was his pool-table scene. The balls were racked, and Fields went through all the motions: took off his coat, hung up his hat, chalked his cue. Then with one quick shot he'd pocket all fifteen balls, put on his coat, hat, and walk off. It was exquisite pantomime by an incredible artist.

Nat Wills's tramp was a happy bum, a genial, outwitting character, in high favor with audiences throughout the circuit. His attire was the conventional patches, the blacked-out teeth, a scrubby beard he scratched matches on. But he was an honest worker who bought his gags, a regular subscriber to *Madison's Budget*, which for twenty years—1898–1918—was a crutch for vaude comics.

The *Budget* was the work of James Madison, an old-timer in the theater who realized he was a better gag man than performer; it was a professional Joe Miller, full of gags, comedy business, and situations. It sold for $1 and if the comic got six laughs out of it he was ahead on his investment. In recent years Madison, whose circulation died before vaudeville—but not much before—sold complete sets for $100 each to Eddie Cantor and Fred Allen, presumably for their radio work. For additional fees, Madison supplied acts with fresh material not in his *Budget*. Cantor, as a vaudevillian, was a client; so was Nora Bayes.

Originally Wills worked with a partner, Bony Dave Halpin, his straight man, unbelievably thin. The act was called "The Tramp and the Policeman," and it finished with a dance by Halpin whose excellent stepping was mimicked by Wills in slapshoes. It was a two-act until about the turn of the century when Wills severed the partnership and built up a single. He was always up with the contemporary scene, using topical stuff continually, and he was a great user of parodies. These were popular with audiences as late as 1910. Wills also suffered from "lifters." It particularly irked him because he bought all his stuff (besides Madison, he hired Vincent Bryan for $100 a week for a time to write his material), and in 1911 he announced that henceforth he would copyright his act. He never did; probably realized it was useless.

For a time Wills appeared with his first wife, Mme. Loretto, as she was known, and after her death he married May Harrison, who died in 1909. A year later he married La Belle Titcomb whose name was Nellie McNierney. She came over from Europe billed as a Frenchwoman, with a spectacular, zany act—pat for Hammerstein's, where she was booked—in which she rode a white horse and sang grand opera arias. After their marriage Wills took her into his act, using a gag whose irony the audience little suspected was so personal: "I should have married the horse," said Wills. They got along not too well.

On a New York Palace bill in 1913, the year the theater opened, Wills followed Sarah Bernhardt. She drew tremendous applause at her curtain and finally was forced by weariness to return to her dressing room. Wills entered to a big hand, some

NAT C. WILLS
The happy tramp

of the applause, no doubt, lingering for the Divine one. As he stood bowing, an usher came down the aisle with an enormous bouquet for Bernhardt and a wag in a stage box yelled, "Give 'em to Wills, he's dying." Four years later he did die—of carbon monoxide poisoning in his New Jersey garage.

That Palace crack at Wills unnerved him so he was scarcely able to go on. He never felt that he was precisely through—but performers worry. Besides, it had all the earmarks of a professional quipster, "dying" being backstage patois and not in the vocabulary of a lay patron.

It had all the earmarks, as a matter of fact, of Johnny Stanley, the greatest "wing player" in vaudeville. Little Johnny, dapper, a good dancer and a good fellow, played a lot of vaudeville with a number of partners. He was never a headliner, but nobody could top him as a sidewalk comedian. It is probably true that he didn't go farther because of his habit of "playing to the wings," that is, making wisecracks or gags that were understood by performers but not by the audience. He'd toss them into his act wherever; and while they were relished by his partners they did the act no good. Example: Stanley was appearing at the Union Square in New York on a night when a stack of stage braces fell. The crash spoiled his line. Said Stanley to his partner, "That was Freeman Bernstein booking an act." Bernstein was a noisy agent; yelled in the phone, pounded his desk, slammed doors—you could hear him up on Washington Heights.

Stanley once came into the Comedy Club, an exclusive organization of vaudeville comedians then on 46th Street near Eighth Avenue, and stopping before a large mirror, carried on a heated argument with his reflection in pantomime. Finally he shouted, "I'll take it!" and walked out of the building. It was a portrayal of the actor having his usual salary wrangle with agent or manager.

All of Stanley's cracks were spontaneous. Among his colleagues he was generally regarded as the best recondite wit in the profession. Here are his two best immediate cracks:

Observing a dejected actor, a friend, Stanley asked the reason for his depression. The actor explained that his wife had run off with a Negro. "Why don't you black up and win her back?" asked Stanley. Again, he was standing in front of the Palace talking with Joe Cook when George M. Cohan, who hadn't seen Stanley in a long while, came over, a smile on his face, his hand outstretched. Stanley turned to Joe with a perfectly dead pan and said, "Here it comes, a touch."

Tinney—and the Blackface Comics.

The blackface acts were brother comics of the tramps and it is no step at all into their dressing rooms where the grease color and occasional accent will be about the only changes found. Topflight entertainers in this group were George (Honey Boy) Evans and Frank Tinney. Tom Lewis can be cast here, too. He originated on the Pacific Coast and cared little about playing Eastern time but friends persuaded him to come to New York. After a foray with Gorman Brothers Minstrels he teamed with Sam Ryan, and as Lewis and Ryan they became a feature two-act throughout the circuit. Ryan in whiteface played a tragedian in sore straits trying to convert a doltish Negro (Lewis) into a tragic actor. Lewis was a prime comic, never overplayed. Ryan foiled him excellently.

George Evans was dubbed "Honey Boy" after his song of the same name. The nickname was a natural. Considerate, charitable, and never a roisterer, Evans was universally liked by players and audiences. He got his early training in minstrels where he progressed from first-part singer to inside end, then to first relay of outside ends, then to principle end and single specialty in the olio. When he quit minstrelsy for vaudeville he at once became a big-time single with continuous booking, yet after a number of highly successful years on the circuit withdrew to go back into minstrels with a show of his own.

Evans delighted in simple amusements and his interest in them was as naïve as a pinafore. A natural pianist, he memorized hundreds of old-time melodies and ballads and at gatherings would challenge anyone to name a song he couldn't play. His most violent dissipation was to collect a few cronies after the show and repair to a Childs restaurant for coffee and collaboration on "nut" songs. It was a sort of game in which each person in turn furnished a line. Songs came out of these sessions, too. "In the Good Old Summer Time," Evans, Ren Shields, and Maximilian created at one of their *Kaffeeklatches*.

Vaudeville was like this: you say one man was the greatest of his type of act, and in a moment somebody gets you down with four names you've forgotten—all of them as good as the one you mentioned. The writer does not purpose to eat his words about W. C. Fields as a comedian, but—it gives one pause when Frank Tinney is announced. In Joe Cook's opinion, Tinney was the greatest *natural* comic ever developed in America.

Some years ago Joe and Tinney were playing a Vanities show. One night Tinney came into Joe's dressing room. "Congratulate me, Joe," he said, "it's my birthday." "That's fine, Frank," said Joe. "I certainly do. How old are you?" "Well," said Tinney, "I tell everybody I'm 48 but I'm really 49."

Tinney's method was the acme of ingenuousness, and he never misused it. In disarming an audience he laid down his weapons. His gags were atrocious: "Lend me a dollar for a week, old man?" "Who is the weak old man?" And strong men laughed like bloody fools. His business of smoking a cigar, and arguing with the orchestra leader about it . . . rehearsing a riddle or a joke with the leader, and having it go haywire ("Now you tell me . . .") . . . his dismal failure in attempting a bit of heavy drama . . . his tragic effort to play the "Miserere" on the bagpipes. ("Show 'em the bagpipes," he'd cry. The spot would then play on them as they lay on the stage, and the audience howled.) All these were hokum sequences that would have earned apathy for another man. For Tinney they earned convulsive laughter, and a top rung as an artist.

Tinney was a Philadelphia lad and, as a child, was exploited by his mother in that city's myriad clubs, churches, and lodge rooms—as a prodigy. All he did was to walk on sedately and play tunes on sleigh bells, bottles, ocarinas—anything his mother could carry that made a noise. His act finished, his mother bundled him up and took him home.

After he had played every hall in Philadelphia countless times, his mother realized his audience was virtually exhausted and hauled him off to Texas—a wise move. No territory was more vaudeville-minded in the 1900's; variety houses dotted the state's immensity like beeves at pasture. Moreover, these houses were booked independently by maverick managers unaffiliated with any circuit and performers not too lazy to change their material even slightly could roam the Texas range over and over.

Blackface had always interested Tinney. He studied these performers closely, cribbing here, pilfering there, but developing a technique of his own that raised his thievery to inherent right of ownership. He became one of the biggest draws in Texas.

One day a performer came in from the Southwest and called on Max Hart, a vaudeville agent with a stable of headliners that made him so strong it led to a $10,000,000 action in the Federal courts—Hart suing and losing to Albee and his associates, whom he had charged with violation of the anti-trust law. This performer told Hart that Tinney was a find. And Hart set out for Texas to see for himself. This might seem a long jaunt to view an act, but big agents frequently scouted talent in Europe. Anyway, Hart saw Tinney's act and liked it. Just to make sure, he saw it three different nights. Then he signed him to a personal play-or-pay contract for one year at $150 a week. Tinney was delighted. He'd been getting $50 a week in Texas and hadn't the slightest notion there was a house in America that could pay more.

Hart booked him into Hammerstein's, where he was a riot. He was reengaged for the second week and Hart jumped his salary to $500. Willie Hammerstein beat his breast but he paid. Hart kept raising the ante until Tinney's salary approached a figure several times the contractual obligation. When the contract expired Hart made new terms with his illustrious seal—a flat 25 per cent on all engagements. Somebody should have told Tinney; mother did not seem to be anywhere.

Often Tinney stepped out of vaudeville into musicals. He worked for Ziegfeld, Carroll, and put on his own show—usually with sensational success. In 1913 he went to London and the difficult music-hall audiences went mad over him. One reviewer wrote that he "was the most irresistible entertainer that America has sent us." All of this astounded Tinney, who, arriving in England, had been so afraid he would not click he went to a small theater and asked the manager to put him on; under the name of Lem Beasley he was such a smash the manager offered him a week at £20.

As a matter of fact, Tinney was more of a salary success in London than in America. In the spring of 1919 he accepted a sixteen-week engagement at Stoll's Alhambra in London at a salary of $2,250 a week, an almost unprecedented sum for an American single. And the following fall on his return to America he rowed with George White, refusing to play in the "Scandals" for less than $1,250 a week. Nor did he; he joined "Atta Boy" instead, presumably at his demand figure. From then on he appeared mainly in musicals, and in "Some Time," produced in 1920, he abandoned blackface. It made no difference in his work; he never used dialect.

On or off stage Tinney was a definite zany and there are innumerable yarns about him, many of them phony. He is said to have had at his Freeport, L.I., home a white horse with gold teeth—supplied by the comedian as a measure of affection. There is the yarn that he would hire an open cab, seat a pony beside him, and then drive around Times Square greeting his friends. "Hya, Bill," and when "Bill," recognizing the voice, turned to answer, Tinney would slump in his seat and the pony would take a bow. One of his early diversions seems to be authentic. To amuse himself on tour he would drop around to a vegetable store and inquire the price, say, of a coconut. "Fifteen cents, eh, and can I leave it here a little while?" Sure; and Tinney would stroll on, not too far, and then back toward the store in a kind of patrol until a cop came along. Then Tinney would dart furtive glances—at the vegetable stand, at the cop—and otherwise act suspiciously until he was sure he had aroused the cop's interest. Then he'd grab the coconut and dash away, the cop after him. After a chase of a block and a half Tinney (who in his early days was athletic; had been a lifeguard at a Jersey resort) would slow up as the cop—and the crowd—closed in on him. Inevitably the dialogue proceeded as follows:

"Thought you could get away with it, eh? You come with me."

"Just a minute, officer. This is my coconut." Then, half to the crowd, "What do you mean by infringing on the rights of citizens in such a manner?"

"Your coconut, eh? Why I saw you steal it."

"How can a man steal his own property?" Then directly to the crowd. "Look here, ladies and gentlemen, is this city of yours in a free country? Do you allow your policemen to go around arresting American citizens for simply carrying their own goods? This coconut is mine and I can prove it. And as an American citizen I demand redress for this unseemly, this outrageous conduct on the part of this policeman."

"I'll give you a chance to prove your ownership, you thief. You come back with me to that store." And they'd march back to the store, the crowd following.

"Look here," Tinney would say to the astonished store-keeper, "that's my coconut, isn't it? Didn't I buy this coconut from you a little while ago?"

"Yes, sir, that's your coconut . . . " And so on, until the cop retreated, discomfited, still suspicious.

Tinney is at a health farm at this writing, and improving.

He made a million people laugh.

Williams and Walker.

Even in the beer halls and wine-room honky-tonks of the eighties and nineties, strictly Negro performers were not too welcome. With the exception of Charlie Case, the Negro performer shuffled along as best he could, usually for throw money. In such endeavor Bert Williams was discovered. In the late nineties Thomas Canary and George W. Lederer had just put on Victor Herbert's "The Gold Bug" at the Casino in New York. It seemed to have a fairish chance so Canary went out to French Lick Springs, Ind., for a holiday.

Coming down from his room one evening he stopped to listen to two Negro comics doing an act in the lobby of his hotel: Williams and his partner, George Walker. The next day the theater-wise Canary sent them on to New York with instructions to Lederer to put them in the "Gold Bug" as a specialty act. Their success was sensational, Williams taking some twenty encores for his song, "Go 'Way Back and Sit Down."

They continued in musicals for a time, enjoying astonishing favor. When their lawsuit against Hurtig and Seamon, who subsequently managed the team, disclosed that their earnings for one season totaled $40,000 the judge almost fell off the bench.

Williams was born in Nassau, of Afro-Spanish descent. When a lad his father brought him to America, subsequently settling in Riverside, Calif. He thwarted his father's educational ambitions for him by joining Martin and Seig's Mastodon Minstrels in 1893, luring George Walker, who had been a song and dance man in a medicine show and whom Williams met in San Francisco, to join with him.

Walker was an unusual fellow—several notches above just a good, straight feeder. It is true he couldn't take success like his more illustrious partner. Before his death at thirty-nine of paresis in 1911, he blossomed out like a Lenox Avenue pimp— a bediamonded Sir James Jewelry (as Irvin Cobb once called Jim Brady) in blackface; wore silk underwear at a time when

American whites were just shedding their red flannels; had his bedroom done in pale-blue satin. In pigment, mannerisms, and character he epitomized his most famous song: "Bon-bon Buddie the Chocolate Drop."

But more than the quiet, gentlemanly, aloof Williams, he had a true understanding and philosophy of what they, as representatives of the Negro race, were trying to do.

Five years before he died Walker stated: "The one hope of the colored performer must be in making a radical departure from the old 'darky' style of singing and dancing . . . There is an artistic side to the black race, and if it could be properly developed on the stage, I believe the theatergoing public would profit much by it."

Again: "My idea was always to impersonate my race just as they are. The colored man has never successfully taken off his own humorous characteristics, and the white impersonator often overdoes the matter."

Williams and Walker were pioneers in the movement to establish the Negro on his own in the theater. Whites and blacks may unite in acknowledging a joint indebtedness.

With careful consistency Walker justified the endeavor of his race to his death. He called precisely the more humane and intelligent trend toward the decently ambitious Negro as early as 1909. That year Walter C. Kelly, whose "Virginia Judge" was a featured act in vaudeville, refused to appear on a bill at Hammerstein's Victoria with Williams and Walker. Said Walker: "The man is foolish. The day is past for that sort of thing. Both white men and black have a right to earn a living in whatever manner they find most congenial, provided they injure no one else in so doing." There is no record of Kelly's rejoinder.

Williams, too, was subjected to racial affronts, at one time by, of all people, the cast of the "Follies of 1910." Ziegfeld had ordered that a substantial part be written in for Williams. When the cast learned that a Negro was to act with them they threatened to strike and Ziegfeld was forced to eliminate the part and substitute Williams's vaudeville specialty. Williams's artistry dissolved the difficulty. He stopped the show—in fact, was such a hit the rejected material was revised and his part restored. This, and the Kelly incident, were exceptional. Throughout the profession for the most part Williams was respected as a man and acclaimed as an artist (he was the only Negro the Keith circuit could book on a white bill in Washington). Nonetheless, it was the audiences of the 1900's, except in the deep South, that changed public opinion toward the Negro actor from hostility to apathy to acceptance.

The deep South rebelled at one of their best musicals, "In Dahomey," expanded from an abbreviated version they had put on at Koster and Bial's with considerable success. The team took the musical to London and there they were a sensation—wined, dined, played a command performance for Edward VII (June 27, 1904), and otherwise royally entertained. The color-lineless Britons referred to them as "those droll Americans."

In vaudeville the team, aside from their songs, presented a crossfire act generally based on the dapper, city Negro slicker (Walker) trying to take over the slow and cautious (Williams);

WALKER: I tell you I'm letting you in on this because you're a friend of mine. I could do this alone and let no one in on it. But I want you to share in it just because we're good friends. Now after you get into the bank you fill the satchel with money.

WILLIAMS: Whose money?

WALKER: That ain't the point. We don't know who put the money there, and we don't know why they got it. And they won't know how we got it. All you have to do is fill the satchel; I'll get the satchel—you won't have nothing to bother about—that's 'cause you're a friend of mine, see?

WILLIAMS: And what do I do with this satchel?

WALKER: All you got to do is bring it to me at a place where I tell you.

WILLIAMS: When they come to count up the cash and find it short, then what?

WALKER: By that time we'll be far, far away—where the birds are
singing sweetly and the flowers are in bloom.

WILLIAMS (*with doleful reflection*): And if they catch us they'll put us
so far, far away we never will hear no birds singin'. And everybody
knows you can't smell no flowers through a stone wall.

After Walker was stricken in 1909 when the team was appearing on tour in "Bandanna Land," Williams continued
in vaudeville—but only in interludes, for he was under a
long-term contract to Ziegfeld. In vaudeville he was even
greater as a single. But in fairness to Walker it must be recorded that during his incapacity, and even after his death,
Williams studied assiduously during his summers in Europe
with the great pantomimist Pietro—"who taught me that the
entire aim of art in the theater was to achieve simplicity."

As a single Williams, who, by the way, always worked in
blackface make-up, relied mostly on his songs and pantomime
interspersed with stories. No one could top him. One of his
most effective—all lost in this relentless type which can give
no hint of his ineffable facial work and manner—was:

Where I'm living now is a nice place, but you have to go along a
road between two graveyards to get to it. One night last week I was
coming home kind of late, and I got about halfway home when I
happened to look over my shoulder and saw a ghost following me.
I started to run. I run till I was 'most ready to drop. And then I
looked around. But I didn't see no ghost, so I sat down on the curb
stone to rest. Then out of the corner of my eye I could see something
white, and when I turned square around, there was that ghost sitting
along side of me. The ghost says: "That was a fine run we had. It
was the best running I ever saw." I says: "Yes. And soon as I get
my breath you're going to see some more."

Best of his pantomime bits was his poker game. On a dark
stage a small spot high-lighted only his head and shoulders.
With a poker hand held close to his face he pantomimed the
draw, the study of the hand, the bets, the suspicious looks,
the raise, the call, the disgust of the loser. It was a classic.

He put over a song as well: "Nobody"; "Let It Alone"; "You Got the Right Church but the Wrong Pew"; "My Castle on the Nile"; "Not for Me!" "The Jonah Man"; "That's Harmony" (which he introduced to give Grant Clarke, an unknown, a break). They could be used today—if you could find another Williams. His last show, and one of his best, was "Under the Bamboo Tree." On tour with it, he was stricken with pneumonia in Detroit and died there, March 4, 1922.

Jewish Headliners.

The racial acceptance of the 1900's audiences is further attested in their hearty response to Jewish character comedy. The faithful will recall Burt and Leon who, with Frank Bush, flourished as Jew comics from the seventies to the nineties. They were the great exceptions. Beyond these there were no Jewish acts of importance during the nineties. There were plenty of excellent Jewish performers, but they were doing Dutch, blackface, or singing and dancing acts. Some of them were good Irish comedians. Indeed, Weber and Fields at one time did a neat Irish act. Ed Rush and his wife (Rush and Bryant) were grand Irish comics, with all the trimmings: cape coats, lace falls, knee pants, and conical hats.

Frank Bush hung on to reap his reward in the twentieth century when his type of comedy was best appreciated. Then he really flowered as a headline attraction. He had the foresight, and the talent, to mix up his characters—his versatility was as amazing as his off-stage character was unique.

According to Bush's own story, he made his first public appearance in the Grand Duke Theatre where, as the reader may remember, Sam Bernard made his debut. It was run by Dave Conroy, who was also stage manager, producer, scenic artist, actor, and played the accordion—his "orchestra"— for accompaniments and overtures. For the most part the performers were newsboys and other kids who did jig dancing, bone solos, blackface acts, and dialect specialties. Bush did a routine of imitations and character bits which were of such

merit he had no difficulty in booking himself into the regular
variety houses.

In his original act he opened in grotesque Jew make-up:
tall, rusty plug hat, long black coat, shabby pants, long beard
which ran to a point, and large spectacles. As a youth he was
tall, thin, and limber—a physique that accentuated his crazy
song and dance and funny gestures. Here is one of his first
songs; a jargon of his own invention, no doubt:

> Oh, my name is Solomon Moses I'm a bully Sheeny man,
> I always treat my customers the very best what I can.
> I keep a clothing store 'way down on Baxter St.,
> Where you can get your clothing now I sell so awful cheap.

> CHORUS: Solomon, Solomon Moses, (Break).
> Hast du gesehen der clotheses? (Break).
> Hast du gesehen der kleiner kinder,
> Und der sox iss in der vinder?
> I sell to you for viertel dollar,
> You will say was cheap,
> Oskaploka overcoats
> For fimpf sehn dollar and half.
> My name is Isaac Levy Solomon Moses hast du gesacht?

His dance was no dance at all; it was more like a Hopi
Indian ritual, except for his spectacles, as he shuffled around
with his hands behind him and peered at the audience over his
glasses. For his exit after the second verse he accomplished a
kind of schottische movement, using his hands and arms more
than his feet. Bush may well have been vaudeville's first
eccentric dancer. Certainly this was the first specialty of its
kind in early variety theaters.

Next he impersonated a German entering a saloon; then a
Yankee farmer; and they were remarkable. They had no
continuity or meaning in relation to story; they were pure characterizations. As the German he made up with a mop of iron-
gray hair, a walrus mustache to match, a straw hat, and a long
linen duster.

Ach, guten morgen, Schwartburger. Ich bin heis. Ich will ein glass bier haben. (*Business of drinking*) Ah-h-h-h, das bier ist gut! Ich bin gangen geworden down sein binz eber ganz Laudenschlager Strasse. Das is two mein alles schwartzzingenpfeifer bicht mein Landsmann unt seden gegeneber. Ich habe mein pantoffel veloren. Wo hast mein pantoffel gesehen? *Wo hast mein pantoffel gesehen?* . . .

And so on; getting louder and faster until exit. The gibberish matched his eccentric performance and was received with guffaws.

His cow-swapping Yankee was an astonishing contrast:

There she be neighbor—not a finer critter in this whole county—sound in eye, wind and limb—not a blemish on her the size of a pin point—kind and gentle, good milker and light feeder—every word I'm telling yeh is true as the noon-day sun—I'll swap even for that roan heifer of yourn if you'll throw in a couple of plugs of store tobacco and come over next Tuesday and help break in a yoke of steers—Is it a swap?—Shake hands on it—The halter don't go with the cow, you'd better fetch along a rope when you come to git her—Goin' down by the cider mill? Reckon I'll go along part ways—Tarnation dry weather, ain't it? (*Exit*)

After this he obliged with a tin-whistle solo. The man was an expert on the tin whistle, which sounds like a gag in itself. Yet Bush got as big a hand for his tin-whistle triple-tongue polka (featured by Jules Levy, the famous cornet soloist) as he did for his characterizations. An eccentric, Bush, between shows, would make a pitch on the street (often near the theater, to the management's embarrassment) and sell tin whistles. With a satchelful of them dangling from his neck, he'd mount a soapbox and when the crowd collected he'd call for tunes: "No trouble to play it, gents. Give me a tune. Look—it's easy . . . " With his gentle kidding and his friendly personality he sold thousands at a dime apiece—no small addition to his performer's salary.

With a poignant attempt to seize the forelock of the times that begat audiences alert to brushed clothes, clean boots, and daily shirt and collar changes, Bush junked his Baxter Street costume and wig make-up and appeared in a dinner jacket, retaining only the spectacles, for a monologue that consisted mainly of stories in all dialects. But he lost caste as the new century drew toward the close of its first decade. And it bothered him, too, that the success of a show he took out on his own, "Girl Wanted," in which he played a protean comedy role, was only middling. He was forced to return to vaudeville. But his oars were gone; there was nothing to rest on. The new generation didn't care what he had been. They saw only a funny old man in a tuxedo who might have looked more agreeably comic in duster and mop wig.

But nothing can take credit from him for surviving through the years of a vaudeville that was changing with a chameleon America. As a pioneer Jewish single he made that type of comedy a staple in our variety theaters. To his moss-green coattails figuratively was tied nearly every succeeding Hebrew comedian. Their ultimate acclaim is largely due to his efforts; and so from 1900 on we enjoyed a wake of Jewish acts that enlivened and diversified vaudeville. Came along after Frank Bush: Hoey and Lee, Gilday and Fox, Julian Rose, Jess Dandy, Joe Welch, Willie and Eugene Howard, Jordan and Harvey, Ben Welch, Fields and Wolley—a score more.

It is of not much point to describe each of their acts because they used parodies, parodies, parodies, and more parodies. Hoey and Lee had a stock of them that apparently was inexhaustible. They—parodies and team—were always good. They worked smoothly and derived their comedy from disagreements on points of etiquette, pronunciations, misunderstandings, and misinterpretations. And they used no exaggerated make-ups.

Jess Dandy had a bit of a run in the vaudevilles and could have kept on. But he was cast for the comic in "Prince of Pilsen" and remained in that hit musical. He also depended largely on parodies, but his make-up struck a new note in vaudeville's Jewish comedy and anticipated Montague Glass's

Abe Potash that came along a few years later: a stout, genial, business Jew, Dandy never whined or deplored but stressed good humor and pleasantries to win his audience.

Julian Rose, a Philadelphian, took an opposite stance with a satirical monologue that criticized the Jew's alleged foibles. But he was a good performer whose attitude gave no hint of malice. Rose, a commercial accountant, started by playing clubs, lodges, and smokers. Finally Tony Pastor gambled on his act and Rose became a headliner almost overnight. His material was excellent; and his pace and gag planting made it irresistible. His best monologue was "Levinsky at the Wedding":

. . . then I got my invitation. It was printed on the back of her father's business cards. Old ones. On the invitation it says, "your presence is requested." Right away the presents they ask for. Sure, Feinberg was there. He stood up all evening. He borrowed a pair of pants and was afraid to sit down in them. He asked me to come over and see him the next night. I told him I can't, I was going to see Hamlet. He says, "bring him along, what's the difference?" He thinks Hamlet is a man! Hamlet is a theater . . . And the supper! Everything was stylish. They had napkins—clean—some of them . . . There was a tough feller there named Finnegan . . . He wasn't invited . . . He came anyhow. Everybody says, "look out for Finnegan. All the time he wants to make a fight."—Poof—He was no fighter. Me and my two brothers and a couple of cousins almost licked him. . . .

Joe Welch, one of the best of the Jew comics, portrayed a mirthless, God-forsaken type; stressed his misfortune. The picture of misery, slow music pointed his entrance, and anyone who has ever seen his act will never forget his opening line: "Mebbe you t'ink I am a heppy man." He began with a street brawl:

I was taking a pair of pants to a customer in a hospital when a couple of loafers bumped into me. One of them grabbed the pants and the other fellow tried to pull them away from him. The pants commenced to rip and I hollered—"Police!" When the cop comes he hits me with a stick and the loafers run off with the pants. The police pushed me in a wagon with a lot of tough guys. One of them says: "What did you do?" I said, "I done nothing." He says, "neither did I. All I did was stick a knife in a Dago's heart." Oy! Such a tough guy. Another fellow says: "What you gonna tell the judge?" I says, "I don't know the judge, what I should tell him?" And the tough guy says, "When the judge calls you, just say, 'Judge, you're a big stiff.' And he'll let you off." They stood us in front of a big counter and when the judge says to me, "What have you got to say?" I said, "Judge, you're a big stiff!" . . . After I got out of the hospital . . .

Ben Welch, Joe's brother, did a lively, fast-talking Jewish pushcart type, in exact contrast to Joe. For a time he teamed with Jules Jordan, of Jordan and Harvey, in which the pair characterized the breezy, jolly type of Jew. Later Ben went into burlesque and became an extraordinary favorite. One night, in the middle of a show, he went totally blind. He retired to submit to treatment, but it never helped him. Rather than place himself on the dependence of friends or charity, he returned to vaudeville in a sketch that required little action. His blindness was not apparent to the audience and he did very well until a complication of ailments took him from the stage for good. A further burden was a conscienceless insurance company. Ben held some kind of policy but the company maintained that his disability did not prevent him from earning his living and refused to pay.

The Single, Two-, and Four-acts after 1900

SOAPBOXING has never been unpopular, but the first decade of the twentieth century was a ten-year binge for the political tub thumpers. Vaudeville, especially the monologists, regarded them as fair game, and from Lew Dockstader and John W. Ransone to Cliff Gordon and Will Rogers the alarm-viewers and pride-pointers were neatly bagged as feathered asses, and thanks for the sport. Rogers's contribution to political satire was immense although it did not reach its intensities until the twenties.

All will recall the untimely death of Rogers, who, when he crashed in Alaska, had sugared Hollywood's sap into the ownership of about half of California. He had known poverty. Years earlier, playing Fort Worth, Tex., on the same bill with Rosy Green, mother of Mitzi, he tapped her for $60. Mary Rogers had just been born and Will had been sending all his money home. So Rosy reached for her grouch bag and handed over. (Most of the girl performers carried a grouch bag; a tiny purse they concealed in their bosoms; probably the origin of "mad money.") Will paid it back Saturday night, and never forgot Rosy. Rosy never forgot him. He referred to the incident so constantly in his monologues and to performers that it became a nuisance to the generous woman, who, each succeeding Christmas, received grouch bags by the dozen from her friends.

Cliff Gordon, brother of Max, lacked the Voltairian terseness of Rogers. This may seem an unfair comparison; it is intended only as a characterization. Gordon's dumb Dutchman had a kindliness and vigor more ingratiating than the sharp-shooting Rogers whose wit, incidentally, was often muffed in the sticks. Gordon portrayed the customary puzzled German, but his personality and explosiveness enhanced his material, of which this is a sample:

Efferbody says there iss a shortness of money. Who shortened it? I didn't done it. Who has got all dis money? I ain't got it. Efferbody says we must have change. I ain't got change for ten cents. We neffer had dese things when people like George Lincoln and Abraham Washington vas superintendencing the gufferment. . . .

The easy delivery of the immaculate Clifton Crawford also featured the vaudevilles, although he was mostly identified with musicals. For his variety monologue he, too, caustically referred to political and social conditions. He had a remarkable change of style and pace. "Never again," he would say, referring to a marital mishap. "I'm through. No more . . . " (Business of blonde crossing the stage. Crawford turns, slowly follows, then quickens his step. Exit.) From this he would turn to a recitation of Kipling's "Gunga Din." No one who heard him will ever forget it, and Crawford, long before vaudeville's demise, wished heartfully Kipling had never written the poem. But the audiences screamed for it, managers insisted, and there was nothing he could do but recite it. He used a conversational tone that he heightened only when the lines demanded emphasis, and generally made his audience feel that they were sitting in a London pub, hearing firsthand the tale of a veteran soldier of the Queen.

There were any number of monologists and "singles": George Fuller Golden, Loney Haskell, Jim Thornton, Chic Sale, ad infinitum. But the bulwark of vaudeville's comedy was supplied by the two-acts, the teams. Among the outstanding pairs were Van and Schenck, Matthews and Bulger,

Clark and McCullough, Montgomery and Moore, Rock and Fulton, Billy Gould and Valeska Surratt, Whipple and Huston, and Melville and Higgins.

Van and Schenck had been respectively conductor and motorman on the Brooklyn trolley lines, and like Cliff Gordon entered vaudeville through amateur appearances before social gatherings. "Entered" is scarcely the word—they were invited in; they did not have to break in. In a short while they became the best, in the opinion of many, of the two-man piano acts. Schenck was a natural pianist and possessed a good voice; Van was an excellent character singer and a wonder at dialect. Their songs were fresh and clean and usually had a neat turn.

Matthews and Bulger began as a blackface act. In their early years they opened with a full set showing a watermelon patch enclosed by a stone wall:

Dim lights, sneaky music. . . . Enter Matthews, a dapper darky, over the stone wall. Cautiously stepping among the melons, he'd tap one or two and listen. Finally he tapped the largest melon, the orchestral cue for a loud, sustained chord. Lights up, the melon burst, and out stepped Bulger as a wench. They then went into a flirtation song and dance. With minor variations, they played this over the circuits for years until claimed by musical comedy in which they were a starring team until the unfortunate breakdown of Matthews who became a hopeless paralytic, broke, but not friendless— George M. Cohan provided for him until his death.

Bulger, who specialized in rowdy comedy, was not the better comedian, but he was good and, continuing alone, became an adept single with a style of his own. He never humored his material; in fact, had no knack for this. He'd just turn it on and let it go with the staccato delivery of an auctioneer. One of his biggest song successes was "Rip Van Winkle":

> CHORUS: Rip Van Winkle was a lucky man,
> Rip Van Winkle went away.
> He slept for twenty happy years
> In the mountains so they say, how lucky!

> Rip Van Winkle was a lucky man,
> Deny it if you can.
> He never saw the women
> Down at Coney Island swimmin'
> Rip Van Winkle was a lucky man.

Bobby Clark and the late Paul McCullough also became musical comedy stars, curiously, rather through burlesque than vaudeville. In their skit Clark, an eccentric comic, played a railroad section hand, fed by McCullough, a passenger on Clark's jerkwater line in a funny folderol at a whistle-stop.

Chic Suratt; Loyal Whipple.

Billy Gould's first partner was Nellie Burt. The pair did a light comedy song and dance and talking act, a popular number in the early days. In the 1900's he teamed with Valeska Suratt, an unknown girl though with vaudeville background who, at the time, was her own excuse for being. A handsome brunette with bedroom eyes and a sapling figure, she was any man's desire. Moreover, she was no horse for a wardrobe but wore her clothes as a flower its petals. Under Gould's coaching, they developed a crossfire and wisecracking act in one in evening dress. They worked with unstudied ease and became a top-flight, three-bracket two-act.

Suratt, a shrewd businesswoman, had ideas of her own. She quit Gould, organized a company, and went out with a new act called "The Belle of the Boulevards," which carried her into legit under Al H. Woods. She was not fortunate and after her show, "The Red Rose," folded she went to Eddie Darling, asking for time with a dramatic sketch. "I'm calling it 'The Purple Poppy,'" she said. "You see, I'm identified with purple." She wanted to open in the Middle West because the stars were more propitious for her then in that territory. Darling was skeptical. But Suratt was a draw, and he shipped her out to a theater in the Ohio chain where, to his surprise, she did a tremendous business.

VALESKA SURATT
"... *as a flower its petals*"

Darling then brought her back east, booking her into the Riverside Theatre in New York. Going up early to catch her sketch, he went backstage where her maid denied him to her dressing room. "You can't see her, she's concentrating." Darling waited and finally Modjeska Valeska came out and struck a dramatic pose. "Please overlook this," she explained, "but I must get into the character fifteen minutes before I go on." Darling went out front for the act. He was unimpressed. But her setting and costumes were in the Suratt taste and the sketch played the circuit for a year.

Drama had clutched her skirts and thereafter she would listen to no other urge. So when Chester Devond wrote a sketch called "Jade," she promptly purchased it so that she could play the part of the Waif. Darling booked her for a try-out at the Fordham (New York) Theatre. At her Monday opening Darling went up—and out. Out, when, interrupting the story about the girl who, finding the piece of jade, must give herself to its masculine owner, the curtain was rung and her leading man came out and sang "They Needed an Angel in Heaven, So God Took Caruso Away." The following morning Darling phoned her the verdict. "You can't go on with it," he said. But she talked him down. "You don't know the finer things in life," she told him. So he booked her at the Brighton Beach Music Hall, then about to close its summer season. It was dreadful.

For some reason Whipple and Huston never clicked as they should have, and it is doubtful, despite his talent, that Walter Huston would ever have achieved more than No. 2 billing had it not been for his astute, persistent, and loyal first wife, Bayonne Whipple. They went over with the audiences; but the managers remained chill. Finally they were booked into the Fifth Avenue Theatre in New York and Darling went to see them. He liked their act but didn't do anything about it. The following year he saw them in another act and liked that. But Darling was new then, had not reached his post as chief booker so he dismissed them on the grounds that if nobody else had done anything about them they couldn't be any good.

One day Darling received a long letter from Huston. It told how they seemed to go over with the audiences but could never get any place, and asked if Darling would kindly book them into one of the better theaters without salary—they would take their chances. Darling recognized the justice of the complaint and the following week booked them into the Riverside (a two-a-day at Broadway and 96th Street, New York) where Eva Tanguay was being headlined. Tanguay's salary was excessive and the bill required an inexpensive act to keep the budget within reason and Albee in his chair. Whipple and Huston were playing "Boots," said to have been written by Huston. Darling paid them $300 for the week and they were successful. The next year Huston changed his act but Bayonne could never get him more than the $300.

At that time the Shuberts were again invading Albee's circuit with their "advanced" vaudeville, buying good acts for their own theaters and—the jazz craze was beginning. "You can never," said Darling to Bayonne, who had again asked for time, "get more than $200 or $300 for that act," and turned away. "What would you advise me to do?" she asked. "I've got to get Walter some money."

To be rid of her Darling replied, "Why don't you get yourself a jazz band?" Four weeks later she returned. "I've got it," she said. "Got what?" "Whipple and Huston and their Jazz Band," answered Bayonne. Darling booked them into the Bushwick Theatre in Brooklyn. He saw the act, and it was good—in it Huston danced, told stories, and played character parts.

"The act is all right," said Darling, "but with your company you would have to have $1,500 weekly and we just are not paying that money, your names are not big enough." Said Whipple, "The Shuberts have offered us $1,500." "Take it," advised Darling. "But if we do," countered Whipple, "we'll never get back; it's only for ten weeks." Said Darling: "They'll take you back [into the Albee fold] quicker than they will rebook people that stick with them."

It was true. Whipple and Huston played out the Shubert ten weeks, and when they finished Darling booked them over the regular circuit for $1,250 a week.

Still Bayonne was unsatisfied; her ambition for her husband burned as bright as the lights she hoped someday to see his name in. "I've just got to get Walter on Broadway," she once told Darling. She did, too, raising in some manner enough money to produce a play called "Pitt." It was not successful. But one night Eugene O'Neill came in and, observing Huston, remarked, "That is the man I need for 'Desire Under the Elms.'" Huston climbed its branches to the topmost bough.

The singles and two-acts we have discussed were some of the really great comedy acts of vaudeville. A few, Bert Williams, Frank Tinney, Joe Cook, were artists of the very top rank. They had that ineffable something that raised them above the standardization with which vaudeville became afflicted in the second decade of the 1900's. From 1910 to its close, save for its few artists, its featured specialties, its "name" acts, vaudeville graded off to specific routines, many of them good, but all of a pattern.

"That Was No Lady . . . "

Take the Dutch comedy or the blackface; we are speaking now of the standard acts, say from 1910. The straight man (invariably): "The way you insulted me at that party last night was something delicious." The comic, right back at him: "Who stole the dishes? Every time you open your foot you put your mouth in it. Better not say anything at all." Bang. A kick in the belly, and lima beans. Same routine: Comic: "What did I do?" Straight: "What did you do? The way you insulted that girl that sat along side of you!" Comic: "What insult?" Straight: "Didn't you ask that girl that sat along side of you if you could dunk your bread in her gravy? Don't you know that's bad manners?" Comic: "Bad manners, maybe, but it's good taste." Bang. A kick in the belly, and lima beans. Raymond and Caverley, who rated a notch above the graded comedy acts, nevertheless used this routine. Made up as two German musicians carrying instrument cases they entered on a street in one and proceeded with tangle talk, misunderstandings, and atrocious puns. (Puns as gags, by the way, were as prevalent in vaudeville as parodies.)

> What for iss it you viggle so?
> Undervear.
> Vat iss under vere?
> I said undervear.
> I ask you—under VERE?
> Dot's vat I said.
> Vat you has said?
> Undervear.
> I don't know.
> Vat you don't know?
> Under vere.
> Look. (*Tapping shirt front*) Under here.
> Oh, under dere.
> Yes, sure.
> Vat iss under dere?
> I am.

In the blackface act the little fellow would open: "Boy, if I don't come around and knock you out." Straight: "Don't talk to me that way. Ain't I always helped you? Didn't I get you a job?" Comic: "Sure. Bathing dishes. That was employment." Then into the fight. It never varied. Same with the white comedy act, the straight politician, say, and the comic. "Hello, Tony (*entering*), you come around tomorrow and I'll get you a fine job." Comic: "Oh, you got me a job all right; manicuring the boulevard."

Even the four-acts, the quartets, had standard routines. They usually included a broken-down legit singer as bass, a Dutch comic as baritone; the lead, or second tenor, was invariably the straight while the tenor supplied more comedy if only because of the customary costume of red socks and peg-top trousers the cuffs of which were fully four inches above the shoetops.

The quartets were favorite acts of Sid Phillips, himself a classy single in vaudeville whose astute observations led to his current job as play and talent representative for Metro-Goldwyn-Mayer in New York. The way the quartets opened always amused Sid—as they do anybody now in retrospect. Invariably the Dutch comic baritone would rush on yelling: "Keep him away from me or I'll kill him!" This was the cue for the straight second tenor who would enter with the lines: "Just a moment, please." Here was the peg-top tenor's cue who, entering with the bass, would cry: "Water, water, Give me water." Somebody would oblige by squirting it in his face and then they would go into a parody. Why, nobody ever knew. The act just wouldn't seem to jell any other way.

The character quartets were also of a piece. Take the boot-black (Willie Howard was one), the messenger boy, the news-boy, and the straight. The straight would come out and say: "Hey, fellows, come here. I got us a job tonight. That big broker I told you about is giving a party and he'll pay us to go up to his home and entertain. What do you say? We'll rehearse right here." And they'd go into their first number, likely to be:

> Roll them bones,
> Roll them anywhere.
> Roll them on the sidewalk,
> Roll them on the square.

Then the finish with "Love Me and the World Is Mine." Exit, falling off, two on each side.

Sid Phillips, incidentally, was an off-stage character him-self. A collector of first editions, he'd browse around the honky-tonks between shows looking for buys. One afternoon in a small Midwestern town he picked up a Conrad first. Return-ing elated to his hotel he found a group of performers lazing in the lobby and told one of them of his good fortune. "He's a louse," said the performer. "Who?" demanded Sid. "That guy Conrad." And Sid, recalling a performer of that name, said, "I don't mean him, I mean Joseph Conrad." And the performer said, "Oh, you mean the guy on the wire." And Sid said, wearily, "Yes, that's the guy," and dropped it.

Two famous four-acts used schoolboy comedy—The Avon Comedy Four and the Marx Brothers, although at the time the Marx Brothers were school-kidding there were five—Gummo (Milton), who later rolled his fifth wheel into the clothing business. The Avon Comedy Four was assembled by Max Hart, as shrewd a picker of talent as Bill Morris. Smith and Dale, still strong, stayed with the act from its start to its finish but the other two members were changed frequently. Their script (if they ever had one) doubtless would read very unfunny. Indeed, their act was the wildest hokum; made no bid for class. But the Avon Comedy Four could close a long bill of headline favorites and "name" acts—and emerge as the hit of the show. Their routine varied little from the familiar "school act" formula: the harassed teacher, the impossible scholars, the questions in geography and history and the ridiculous answers, the slapstick and dunce cap. A reader might well ask how an audience that could read, write, and dress themselves could derive amusement from all that. Amusement? The audiences rolled in the aisles.

The Marx Brothers began with an act called "Fun in Hi Skule." They sang, danced, and played, a conventional vaudeville comedy act. According to Chico (Leonard), they inaugurated their specialty of kidding their own act, themselves, and everybody else, in Texas. Chico says that at the time they were playing this Texas town a mule outside the theater was demolishing a cart and the audience rushed out, on the reasonable presumption that the mule was more fun than the show. Playing to empty seats, the brothers went into a hilarious razz of their own act which eventually lured back the customers. They were forced to retain their zany style, says

Chico, when, in Brownsville, the sheriff seized all their costumes and scenery. The Marx Brothers were never headliners in vaudeville; their act was an anachronism. Vaudeville after 1910 was becoming just too, too lahvely; leaned toward the sissy. In this setting the brothers' toothy disregard for convention, theatrical or social, was wasted. They were redeemed by a happy coincidence.

Will B. Johnstone, news cartoonist of the New York *World-Telegram*, and his brother Tom had written a show called "I'll Say She Is," and with Joe Gaites supplying the shoestring they looked about for a comic. Not for long, because Tom already had four in mind—those zanies. But when Tom and Will suggested the Marxes to Gaites you could have thrown a stone through the silence. A night later they lured him over to a Brooklyn grind where the Marxes were playing four-a-day. They were signed for the show and the rest is N. Y. to L. A.

Character acts—usually singles—were bathetically satisfying to the 1900–1915 audiences. These were sops for the sentimental reactions of the time, a boo-hoo period replete with such handkerchief melodies as "Won't You Come Over to My House?" (And Play That You're My Little Girl); "Two Little Bright Eyes Stood Out All Alone" (the orphan kid watching the others get presents from home); or "Mother Has a Sweetheart, Daddy Is His Name." The vigor of vaudeville's audiences seemed to die with the slapstick and rough stuff. Albee's tinseled temples actually cheaply veneered also his patrons. There were a great many hammy impersonators of various types, but the top character artist was rare. Of these we shall set down three (not all sob purveyors) who were headliners for years: Junie McCree, Walter C. Kelly (the "Virginia Judge"), and George Beban.

McCree was a Pacific Coast performer with extraordinary versatility, but he will doubtless be best remembered for his dope fiend in a sketch called "Sappho in Chinatown." Assisted by two women, McCree impersonated a carefree drug addict. One of the women complains of the indifference of her husband. She decides to make him jealous and accordingly sends out her best friend to gather in a likely-looking gent for this purpose. The friend then brought in McCree, a bit seedy but somewhat dignified dope with an inexhaustible fund of picturesque slang.

McCree, on or off, was an interesting character. He wrote his own material and at the time he served as president of the White Rats, opened an "authoring" office at Broadway and 47th Street where other performers could buy gags, routines, or one-act skits. His impersonation of the hop-head was occasionally cynical. At times he'd throw in a couple of gags in the argot of the addict and known only to them. "A laugh here or there," he used to say, "and I could spot the hops in the audience."

Walter C. Kelly, a native of Philadelphia and a brother of George Kelly, the playwright, at one time operated a café in Newport News, Va. There he met the prototypes of the characters he afterward presented in vaudeville as the "Virginia Judge." He worked in one, wore a baggy black alpaca coat, stood behind a pedestal, flourished a gavel and "tried cases." His dialects were perfect—Southern gentleman, Negro, Irish.

George Beban's "My Leetla Rose" may not be our dish today, but it was effective in the 1900's; the audiences dabbed unashamedly, even as we do now at tear-jerker movies. But Beban's was by no means a crying act. He could impersonate odd types, many of them topical, superbly. The audiences wanted to cry and demanded "My Leetla Rose" so often he was forced to expand it into a sketch. New-fashioned for three persons—himself, a woman, and a little girl—it became an exceptional feature. But it nearly wiped out his versatility and utterly dissolved the subtle note of criticism in his work.

Magic, Mental Acts, Wire Turns, and Animals

T HE great magic and mental acts of vaudeville were excellent draws, and in the gullible 1900's few bills were presented that did not offer one or the other. The greatest of the magicians—Kellar, Thurston, Herrmann—did not remain with vaudeville. When an act like theirs clicked the performers at once organized a unit and played the legit houses with a full two-hour show. Indeed, many of the old-timers cannot recall ever playing with Kellar on the bill. He was, however, one of the most accomplished magicians of his day, and since he left his bag of tricks to Howard Thurston, a vaudeville headliner, he rates mention.

Harry Kellar's sleights were well-nigh perfect, few could approach him in deftness of touch; remarkable, for he was an awkward, powerfully built man with such enormous hands his apparatus had to be specially made for him. Admittedly the magicians' magician, he was second in popularity to Alexander Herrmann, probably because Herrmann was a fine showman, on or off, and had an excellent sense of comedy. Kellar was a pleasant man, but he was serious in his routines and never clowned—a slave to his work. His patter was often ungrammatical, and once Alan Dale, belligerent Hearst dramatic critic, blistered him for it in a sarcastic review. Kellar, instead of being angered, subscribed for the International Correspondence School course in English. He always said he was grateful to Dale for the criticism, and there is no reason to believe his remark was ironic; irony was no part of his nature.

Kellar admired Thurston immensely, but as Thurston grew in drawing power (latterly he outdrew Kellar), he became arrogant before his audiences and Kellar's admiration waned. He told friends that Thurston "fought his house," which was true, and a grave fault to the faultless Kellar. Yet this generous man, who never failed to help a competitor, apprised Thurston of his arts before he quit to idle his last days comfortably in Los Angeles, living on annuities he had sagaciously purchased while the money was rolling in.

Kellar's levitation, his most applauded trick, was the envy of other practitioners. Instead of booms he used wires, which were more effective, and his "blue room" illusion, a variant of the London Ghost Show, was perfect. He was one of the first to do the spirit cabinet exposé.

Herrmann, who billed himself as Herrmann the Great, was a son of Carl Herrmann, a European magician. The Great's performance was indifferent but its very casualness made his sleights seem as good as Kellar's. And he had the acumen to vary his unit with a couple of vaudeville acts, jugglers, or other germane performances. His wife, Adelaide, was his chief assistant.

After Herrmann's death, Adelaide brought over Leon Herrmann who was announced as the Great's nephew. Leon had a thick accent and little humor. Adelaide booked a route for him which, in his stolid way, he completed and then returned to Europe, a flop here. The resourceful Adelaide then framed up a small act, mostly press-the-button stuff, adding a minor illusion and closing with an original suspension. "Press-the-button" stuff was performers' patois for "magic" achieved by mechanical means instead of sleights. The "original suspension" can be seen today in Coney Island ballyhoos. A girl stands on a low box, and is propped up by a pair of crutches.

She is then "hypnotized" and the box and crutches are removed, but she stays put, gripped by a metal harness. She can be raised or lowered in the harness by mechanical means, unseen, or unnoticed by the audience. This was the earliest suspension act known and was used years before levitation was perfected by Kellar.

Horace Goldin was discovered by Bill Morris, who picked him out of a dime show one day on the road from the ferry to Ambrose Park, Brooklyn, where Buffalo Bill had pitched for the season. Goldin was uncouth, but he had some good tricks and Morris got him work at Pastor's, then in decline, and in the honky-tonks, where his lack of finesse didn't much matter. Under Morris's prodding he eventually reached Hammerstein's Victoria and some of the Keith houses, but he was always a small-timer until . . .

Probably chagrined at his mediocrity here, he went abroad and presently word came that he was a knockout in Europe. The news was received with skepticism by Broadway's theatrically recondite, but when he came home and appeared at Hammerstein's the boys gasped. In twenty minutes, without opening his mouth, Goldin performed as many sleights and tricks as the average magician would make in a two-hour show. A smash.

When the first World War broke out, Goldin was touring India and the Eastern colonies. Maybe he talked too much off stage—nobody ever knew how it happened, but he was interned as an enemy alien. It proved a sad end to his career in America. Audiences had forgotten him when he returned. He made a partial comeback with sawing a woman in two, but a flood of exposé copies put him down. He died in London in 1939.

The woman-in-two trick should be explained. Two girls are used, one in each half of the box. One sticks her head out of a hole in one end, the other thrusts her feet through a hole in the other. The excess girl is hidden by the platform upon which the box rests.

Thurston, although befriended by Kellar, actually owed his start to the Great Herrmann, who, viewing Thurston's act in a Western honky-tonk (where Thurston probably would have stayed if this incident had not happened), asked him to explain a trick. He did explain it, and came east billing himself as "The Man Who Mystified Herrmann the Great." It was the rising-card trick, so simple it fooled others besides Herrmann. Its only "mechanism" was a piece of black thread and two stagehands, one either side of the stage. For a couple of years after the turn of the century Thurston did an ordinary act. Then he blossomed out with a set of showy illusions and was made.

Bautier De Kolta played two long engagements here and toured the circuit once, but never got over although his act was showy—and his own. He was the inventor of two excellent illusions, La Cocoon and Cremation (burning a live woman). For his Cocoon routine he used a light frame of a box suspended above the stage by ribbons which concealed piano wires. He then pasted paper over the front upon which a cocoon was drawn. The box suddenly becomes heavy, the wires sag a couple of inches, the paper is torn away, and a girl emerges. For his Cremation, De Kolta used a girl covered by a sheet. The sheet is fired and collapses to the stage. As the girl goes down through a trap, a wire frame retains her outline.

Enter now one of the most picturesque personalities in the business—Harry Houdini. Harry started in the dime museums as a "platform" act, meaning he worked the curio hall of the museums, not the theater side. His first act was card tricks and a trunk escape which he called "Metamorphosis," and had a difficult time pronouncing. Throughout his early years his great desire was to head a medicine show. The graft in a medicine show goes to the "doctor" who "practices" on the side. But in Harry's day the law was catching up and most states required that the doctor hold a license from some authentic body. So to keep the graft in the family Harry staked his brother Leopold to a college and medical school education. By the time Lee graduated, Harry had gone into the four-figure salary class with his handcuff work and Lee became one of the most expert X-ray specialists in New York. So they forgot the medicine show.

The origin of Harry's handcuff trick was always a touchy point and there are a number of stories about it, none of which has ever been proved. The least apocryphal—at any rate, the one that makes sense—concerns a Boston inventor of magic. The Bostonian had a set of three keys which would unlock any handcuff except one. He intended to make three sets and sell one each to an Easterner, a Midwesterner, and one on the Coast. He showed them to a number of magicians, one of whom later sought to buy a set only to be told that all three had been sold to one man for $1,000. Soon after this Houdini broke in his handcuff act in the West.

He brought it to New York—and flopped. "Interesting," said the wise boys, "but there is nothing to show that it's on the level." Bitterly disappointed, Harry, left town and did not return until he had perfected a number of routines. He arranged a demonstration in Yorkville Prison, New York. He stripped nude, and was thoroughly examined even to inspection of his rectum. He then entered a cell, the door clanked and was locked. Almost immediately he emerged. The lowdown, or anyway the explanation gossiped about Broadway, was that just before he entered the cell Mrs. Houdini kissed him "for luck," slipping the key from her mouth to his.

Harry realized that handcuffs alone did not make a well-rounded act, so he developed and added a number of escapes to his routine. They were the escape from a packing case, built on the stage by a crew from a local store, the milk can, tank, and others; they have not been duplicated since. He also added the escape from a straight jacket, his medical brother teaching him how to make the necessary shoulder dislocations. He also permitted himself to be thrown into the East River, heavily shackled. This was declared perfectly safe, but his family were always in a fever of anxiety until a phone call assured them all was well.

Once Harry was playing Baltimore. Loafing in front of the theater before the show, he was accosted by a chap he did not know. "Want to see the show?" the fellow asked. "Why, yes," said Harry, taking the proffered ticket, "thanks."

"There's just one thing I'd like to ask," continued the stranger. "There's a girl on this bill, a singer, and she's great. I want you to give her a big hand, and when she finishes her song I want you to call out a request number, 'Lovey Joe.'" Harry said all right, and strode into the theater. Continuing on backstage he learned that his own act followed the girl's. He said to the stage manager, "Give her all the time she wants. But nobody goes on that stage after my card is up."

The girl would have gone over normally. But the "packed" house gave her a tremendous reception and she took bow after bow. Finally Houdini, waiting in the wings, said to the stage manager, "Put my card up." It was done and Houdini walked on, the din crabbing his entrance. He raised his hand and succeeded in getting quiet. Then he said:

"There seems to be some doubt about your wanting to see me. If you will let me go on with my act, I will be glad to do so. If you don't want me to I'll walk out. But if I do, I'll never play Baltimore again as long as I live." The audience subsided and Harry went into his act. The girl who had nearly ruined him was Belle Baker, who later rose to a $2,500-a-week headliner. The "shill" on the sidewalk was Lew Leslie, her husband. In passing: Houdini's threat to waive Baltimore was no pompous peeve. At the height of his career he was the No. 1 draw of vaudeville. Eva Tanguay always claimed the box-office record. Not so; it was Houdini's.

Another point: There was one challenge he would never accept—that of a Gloucester fisherman to tie his thumbs behind his back. Even Houdini couldn't get out of that. And he knew it.

They all fade. Houdini in afteryears wound up lecturing.

Coming through Cleveland during his decline he stopped to
see John Royal and the new Albee house. The doorman refused to let him backstage. Later Royal booked him for two
weeks. It was successful because Royal tied his appearance to
an exposé of spirit-medium frauds then being advertised in a
local newspaper. A rival print, the Cleveland *Press*, took up the
crusade and gained important circulation.

Houdini's real name was Weiss; he took his stage name from
Robert Houdin, a French conjurer, whose "Life of Robert
Houdin," fascinated him. Someone told him that Houdini
meant "like Houdin." Harry always wanted to write a new
work which would amplify and complete Houdin's autobiography. He bought dozens of books and hundreds of old
programs before he found out that Houdin was an unmitigated
liar. So he wrote "Robert Houdin Unmasked."

During his career Harry purchased or obtained the patent
papers of every lock patented in the United States, Great
Britain, France, and Germany, and he knew more about
locks than most locksmiths. He was an expert on spiritualism,
being advised in these media by Joe M. Dunninger who
umpires the claims of those seeking the reward of the Society
for Psychical Research for bona fide demonstrations. He made
a number of films, but he lacked a good picture personality
and they were not too successful.

In his lifetime Harry gave his old stuff to a brother, Hardeen,
whom he put out as a sort of No. 2 company. At his death,
Hardeen inherited all Harry's tricks but never did much with
them.

Houdini died in Gray Hospital, Detroit, October 31, 1926,
after two operations for a burst appendix. It was ruptured by
a blow delivered by one of a group of students in Montreal
twelve days earlier. The students had assembled to hear
Houdini's address on spiritualism and to watch his exposé of
tricks. A reception followed, and Harry told them of the
splendid development and unusual strength of his stomach

muscles. Thereupon, a student, without warning or giving Harry time to tauten, struck him twice in the stomach. One of the blows burst his appendix, but so remarkable was the man's constitution he did not feel the effects until he boarded a train for Detroit.

The Great Lafayette (a name he had made legal in the courts) called himself a magician, but he was master only of the simpler tricks and relied mostly upon an illusion, "The Lion's Bride," which he bought from an unsuccessful conjurer named Bancroft. It was a good act and Lafayette was a headliner until his untimely death in a theater fire in England. Through the flames he dashed down under the stage to rescue his dog, Beauty, which seemed to be the one thing in the world he cared for.

Most colorful of the conjurers was Herbert (Bert) Albini. His sleights were excellent—coins, cards, small objects—and his egg-bag trick was unbelievable. He played the circuit pretty consistently and was never out of work on the Sullivan-Considine time (Washington, Oregon, Vancouver). The story is that Albini walked into the trial of John Considine and, as a surprise witness, testified that Considine's shooting of a policeman was in self-defense. Considine was freed, and thereafter Sullivan and Considine booking was Albini's. He could play the time whenever he liked and was under no obligations to take lip from the managers—dangerous license, for Albini did almost as he pleased anyway and to give him carte blanche was to feed him raw meat. More than Thurston, Albini fought his audiences—badgered and baited them. He'd come off stage, walk up and down the aisles, and work his sleights literally under the noses of his audiences, the while keeping up a running fire of banter and insult. He'd take a hat from a man about to be seated and ask: "What is in this hat?" answering himself: "Nothing." Then he'd tap the poor chap's head and remark: "Just as I thought, there never was anything in it." He not only invited hecklers; he dared them, in a high, rasping voice that enhanced his invective. No one was ever known to top him. A terrific drinker, he virtually soaked his bread in liquor. He took a fancy to Joe Cook in Joe's early days and occasionally Joe would chaperon him around, for Albini, although he had plenty of money, never could assume financial responsibility. He'd give Joe $100 and they'd start out, buying wine for the crowd in the first saloon they'd enter.

Albini came to America from England with his wife, Nellie Maguire, and for a time they appeared on the same bills although not in the same act. Nellie was a character singing comedienne. Good, she was, too, but her types never got over. Latterly she dropped out and Albini went it alone until he bottled himself into the grave. Albini was the only man in vaudeville, or any other activity for that matter, who could deal a poker hand while asleep.

Three other magicians, lesser lights, but good in their ways, are T. Nelson Downs, Elmer Ransom, and Imro Fox. Downs billed himself as the "King of Koins." He was, too. He was the first magician to specialize in coin palming and to build this one routine into an acceptable full act. He could palm twenty coins without showing and produce them one at a time, a feat the writer has never seen equaled. Poor Downs's specialized skill ruined him. It was impossible to freshen his act. He quit and went back to run a picture house at Marshalltown, Iowa. It was sad to read of his death in 1938.

Ransom's was chiefly a club act, but unique. So far as known, he was the first to exploit the physical whimseys of liquid air on the stage. He was a remarkable Punch and Judy worker, quite the best in America, and at Christmas and other holidays frequently played as many as five engagements a day.

The tricks of Imro Fox were mainly elemental, but he was a good comic and did well on the circuits for years. He had been a chef in Washington, D.C., and picked up magic for himself, trying it out at benefits. Once he filled in for a professional troupe. He was successful and kept going.

"If the Gentleman Will Concentrate."

The mental, or "mind-reading," acts were every bit as elaborate and complicated as the magicians' routines; sometimes more so. The biggest money-making mental act, although by no means the best, was that of John T. and Eva Fay. John was the son of Anna Eva Fay, who described herself as a psychist. Anna, with reason, was frightened of New York and stuck mostly to the medium towns of the East and Midwest. About 1900 John broke with his mother, married, and built up a flashy mental act mainly adapted from hers. His wife was the brains of the act, and through her remarkable ability the team developed a performance astonishing in its cleverness and finesse. Kellar, who once tried to hire her, said, "If I had, I would have produced the most marvelous second-sight act of all time." Based on a psychology that couldn't miss —the blind belief of a sucker public—the Fays kept going for years on full time at salaries that ranged from $1,500 to $3,000 a week.

Their methods were so simple it is outrageous anyone was fooled. The act of John and Eva was in two parts. First the exposition:

With Mrs. Fay seated on the stage, the lecturer began a grandiloquent spiel. Mrs. Fay, ladies and gentlemen, could read any clearly formulated question, but it was necessary that the questioner concentrate on his inquiry. Now the best way to concentrate is to write out your question. For the benefit of those who have not brought paper with them the aisle men will now distribute pads . . .

These pads consisted of three or four sheets of common newsprint, stapled to a square of hard celluloid about five by six inches. All sheets were alike, except that the second sheet was lightly coated with wax on the underside. Hard pencils were supplied, and the question was transferred from the bottom of the second sheet to the face of the third without becoming apparent because the wax was colorless. The subject was instructed to write out his question, tear the sheet off, and hand the pad back, retaining the question to help him concentrate at the proper time. The curtain fell, and the pads were "developed"—the third sheet was lightly dusted with powdered graphite. The graphite did not adhere to the waxed lines, and the question could be faintly discerned. All pads were marked to indicate the section of the house from which they came and this mark was transferred to the question sheet. The curtain rose on the second part.

Mrs. Fay was discovered seated on stage, but this time the high-backed armchair she used was plugged into an under-stage telephone that ran to a receiver over one ear, the receiver being concealed by her hair. She was then elaborately blindfolded and the answers started.

Hundreds of the questions suggested their own answers, but some were "blind," as "What is the number of my watch?" With such a one the understage man would phone up, "Guy on the left wants to know the number of his watch." Very pleasantly, Mrs. Fay would announce: "A gentleman on the left wants to know the number of his watch. But he is not giving me much help. He is not concentrating." This was the cue for an aisle man to dash up and suggest that if the gent would kindly write down the number of his watch on this pad it would aid him in concentrating. The patron retained the slip, of course, but gave the aisle man the number. He retreated to the head of the aisle, wrote it out and slipped it to the middle aisle man who was continually patrolling his section. The middle man would slip it to the leader of the orchestra (the Fays carried their own leader), who passed it understage. The number would then be telephoned to Mrs. Fay. "Ah," she would say, "I am getting better help from the gentleman on the left. Yes, the number of your watch is ———" and she would dish it out. Fay would yell "Right?" And the gent would nod, embarrassed, astonished. Other "blind" questions were handled in the same way. Now and then the aisle men would cross a recalcitrant, but it was easy to stall them. Most were obedient, really enjoyed their part in the act.

Often help was obtained from some well-posted local man,

the house manager, for example, who would point out to the aisle man, say, a well-known citizen who had recently been divorced. If he asked, and they usually did, oddly enough, "Will I be married soon?" Mrs. Fay would answer: "Not too soon, for your decree will not become final for another nine months." The elder Mrs. Fay, Anna, that is, a conscientious worker, used to send a man ahead of her towns to glean these personal details the week before she came in. John T. never bothered; just shouldered through.

While playing at Hammerstein's Victoria, their two leading aisle men, Louis M. Granat and Chauncey Herbert, rowed with the Fays and quit. Still sore, they cooked up an exposé. With Mrs. Herbert in the role of Mrs. Fay, they put it on at the New York Roof, almost across the street from the Fays. Nobody paid any attention, and after a futile four weeks the boys were canceled. The popularity of the Fays was tremendous; their audiences wanted to believe and looked on the exposé as heresy.

A part of the income in both Fay acts was the sale of booklets on fortunetelling. Each carried a coupon good for one question to be answered by mail. The booklets sold for a dollar each and hundreds were disposed of. In their spare time the aisle men would fake the answers to the mailed questions, especially those that could be answered with generalizations, as most could. Once a woman asked about a lost ring. She was advised: "Your first suspicion was correct." Whereupon the woman had her maid arrested and the terror-stricken girl hanged herself in her cell. Later the mislaid ring was found. It is a justifiable conjecture that many families must have been broken up, grievances multiplied, or difficulties enhanced by the answers, since nearly all the questions were personal and almost invariably involved relatives or sweethearts.

Another type of transmission act was "second sight." As originated by a man named Heller, it is still common in dime shows in the honky-tonks, but it was brought to an amazing stage of perfection by Julius Zancig and his wife.

In the simplest form of the routine (not the Zancigs') the

aisle man (only one) caused the blindfolded person on the stage to identify articles presented to him. It was done with vocal cues, each form of question meaning a definite object. "What do I hold?" might mean a handkerchief; "What have I here?" would be a knife. The cues ranged, on the average, from fifty to a hundred.

The Zancigs used many more and had several sets which could be switched on signal. Just as an auditor, or maybe a spy from a competing act, would discover that "What is this?" meant a watch, Julius would switch and that question became a necktie. It was impossible to catch him.

The Zancigs were an intelligent couple; Mrs. Zancig, a hunchback, was an extraordinary woman. When they developed their idea they practiced it one full year ten, twelve, and sometimes fourteen hours a day, before they attempted to sell booking time.

An important factor of their act was that it required so little help from the audience. With his wife on the stage, Julius would go through the aisles, talking to her with lightninglike gestures that were so natural they were unobservable except to the most recondite. They used gestures for common phrases, gestures for numbers, gestures for days of the week, the month, the year, for apparel, and for colors; it amounted to a rhythmic, physical shorthand. Approaching a man or woman, Julius would make a casual adjustment of his tie, or touch his left ear, or his right, and thus would give Mrs. Zancig pages of characterization about the subject and his question. Constant practice enabled the Zancigs to work rapidly and surely. They never approached the Fays in drawing power, but they enjoyed a distinction in the profession far beyond any the Fays ever earned.

Another clever stunt of the Zancigs was their reading routine. Julius, in the audience, carried a book similar to one held by Mrs. Zancig on the stage. She would, on demand, read from any page starting at any line or word. This was sent by number. It was also done by counting. A slight cough by

Julius would start Mrs. Z. counting. Another sound stopped her at the proper number. They could count to 100 or more without falling behind or advancing. It was most mysterious and the Zancigs were a riot in India, tremendous favorites with the native princes.

One of the Zancigs' experiences illustrates the blind allegiance of those who want to believe. The Zancigs were too clever to capture a great following, but to his death Sir Arthur Conan Doyle believed in them with childlike faith. On one of his visits to America he attended a bill on which they played. Entranced, he went backstage to meet them. He was so lavish in his compliments the gentle Julius was forced to remonstrate. "But, my dear Sir Arthur," he said, "I am sorry to disillusion you but our act is a fake. We rehearse it. It is done by signals." The novelist-spiritualist would have none of it. "You are psychic," he insisted. "You may not know it, but you are positively psychic."

At their pinnacle Mrs. Zancig died. Julius, heartbroken, tried to break in a couple of assistants but they could not bring to the act the superlative artistry of Mrs. Zancig. So he quit vaudeville and went to California where he made plenty of money as an astrologer. Carried a side line of crystal balls which he sold for $5 and $10 each, "with full instructions."

Poor Julius's retirement suggests the old yarn about the ventriloquist who had had a row with Albee. When you rowed with Albee you were out. This man could not get time anywhere, so he set up shop as a medium in Los Angeles. He was an excellent ventriloquist, an art he adapted to his new line. One day a lady begged him to permit her to hear the voice of her departed husband. She was in tears as she pleaded. "If you will only let me hear the voice of my beloved husband, if you will only let me talk to him, I will pay you $25."

"Lady," said the ex-performer, unconsciously going into his act, "for $25 I will drink a glass of water."

Another form of transmission, the "number" act, was

successfully exploited in vaudeville by the Svengallis. Svengalli always contended that he was really Slade, a notorious spiritualist and medium. He worked the aisles and was assisted on stage by a boy and a girl while Mrs. Slade was concealed behind a screen of black scrim through which she could read Svengalli's signals with opera glasses. The patron would whisper to Svengalli what piano piece he desired the girl to play, or the name of a celebrity he would like the boy to impersonate. Svengalli would indicate, and Mrs. Slade would translate the cues to the boy and girl. The transmission, which was absolutely silent, was done by dividing the face and torso into nine parts. For example, the left side of the forehead was 1, the center 2, the right 3; the left cheek was 4, the nose 5, the right cheek, 6; the left of the chin was 7, the center 8, the right 9. The left shoulder was 1, the center of the chest 2, the right shoulder 3; the left lung was 4, the solar plexus was 5, and the right lung 6; the left of the abdomen was 7, the center 8, the right 9. All these numbers referred to specific piano pieces or impersonations and could also be cued to mean words. The pianist and the impersonator were not privy to the code, merely doing what Mrs. Slade told them. For some time the act was a hit but, contrary to the experience of the Fays, when exposed by the newspapers, audiences lost interest and the Svengallis dropped out.

"Ah! Oh! Wonderful!"

There were never many funambulists in vaudeville, because the tight wire works best under canvas. Most of its exponents were circus, fair, or carnival performers, but a few ventured the narrow confines of the vaudeville stage, and as the slack wire was developed these increased. The slack was better suited for shorter lengths and, though easier to negotiate than the tight wire, was more showy and appeared more dangerous. More tricks could be performed on it than on the tight wire.

Most famous of the tight-wire experts was the Frenchman,

Charles Blondin, because of his feat in 1859 of first crossing the gorge of Niagara Falls. Another capable tight-rope walker was Ella Zuila, who later teamed with her daughter under the billing "E. Z. and Lulu." They played a few halls for winter revenue when the circuses closed.

By lowering the tight wire the Meers Brothers successfully worked the vaudevilles, in fact, became so adept it is hard to recall an act, beyond the incomparable Bird Millman's, that excelled theirs. The brothers, Alf and George, came from an old English circus family. Alf was the feature, a highly finished performer, the first to accomplish a cartwheel on the wire. He used George as a breather and for double passing. When George married a girl in an English musical and went off with the show Alf took on a younger brother, Fred, who is currently manager of the Eden Musee in Coney Island. Later Alf added George Omo to form the Three Meers for an act in which he let the other two do the hard work while he clowned it. Alf also originated the "endless wire," a wire loop passing over pulleys, given motion by a crank at one end and with a sort of bicycle arrangement at the other. The only trick possible with this gadget was running, but it gave a fine two-minute finish to the act for "Ahs! Ohs!" and applause.

Of the girls, Virginia Aragon, a Spanish lass of willow-branch grace, and Millman were the best. Virginia worked the high wire and was a bit skittish of vaudeville stage dimensions. She was a natural. Of a long line of wire walkers, her mother told an old friend of the writer that she had done her wire work until within three weeks of Virginia's birth, concealing her condition with fluffy skirts.

Bird Millman began with her parents as the Millman Trio, working circuses and Midwestern honky-tonks. When she passed the S.P.C.C.'s age restriction her parents wisely put her out solo; she had gone so far beyond them they would have hammed her act.

The present topper among wire performers is Con Coleano, the first to discard all balancing aids. Few vaudeville audiences saw him. He preferred to work abroad, although he circused America often.

Performers—Tooth and Claw.

Animal comedy was the surest of laugh material, provoking alike the risibles of sap and savant. The only time anyone ever caught Bill Morris laughing was at the antics of Berzac's trick mule. Animal acts were standard in vaudeville, nor was it solely because of their humor. The idea of a trained brute, or lesser animal, imitating man, his so-called master, and presuming upon his mentality was also compelling—a point recognized, if not understood, by the managers.

Throughout the span of vaudeville all kinds of animals were shown at one time or another—dogs, ponies, elephants, lions, tigers, goats, cats, pigs, snakes, seals, bears, monkeys, and birds—cockatoos, parrots, even canaries.

In the dog acts (which predominated), mutts were much the best. Real trainers know that the mixed breeds make the best "students." They learn more rapidly the greatest variety of tricks, have more impudence, health, and confidence than the nervous, temperamental thoroughbreds. Yet the mutts must be selected—cast, in fact—for certain breeds are fit for but one thing, others are more versatile. The greyhound is a wonderful leaper, but that is all he can do. The small white poodle is bright and willing and can be taught a number of pretty little tricks—but nothing sensational. The large black woolly French poodles are natural clowns. Frequently they unconsciously introduce some bit of comedy which, of course, the trainer always leaves in. Collies, spaniels, chows, Dalmatians, were never practical as performers. Pointers and setters were used only for posing in hunting scenes and tableaux; St. Bernards made a wonderful appearance pulling a wagonload of dog passengers; and occasionally great Danes and mastiffs appeared as "police"—which let them out. They were too slow and cumbersome. Best were the fox terriers.

All performing animals have to be cued for their tricks.

This is done in many different ways: by a snap of the fingers (unseen by the audience), by the tone of voice, by holding the riding whip in a certain position, tapping the foot, or whispering. Coin's Dogs, one of the best animal acts in vaudeville, presented a village episode in a miniature set without trainer or assistants in sight. The dogs were cued off stage, each performing his role as directed behind the set.

Bears were mainly used for comedy. Usually they work willingly but are subject to occasional sulks and then are dangerous. Spissardy, whose troupe of bears was outstanding, was once badly torn when playing with the pet of his lot between shows. Apdale, who had a mixed animal act, presented a lump of sugar to his most playful and gentlest bear, who promptly bit off a finger. With bears the trainers could only take chances; no sense in beating them. In passing, animals in vaudeville acts were for the most part treated kindly, if only as a matter of business. A beaten dog cringes; can't perform, or if he does shows his lickings in perfunctory stunts.

Trainers say that tigers and leopards are worse to work with than lions. Fearlessness, and liking for the fierce felines, are the trainer's best assets. He has his loaded cane or pistol or protective chair or stool. But the best defensive is a stream from a firehose.

The domestic feline—the writer, who adores them, regrets to say—never graduated with high honors in vaudeville although there were a number of successful cat acts. Of course, these cats are not dangerous, but they are unreliable, merely because they are supreme individualists, preferring to do the thing they want at the time they want to do it; which should be understandable.

Best of the cat acts was Tetchow's. Tetchow carried about thirty cats and two assistants. No babe in arms received better care than these mousers. All were common animals; no haughty Persians, snooty Angoras, or petulant Siamese—just good, healthy toms and tabbies. Tetchow combed and brushed them, kept them in spotless cages, fed them milk, raw eggs, and chopped meat, and exercised them regularly. Yet even he could get from his pets, for indeed they were that, but one trick each. His star performer was a tom who ran from the wings, scrambled up a rope hanging from the proscenium arch, got into a basket attached to a parachute and came floating down to the stage.

It may be unnecessary to say that goats are difficult to work with and more unreliable than cats. It would certainly be an unpleasant reminder to Charles Andress, who had an excellent goat act. The poor man never knew from one performance to the next what his goats would do. Once a goat in his troupe jumped nimbly over the footlights, trotted leisurely down the center aisle, stopped midway casually to regard the audience, then frightened a woman patron witless as he lunged toward her. Billy only wanted to nibble at her program. Another time one of Andress's goats walked out on the show, butted his way through the stage door, ran around to the front of the house, eased the doorman out of his path, entered the theater, loped up to the balcony, trotted down the aisle to the rail, took stance and calmly viewed the act of his fellow goats. Goats are never frightened, just unconventional.

A phase of animal-act training likely to be forgotten by the lay audience is that the animals must be accustomed to them—to the audience. After finally obtaining mastery of the routine —it may take years—the trainer must make his animals unmindful of applause, laughter, noise, and music. After their long training in quiet places they are rehearsed with footlights, synthetic laughter, applause, and music before the act is presented to the public.

BOOK IV
The Revels End

Madames of the Marquee

THE great feminine names of vaudeville—Tanguay, Bayes, Janis, Franklin—were those of specialized artists whose talent and personality were unique. There were others, fine performers all, but these four were tops in box-office draw and acclaim.

The terrific Tanguay was an electrified hoyden, a temperamental terror to the managers, a riotous joy to her audiences. A singing and dancing comedienne, it is easy to analyze her act: it was assault and battery. She cared no whit for anyone and under the very nose of Albee got more sex into her shouted numbers than could be found in a crib street in a mining town.

One of her earliest ventures was in a musical farce George M. Cohan wrote for Smith and Scott, a male team of variety comics. Paired with Nellie Lawrence (later Monroe, Mack, and Lawrence), Eva did a double singing and dancing specialty in the show which opened in the New York Star Theatre, Broadway and Fourteenth Street, near the old Morton House. This was in the late nineties when Midwestern stock and one-night tank shows flourished. So when the Cohan show closed, Tanguay set out for the Midwest where she took on rowdy-dowdy soubrette roles in repertoire, including some of Harry Blaney's ten-twent'-thirt' thrillers.

Her rise thereafter is unexplainable. When she finished soubretting she played a few Western vaudeville dates as just another noisy hoofer when, out of nowhere, she "flared in the lights." Her salary jumped from the $40 class to thousands and when Mike Shea sought to book her in Buffalo she demanded $2,500 a week, an incredible figure for the early 1900's. She and Mike abused each other until Tanguay finally offered to "buy the house," that is, play the week and take for her share everything over the average weekly receipts. Shea agreed. And she cleared more than $12,000 for her share. Then Shea offered her the following week in Toronto, (where he controlled a house managed by his brother) at $2,500. Tanguay laughed long, loud, and harshly.

It is virtually impossible to overestimate Tanguay's personality, or her influence in vaudeville. In the years she was tops this incredible woman alone jolted the maudlin period of the early 1900's away from its eye-dabbing with the vigor of unashamed sex. Precisely when the vaudeville public was listening to such treacle as "You'll Be Sorry Just Too Late," Tanguay was screaming "I Want Some One to Go Wild with Me"; "It's All Been Done Before but Not the Way I Do It"; and "Go as Far as You Like." These naughtily suggestive titles she developed in her brassy delivery almost to physical fulfillment.

Keith was often chagrined by her deliberate flaunting of his Puritan policy and she had many rows with the United Booking Office. They were always sorry they brought it up, for Tanguay was not only a turkey-talker, she was box office and they knew it. She was in constant difficulties with the management; with audiences. In Pittsburgh a bit of comedy she introduced (a short "blue" monologue about a chicken) was tossed out by the authorities. The unabashed Eva, at the reputed salary of $3,000 a week, proceeded with "Nothing Bothers Me" and gaily continued to shake her torso and wriggle her thighs, explosively shrieking "I Love to Be Crazy."

She announced repeatedly "In Vaudeville I am second to none," and insisted on billing that labeled her "The Girl Who Made Vaudeville Famous." Some of this was justified. She was variously called "The Sambo Girl," "The Cyclonic Comedienne," and the "Evangelist of Joy"—everything but "Miss Brainstorm," which seems to have been an oversight by the chroniclers of the time. The newspapers kidded her, but she loved it, and so did the public. She never cared what the papers printed about her. The perennial lost-jewel stories of her press agents always gave the boys a twit or two and of one the *World* wrote: "With the vaudeville season right at hand that melancholy business of recovering $10,000 worth of lost jewels came up again yesterday to bother Eva Tanguay . . . "

It was no bother. She was a master of publicity. The times she was "kidnaped" when failing to appear at some honky-tonk in the sticks were legion. She can scarcely be challenged as the most dynamic personality developed in vaudeville and to the fanfare that fed this characterization she added a surprising frankness. She once told an interviewer that her entire success had been due to the exploitation of her personality. "That's all there is to it," she said. "As a matter of fact, I am not beautiful, I can't sing, I do not know how to dance. I am not even graceful." It is a matter of fact.

Eva rowed with everybody. Rowed? They were brawls, and more than one got into the courts. Presumably, her first husband was Johnny Ford, but she may have had an earlier, named Leach. At any rate, a man so named was arrested with her after an altercation with a brakeman on a train in which Leach drew a gun. Des Moines police let them go.

Her energy was no artistic illusion. In Louisville she tossed a stagehand down a flight of stairs because "he was in my way" when she was taking a curtain call. Hurt him, too, and he hauled her off to court where she was fined $50. She paid with a $1,000 bill. (This was no gag—$1,000 bills were a Tanguay gesture; she often carried five to fifteen of them in her purse.) The civil suit that followed she settled for $1,000. In 1910 when starring in "My Lady" she tore into a chorus girl named Jeannette Jordan, grabbed her by the hair, flung her against the stage wall, and stalked out of the show. Said Jeannette jeered at her and made nasty cracks, probably about her rumored associations with other performers and managers. Her name was linked to many. Ford in his counterdivorce action accused her of intimacies with numerous men. But "Nothing Bothers Me" trilled Eva. And soon after she announced (prematurely, as it turned out) the writing of a book, "A Hundred Loves" which she admitted was to be semiautobiographical. "Some people," she said, "will recognize instances and situations."

In Evansville, Ind., in 1905, deciding not to play the matinee, she slept blissfully through the afternoon and the manager hung a $100 fine on her. Incensed, she seethed through her evening performance and at its conclusion shredded the asbestos curtain with a dagger. She settled this for $15. Playing Morgan's Grand Theatre in Sharon, Pa., in 1914, she bawled out the audience for hick-town saps and cursed the management from the footlights because her dressing-room mirror was not only not beveled but was twelve by eighteen inches instead of fourteen by twenty-four. This house was run by a tough Irishman named John Murray who happened to be in the audience. He ordered her off stage, rang the curtain, and refunded his patrons' money. Then he went back to see Eva. Both survived, and it is still a miracle on Broadway.

She was constantly walking out of shows because managers wanted her to share billing. This brought about her most serious row with the New York Palace management. The late Walter Kingsley, press agent for the house, inadvertently sent out news releases for a future bill featuring a Gilbert and Sullivan chorus and mentioning Tanguay as "among other acts." Enraged, she hauled her trunks out of the Palace, but this time Manager Elmer Rogers beat her to it. Guessing her reaction, he had already arranged for Frank Tinney to go on in her place. And that there were no casualties is another Broadway mystery.

So tempestuous and undependable was she that even the gentle Percy Williams (who named a theater for her) when booking her at his theaters exacted a $5,000 cash bond from her to keep the peace—and her engagements.

Her most publicized act was "Salome" which she put on in 1908 in a costume called "two-pearled." This aroused the hair shirts from Brooklyn to Vancouver. Disdaining the protests, she kept it going and made a lot of money with the act.

Eva was born in Marbleton, Canada, of a Parisian physician and a French-Canadian mother in 1878 and in forty years of trouping she never lied about her age. Her estimated earnings in vaudeville were $2,000,000, which she lost in the 1929 crash. Thereafter she eased slowly down the skids to comparative obscurity, dabbling in Los Angeles real estate and other ventures until virtually blinded by cataracts.

The Banner of Janis.

Almost as great a draw was the kindly, gentle Janis whose appearance you could set your watch by, who only once caused the slightest headache, and who was generally adored by managers, performers, and audiences. Elsie had but one thing in common with Tanguay: Janis, too, never lied about her age. She was born in Columbus, Ohio, in 1889 and from her Fauntleroy roles as a child of six she was managed by her mother, Mrs. Josephine Bierbower (Elsie's real name), until her mother's death.

Up to 1905 she was mainly identified with East Lynne-Two Orphan honky-tonk stock. Thereafter she played mainly musicals in one of which, on the New York Theatre Roof, "When We Were Forty-one" (*sic!*), she interpolated her first professional attempt at mimicry. Her success was instantaneous and she developed her imitations to an art form only equaled by Cissie Loftus. With song, dance, and imitations she carved out a captivating act that graced vaudeville for years.

The week of April 14 in the season of 1923–1924 was Holy Week, the worst week in the theatrical year. To bolster his bill at the Palace, Eddie Darling booked in Elsie Janis, Jim Barton, and for added measure, Bard and (Jack) Pearl, a fine comedy team that was laying off for the week in one of the Shubert "Passing Shows." All appearances of Janis at the Palace, as per contract, were heralded by an enormous banner, with her name alone across it, which was hung over the marquee. The thing was as big as a twenty-four sheet and Barton, aware of Janis's special billing, agreed not to top it, but insisted that his name appear in equal size type on the same line. He wanted this in writing but when Darling pledged his word Barton waived the contractual clause.

Bard and Pearl, although they agreed to take third billing, also insisted on the one line and equal size type. Done and done, and Darling cautioned Rogers that all must be arranged as per agreement.

The week opened with the biggest Monday ever registered for Holy Week in the Palace's history. The next night Darling called on Janis backstage. "What about the banner," asked Janis, "that it isn't up?" She told him that she had spoken to Rogers about it and he had promised. So Darling went to Rogers and asked how come? Rogers said he was just stalling her.

Thursday morning Darling received a note from Mrs. Bierbower. If the banner was not up by noon of that day, she wrote, Elsie would not appear again. It was not up by noon and Elsie did not appear (did not appear, for that matter, on any Palace bill thereafter).

Janis's walkout was immediately telephoned to Albee, who was ill at his home. He dictated a notice that, since Miss Janis had no regard for her contract(!) and still less for her public, she would never again be booked at the Palace. The notice was blown up and prominently displayed in the Palace's lobby where it drew large crowds and much comment unfavorable to the management. The public suspected that Janis was right.

Darling tried to persuade John Murdock, acting for Albee, not to post the sign and thus give Janis the first black mark of her career; explained also that it was not her fault. Murdock took no heed. But that night when Darling went to the theater the sign was gone and he asked Walter Kingsley for an explanation. "The thing created an awful stink," said Kingsley. "The newspapers are very sore that such a thing should be done to Janis. So I phoned Albee and he ordered it out and burned."

The next day Ted Lauder, Albee's son-in-law and vice-president of the circuit, read Darling a letter that Albee was sending to Janis. Albee expressed his indignation at her treatment from his underlings; said that if he had been about the incident would never have happened, placed the entire blame on Darling, and enclosed a check for $3,750, her salary for the unfinished week.

This humiliation Darling refused to accept. He went to Janis and her mother at the Algonquin and told them the truth. Also that the check was but a gesture and Albee expected her to return it. He advised her to keep it, and she did.

Next day came one of those "interoffice communications" from Albee to Rogers and Darling. As both were to blame, so Albee put it, they could send him their checks for $1,875 each as their share in redeeming the mistake. Darling didn't pay.

Nora, the Fantastic.

Nora Bayes was the American Guilbert, mistress of effortless talent in gesture, poise, delivery, and facial work. No one could outrival her in dramatizing a song. She was entrancing, exasperating, generous, inconsiderate—a split personality; a fascinating figure.

Her real name was Leonora Goldberg and she was born, presumably in Milwaukee, in 1880. Contemporary pieces about her vary the town, fixing it as Los Angeles, Joliet, or Chicago. The trio of errors can scarcely be casual and may be significant. George Ade in an article on Bayes gives her birthplace as Milwaukee. And, for whatever it may mean, in twenty years of vaudeville trouping she would never play the Wisconsin city.

Jay Rial of the Chicago Opera House is said to have given her her first chance at $25 a week in 1899. In 1907 she sang in the Cadillac Hotel in New York. Her response was only so-so, but Al Fields, of Fields and Lewis, gambled on her development, became her manager. Later Bayes and Fields opened the Fifth Avenue Theatre (with Lily Langtry headlining), and she clicked. Her success was short-lived for Fields, for soon afterward she met Jack Norworth, fell in love with him, and they teamed for an act that was one of the greatest in vaudeville in artistry and financial yield. They opened in Atlantic City in 1908 and were received with such acclaim Percy Williams booked them into the Colonial in New York at $2,500 weekly.

The following year they went into the "Follies"—and out. Suspecting Norworth of too friendly an interest in one of the girls, Nora quit and Norworth followed her. (Tanguay replaced her.) Thereafter, despite a succession of nuisance injunctions first by Ziegfeld, later by Werba and Luescher to whom they were under contract in 1911, they continued in vaudeville, billing themselves as the "stage's happiest couple," an ironic designation erased in 1913 when Nora divorced Norworth.

Within two weeks after the final decree Nora married Harry Clarke, her third husband. (Otto Gressing, of Chicago, had been her first.) But Clarke did not accompany her when she went to London in the spring of 1914 to play the Empire under the management of Alfred Butt. She failed, and so did her health, and she went to Kissingen, Germany, to recover from what may have been the first manifestation of the cancer that was to eat out her life. As a further aggravation, Norworth, who played the Hippodrome in London at the time she was flopping at the Empire, was a tremendous success.

Restored at the German resort, Nora returned to America and on September 21, 1914, began a thirty-week tour of vaudeville at the Palace. She was billed as "The Greatest Single Woman Singing Comedienne in the World" which was almost as good as the billing she had insisted on when, as a two-act with Norworth, she was headlined:

NORA BAYES

Assisted and Admired by Jack Norworth

Her United Booking Office contract called for a salary of $1,500 weekly and this she forfeited, January 16, 1915, when she demanded $75 more. It was refused and she quit the tour, tossing away $33,000 worth of appearances. She further punctuated the year by divorcing Clarke.

Patching up her row with Albee, she returned to vaudeville and behaved herself until Thanksgiving Day, 1916, in Philadelphia. All Keith contracts for Philadelphia and Boston contained an ironbound clause that the performer was to play a third show on Thanksgiving Day and New Year's Day. Not Bayes. "I just won't play it," she told Manager Jordan. Eddie Darling was brought in. She told him: "That is the way I get ahead. They'll listen to me now. But when I lose my voice they won't do anything for me."

"But you had a contract!" exclaimed Darling.

"That was Nora Bayes," she answered. "I didn't do it."

Her irritability increased as her health declined. Her friends, and she had hosts, never heard a complaint, were still under her spell; still were received and royally entertained by a gracious woman at her brownstone-front home, 624 West End Avenue, in New York, where her household was managed by Ada Patterson assisted by her two colored maids, Ida and Belle. In her top-flight years her annual earnings must have averaged $100,000. She saved little.

In the last years of her life Frank Sullivan, gentleman and

NORA BAYES

satirist, became one of her closest friends. The friendship developed in characteristic fashion for both. At the time (about 1923) Frank was on the staff of the old New York *World*. In one of Nora's publicity yarns it was announced that she could not practice her songs in a Pullman which was why she had to have a private car. So Frank was assigned to find out from Nora why she couldn't sing in a Pullman. He phoned Edna Haskins, Nora's secretary, for an appointment. The frigid Haskins put him off, but Frank went back and wrote the piece anyway. Made it kind of mean, too. After its publication Nora wrote him a note. It was friendly, with no reference to the ribbing. Frank answered it—the initial note of a long and delightful correspondence which Nora subsequently had bound. It was almost a year before they met.

By this time she had acquired a fourth husband, Arthur Gordoni, and had adopted three children, Norman, Leonora, and Peter. Her marriage to Gordoni ended in 1922 after two years, and in 1924 she was slipping badly—played the Palladium in London for Charles Gulliver in a ten weeks' contract for $300 a week, three shows a day.

She had messed her act, too; used a dramatic technique and business foreign to her style and insisted on talking about her adopted children. Albee told her to stick to her songs and comedy. She refused. And although she was receiving $2,000 weekly, Darling finally had to put her in No. 3 position on the bill, a lowly spot. Ultimately he told her he wouldn't book her any more.

She made a surprising recovery in 1926, succeeding, by a ruse, in getting back on the Palace bill and the Keith circuit at $2,500 weekly. Darling had booked in Cissie Loftus (at $1,500 weekly) and he suggested to Nora that when Cissie who was living in Nora's home at the time, did her imitation of Bayes, Bayes go up on the stage and do it with her. They had introduced this at the Palladium in London and it had gone well. "I'll do it if you'll book me at the Palace next week," said Nora. Which is how she returned to the circuit.

Meantime Nora had married a fifth husband, a wealthy businessman named Benjamin Friedland. Generous, he did not wish her to continue, yet never attempted to keep her out of the theater. It seemed now, despite Friedland's devotion, she had no place else to go. Previously she had gone out to Cleveland, where Norworth was playing an engagement on the same bill with Trixie Friganza, to plead with him to rejoin her. Norworth refused.

But she had smoothed her troubles with Albee and Darling and 1927 seemed like old times. In that year Darling booked her through to San Francisco where she was as big a smash as she had been in the old days. On the bill was a young chap named Jack Benny, drawing $450 a week as a singing single. (That was his West Coast salary; in the East he got $350.) Benny suggested to Bayes that she do an afterpiece with him and at first she indignantly declined. Then, thinking it over— maybe . . . Finally she consented to try it, and a pair of obscure hoofers known as Burns and Lynn (Burns: brother of George of Burns and Allen) were included in the piece.

The sketch was tremendous and they played it three weeks. They went on to Los Angeles, and thence to Chicago, with the afterpiece a smash in both cities. Max Gordon, who saw it in Chicago, said it was the best he had ever heard. Meanwhile they were preparing for N.V.A. week at the New York Palace. Set for Easter Week, always a sellout for a good show, this was to be especially gala. Darling had booked Nora Bayes, Jack Benny, Ann Pennington, Brooke Johns, the Avon Comedy Four, and Burns and Lynn, with Frisco as the guest star.

Sophie Tucker had just returned from Europe. Sophie was a client of Bill Morris who asked $3,000 a week for her. The money didn't matter but Morris, foe of the Albee circuit, did, so Darling traded on her friendship. Would she appear at the first matinee—it was for N.V.A.—for nothing? Certainly, if Darling would give her a banner out front like Janis's. All right. "And where would you like to appear on the bill,

Sophie?" "Any place you like," said Sophie. So Darling billed her to close the show. Easter Monday morning Sophie's sister called Darling. Sophie would just love No. 5 spot because she was bringing in Eddie Elkins's band from her night club with her. Darling changed the bill accordingly.

An hour later the sister called again and said Tucker wanted to close the show. Ten minutes later she wanted to close the first half. Wearily Darling said O.K. and revised his bill so that Frisco closed the show; not too good a spot for Frisco who, although a splendid comic and well able to hold it, was trying a new act. Just as Darling was leaving his office for luncheon at 1:45 P.M., Frisco was shown in. He was so mad he couldn't talk at all, and at first Darling thought it was a gag. Finally he told Darling he was not going on. "Why not?" asked Darling. "Miss Bayes ain't gonna change no show for me," said Frisco. "How can that be?" countered Darling. "Bayes hasn't even arrived yet. Her train isn't due until 2 P.M." But Frisco, suspecting trouble, remained firm. Frisco was a valuable player. Moreover, he was getting a special salary of $800 a week for the act. Again Darling turned on the charm. No. Then Darling told him that if he walked out he would have to forfeit his salary. Frisco took out his wallet and laid $800 on Darling's desk. Darling brushed it back. "I know that you will be as big a hit as anybody on that bill," coaxed Darling, "and if you will go on that closing spot just this afternoon you can call your own position thereafter if you are not satisfied." Reluctantly Frisco agreed.

Promptly at 2:05 that Easter Monday afternoon the Palace curtain rose. The first two acts went over well. But during the third number an usher came to Darling, who was in the audience, and told him Manager Elmer Rogers wanted him backstage. He went back, and walked into a terrific argument between Bayes and Tucker. Just as Tucker had arrived with her band, Bayes strode to the wings and announced to the rest of the performers that she was the headliner and would not permit Tucker to go on before her. Darling first went to

Tucker. Then he pleaded with Bayes. "Nora," he said, finally, "the years have straightened things out. There shouldn't be any more trouble between us." She told him to go to hell. He did not have to take that. But he could not help thinking of Burns and Lynn who had canceled all their Orpheum time for this great break to do the afterpiece with Bayes. It would have been a sure smash, taken them out of the small-time hoofing class. And Darling renewed his plea but Bayes insisted she was going on before Tucker. Yet while she was speaking the stagehands were striking her set and putting up Tucker's scenery as Benny was finishing his number in one. "You'll have to give in to Miss Tucker," Darling told Bayes. She replied: "Your stomach is a little bad." And Darling, who had never liked her, recalling her inconsideration for the people who had canceled their time, her disregard for her public, decided that in no circumstances, if it cost him his job, could she go on. He led her to the stage door, pushed her through it, and closed it.

Two masters of ceremonies announced this benefit: Robert Emmet Keane and Burr McIntosh. It was Keane's turn when Darling came back to the wings. He drew Keane aside: "I want you to go out on that stage and repeat everything that happened here. I do not want you to say Miss Bayes is ill. Repeat everything that happened, but without the profanity." At first Keane refused; said he would not belittle any artist before the public. But he was being paid $100 and was therefore under obligation to carry out Darling's instructions. Keane went out on the stage describing everything as Darling had told him to. Then Tucker went on and was a riot. And the heartbroken little Burns and Lynn, who had gambled their Orpheum time for this one big Palace chance, went back to the sticks.

Darling was now shy an act for the evening performance. About 6 P.M. he telephoned Miss Tucker, to ask if she would appear again. "Anything for a pal," said the agreeable Sophie, "but come up and have a bite with us." He did and found some dozen people, including her family, about a well-laden table. At the finish of the meal Darling asked Tucker what she would ask to play out the week and she said, "I don't want anything. You did me a favor and I'm doing one for you." At this point her brother, Phil Abuza (Abuza was Sophie's real name), delivered a lusty kick against Darling's shin, intended, of course, for Sophie. Later one of those present told Darling that when he (Darling) had left, Phil called Sophie's agent, Bill Morris, and asked what she was going to be paid.

Each day up to Thursday, which was the dead line for the following week's show, Darling asked her to name a salary and each time she declined. Darling then told her he was holding her over for a second week and the next day, Friday, Bill Morris came to Darling and asked, "What are you going to pay my star this week?" Darling told him she had repeatedly declined all offers. "You didn't expect a woman like Sophie Tucker who is packing them in to work for nothing, did you?" asked Morris. Morris then told Darling that Sophie had instructed him to say that unless she was paid $5,500 for the two weeks she would not go on. "I guess we'll have to give it to her," said Darling, and made out the contract. "That's the way to do business," said Morris, "No," said Darling, "she should have mentioned salary at the start and I would have given her the $6,000 you asked for." Then Morris asked if there was anything Darling cared to say to Miss Tucker. "Tell her," he said, "she will never play the Palace again so long as I am booking it."

They were always talking like that. A year later Sophie called Darling, explained that she had acted only on Morris's advice and since they were her agents she felt obliged to obey. Darling (who needed a headliner) told her the only way she could adjust matters would be to play the Palace the following week, for free. Sophie agreed. And at the end of the week Darling sent her a check for $2,500.

Bayes's difficulty with Darling must have seared her; she

declined tragically. On the night of March 16, 1928, she telephoned Darling. She said she was giving a party and please
wouldn't he come? About midnight. When he arrived Nora
received him alone, in her dressing gown. She sang some of her
old songs, a thing she would never do. She said she was going
away for a week with Mrs. Condé Nast and would Darling
please do her a favor? Would he please (she had never pleaded)
put up a set of her photographs in the lobby of the Palace and
announce her as coming the following week? She would accept
any salary. Next day the photographs were duly mounted in
the lobby, and two days later, March 19, 1928, she was dead.

The Resourceful Petrova.

In the season of 1912, Jesse Lasky, a successful producer of
vaudeville acts, attempted a new vaudeville diversion along
Continental lines at the Fulton Theatre in New York. In
association with William Harris, he opened a cabaret—a
variety of sketches and acts comparable to our contemporary
night clubs except that there was no dance floor. He called it
the "Folies Bergère." New York muffed its Parisian fling; it
was far too advanced for a public that liked its vaudeville
straight and its comedy more snappy, less Gallic. But a minor
cause of the failure may have been a "Russian" woman
(imported for the show by Harris) whom audiences greeted
with cheers—Bronx brand.

It was not wholly the fault of the girl. Her appearances were
badly timed; her act, a dramatic sketch, was usually performed to the obligato of rattling dishes in the arms of
scurrying waiters. When the "Folies" closed, Lasky asked
Darling if he would give Olga Petrova a chance on the circuit.
"Who is Olga Petrova?" asked Darling. "She was that Russian
girl in the Folies," said Lasky. "She was a failure," said
Darling, "what do I want her for?"

Two years later, in 1914, George V. Hobart induced Darling to go up to Poli's in New Haven, Conn., to see a new act
of his called "Night of the Party" in the hope Darling would

give it a route. On the bill was Petrova. Among other musical numbers she sang "My Hero" from "The Chocolate Soldier" in four different voices and gave an imitation with a full stage set of Lena Ashwell in "The Shulamite." Darling considered her sensational and so did the audience: she was tall, shapely, her reddish hair flamed, and she wore gowns like a Lanvin dream girl.

Darling, who was then booking Proctor's Fifth Avenue Theatre in New York, told her he would engage her for the following week. She said she would appear on certain conditions. "What are they?" asked Darling. "Well," Petrova said, "I don't want any money and I don't want any billing." Then she said that if she was a success she would ask to be held over the second week at $125. Darling, much puzzled, agreed.

The Tuesday after her opening the theater began receiving phone calls: who is this woman who cries such real tears in "The Shulamite" and sings so wonderfully and why is she not named on the bill? At the close of a second phenomenal week Petrova said to Darling, "Unless I am billed as the headliner I cannot play the third week." And Darling told her, "Well, we have a man, an English performer, that we've got to headline next week. But I will explain the circumstances of your coming in here. I think he'll step aside for you and take second billing." "All right," said Petrova. "But please remember that it is very important that I be the headliner next week. I don't mind going down to second billing the fourth week, but next week I must be the headliner."

Darling went to the English performer. He was R. A. Roberts who had made a considerable success in American vaudeville with sketches and characterizations from Dickens's novels. He was always headlined and was paid $1,250 a week. "Who is she?" asked Roberts. "It is nobody you know," answered Darling; "a woman named Olga Petrova." Roberts, who was quite charming, agreed to second billing on condition his name be in the same size type. When Darling returned to Petrova she asked, "Did you tell Mr. Roberts it was I who asked to be headlined?" "Yes," said Darling. "That is very nice," said Petrova.

About noon before the opening Monday matinee of the third week Roberts telephoned Darling. "Why didn't you tell me it was that woman?" he demanded. "If I had recognized her name I would never have consented. I am walking out on the show." He did, and Darling went to Petrova. "I was quite sure he would walk out," she said. "That is why I wanted the headline. Let me tell you a story. My name is Muriel Harding. I am a London Cockney girl. When I first started in the theater I got a job in this man's company on a tour of South Africa. It was the most miserable year of my life, and I vowed that someday I would make him pay for the way he treated me. It was quite interesting when I met him at rehearsal today. I went over to him and said, 'How do you do, Mr. Roberts.' And he said, 'what are you doing here?' And I said, 'I am the headliner.' And he walked out."

This could be done in 1912–1914, when only play-or-pay contracts were in force. The Keith-Albee offices could have required Roberts to play, but he was so incensed that Darling felt it was better to let him go. He canceled his tour and never played again in America.

Still receiving $125 weekly, Petrova was booked through the Middlewest where, playing Keith's theater in Indianapolis, she fell ill. The house physician, Dr. John D. Stewart, was sent for. The association developed a romance that led to marriage. Before his death in 1938 Dr. Stewart became a leading New York surgeon.

Petrova continued in vaudeville until, taking the eye of the Shuberts, she appeared on Broadway in two legitimate plays: "Panthea" and "The White Picture." She did not make a lot of money, but it is a safe wager she did not lose much. As a matter of fact, the plays pegged her for the silent movies in which she made a fortune, drawing, at one time, the incredible salary (for 1916–1917) of $10,000 a week.

But in 1917 Petrova again came to Darling. She said she

had been told in pictures: "You are through. You don't draw any more. In certain towns you do not mean anything." She asked, "Can you get me a ten weeks' engagement?" And Darling told her, yes.

"But," she added, "I only want to play these towns: Providence, Oklahoma City, Columbus, Indianapolis, Fort Worth, and Houston."

"You couldn't make those jumps," said Darling.

"I will make them," she said. She then inquired about top salaries.

"In Columbus we played Nora Bayes for a test at $1,500," said Darling.

"Then give me $1,501, and I shall be the highest paid performer in that town," she said. Darling told her that in Providence Ethel Barrymore drew a top of $2,500. Petrova then asked $2,501 for Providence.

They were a curious series of contracts, all of them reading "plus $1," violating the standard Keith-Albee form, so Darling kept them from Albee. He asked Petrova if he could not make one out for the Palace in New York, but she declined.

Well (somehow making the jumps), she played the towns she asked for to tremendous business using her old act of songs, imitations, and "The Shulamite" interlude. Albee, checking returns, said to Darling, "I want that woman booked into every house on the circuit." And Darling could only reply, "She won't play them."

Only once did Albee interfere with her and the rift almost severed their relations, for Petrova was as determined as he. The row was over the recitation of her verses, "To a Child That Enquires." Here is the poem:

To a Child That Enquires

How did you come to me, my sweet?
From the land that no man knows?
Did Mr. Stork bring you here on his wings?
Were you born in the heart of a rose?

Did an angel fly with you down from the sky?
  Were you found in a gooseberry patch?
Did a fairy bring you from fairyland
  To my door—that was left on the latch?

No—my darling was born of a wonderful love,
  A love that was Daddy's and mine.
A love that was human, but deep and profound,
  A love that was almost divine.

Do you remember, sweetheart, when we went to the Zoo?
  And we saw that big bear, with a grouch?
And the tigers and lions, and that tall kangaroo
  That carried her babes in a pouch?

Do you remember I told you she kept them there safe
  From the cold and the wind, till they grew
Big enough to take care of themselves,
  Well, dear heart, that's just how I first cared for you.

I carried you under my heart, my sweet,
  And I sheltered you, safe from alarms,
Till one wonderful day the dear God looked down—
  And I cuddled you tight in my arms.

Albee called it "indecent" (and so might others, albeit for other reasons) and demanded she cut it from her act. "I want nothing like that in my theaters," he stormed. "What are you running, a Sunday school?" asked Petrova. But Albee won.

In 1919 Darling finally induced her to play the Palace. She played to sensational business. One night Darling came back to see her.

"I don't understand it," she began. "Seven years ago when I came to America I was doing the same act. But instead of applause they jeered me. Now I have some news for you. I am retiring from vaudeville. I have only stayed in the theater to find out why I was a failure. Well, I found out that everything that made good was a noisy fake. So I assumed an accent and took a Russian name. Now about those towns I insisted on playing: I was told I would flop in those towns. Well, you know the tremendous business I did on the tour. And here is the proof of it." And she showed him photographs she had taken of the box-office lines in each of the cities.

The Ascendant Female.

As vaudeville rounded into its greatest expression in the 1910 period the women performers became more dominant; indeed, in a number of instances outrivaling the men in artistry and appeal. The distaff side had been a steady development, inspired by such grand performers as Elfie Fay, Irene Franklin, Gertrude Vanderbilt, Gertrude Hoffman, and those whose careers have been detailed.

Elfie Fay was the daughter of Hugh Fay of the team of Barry and Fay, Irish comics, hilarious purveyors of "McKenna's Flirtation." Elfie grew up in show business and became a sprightly hoyden as a riotous single. Her specialty, Al Smith and his contemporaries will recall with delight, was "The Belle of Avenue A." The song became her trade-mark.

Irene Franklin, although beginning as a child artist, never used childish material. It must have endeared her to her audiences. The adult routine seemed strange, but so marvelous was her talent for handling gags and crossfire that few thought of her as a juvenile. One of her earliest bits was the tough streetcar conductor and the timorous passenger who wished to alight at Watt Street—a standard routine today in the honky-tonks:

> Let me know when we get to Watt Street.
> What street?
> Yes, Watt Street. That's where I'm going.
> Where are you going?
> Going to see my cousin. He lives there.
> Lives where?
> Watt Street.
> How do I know what street he lives on? . . .

ELFIE FAY
"The Belle of Avenue A"

Irene soon got out of that class and developed some lovely characterizations: the giddy girl returning from a picnic; the slangy waitress in a quick-and-dirty; the old lady asking innumerable questions at a railway ticket window, and then deciding not to make her journey until she sold her cow. . . .

Soon after she became established she went to Australia for a tour. Her mother, who accompanied her, died during her engagement, and shortly thereafter her father, who had remained in New York, died here. She came back, and carried on alone. She wrote nearly all her own material, incorporating satirical twists of current fads and local events. No one will ever forget her song, "Red Head." (And what a darling she was in her romper costume! or anything else, for that matter.)

Irene frequently played Pastor's when Burt Green was the pianist there, and a warm friendship that ripened to love soon developed between them. It was an artistic liaison as well; Burt was not only an excellent pianist, he made orchestral arrangements for Irene's songs that not only were of musical value but enhanced her presentation.

Burt Green was married at the time to Helen Van Campen, who had sealed, fished, and hunted in Alaska, placer-mined for gold in Mexico and, although poking about in odd corners of the world and invariably involved in some unusual stunt, generally managed to return to the Broadway she knew as well as George M. Cohan and loved more. She was not only a prolific writer, she was excellent at characterizations and her column in the *Morning Telegraph*, which in the early 1900's shared its racing news with Broadway and the theater, was a gem in portraying the types she knew so well. Some of her columns carried stock heads: "The Telephone Girl"; "The Actors' Boarding House"; "A Studio Tea"; "In Gay New York"; "First Nights," and "Vaudeville."

Van Campen, whose social philosophy was years ahead of her time, favored advanced marital conditions: separate apartments, meetings by appointment only, no questions asked—or answered. Van Campen knew Irene and liked her

"What Have You Got on Your Hip?" One of her best characterizations

immensely, despite the fact that she knew, too, of Irene's affection for her husband. One day she told Burt that if he would promise to marry Irene she would divorce him. He promised, and the details were accordingly arranged at a round-table conference at which Bill Hines, Earl Remington, and other interested parties and friends were present. Van Campen established residence in Reno, and while awaiting her decree wrote a short story plotted on the above situation. After the divorce Burt and Irene were married and he joined her act as pianist, playing solos while she made costume changes. They were an extremely popular pair, socially and professionally. In the last war they went to France with an entertainers' unit, working in the open and using a truck for a stage. Returning to America they resumed their vaudeville time and continued until Burt's death. Irene kept on for a while. She married Jerry Jarnagan, an excellent pianist who teamed with her. But her act was never quite the same. The flame became an ember, and went out altogether in Hollywood with Jarnagan's suicide. Before Jarnagan's death Irene played legit musicals but never remained long with any of them. Not running her own show in her own way she was lost.

Marilyn Miller was also a graduate into musicals after her original vaudeville act as one of the five Columbians. Marilyn, however, stuck mainly to Ziegfeld and the legit stage—once was forced to by Albee. Ziegfeld had a contract to star her for the season of 1920–1921 with her husband, Frank Carter, featured in the cast. Soon after the contract was signed Carter was killed in an automobile accident near Cumberland, Md. Marilyn went abroad for the summer, returning in early fall for rehearsals as her contract required. But Ziegfeld was not ready for her and asked Darling if he would persuade her to do a few weeks' vaudeville until he had something ready. ("Something" was "Sally," her greatest success.) Ziegfeld, as the contract provided, had to pay her for her idle time and he was anxious to be relieved of the load.

Marilyn wasn't interested in vaudeville, and it required a

deal of persuasion on Darling's part even to get her to discuss the venture. She had no worries, the money was coming in regularly from Ziegfeld. Finally, after Ziegfeld agreed to let her use songs from some of his past "Follies" in which she had been featured, together with any scenery she desired, she consented to play six weeks at a weekly salary of $2,500. Elated at landing so great a headliner (Marilyn was at the peak of her appeal), Darling rushed joyfully to Albee and told him of the difficulty he had had in persuading her to appear. Albee replied, "This office is not paying that kind of dough for your pleasure. If you have so much friendly influence over her, get her for $1,500—not another nickel." It was a tough spot for Darling, who had already closed for $2,500. Marilyn didn't care; Ziegfeld had to pay her just the same; she agreed to cancel. And Ziegfeld, who had always hated Albee, hated him more. Albee's petulance almost ruined him as a showman. He was unpredictable, which, of course, is a quality in show business. They all had a streak of it. George M. Cohan tossed the script of "Peg O' My Heart" at Laurette Taylor and told her to take it out of his office.

In 1925 Laurette appeared on a revival bill at the New York Palace—a bill that in action, anecdote, and draw high-lighted the famous house, front and back. Darling signed Weber and Fields who, though they had not drawn too well in their later excursions into vaudeville, were at the moment in the public eye through their autobiographies which were running in the *Saturday Evening Post*. At best, revivals of plays or personalities are a gamble and Darling had his fingers crossed, though the salary he was paying—$3,000 a week, and more than fair to a team which would have to be introduced to 30 per cent of the 1924 audience—hardly indicates skepticism. They were the headliners; with whom to surround them presented difficulties. But some weeks before their scheduled appearance, Cissie Loftus dropped into Darling's office, casually observed that she had seen Weber and Fields's advance photographs in the lobby. "It made me think of the times I used to play with them," she said. "You've given me an idea," said Darling, and promptly signed her for the first addition to what was to be an "old-timers' week." In a short time he had signed Marie Cahill and Emma Trentini, a diminutive singer who had been the toast of the town in the first production of "Naughty Marietta." With extraordinary good fortune he was able to obtain Eric Zordo, a pianist and Trentini's accompanist, a clever chap with a superlative knack for putting her over. For youth and balance he added Dr. Rockwell, Blossom Seeley, and Bill Robinson.

Well, the bill was a beautiful draw, surprising everybody, which is a surprise in itself. Why should it not have been, with those artists and their wonderful material? Darling rebooked it for another week—the week, he had momentarily forgotten— for which he had signed Laurette Taylor for her vaudeville debut. It was to be a gala première in which the renowned Miss Taylor was to do her Pierrot scene. Darling begged her to defer her opening. He told her how the old-timers had taken hold and said it would not only be showman's folly to disturb the bill, it would do Miss Taylor no good to enter at such a time, since it would diminish her publicity and possibly detract from her act. Again he named the performers on the bill. "Well, who are these people?" asked Miss Taylor. Darling, who was familiar with this sort of temperament from legitimate actors, then outlined the financial side. With his weekly budget of $8,000 he could not afford to put her on that week; indeed, her salary exceeded the $3,000 he was paying Weber and Fields. Said Miss Taylor, "I will play the week." So Darling went to the performers.

"Look," he said, "I have to save $2,500 on next week's bill because Miss Taylor insists on coming in. Will you take a cut?" Everyone agreed except Lew Fields. "All right," said Darling, "I'm sure Joe Weber could get along without you." "All right," said Fields, "I'll take the cut for next week."

Then the dressing-room headache. "I would die," said Marie Cahill, "if Laurette Taylor has a dressing room ahead of me." Darling told her of "the lovely room on the top floor" (really excellent and the Palace had elevators), but Miss Cahill said no. "I want the first room. It is small, but it is first and that is all that counts." And Darling said excuse me, slid over to the Palace, and had buckets of paint put in every stage-floor dressing room to show that they could not be used because of redecoration. It worked, too. But the week was a fever of petty jealousies, bickerings, and temperamental tantrums. When it was over Darling said good-by to all of them with a sweet sigh—only to jam into Albee who had been checking box-office returns and had discovered that the bill that followed was earning far less than the old-timers.

The nerve-racking job of wet-nursing a troupe of stars, wheedling, cajoling, humoring, soothing, with an occasional veiled threat to restore their senses, if any, Albee could never understand. To him an actor was merchandise. His appraisal of acts was a standard gag on the circuit: "Good at forty, fair at fifty, lousy at sixty"—dollars a week.

Nudged by Albee, Darling began scouting for another old-timers' bill. He re-signed Weber and Fields and Cissy Loftus, but Miss Cahill was cagey. "Who have you got?" she asked. Anyway, she signed. And so, eventually, did Marie Dressler, whose coy refusals ("Oh, dear, no; they don't want me any more") were overcome with $2,000 a week. He recruited Blanche Ring, whose style in putting over such song hits as "Bedelia" and "Rings on My Fingers," drew raves from a delighted Broadway, and Charlie Winninger whom younger readers will remember for his radio "Show Boat" captain not so many years ago. And then Darling's recollections brought up Fay Templeton, famous for her role in George M. Cohan's "Forty-five Minutes from Broadway," and a public sweetheart for years. Joe Weber advised against it, but Darling wrote to her in Pittsburgh. At first she declined. Darling persisted, and she said, "If you will get the consent of Weber and Fields to allow me to appear with them in some of the things we have done together, I'll feel at home and I'll do it." They consented. And then there was the devil's own time devising an act, for Fay had become a mountain of flesh. But her voice —that wonderful low note she alone could deliver—age had impaired but little. Together they rehearsed a number of scenes, but all were abandoned, even Darling's suggestion that they do the old poker game that, with Lillian Russell, Dave Warfield, Weber and Fields, and Fay, was a hilarious act from their old Music Hall.

Then Weber and Fields, who, Darling says, had not been helpful, possibly because they thought Fay interfered with their own act, said to her, "We'll wheel you out in one of those wheel chairs and you can get out and sing." And Fay said, "I would rather not do that, I want to be myself." But they wheeled her out, and at the opening matinee the chair tipped and they let her fall—quite by accident, of course. She rose slowly, steadied herself at the chair, and stood, facing the audience which, momentarily stunned at the mishap, responded with an ovation that restored her confidence. She began her song, and when they heard those deep velvet tones they cheered and sang the second chorus with her. After Weber and Fields concluded their pool-room scene she returned as Bunty in a lovely costume that draped her immensity with grace, and with Weber and Fields on either side holding her wrists, did an imitation of Lillian Russell singing Lillian's famous Music Hall song, "My Evening Star." At the half she broke down. The poor soul, thought the audience. But it happened more than once and Darling became suspicious. "She was never like that, she couldn't be that ham, to play so cheaply on a house," he thought.

The bill again ran a fortnight with great success. Everyone came to see Fay; old professional friends beat a path to her dressing room—except George M. Cohan, for whom she had worked so long. It hurt her. She had had words with Cohan while under his management. "And I guess he never forgave me," she said. And when it was over she said to Darling, "Now I will tell you why I cried at the performances of the song.

It wasn't because I was affected giving the imitation of Lillian Russell, who was one of my dearest friends—I felt they didn't want me," she said. A lovely Buttercup, Fay in 1926 played that role again in a Shubert revival of "Pinafore" and, still later, in straitened circumstances, took a part in Max Gordon's production of Jerome Kern's "Roberta." She was unhappy. A star, she had long set. She knew it. But everywhere, and by many who should have been kinder, she was confronted with constant, cruel reminders. She died in 1939 in San Francisco.

This old-timers' bill had one happy repercussion—it rejuvenated Marie Dressler. During her engagement she told Vincent Sardi, genial theatrical restaurateur in West 44th Street, of her intention to retire and live out her life in Capri. Almost the next day came the wire from Hollywood. There she died, but not before she fed again upon fortune and fame, and —that seventh heaven of superannuated stars—acclaim by a new generation.

Sketch Writers and Players

THE prettified and stenciled vaudeville of the second decade of the 1900's achieved its best expression (and perhaps its excuse for being) in the perfection of the one-act sketch, notably in the sketches of George Kelly. Kelly's contributions (to vaudeville) were not numerous—"Finders Keepers," "The Flattering Word," "Mrs. Ritter Appears," "The Show-Off," etc.—but they were unique. Each was a gem from a talented pen, and they were shots in the arm for a declining vaudeville, causing hasty reconstruction in billing by the managers who heretofore had centered their programs on name acts and headliners. When Kelly, who starred in his plays, was booked, the bills revolved around his sketches. They were not just another number. More, they were unusual in theme: tragedies, psychological studies, acidulous satires set down in aloes. This was heady stuff for vaudeville, and it is small wonder that Kelly, after a brief five years in the two-a-day, took himself into the larger field of the legitimate theater.

Two of Kelly's one-act vaudeville plays are now included in the literature of the theater: "Mrs. Ritter Appears" and "The Show-Off." Both were rewritten into full-length comedies. "Mrs. Ritter Appears" became "The Torchbearers." Their histories are interesting. "Mrs. Ritter Appears" opened in a Keith circuit house in Jamaica, Long Island. It was so funny the management withdrew it at once for presentation with an all-star cast in the belief that more money could be made with it in this way. Almost at once difficulties arose. Much time was lost in attempting to cast it. Finally Kelly, irked by the delay, withdrew it altogether to reshape it into a legitimate comedy.

The day after it opened as "The Torchbearers," the late David Belasco, then staging "Deburau" with Lionel Atwill, came to Kelly, who had directed "Torchbearers."

"You gave me a pretty bad turn at the opening last night," he said. "Do you know you had about twelve people moving and landing points at the same time? Where did you learn to do that?"

"Vaudeville," said Kelly, giving decent credit to a fine school.

"The Show-Off" opened in Port Richmond, Staten Island, and was equally successful. But unlike "Mrs. Ritter Appears" it continued to play the circuit; continued, even during the New York run of the full-length comedy Kelly had fashioned from it. For weeks after it came to Broadway Kelly received mail daily advising him that a pirated abridgment of his play was being toured in vaudeville. The reason was that contracts for the route had already been signed and had to be fulfilled.

It may have been Paul Armstrong's influence that led Kelly into the satirical field. At any rate, Kelly began his vaudeville career in an Armstrong sketch called "Woman Proposes," a vinegary one-acter, the only play in which Kelly appeared in vaudeville not written by himself.

The satire and psychology both Armstrong and Kelly introduced into their work were of a piece with the trend of those war times (1914–1918) and a thoughtful advance from the rube-type sketches and stylized comedies which clowned up the vaudeville bills of the early 1900's. These, too, were later patterned even as the comedy teams and four-acts were standardized.

Usually the standardized sketches were developed from the

hokum of mistaken identity. When the curtain rose, discover the maid with the abbreviated French costume busily engaged in dusting. She would turn on the light and, enter madame: "Master is not home, yet?" "No, madame." Enter, the master. Inevitably he carried a carefully folded newspaper which he used throughout the entire week; one of his gloves would be on, the other off; and invariably his opening line was: "Gad, but I'm tired. I had a difficult day at the office. By the way, I'm expecting my rich uncle, whom we've never seen, for dinner tonight and if we make a good impression we'll be wealthy when he dies." (Postman's whistle, off stage.) "Don't bother, I'll go." The door opens a crack and the grimy mitt of of a stagehand thrusts a letter through the crack. Master opens it; reads. "Hello, what's this? An escaped lunatic and he's coming this way. We'll take care of him." Enter, uncle, who is promptly mistaken for the escaped lunatic and treated accordingly (to his indignation) until the mystery is cleared. No one has ever been able to figure out how or why master got the letter about the escaped lunatic.

One of the most prolific of the vaudeville sketch writers was Will M. Cressy, an admirable creator of rube types. A native of New Hampshire, he stunned his parents when he forsook the flour, feed, hay, and grain business operated for years by the Cressy family to run off with a repertory troupe. In the early 1900's "types" were in special demand by the vaudeville managers and Cressy, who conformed to their desires *au naturel*, became an immediate success with his wife, Blanche Dayne, in character sketches of his own writing. They were a series of friendly bucolics; friendly is precisely the word. They never tossed anybody in the aisles and there was scarcely a belly laugh in any of them. But they offered real entertainment in characterizations that were widely understood and liked.

Cressy gave much attention to detail; one of his early sketches was so scenically complete it would have pleased the realistic masters of today. It was a crossroads grocery store showing the crowded shelves, miscellaneous merchandise, and homemade counter, and oil lamps suspended from the ceiling. During the action Cressy, as proprietor, receives a letter stating that an old friend who had passed requested that his baby girl be sent to Cressy, and that presently she would arrive in charge of the conductor of the train. It is a bit of a blow, but he takes it philosophically, turning for guidance to a book, "Advice to Mothers," from which he reads a few passages on proper diet and hygiene. Rising, he mumbles phrases from the book, and then strings a line across a corner of the store, thoughtfully adding a few clothespins. Then he resumes his reading until interrupted by the arrival of the "baby"—a full-grown young woman, Miss Dayne.

This is really tough.

CRESSY: I don't know where I can put you to sleep, unless you don't mind bunkin' in with the station agent.
DAYNE: Sir! I am a lady!
CRESSY: So is the station agent.

Although Cressy's forte was the rube-type act, he was not unfamiliar with other expressions and a knack for comic situations enhanced his versatility. Among the numerous skits he wrote for other performers, one for Foy and Clark is of especial interest for its illustration of his talent for comedy bits other than dialogue. This was an undersea act played behind a scrim drop representing the bed of the ocean, seaweed, wreckage, rocks, and shells. Foy, a sailor, presumably falls from a passing ship and sinks into the scene, holding himself down by grasping an anchor. Miss Clark appears as a gorgeous mermaid. Throughout their dialogue fish swim about, steamships are heard passing overhead; bottles, cans, and varied bits of rubbish fall from them. References are made to the Fall River and Joy lines. Finally, the mermaid attempts to persuade Foy to remain with her. But he is not too friendly, and presently an anchor and cable swings into the scene and vanks him out of the picture.

JOHN HYAMS AND LEILA McINTYRE
"Subtle crossfire, dainty flirtation . . ."

Cressy and his brothers inherited the New Hampshire hay and grain business which this energetic man, despite his vaudeville tours and skit writing, never forsook. He was a member of the Feed Men's Association, attended their annual dinners, and is probably the only actor on record who baled hay for a side line.

Sketch acts that were noted for their smartness in direction, dialogue, presentation, and finesse were termed "classy" by the performers. An outstanding act of this character was that of Hyams and McIntyre. John Hyams broke in as a blackface song and dance man touring with minstrel shows. Later he joined a male dancing sextet at Hoyt's Theatre in New York, a specialty number interpolated in Hoyt's famous comedies. An impressive performer, he was signed by Klaw and Erlanger for "Beauty and the Beast" (as was Victor Moore). In the cast was Leila McIntyre who had been engaged to play the role of Beauty, an illustration, incidentally, of perfect type casting. Miss McIntyre previously had toured the vaudevilles as a member of the well-known team of Linton and McIntyre, performers of an entertaining potpourri of singing, dancing, banjo playing, and light comedy. Hyams's response to the McIntyre allure was immediate and during the run of "Beauty" they were married. After a joint starring venture in a Joe Spears musical comedy, they fashioned a vaudeville act with a photograph studio for a setting. This was livened with subtle crossfire, dainty flirtation, and interpolated single and double specialties. It became an overnight success and Hyams and McIntyre remained a featured team as long as vaudeville lasted.

In point of interest, technique, and sophistication, vaudeville sketches developed so rapidly they caught up with and occasionally got away from the managers who had the devil's own time watching them for blue gags and allusions.

During a week in Cleveland, John Royal, Albee manager there, penciled out some of the monologue of Robert Emmet Keane. Keane yelled lustily. "There is an act next week you won't cut," he snarled. "And what would that be?" asked Royal. "Frank Keenan." Now Keenan, a wheel horse of the American stage, was no one to monkey with. But Royal said that if his sketch violated the rules about cleanliness (so called) the offensive line or lines or situation would be eliminated.

Thus forewarned, Royal looked to his next week's bill apprehensively, and when the time arrived went out front to catch the Keenan play at the Monday matinee. The scene was the Governor's office in an unnamed state. At his desk sat the Governor when, enter, an orderly. "There is a man outside, sir, who would like to see you. He is an old soldier." The orderly is instructed to admit him and, enter, Keenan as a Confederate soldier. Well, the Governor had served on the Union side and after some hatchet-burying dialogue Keenan came to the point. "It's about my boy, Governor. You are going to hang him next week." He mentions the name of his son and the Governor stiffens. "But, Governor, my son is not a bad boy. He never did anything wrong before in his life, Governor. A good lad. I don't think you know how it happened. You see this man spit on the picture of Robert E. Lee, and—God damn him—my boy shot him." Of course, it electrified the audience, and Royal's hair looked like a fright wig. He ordered the line cut, which killed the scene.

Keenan refused to comply. Both wired Albee. "It's enough to make Keith turn in his grave," telegraphed Royal. Albee wired back: "You run the theater, we'll take care of Keith's grave." And the curse stayed out. Yet Albee permitted the Lady Godiva act uncensored time on the basis that audiences "ought to have a little fun."

Audiences never realized how rigid was the censorship of Albee and his crew until as late as 1923, when Albee canceled Mme. Alla Nazimova's one-act play, "The Unknown Lady," after two performances at the Palace Theatre in New York. The play, written by George Middleton, exposed the fraud of collusion and pleaded for more sensible divorce laws. Albee killed it on the protest of the Reverend John B. Kelly, chaplain of the Catholic Writers Guild. When newspapermen asked him to discuss his objections Father Kelly declined, stating that his position in the Church (he was an assistant in the Church of the Blessed Sacrament, Broadway and 71st Street) prevented comment. It hadn't prevented his protest, however, and Albee, a Milquetoast when plagued by pressure groups of any standing or numbers, hurriedly knifed the act.

Among those who rallied to Middleton's support was Ben B. Lindsey, Denver Juvenile Court judge who had seen the play under its first title. Said Judge Lindsey, in a wire to Mme. Nazimova:

This country has never witnessed a more outrageous piece of intolerance than cancellation of your sketch The Unknown Lady high time people assert themselves against interference free speech expressed through art theater platform or press your sketch is strictly within the law and one of the finest productions ever presented in interest of public morals I wish to go on record publicly as protesting against this triumph of ignorance and intolerance.

What really happened was this: Under the title "Collusion" the play had been a smash on the Orpheum time and Albee sought it for the Eastern Keith circuit with a debut at the New York Palace. Contracts to this effect were dispatched to Nazimova. Now the Keith contracts contained what was known as the "elimination" clause. This clause was the keystone of the Keith-Albee vaudeville policy. It gave the managers authority to censor any word, line, lines, business, or costume that violated the Keith-Albee idea of "cleanliness."

Nazimova crossed out the clause and wrote in her own to the effect that not one line or bit of business was to be tampered with and that the act was to be presented exactly as she played it. With these changes she signed the contracts and forwarded them to New York where they were filed—unexamined. That any performer, from Bernhardt and Bayes to a honky-tonk hoofer, would dare to scissor this clause, let alone change it, was inconceivable in the Keith-Albee offices.

So when the righteously indignant Albee (after the prodding by Father Kelly) descended on Nazimova she produced her copy of the contract and bade him look at his. He did, and paid her $11,000. The sum included not only her salary for the truncated week at the Palace, but for the entire booking time.

The one-act play in vaudeville was of considerable importance. It not only required a precise technique, it demanded expert acting. Thus it was an excellent medium for the development of writers, and the finest of schools for actors. George Kelly, for example, at one time followed Chic Sale on a Palace bill after Sale had exhausted an audience who would not let him go for an hour—followed him, as a matter of fact, in "Finders Keepers," a tragedy. Spots like this sharpened an actor—if he could be sharpened. Many a legitimate star, excellent in the more leisurely drama, fell by this test when taking a vaudeville fling. The vaudeville performer who could meet it remained as a respected player or entered the legitimate theater in featured roles. William Gaxton is a sketch-act graduate, matriculating in Broadway musicals largely through the assistance of Eddie Darling who prevailed upon Al Lewis and Gordon to sign him for the "Second Music Box Review." Another is Tom Fadden, who with the late Gregory Kelly was an outstanding sketch player and is today one of the best of our character actors on stage or screen.

New Names for a Closing Show

Even the waning vaudeville of the 1920's developed new stars. Some of these were Eddie Cantor, George Jessel, Lou Holtz, and Moran and Mack. That these performers, whose names are so familiar today, are dealt with briefly here is no reflection on their several talents. They served vaudeville well, however limited their tenures, but circumstances, the changing social expression, and the advance of mechanized entertainment decreed that they achieve their victories in radio and movies. Walter Winchell, who (Cantor and Jessel, too) at one time was a hoofer in a Gus Edwards act, and then teamed in the two-act of Winchell and Green, went on to become a highly controversial keyhole commentator; financially the most successful syndicated columnist in America. Winchell was no Astaire on his feet. But he has never laid claim to vaudeville fame. His foray into the field was fleeting, and when he realized his inclination was for the not-too-poisonous pen he got out. After the World War he wrote first for *Billboard*, show business trade paper, for which he typed a column called "Stage Whispers," signing it "By the Busybody." In a characteristic letter to *Billboard* printed in the weekly's fortieth anniversary number in 1934, Winchell acknowledged that the paper gave him his first opportunity and added a significant reference to his earlier hoofing:

"Except the newcomers, most of the gentlemen and gentle-women of the show shops can remember away back when 'that' Winchell person flopped in the deuce spot in any theater on the W.V.M.A. (Western Vaudeville Managers Association), Gus Sun, Sullivan and Considine, Loew and Pantages chains. It was a grand apprenticeship, too, being rebuked and rebuffed by critics, stagehands, house managers and baggagemen. And, of course, audiences . . ."

Later he became an advertising solicitor for *Vaudeville News*, the official organ of the N.V.A., then headed by Glen Condon. He also conducted a picture feature, like the inquiring reporter columns, for the *Vaudeville News*. His next move was to the (New York) *Graphic*, a fierce tab, now happily dead, where he began his present vivid, picturesque, and acidulous style.

Moran and Mack featured a decadent vaudeville, but preserved the comedy elements that made sprightly and effective the variety of a happier day. The slow and stupid comic (Mack) made ridiculous observations fed by the spruce and energetic (Moran) straight man:

MORAN: I hear you folks are getting rid of all your horses.
MACK: Only the white horses, they eat too much.
MORAN: You mean to say the white horses eat more than the others?
MACK: Yes, the white horses eat twice as much as the black horses.
MORAN: How do you explain that?
MACK: There's twice as many of them. We have four white horses and two black horses. So we're getting rid of the white horses and are going to get black ones . . .

Mack (there were a number of Morans) was killed in an automobile accident in 1934 and the act was no more.

Eddie Cantor is so well known it is scarcely necessary to set him down here except as a latter-day vaudeville artist of importance. Cantor's wide variety of social and political interests is the new expression of the actor in the world of reality, acutely aware of his off-stage role and his relationship to society generally. Cantor has been a leader in actors' union circles and has contributed money and time to movements designed for the performers' betterment. Although on the West Coast in 1939 at the time of the threatened actors' unions strike against the attempted domination of the performers and artists by the stagehands' union, The International Alliance of Theatrical Stage Employees, he supported the actors vigorously and his telegrams, opinions, and advice to the New York and Atlantic City conferences during the crisis were influential and constructive. As a performer his youthful vigor, still apparent in his work, was appealing to audiences, and he could dynamite a song like a masculine Bayes. His natural wit and inherent response to comedy are fortifications only the best artists enjoy. When told that Sophie Tucker, then president of the outlawed American Federation of Actors, sobbed at a meeting that heckled her, Cantor observed, "Sophie would cry at a card trick."

The feature of George Jessel's vaudeville act was a telephone conversation with his mother: he knew nothing about the money missing from the bureau at home, didn't take the cake from the cupboard, etc. Since the collapse of vaudeville, Jessel has played radio, shows, and pictures like a checkerboard, flitting casually about with easy adaptation.

Lou Holtz was the discovery of Ma Janis, Elsie's mother. This gracious lady was constantly on the watch for talent and aided generously any obscure act she thought warranted it. Thus, when she observed a minor three-act—Boland, Holtz, and Harris—during a West Coast tour, she brought them east to the attention of Eddie Darling who booked them at the Palace. Little Rita Boland was a lovely thing and it has always seemed to the writer that some sinister influence on the part of the late Arnold Daly, who was on the bill at the time, withered her bloom as a performer. At any rate, she left the act for a small part in one of Daly's plays and never rated thereafter.

After Harris also withdrew, Holtz continued as a single. He was an extraordinary comic with immediate reactions that made him superb as a master of ceremonies, but he continually slipped over the blue line into a vulgarity that often destroyed his effectiveness. During his short vaudeville tenure he was a constant distemper to Albee and Darling. Repeatedly they cautioned him to clean up his act. Five years earlier Albee would have barred him from the circuit, but Albee was as old as vaudeville and, like the Palace, dying. Holtz never needed the goosing stick, and it is pleasant to report that today he realizes this. His broadcasts are excellent and in the writer's opinion he rates as one of radio's few really funny men.

Holtz was master of ceremonies during the Cantor-Jessel nine weeks' run at the Palace in 1932. Eddie Darling had retired but still retained an interest in the grand old theater he had done so much to develop and when Manager Elmer Rogers asked him to come up and see the show he consented. Arriving in the lobby he met Mark Luescher, who was handling the publicity, and asked for his tickets. Luescher returned from the box office with one ticket. "I feel awful," he said, "but there is a $2.20 charge." Darling paid and entered. Men, sloppily dressed, many in shirt sleeves, lounged in the boxes; the curtain folds and drapes were heavy with dust. Darling took his seat.

Holtz was introducing celebrities in the house as Billy Gaxton came on the stage. "And now, ladies and gentlemen," said Holtz, "there is one more person I'd like to have you meet here, someone who really did more for this theater than anybody else in vaudeville . . . " And Darling wondered, "Can he mean me?" Holtz continued, "He is responsible for my being here today," and began to tell the story of Darling. Gaxton interrupted with "Get out of here," and Holtz turned on him, "He helped you, too, didn't he?" "Yes," said Gaxton. Turning to the audience, Holtz said, "I want you to meet Eddie Darling," and asked Eddie to stand. There was tremendous applause, but a sickening thought came to Darling: it was for Eddie Dowling—confirmed when a chap in the gallery yelled, "Sing 'Honeymoon Lane' or sit down!" Darling asked Holtz to spell his name, and Holtz, though reluctant, finally spelled it. Then Darling referred to the con-

FRED AND ADELE ASTAIRE
A heyday dance team—favorites at the Palace when Ginger Rogers was bottling

fusion between his name and that of the actor-producer, adding, "I guess all that applause was for him." Whereupon two little old ladies, seated next to him, cried, "No, No!" and applauded, but over their feeble patting came the raucous repeat of the gallery dope: "Go on, sing 'Honeymoon Lane.'" Darling sat down.

The Curtain Lowers

As early as 1915 Bill Morris predicted vaudeville's doom. Stifling his pride to save an industry he had done much to develop, he went to Albee and declared himself.

"In view of the conditions," he began, "it would be a smart thing for you to reorganize and install George M. Cohan as the head of the circuit. Makes no difference if it costs a million dollars. We could pull out of it because I will go to Europe and book enough novelty acts to freshen up the bills; get new life and talent into the business."

Albee looked up at him as though Morris was mad.

"To hell with your proposal," said Albee. "I am vaudeville."

Morris returned to his office and phoned the Cunard Line to cancel his passage. It was on the *Lusitania*—her last crossing.

Morris then was known throughout the entertainment world as the Napoleon of vaudeville. Although frozen from the Keith-Orpheum time, he had managed to book, pretty continuously, the American Music Hall, the New York Roof, the Plaza Theatre and at one time operated a venture of his own—Wonderland, an indoor Coney Island. The Morris Agency is today the largest bookers of entertainment talent in the world.

France recognized Morris's distinguished efforts and decorated him as an Officier de l'Instruction Publique for promoting good will in the amusement world of both countries.

In 1924 he founded the Jewish Theatrical Guild of America to memorialize the death of Barney Bernard, and became its first president. On November 2, 1932 (the year the Palace folded as a two-a-day), he entered the Friars Club, then at 110 W. 48th Street, and sat down to play pinochle with Walter C. Kelly, Lou Riel, and Munro Goldstein, a lawyer. He led a card, slumped against the table, dead. That afternoon he had planned to see John D. Rockefeller, Jr., hoping to interest him in bringing over the crown jewels of Great Britain for museum display.

Morris's great confrere in the battle against Albee was Sime Silverman, who on December 16, 1905, published his first issue of *Variety*. It hit Broadway like a thousand of brick: an honest publication whose summaries of acts and plays were fearless and uncompromising, one that flayed an act with a left-hook critique, often printed in the same issue containing the act's paid advertisement.

Sime had worked for his father's financial concern, the Fidelity Security Company, and his interest in vaudeville (his other love was baseball) grew out of his association with the firm's theatrical clients. When the interest carried him into the writing phase of the industry his father fussed, for the son was an expert appraiser of furniture, chattels, etc. Sime got his opening in vaudeville in 1899 when George Graham Rice founded the *Daily America* in opposition to the *Morning Telegraph*. Rice drew from the *Telegraph*'s staff as many as he could for his new paper, including Leander Richardson, who had been editor. Richardson's secretary, Joshua Lowitke (who subsequently changed his name to Lowe), suggested to Sime that he take over vaudeville criticism for the *America*. Sime accepted and began writing under the signature "The Man in the Third Row."

The job didn't last long. Rice's only interest in the *America* derived from the fact that in it he could publish without restraint advertisements of his turf tipping bureaus, chief of which was Maxim, Gay & Co. Daily Rice announced the winners supplied by his bureaus. The Post Office authorities cracked down on him and the paper soon folded. Richardson went back to the *Telegraph* and Sime, knowing that Epes W. Sargent had quit the *Telegraph*, applied for Chicot's job as vaudeville critic. He got it and this time began writing under the pseudonym "Robert Spear." After his first three reviews he was cautioned to ease up on his criticisms. Sime disregarded the instructions and in his second week was fired by Bill Lewis, the managing editor.

"You can't get away with that kind of stuff," said Lewis.

"I'll show you that I can," answered Sime. Thereupon Sime borrowed $1,500 from his father-in-law in Syracuse and, consulting with Chicot in Pabst's Columbus Circle restaurant, drew on the tablecloth the masthead of *Variety* as it appears today. He rounded up John J. O'Connor, a vigorous lad who had been an usher at the Alhambra (and at this writing Fred Waring's manager) and Al Greason. With this staff, and appointments purchased from a secondhand furniture store in Sixth Avenue at a cost of $40, he opened a one-room office in the Knickerbocker Building, Broadway and 38th Street.

Sime—and *Variety*.

Soon after its first issue *Variety* caught on and early in 1906 Sime appointed Johnny O'Connor an advertising solicitor, hired Joe Raymond in the same capacity, and made Sam Mitnick his circulation manager. Loosed from the office, O'Connor set out for his first love, the Alhambra, where he encountered Matt Keefe, a singer, and Tony Pearl, a harpist, both of whom he tapped for ads. Said Pearl, "What the hell is the sense of advertising in *Variety?* Everybody knows who we are." Johnny had better luck at Proctor's Fifth Avenue where Grace Cameron bought the first page ad for $50. The grateful Sime printed her photograph on the cover.

For a time Sime ran the cover photographs (a center oval with a grouping of four small head circles around it) for free, but O'Connor, who received 25 per cent commission on each sale, talked him into selling this space also. One of the first to buy the cover was Joe Cook, whose initial investment cost $25. A few years afterward Johnny sold Joe the same space for $2,500.

In 1907, two years after *Variety* started, Sime sent O'Connor on a fourteen months' intensive exploitation campaign throughout the United States and Canada. When O'Connor got to a town he'd rent a bicycle, pedal to every news dealer, deliver a pep talk, and arrange with the dealer to display as many copies of *Variety* on his stand as he did of the *Clipper*. He also tacked cards backstage announcing the availability of the weekly, and appointed correspondents in each town to supply news to *Variety* for the privilege of getting into the theaters on passes. These correspondents were later replaced by newspapermen who were paid space rates for their copy. After opening branch offices in San Francisco and Chicago, O'Connor returned home where already the effects of his campaign were being felt in mounting circulation. Sime increased ad rates, drawing in the music publishers for half- and full-page ads—revenue which carried the paper for some time.

A rate card for long-period advertising was inaugurated. The first act to come in under it was Ed Reynard, the ventriloquist. It was a two-inch ad to run a year and cost $145.60. With the ink wet on the contract Sime tossed Reynard double or nothing. Sime lost. He then matched Reynard one flop for $500 or an ad for the life of *Variety* and Sime lost again—his first long-time ad bringing in nothing. Later, when Albee black-listed all performers who failed to withdraw their advertising from *Variety*, Reynard begged Sime to discontinue it. Sime did. But by this time he had built up a sizable advertising revenue from acts that splurged—and occasionally squawked; nice ad, but a bad notice. It didn't add up for the performer.

The staff grew with the paper. Joshua Lowitke, or Joe Lowe, was hired as a reviewer. He coined the phrase—"good for the small time"—which became a vaudeville cliché. Lowe signed his copy "Jolo." No signature, with few exceptions, exceeded four letters, in deference to *S-I-M-E*. Others who joined the paper included Charles and Jesse Freeman, Sime's brothers-in-law, Fred Schader, and Leo Carillo, then a Chinese impersonater who was by avocation a cartoonist.

Sime's scathing editorials lashing at the vaudeville trust blistered Albee, who was constantly besieged by angry performers whose acts had been panned mercilessly, if justifiably, by the "muggs," as *Variety* reporters are still dubbed. Albee summoned Sime and laid down the law. Said he would dictate Sime's editorial policy, or else. Sime told him to go to hell. "All right," said Albee. "I will break you." And from 1910 to 1914 the fight raged, with no holds barred.

Albee's first act was to announce that any performer who failed to withdraw his advertising from the weekly would be considered an enemy of the U.B.O. This meant the dreaded black-listing and performers immediately sent in cancellations. So great was Albee's influence he was even able to induce the music publishers to withdraw their ads—a body blow. Next he pulled out Sime's staff. He presented Fred Schader with an agent's franchise and Schader quit. He offered similar franchises to Joe Lowe and Joe Raymond, and they quit. But he never sought to buy O'Connor or Al Greason, apparently knowing they would have told him off. The defections never troubled Sime; indeed, he took some of the boys back, including Joe Lowe who at this writing manages *Variety's* London office.

Sime was broke, and going weekly deeper in hock. One morning after Albee's raid, he walked into the office and found only Greason and O'Connor. "What do you think we ought to do?" asked Sime. "Are you fellows going to stick?" They said they would. "All right," said Sime, "let's see if he can break us while we're still young. If he can, O.K. We can get jobs somewhere."

During the fight the Technical Press, a printing establishment, slapped a judgment on Sime and attached his accounts receivable. Sime went to the Sands Street Press, and later to C. J. O'Brien, head of a Park Row printing house, who extended him credit. Many of Sime's friends came to his aid, and among his chief supporters was Joe Tooker, a theatrical-poster printer.

Few knew what lay back of the enmity between Albee and Sime. The basic reason was, of course, Sime's crusade for independence, but Albee contended that Sime attacked him because the United Booking Office financed the paper for a time, taking *Variety* stock as security; that when Sime eventually put the paper on its feet and bought back the U.B.O. loan, he maliciously attacked Albee because he regretted the financial obligation and sought to erase it from his memory. It hardly makes sense. To his death Chicot held that the fight was secretly initiated by Albee's own associates who regarded him as a menace and wanted to ease him out, using Sime as the mouthpiece for their cause. This doesn't make sense either, not because of the suggestion that Albee's colleagues might double-cross him, but because the role just doesn't fit Sime.

Anyway, the plight of the paper rapidly became worse. Its only revenue now was a few paltry dollars from acts already black-listed. The debt steadily mounted. As a last venture, Sime went to the president of the Mutual Bank at Broadway and 32nd Street and asked for a loan of $10,000. He had no security and no hope that he could get it solely on his signature. "I like your paper and the fight you are putting up," said the president, "you've got guts." And Sime walked out with the money.

Some time after (the fall of 1914), O'Connor put the situation squarely to J. J. Murdock, Albee's associate, and talked him into a submissive attitude. Murdock agreed to confer with Sime if other representatives were present. A few days later Albee, Murdock, Maurice Goodman (the Keith-Albee lawyer), Sime, and O'Connor met on neutral ground, and a truce was declared.

Meantime *Variety* was approaching its December anniversary number and O'Connor, now business manager and secretary for the publication, suggested to Murdock that all agents be notified that *Variety* was in good standing and to pass this on to their acts. Also theater managers were to be told that muggs were again welcome, back and front. Murdock agreed and signed the order in O'Connor's presence. O'Connor asked that the agents be directed to give him their stationery and list of accounts and said he would have his own staff send out the notification, thus saving Murdock's office much clerical labor. And to this Murdock agreed.

Forthwith, O'Connor drafted a note on the agents' letterheads: "*Variety* is preparing its anniversary number and I have reserved a large portion of space for my acts. I am enclosing a rate card and would suggest that you confine your holiday advertising to *Variety*." The notes were signed by agents and promptly mailed to the performers, timed so that an act in San Francisco received the notice on the day those in New York got theirs. Within thirty days *Variety* issued one of its biggest anniversary editions, piling up funds that enabled Sime to pay off a number of creditors. But the other papers yelled long and loud.

A week later Albee summoned O'Connor to his office where he found Sam McKee of the *Morning Telegraph*, C. F. Zittell, of the *Journal*, W. H. Donaldson, publisher of the *Billboard*, and Albert J. Borie of the *Clipper*. They were somewhat annoyed about O'Connor's use of the word "confine" in his notice. Albee dramatized the occasion with his customary profanity. But nothing could be done and Albee dismissed the complaint committee, holding O'Connor for further abuse. But *Variety* continued the practice.

How far Sime was swayed to Albee's camp after the brawl was over one cannot determine. Sime was putting out a paper that reflected his views and if the man changed his mind, how can you prove anything in court? It is a matter of record that in a complaint made public May 14, 1918, by the Federal Trade Commission he and his paper were cited as being under control of the vaudeville monopoly enjoyed by Albee and his colleagues.

The commission charged that Sime published propaganda for the manager members of the United Booking Office which, in turn, forced performers to advertise in *Variety*. The complaint alleged that *Variety* in its "special" numbers sometimes issued as many as 200 pages of performer ads for which the actors paid $125 a page. Earlier, in 1916, the White Rats sued *Variety* for $100,000, charging unfair discrimination. Nothing came of either action.

In the early days, after he had rowed with Sime and quit, Chicot suggested to Albert J. Borie of the *Clipper* that he hire him and give Sime a fight. The *Clipper*, then (1907) well established, was owned by the estate of Frank Queen, a Philadelphia oculist who had founded it because of his interest in sports. Although essentially a theatrical trade paper, it had many departments devoted to sports, including a column on cockfighting. Borie's reply to Chicot was that the *Clipper* was too firmly established ever to be annoyed by *Variety*. Seventeen years later, in 1924, Sime bought it, but it was too feeble to be revived and he let it die. At the time of the purchase Sime permitted the muggs to buy stock in the paper according to their desires, and most of the staff did. When the twenty-fifth anniversary edition of *Variety* appeared in 1930, carrying a huge block of advertising and putting Sime in funds, he paid back to each of the staff all the money they had invested although he was under no legal or moral obligation so to do.

The Formidable *Billboard*.

Sime never recognized, or pretended not to recognize, the competition of the more expansive *Billboard*, an older weekly journal devoted to every department of entertainment. *Billboard* gave, and still does give, much space to circuses, carnivals, and fairs, and Sime for a while sought to invade this field. But in these branches *Billboard* was entrenched. Sime found that out, and forgot it. The *Billboard*, founded by W. H. Donaldson and James Hennigan in Cincinnati in 1894, was first issued as *Billboard Advertising*. It catered to the interests of billposting,

poster printing, and advertising agencies, neglecting the theater until 1901 when legitimate shows and vaudeville were given
space which was subsequently developed into sizable departments. Less terse than *Variety*, much more discursive, under
Elias E. Sugarman, its theater department editor, it became
equally forthright in its opinions.

In 1921, C. F. Zittell, a theatrical columnist for Hearst,
inaugurated *Zitt's Weekly* in direct competition with *Variety*.
Zittell considered that Sime was slipping. He had some basis
for the belief, for Sime again was gunning for Albee and sharpshooter Albee was returning the fire. This time the fortunes of
war were on Sime's side. Marcus Loew, then ascending rapidly, had little use for Albee and chortled with glee at each
of Sime's blasts against the one-time all-powerful vaudeville
magnate. Moreover, he paid for his laughs, placing with
Sime not only the lucrative Metro advertising, but inducing
Paramount and the Schenck interests to follow him into
Variety's till. This was fine for Sime but not so good for Zittell,
who promptly went after the department store advertising,
presenting the reasonable, if sometimes thwarted, argument
that showfolk, too, must dress. Although unimportant as a
theatrical journal of opinion, Zittell's snappy copy and publication of vaudeville charts, printed in the manner of horse-park
past performances, kept his weekly going until 1938 when,
after weathering several spotty years, it closed.

Albee's control of the New York Hippodrome (1923) led to
another minor row. Sime printed a story in *Variety* about the
low wages paid the scrubwomen. Albee squawked and again
Sime told him to go to hell. Albee replied, "Someday I will
dictate the editorial policies of *Variety*." Unless the Federal
Trade Commission's charges were correct, he never did.

Sime was a colorful figure and his terse, hell-flung chin-up
Variety reflected the man. He was so much Broadway in person
that James J. Walker, former Mayor of New York, once suggested that the town's nationally known theatrical mart be
renamed "Sime's Square." His picturesque paper was read by

many outside the profession because of its earthy, flaunting style that Sime flung into type without regard for syntax, grammar, or the King's English. He turned nouns into verbs with the ease of an agent deducting commission: "panicked," "high-hatted," "authored," "readied"; and as a coiner of slang terms and phrases was exceeded only by one of his saltiest reporters, Jack Conway, whose "varicose alleys" to describe the legs of a passé burlesque girl—describes the legs of a passé burlesque girl. He not only wrote vaudeville's jargon, he improved it with such inventions as "nuts," "palooka," and "scram." In that fateful week of October, 1929, when the crash cleaned the stock market, Sime's classic head told the story in an epitaph: WALL ST. LAYS AN EGG. His influence lived, for but a few years after his death *Variety* nimbly topped a lead story of the picture industry's policy in feeding rube films to the farmers with: STICKS NIX HICK PIX.

Sime was a genius for getting color into copy. He could take a prosy paragraph, and with a word here and a phrase there make it sting. He picked men for their ability as newsgetters; he wasn't fussy about their style, knowing that they could soon catch the racy touch or that he could give it to their copy. The only instructions he ever gave a new man were: "Go out and dig some news." His own method of reporting was unique. He carried in his side coat pocket tiny pads of paper and a pencil and taught himself to make notes without revealing the fact to the interviewee. Apparently, with hands in pockets, he was merely engaging the subject in a casual conversation. Occasionally Sime slipped into error, all men being fallible. He was prompt with retraction: "Joe Blotz is not a dope addict as reported. Joe says he hasn't hit the stuff in years."

Sime was an indefatigable worker. He drove his men, but no harder than he drove himself. *Variety* became the family crest. Besides the in-law Freemans, Sime put his wife, Hattie, on the staff to write woman's-angle stuff under the signature "Skirt." His son Sydney (Syd) began at the age of seven with a kid's response column under the nom de plume "Skigie." Sime had a curious, boyish facetiousness that never left him. In 1928 he went alone to the composing room—the office was then at its present location, 154 West 46 Street—and himself inserted this in the Broadway "Chatter" column: "When Syd Silverman reads this he will know that he is president and editor of *Variety*." Next day he moved his desk from the dais which was, and still is, the editorial sanctum of *Variety*. It had once been the display stage for a French couturier.

Sime died of a lung hemorrhage, alone and unattended, in the Ambassador Hotel, Los Angeles, in September, 1933. His death panicked Broadway; you should have caught them at the funeral in Temple Emanu-El. He left a net estate of $33,254. And he willed 300 shares of stock in *Variety* to eight employees: to Harold Erichs, Hal Halperin, Louis Rydell, and Editor Abel Green, each 50 shares; to Jack Pulaski, Robert Landry, Joshua Lowe, and Joseph Bigelow, each 25 shares. O.K., Sime.

The Show Is Over

During the ten years that followed the organization of the United Booking Office in 1900 Albee was so busy hamstringing the performer that no further action was taken in extending the Keith-Albee circuit. But in 1910, temporarily free for larger affairs, he and his associates made their first inroad into Midwestern territory with the acquisition of the Columbia Theatre in Cincinnati. Soon after they took over the Mary Anderson Theatre and the Grand Opera House in Louisville, Ky., properties valued at $3,000,000.

Then individual money-taking and internecine warfare again halted them and impending absorptions, earlier determined upon, were delayed. No corresponding deals ensued until two years later when the Percy Williams circuit, a small but exceedingly profitable metropolitan chain, was acquired in 1912.

In the succeeding twelve years there were three (four, if the Cleveland Palace be remembered) important acquisitions following rapidly each upon the other. In 1920 the Keith-Albee interests announced purchase of a half interest in the B. S. Moss theaters, a chain of eight houses in Greater New York together with a booking arrangement relating to sixteen additional theaters with a total seating capacity of nearly 50,000. Three years later, December 18, 1923, the New York Hippodrome, for years the site of lavish spectacles presented by Thompson and Dundy and afterward by Charles Dillingham, was converted into a vaudeville house at a renovating expense of $500,000.

In 1924 Albee extended his influence into Canada by obtaining control of six theaters (Canadian United Theatres) operated by Mike Shea and Joseph Franklin. It may read smallish as a venture, but the deal involved $5,000,000 in property holdings and rights. And none of these deals had anything to do with the muscling in on theaters which were forced to book U.B.O. acts.

Albee constantly impeded the building of his own circuit. Had he recognized the right of the actors to organize, in short, had he played fair, he would have realized his financial returns earlier and in larger volume; and he, Keith, Murdock, Beck, Meyerfeld, Williams, Proctor, Shea, *et al.*, would have reaped a harvest greater than the millions they did take.

There were other ways in which Albee showed himself a reactionary of the first water. His dealings with his own performers corresponded with his attitude in the Equity strike in 1919. This affected the legitimate stage and need not concern us, save for Albee's dismal, though continuously denied, participation.

In the first Equity threat against the managers Albee allied his interests with those of the legitimate stage executives under the banner of the United Managers Protective Association of the Amusement Interests of the United States, an attenuated title that suggests legal nomenclature rather than that of showmen with lights over a marquee. Albee, who was second vice-president, announced its mission to be the protection and well-being of the theater and the resistance of the "unreasonable demands of labor unions."

In 1919, when the actors struck and formed Equity which protects them today, Albee's advice was continually sought, although his direct interest was not indicated until a dramatic ratification of Equity's contract was signified at a meeting of

1,500 actors in the Lexington Theatre in September of that year.

A lone chorus girl, who had served intermittent time in vaudeville, arose timorously and stated her fear of vaudeville reprisal at Equity's action. Whereupon the late Marie Dressler, president of Chorus Equity, jumped to her feet and exclaimed:

"I don't think Mr. Albee will discriminate against you. Mr. Albee's time is coming."

It was, but not then nor through those channels.

Five years later, in May, 1924, when the Equity contracts were up for renewal, William A. Brady told Albee off with the statement that the inharmonious condition between actors and managers was directly his responsibility. Albee ignored the statement, preferring to let Sam H. Harris deny the accusations. But John Emerson, Equity president, supported the indictment.

Further Errors of Albee.

Throughout his career Albee misjudged vaudeville as a type of entertainment. There is scarcely an indication that he was ever aware of its essential function as a critical, satirical summation in topical humor of the social, economic, and political trend of the time. Instead of seeing it as the specific thing it was—a people's escape—he constantly used it as a medium for propaganda. A theatrical hat-passer, he often had the effrontery to beg from his audiences for funds to support his company union, the National Vaudeville Artists; and his perpetual tie-ups with the government and politics were not relished by audiences who came to his theaters to forget, not to be reminded. In 1921 he went so far as to obtain permission from Herbert C. Hoover, then secretary of commerce, to report the industrial bureau's monthly tabulations of the status of various trades, industries, and financial activities as they related to widening business conditions.

Perhaps Albee realized that an unfettered vaudeville would

challenge his propaganda policy. Thus, after the World War when the Y.M.C.A. came in for its share of ribbing from vaudeville's comics because of alleged mismanagement, Albee halted such gags on the protest of one A. G. Knabel, associate general secretary of the Y.M.C.A. in New York. "Such criticism," wrote Albee, "is un-American, un-Christianlike, and a blot upon the intelligence and upon our gratitude for what the organization has done." Well, there were plenty of complaints against the "Y" by the returning soldiers. And anyway the suppression by Albee in itself was un-American.

But his prohibition of the booking of notorious nonperformers for exploitation is understandable as a matter of taste. Thus, he canceled the appearance of Mrs. Florence Carman, who had been acquitted after a sensational murder trial in 1915. She was booked at the Prospect Theatre in Brooklyn, and Albee, upon his return from a Western tour, yanked her immediately and issued this order from the United Booking Office:

To representatives of acts: We understand that some of you have been offering persons as vaudeville acts who have recently gained notoriety through criminal court trials. Such acts have nothing to commend them but their notoriety, and in order that you may know our disposition regarding acts of this character, we hereby notify you that we do not desire them, would not play them under any circumstances, and consider it an insult for you to offer them to our company. Please, therefore, do not even suggest acts of this character to this office in the future.

Sometimes Albee's quirks even inspired generosity. In Cleveland one afternoon John Royal was handed a telegram from Albee: "Give Jack Norworth Two Thousand Dollars." Norworth was not playing Cleveland, but what astonished Royal was that Albee would loosen to Norworth, a performer with whom he had been unfriendly for years. Norworth was finally traced in St. Louis and the money wired to him there. Later he told Royal that he was broke and had tapped everyone for the loan in vain. "I couldn't get it from my friends," said Norworth, "so I thought I'd ask Albee, just for a gag."

Albee, whose town house was in Central Park West, later removed to Larchmont, a suburban town on Long Island Sound in Westchester County, N.Y., within commuting distance of New York City. As a member of the Larchmont Yacht Club he met the Reverend Dr. Richard Cobden, rector of St. John's Episcopal Church in the town. A friendship developed that carried Albee into the church—an amazing capitulation which his associates could only ascribe to the softening impulse of the forthcoming marriage of Albee's daughter Ethel to Dr. Edwin Lauder, a Philadelphia dentist.

After he got religion a change came over the blustering, profane, and relentless Albee. He gentled his staff and his managers, and conducted his office in a halo atmosphere. "Let us do as the Nazarene would," was his pretty prelude to discussions—except for occasional detonating reversions. A representative of some interest, aware of Albee's conversion and slowly tightening the screws in a money deal, would be immediately halted by Albee's: "Listen—you ——." But the outbursts grew less frequent. The warrior was soon to lay aside his armor, exposing his tired limbs to the enmeshing celluloid.

Albee (again the reactionary) consistently defied motion pictures, which by the early 1920's were seriously encroaching upon vaudeville. His attitude may have led to the rift with his closest associate, John J. Murdock, for Murdock as consistently supported them, and is said at one time, unknown to Albee, to have plotted a deal with Adolph Zukor by which Paramount was to be put on the pictures and Murdock the vaudeville over the Keith-Orpheum circuit.

But Albee was having other troubles. In 1907, as heretofore stated, an English performer, Harry Mountford, came to the United States. In London he did a talking-song act and was the first music-hall performer to work in evening dress. He had served as chairman of the National Alliance of Actors,

Stagehands, and Musicians and had fought a strike in England, which won black-listing for him when the managers there triumphed. Soon after he reached this country Albee sent for him. "You came here to get work," he said, "and we can make you very comfortable here. But we don't want any disturbers." Mountford replied, "You mean, of course, you want me to keep my mouth shut. The same offer was made to me in England and I refused. I didn't come 3,000 miles to accept it here." So Albee marked him. And the actors invited Mountford to reorganize the White Rats.

The Lost Cause.

In addition to the problems of the moribund Rats, Mountford was confronted by the necessity of fighting the Actors National Union, an organization set up by the managers to act as buffer and confuse the issues. Although it had a charter from the American Federation of Labor, most performers paid no attention to it. But when Mountford proposed a closed shop for vaudeville, demanded an equitable contract, and sought restrictions to make agents responsible for their misdeeds he was opposed so vigorously by the Actors National Union that he determined to extinguish it. Accordingly, on June 20, 1910, he applied to the A. F. of L. for a White Rats charter which, he told Sam Gompers, then A. F. of L. president, was necessary because of the Actors National Union. Mountford convinced Gompers that the managers were underwriting this union, and the labor president forthwith canceled its charter and compelled an amalgamation into an international called the White Rats Actors Union of which the White Rats of America was a branch. The new charter was issued November 7, 1910. Mountford kept pounding at the Vaudeville Managers Association and its U.B.O. They retaliated by black-listing every actor they knew to be a member of the White Rats. This and a series of minor brawls kept the feud simmering until the lid blew off in 1916.

Albee had previously challenged any actor to prove that

he was forced to pay more than the 10 per cent agency fee and in 1913 gave the New York *World* an interview in which he set forth the aims of the U.B.O. with his customary public altruism. As a subscription to the interview the *World*, in bold-faced type, printed this notice:

This article was shown to several of the leaders in the actors' organizations who were offered space to set forth their charges against the United Booking Office. All declined, stating that the controlling power of the organization was so great they dared not antagonize it in fear of being black-listed.

This precipitated another series of minor strikes, but nothing serious developed until 1916 when Albee and his colleagues formed an organization called the National Vaudeville Artists. Overnight a staff of officers was recruited and at the U.B.O. a new contract was drawn up containing this clause:

The actor hereby guarantees that he is not a member of the White Rats Actors Union and that he is a member in good standing of the National Vaudeville Artists. In the event that either of these statements be found untrue this contract is automatically canceled.

This was a deliberate flouting of basic American labor principles, and Mountford called a nation-wide strike of all performers, notices to this effect being published in every important American newspaper.

The strike began in Oklahoma City before its announced time, and in aid, ironically, of the stagehands who, although giving necessary assistance to the Equity strike in 1919, aided the White Rats not at all throughout their fifteen-year fight for improved conditions. In Oklahoma City the Greek manager of a theater, one Sinopoulo (who had painted this sign over his stage door: "Don't send your laundry out until after the first performance") fired his union stage crew and hired scabs. The discharged crew appealed to Mountford, who at once called the actors out in sympathy. It was the forerunner of similar White Rats strikes in New York and Boston.

In New York the actors' strike was immediately effective—
for the stagehands. For six years the stagehands' union, The
International Alliance of Theatrical Stage Employees, known
as the I.A.T.S.E., had sought to unionize the Loew, Moss,
and Fox circuits. When the White Rats struck on those circuits
the managers signed a union-shop contract with the stagehands the following day, and the stagehands immediately
went out and picketed the actors. In New England on the
Poli circuit, with the exception of Waterbury, the stagehands
in paid advertisements announced to the public that the Poli
theaters were union theaters and called the actors city agita-
tors who were trying to destroy the friendly relationship between the stage crews and the management.

Comparable moves were made in Boston where no stage-
crew union shop was in force until the actors walked out. A
union contract was then signed and motion pictures of the
signing were immediately shown in the Gordon and Keith
theaters with captions that read: "This is an A. F. of L. house
and the manager is a friend of labor."

Mountford, in January, 1917, and during bitter weather,
sought a conference with Charles C. Shay, president of the
I.A.T.S.E. It was attended also by Joseph N. Weber, president
of the American Federation of Musicians; the president of the
Boston Central Labor Council; James W. Fitzpatrick, president of the White Rats, and Mike Fenton, president of the
Teamsters' local in Boston. Mountford demanded of Shay
why he had withheld aid after promising cooperation with
the White Rats.

SHAY: Yes, I promised to help you, but I never promised to pull my
    men out.
MOUNTFORD: I pulled my people out for you.
SHAY: Well, I have contracts with these managers and I can't
    break them.
FITZPATRICK: You didn't have those contracts a week ago.
WEBER: Shay, if you pull your men I'll pull mine out.
SHAY: No, I have contracts and I cannot break them.

FENTON: Oh, cut it out. I know when you made your contracts.
But I have a contract here which I have had for ten years. Shay,
if you will pull your men out I'll tear up my contract and not an
ounce of coal will go into those theaters and they'll be freezing
to death in forty-eight hours.

Shay left the meeting, silent.

This strike, last of the series, was also lost. And Albee began
reprisals. The White Rats had built a beautiful clubhouse at
227–231 West 46th Street. Directly opposite the managers
rented quarters where agents were placed to take down the
name of any performer seen entering—for black-listing. This
was coincidental with a campaign of vilification against
Mountford.

Both *Variety* and *Billboard* published cartoons of him in a
brothel with a girl on each knee and a $1,000 bill in his hand,
the caption reading: "What Does It Matter? White Rats
Money." Another depicted him staggering from a saloon with
a cigar tilted in his mouth with the same caption: "What Does
It Matter? White Rats Money." Mountford did not drink
nor did he smoke cigars. He and Fitzpatrick both were
accused of diverting funds, accusations which were not
criminally proved.

Though he sought it for years, Albee was never successful in
obtaining the White Rats five per cent levy list. (The levy
was exacted of members to finance the strike and $29,000 was
raised.) Later, before the Federal Trade Commission, Pat
Casey, labor executive for the managers and close associate
of John J. Murdock, admitted the strike cost the managers
$2,000,000. Mountford was summoned to produce the list
and threatened with contempt of court if he did not comply.
He could not produce it. Barry Conners had tossed it into one
of the foundations of the Golden Gate Bridge in San Francisco
while the cement was still soft. It was lucky for a number of
still living Hollywood and Broadway stars, who, had their
names been revealed, might today be mooching dimes for
coffee. Albee would have black-listed them for life.

The managers' spy system gradually produced results. Knowing of the careful watch over their clubhouse, no White Rat who wanted to keep playing dared enter. The membership dwindled and receipts dipped from $2,000 weekly to about $65. All the furniture was mortgaged. And in 1917 the club defaulted on the first-mortgage interest to the Mutual Bank. The bank officials sent for Mountford, who told them that if the bank's client would assume the White Rats' commercial debts they, the White Rats, would abandon the building. The bank agreed, and the White Rats walked out singing "The Emblem." Soon after the property was acquired by the 229 West 46th Street Corp., a front for the National Vaudeville Artists who came in and took over.

Twenty years later, in 1937, the N.V.A. members who were loyal to the Rats walked out also singing "The Emblem." When vaudeville was in its death throes in the mid-1920's and there had for some years been no need for a company union Albee lost all interest in the N.V.A., (an abbreviation, cracked Wilton Lackaye, for Never Vex Albee), left not a nickel to the organization, asserting in his will that those in charge "have summarily dispensed with my services, support and cooperation."

Your Motley, Fool.

Although the *coup de grâce* to vaudeville has been assigned to many hands and agencies, Albee himself delivered a body blow to the faltering expression when, in the 1920's, he forsook his one-time beloved two-a-day for "presentation" five-a-day shows. This "generosity" at the expense of the actor bled thinner its arteries. It ate up material faster than the writers and gag men could supply it. And a weary public, tired of stale jokes, offended by the lapse into vulgarity, sick to death of the same old pans and the ancient sets, turned to movies and sports.

That is one theory for the decline of vaudeville. It cannot be ignored. Another is also directly the responsibility of Albee.

The backbone of vaudeville was low comedy. When dialect, eccentric, and nut comedians in exaggerated costumes and facial make-ups predominated, the dumb acts and sensational presentations gave balance to the bill. When dinner coats, white tie and tails, and evening gowns replaced the baggy pants, slapshoes, and fright wigs; when faces were made beautiful instead of grotesque; when wisecracks, risqué gags, and the goosing stick were substituted for dialect jokes; when manufactured acts, consisting of a number of girls who changed costumes frequently, ousted the really nimble and effective old-time dance acts; when fashion-plate comics entertained between numbers instead of a roaring slapstick turn—vaudeville was devitalized. Cycloramas, drapery, and gorgeous drops added to the glamour, but not to the comedy.

Albee was responsible for much of this. He dressed up vaudeville fit to kill and it committed suicide. It became something that was neither variety, burlesque, nor review. On some of Albee's later bills you couldn't find a wisp of crepe hair or smudge of grease paint from opening to closing. The tramp, rube, padded Dutchman, bewhiskered Irishman, clown, crazy juggler, and comic cop had vanished. The performers, forced to dress to match Albee's million-dollar theaters (which were too large for comedy), looked no different to the audiences who could see tuxedos anywhere and for nothing. Anyway, the customers stopped coming. Had they liked the new type of presentation better than the old, possibly they would have been coming yet.

If Albee had had sufficient vision he would have agreed to the unionization of vaudeville. And no actors' union would have permitted five shows a day given in such circumstances and for the average salary that prevailed for standard acts on Keith and Orpheum time.

Just before Albee's death this was dramatically called to his attention by Marcus Heiman of the United Booking Office. When the men met in Palm Beach, where Albee died, March

11, 1930, of a heart attack, Heiman said, "You killed vaude-ville, Mr. Albee."

Dazed, the ailing Albee, who for years had smilingly accepted the accolade for developing vaudeville as America's greatest form of entertainment, could scarcely mutter, "What do you mean?" And Heiman told him how ruinous his flogging five-a-day had been. Unable to comprehend, Albee stood and stared.

He had been retired nearly a year—beaten and broken, and as he suspected, double-crossed.

In 1928, Joseph P. Kennedy, at this writing ambassador to England but then with the Film Booking Office, a motion-picture company, suggested to Albee that he sell out. Kennedy is reported to have offered Albee 21 for his Keith-Orpheum stock which was then quoted at 16 on the Exchange. Albee declined but weakened on the advice of those he thought were his friends. He sold. In three months the stock soared to 50.

Albee was continued with the organization as president but, unknown to him, his power had been taken away. He entered Kennedy's office one day to make a suggestion. The conversation, according to associates, was short:

"Didn't you know, Ed? You're washed up, you're through."

Albee understood, quit, died. He was brought back and buried from the Cathedral of St. John the Divine, to whose building fund he had contributed so liberally. A corporal's guard attended the service.

Appendix

Fifty Years of Standard Acts (1880–1930)

Adams & LeRoy, blackface act
Adgee's Lions
Ahearn, Charlie, comedy cycling act
Ahearns, The, breakaway ladder act
Alburtus, Morris, and Jessie Millar, novelty musical jugglers
Aldon & Co., jugglers
Alhambra Sextet, song and dance
Alma, Mme., electric globe performer
Almond, Tom, eccentric dancer
Althea Sisters, seriocomics
Amazon and Nile, contortionists
Amoros Sisters, novelty song and dance
Andresens, The, risley act
Andrews, Pearl, comedienne and mimic
Angela Sisters, singing and whistling act
Angeles, Aimee, mimic
Anselsmiths, The, iron jaw stunt
Apollon, Dave, musical and dance specialties
Arbuckle, Roscoe "Fatty," monologist
Arniotis, Mary, strong woman
Arnot Brothers, acrobats
Astaire, Fred and Adele, dancers
Astella Brothers, comedy acrobats
Aug, Edna, character comedienne
Austin and Dailey, blackface comics

Austin, Gene, songs
Austin, George, comedy wire act
Austin, Rose and Aimee, novelty trapeze
Austins, Tossing, comedy jugglers
Australian Woodchoppers

Babu Abdulle, Hindu conjurer
Bagesens, The, jugglers
Baker, Phil, comedian
Balabanows, Five, musical act
Baldwin and Daly, "Hottentot" act
Ballard, James, bard (Billed as only rival of the Cherry Sisters)
Baptiste and Franconi, gymnasts
Barber, W. H., trick cyclist
Barbette, novelty female impersonator
Barclay, Don, comic
Barnes and Robinson, songs and crossfire
Barnold's Dogs
Barry, Mr. and Mrs. Jimmy, comic sketch team
Barry, Lydia, seriocomic
Barrymore, Maurice, sketch player
Barto and Mann, comedy dance turn
Barton, James, eccentric dance comic
Barton and Lovera, dance act
Beaumont Sisters, song and dance
Bell, Eva, English song and dance
Bell Family, musical and dance act
Belloc, Robert, and Mlle. Aouda, jugglers
Bennett, Laura, comedienne
Bennington's Harmonica Boys
Berle, Milton, monologist
Berlin and Snyder, singing composers
Bernard, Sophie, seriocomic
Bernie, Ben, violin act
Berrens, Fred, musical novelty
Berzac, Cliff, trick mule
Bessinger, Frank, baritone
Beverly, Maude, seriocomic
Bickel and Watson, comics
Bigelow, Charles, comic
"Big Three Minstrels," songs and comedy
Binns and Burns, instrumentalists

Blanchard Brothers, musical novelty
Blocksam and Page, knockabout comics
Blue, Ben, eccentric comedy
Boehm, Elsie, female baritone
Boganny Troups, "Lunatic Bakers"
Boley, May, "The Village Cutup"
Bordeaux Sisters, songs, dances, imitations
Boreo, Emile, French comic singer
Boston Fadettes, musical
Bowen, Sibyl, songs in character
Boyd and Wallin, wire stunt
Boyle, McCarthy & Co., musical comedy sketch
Braatz Brothers, novelty balancers
Branford, Tom and Bertie, sketches and imitations
Brendel, El, and Flo Burt, crossfire Swede
Brice, Fannie, comedienne
Britton, Frank and Milt, xylophones
Brown Brothers, Six, comedy saxophone act
Brown and Nevarro, character changes and songs
Brown and Wright, Lancashire clog dancers
Browne Sisters, musical act
Brownings, The, novelty songs and skits
Bryant, Harry, ventriloquist
Bryton, Georgia, male impersonator
Buffons, Three, pantomimists
Burke, Johnny, monologist
Burns, Harry, & Co., Italian comics
Burns and Kane, comics
Bursel, Maggie, rope skipping jig
Bush and Gordon, acrobatic comedians
Byrne, Gypsy, male impersonator
Byrnes and Helene, sketch and crayon drawings

Cansinos, The, novelty dancers
Caprice, Lynn and Faye, song and dance
Carletta, contortionist
Carmencita, Spanish novelty dancer
Carr, Alexander, comic
Carr, Jules, performing bear
Carroll, Lew, Dutch imitations
Carter, Thomas J., and Lizzie Anderson, society sketch
Cartmell and Harris, song and dance

Cartrell, Bud, lariat spiel
Carus, Emma, singer
Carver, Annette, equestrienne
Castle, Vernon and Irene, dancers
Catlett, Walter, comic
Cawthorne, Herbert, comedian
Cecil and Van, wire and dog act
Cello, Van and Mary, risley act
Chandler, Anna, seriocomic
Chaplin, Charles, comedian
Chappelle and Carlton, acrobats
Chip and Marble, comedy sketch
Cinquevalli, Paul, juggler
Claire, Ina, mimic
Clark, Amy Ashmore, "Crepe Paper Girl"
Clark, Leoni, animal novelty
Clayton, Bessie, dancer
Clayton, Jackson, and Durante, nut comics
Clayton, Jenkins, and Jasper, character comedy
Cline, Maggie, Irish seriocomic
Clipper Quartet (Ward, Campbell, Howard, and Gale), burlesque specialty
Cole and Johnson, Negro comedy songs
Colibris' Midgets, novelty wire act
Colleano, Con, wire artist
Collins, Lottie, seriocomic
Collins and Peterson, song and dance
Connolly, Dolly, seriocomic
Conroy and Lemaire, blackface
Conroy's Diving Models, tank act
Consul, the monk
Conway and Leland, song and dance
Cook, Pauline, and May Clinton, sharpshooting act
Cook and Vernon, comedy act
Cooper, Fitch, trick novelty
Corrigan, Emmet, dramatic sketch
Coulson Sisters, rope skipping
Craig, Marsh, equilibrist
Creatore, bandmaster
Cronin, Morris, juggler
Curtis and Garden, bag punchers
Cutty, Frank, musical
Cyrene, contortionist

Dalrymple, Jean, and Dave Jarrett, sketch team
Daly, Dan, comic
Daly, Dutch, concertina player
Daniels and Eames, comedy impersonators
Darras Brothers, equilibrists
Davies Family, gymnasts
Day, Harry and Daisy, musical sketch
Dayton, Julian, & Co., comedy sketch
Dazie, Mlle., dancer
DeBar Brothers, contortionists
DeFelippi, M. and Mme., transformation dance turn
DeGranville, Mlle., iron jaw act
DeHaven, Carter, comedian
Demarest and Deland, piano comedy
Dermot and Doyle, knockabout comedy
DeVan Sisters, ladder act
Devere, Sam, banjo soloist
DeWitt, Josie, violin
Dixieland Jazz Band
Donahue, Jack, dancer
Donald and Carson, Scotch comic singers
Doner, Kitty, English comedienne
Dooley, Ray, John, and Gordon, knockabout comics
Dowling, Eddie, comic
Downey, Morton, songs
Dresser, Louise, seriocomic
Dressler, Marie, comedienne
Drummond-Staley and Belle Birbeck, musical blacksmiths
Duncan, Charles H., monologist
Duncan Sisters, song and dance
Dupree and Dupree, cycling act

East and Dumke, singing comics
Eddys, The, Willie, Arthur, and Emily, tumblers
Edgeio, juggler
Edwards, Carrie, and Libbie Ross, female boxers
Edwards, Cliff, uke player
Eichbrette, Mlle., monkey troupe
Eldridge, Press, monologist
Electric Three (Callan, Haley, and Callan), song and dance comics
Elindre Sisters, comedy songs
Elta, Mlle., and Chase, mental act

Eltinge, Julian, female impersonator
Emily Sisters, trapeze act
Englehart, lady fencer
Errol, Leon, eccentric dancer
Etting, Ruth, songs
Europe, Jim, jazz leader
Evans, Charles, & Co., sketch act
Evans, Ollie, and William Barry, Jr., novelty acrobats
Evans and Perez, acrobats

Farro, shadowgraph artist
Fay, Frank, monologist
Ferry, the Frog Man
Fink's Mules
Fisher, Harry, comic
Fitzgibbon, McCoy, and Fitzgibbon, comics
Five Martells, bicycle act
Flemen and Miller, patter and songs
Flippen, Jay Co., comedy and M.C.
Fontaine, wire act
Forber, M., slackwire and juggler
Ford Girls, Mabel and Dora, dance act
Forgardus, Mlle., educated cockatoos and dogs
Fostelle, Charles, female impersonator
Four Athletes, strong women
Four Emperors (Howard, Russell, Powell, and Blackford), musical act
Fox, Madge, "Flip-Flop Girl"
Fox and Ward, blackface comics
Foy, Eddie, comic
Franklin and Royce, sharpshooters
Franklins, The, John, Lillie, and James, Irish character act
Friganza, Trixie, seriocomic
Frigoli, change artist
Fyffe, Will, Scottish comic

Gabler, Harry, glass eater
Gallagher, Billy, and John Gannon, knockabout Irish act
Gamble, Valand, lightning calculator
Gautier, Emile, equestrian
Gautier's Toy Shop, animal act
Gehrue Sisters, toe and buck dancing
Ghezzi's, Les, equilibrists

Giguere, Eddie, trick vocalist
Gilbert, Bessie, cornetist
Gilbert, John, monologist
Gillingwater, Claude, impersonator
Gilmore and Leonard, instrumentalists
Glass, Bonnie, ballroom dancer
Glockers, The, novelty juggling
Goetz, Joseph, revolving globe act
Goodrich, Mamie, and Harry McBride, clog dancers
Goodwin, Myra, song and dance novelty
Gordon, Frank E., magician
Gordone, Robbie, poser
Gorman, Professor, ventriloquist
Gorman, Ross, novelty musician
Grais, Herr, novelty animals
Granat, Louis, whistler
Granville, Bernard, recitations
Granville, Taylor, comedy sketch
Grapewin, Charles, comic
Green, Harry, comedy sketch
Grey, Mamie, blackface comedienne

Hadji, Ali Co. freak act
Hajos, Mitzi, singer
Hale and Francis, juggling and hoop act
Hale, Willie and Francis, hoop rollers
Haley and Flynn, Irish comics
Hall, Al K., comic
Hallen and Hart, comedy duo
Halperin, Nan, seriocomic
Hamilton, Frank, character songs
Hampton, J. W., educated dogs and geese
Hanneford, Poodles, clown
Harbeck, William, Negro acrobat
Harrigan and Johnson, blackface comics
Hart and Walling, novelty song and dance
Hartines, Four, tight wire
Hartmans, The, Paul and Grace, dance satirists
Harvey, Josephine, trombonist
Hathaway, Belle, monkey turn
Haveman's Animals
Hawkins and Kelly, Dutch-Irish comics

Hayden, Ola, female baritone
Hazard, Jack, monologist
Healey Brothers, blackface team
Healey, Ted and Betty, songs and crossfire
Healy, Dan, dancer
Heather, Josie, English character act
Hemstreet Singers, girl quartet
Hengler Sisters, song and dance
Henry's (Charles) Pets, dog act
Herbert and Goldsmith, song and dance
Herman, Al, blackface comic
Herne, Sam, rube comic
Hewitts, The Two, rolling globe performers
Hill, Gus, Indian club act
Hodge, William, monologist
Hodges and Launchmere, blackface act
Hoey, James F., monologist
Hoffman, Gertrude, dancer
Holcombe, Curtis, & Co., comedy burglar skit
Holmes, Pollie, "The Irish Duchess"
Holmes, Taylor, monologue and imitations
Horseshoe Four, voice harmony
Howard and Fox, jig and reel dancers
Howard, The Great, ventriloquist
Howard, Harris, and Leroy, comedy act
Howard, James and Co., drunk specialty
Howard, Willie and Eugene, comics
Hunter, Georgie, comedy songs
Hussey, Mr. and Mrs. George W., novelty ventriloquists
Hyman, Harry, novelty hypnotist

Inaudi, Jacques, lightning calculator
Ingliss and Breen, comedy songs
Irwin, Leo, and Beatner, Australian athletes
Isham's Octoroons, colored singers

Jans and Whalen, nut song comics
Jee, James H., slack wire
Jemima, Aunt, blackface singer
Jewell's Manikins
Johns, Brooke, banjoist
Johnson, Charles, eccentric dancer

Johnson and Dean, song and dance
Johnson and Richards, knockabout acrobats
Johnstone, Ralph, novelty cyclist
Jones, Walter, tramp act
Juliet, violinist

Kahne, Harry, novelty sketch
Karno's Comedians
Kavanagh, Stan, comedy juggler
Keating and Flynn, song and dance
Keatons, Three, comics
Keene, J. Warren, sleights
Keith and Kernan, sand pictures
Keller Sisters and Lynch, song and dance
Kelly, John W., clog and Irish reel
Kelly and Murphy, sparring team
Kemmys, Three, equilibrists
Kendall, Ezra, rube comic
Kennedy and Warren, blackface act
Kenney, Bert, novelty monologue
Keno and Green, song and dance
Kernell, Daisy, song and dance
Kherns and Cole, Dutch comics
Kimberley and Page, comedy and song
King and Brice, song and dance
King, Charles and Nellie, song and dance
King, Hetty, song and dance
King, Mazie, ballet
Kiyose Nakae, jujitsu
Kohlmar, Lee, comedy sketch
Kolb and Dill, Dutch comics
Kouns, Nellie and Sara, twin-voiced sopranos
Kramer, Harry and Jennie, trick cyclists

Lamartine Brothers, somersault act
LaPetite Onre & Co., bicycle stuff
LaRose, Harry, Indian club tosser
LaRue, Grace, seriocomic
Lashwood, George, "English Dandy"
Lasky's (Jesse) Musical Novelties
Latell, Alfred, animal impersonator
LaTour, Babe, and Sid Gold, song and dance

Laurent, Ada, change artist
Laurie, Joe, Jr., monologist
La Vars, Paul and Walter, balancing act
Laveen and Cross, novelty acrobats
Lawson and Namon, bag punching and bicycle riding
Lean, Cecil, and Cleo Mayfield, singers
LeClair, John, juggler and shadowgraphs
Ledeaux and Louise, wire act
Lee, Henry, impersonations
Lee Tung Foo, Chinese baritone
Leo, Jessie, song and dance
Leonard, Eddie, minstrel singer
Leonidas, Professor, animal act
Lester, Florence, whistling act
Lester, Frank, monologist
Lester, Harry B., songs and imitations
Lester and Williams, song comics
Levey, Ethel, singing comedienne
Levy, Bert, cartoonist
Levy, Maurice, bandmaster
Lewis, Ada, comedienne
Lewis, Mabelle, and Paul McCarty, song and dance
Lewis, Ted, jazz band
Lina and Vani, acrobats
Linton, Guy, character song and dance
Litchfield, Mr. and Mrs. Neil, rube comics
Livingston Trio, comedy acrobats
Lloyd, Herbert, "Diamond King"
Lloyd and Wells, eccentric dancers
Lockhart's Elephants
Loftus, Marie, seriocomic (Cissie's mother)
Long, Nick, and Idalene Cotton, comedy sketch
Lorimer, Jack, Scotch comic
Lorraine, Oscar, eccentric violinist
Loyal, Sylvia, and Pierrot, bird act
Lucille, Mlle., and Cockie, trained cockatoo

McAvoy and Hallen, comedy team
McCloud and Karp, violin and banjo specialties
McDonald, Maybelle, ballad singer
MacDonald, Polly, seriocomic
MacKechnie, Peggy, mental act

MacLeod and Laird, Scotch comics
McMahon and Chappelle, blackface comics
Madie and Ray, novelty act
Maffet, James S., pantomime
Magyfy, fire-eaters
Mahoney, Tom, Irish comic
Mahoney, Will, comedy dance
Mandel, William and Joe, comedy acrobats
Manhattan Comedy Four, songs and skits
Marck, George, lion tamer
Martells, Five, bicycle act
Martin and Fabrini, novelty dancers
Martinetti and Sylvester, knockabout acrobatic turn
Marzelo and Millay, novelty bar and wrestling
Matsada Sorakichi, Japanese wrestler
Matthews, Professor A., performing goats
Maurice and Parker, acrobats
Maxellos, Five, rislcy act
Mayfield, Cleo, singer
Mayhew, Stella, singer
Mazuz and Abacco, tumblers
Meade, Jennie, seriocomic
Medrano and Donna, ballroom dancers
Medranos, acrobatic act
Mehlinger, Artie, and Walter Donaldson, piano and songs
Melville, Jennie, seriocomic
Merle, Miss, & Co., bird act
Michels, Karl, the German Sampson
Miller and Randolph, male musical duo
Mills, Jock, Scotch comic
Milo, Brothers, acrobats
Milo, tramp comic
Milo, Irma & Co., posing and dance act
Mizunos, Three, Japanese jugglers
Monroe Brothers, novelty acrobats
Montrose, Louise, and Auto Girls, novelty singing act
Mora, Helen, trick singer
Morello Brothers, head balancers
Morley Trio, musical novelty
Morris, Kittie, coon shouter
Morris, Lilly, English comedienne
Morris and Coghlan, character songs

Morrissey and Rich, comedy sketch
Morton, James C., & Co., comedy skit
Mosconi Family, dancers
Mulcay, Gus, harmonica
Muldoon, Billy, wrestler
Murphy, Mr. and Mrs. Mark, comedy sketch
Murphy and McNulty, gymnasts
Murphy and Wilson, comedy
Murray, Eline and Kathleen, songs and uke
Murray, Mae, dancer
Murray and Mack, Irish comics
Murray and Murphy, Irish comics

Nahm, Anthony, one-armed cornetist
Nelson, Glinsereti, and Demonio, novelty acrobats
Nelson Family, acrobats
Nelson's Boxing Cats
Nelusco and Hurley, magic and shadowgraphs
Nesbit, Evelyn, and Bobby O'Neill, song and dance
Nevins and Erwood, blackface
Newell and Niblo, novelty instrumental act
Niblo, Fred, monologist
Nichols, Jessie Lee, animal act
Nichols, Lulu and Mabel, plantation songs and dances
Nolan and Nolan, comedy juggling
Norman, Mary, monologist
Norvelle Brothers, acrobats
Nugent, Maude, seriocomic

Oberita Sisters, Three, novelty dance
Olson and Johnson, comics
Olympia Quartet, plantation four-act
Orpheus Comedy Four, singing four-act
Osterman, Jack, comic
Osterman, Kathryn, comedy sketch

Paine, Chevalier Ira, sharpshooter
Pantzer (Willy) Troupe, acrobats
Parker, Harry M., dog and cat circus
Patterson, Burdella, picture poses
Pennington, Ann, and Stewart Sisters, song and dance

Perry and White, songs and crossfire
Petching Brothers, The, novelty musical act
Petrie and Elise, eccentric comedy
Pettingill, Mac, dog act
Pollard, Daphne, comedienne
Powell, magician
Powell, Jack, trick jazz drummer
Powell, Louise, and Robert Cottrell, bareback riders
Powell and Phillips, wire act
Powers' Elephants
Powers, Mr. and Mrs. John T., song and dance
Preisser Sisters, Junie and Cherry, acrobatic dancers
Prince, Arthur, ventriloquist
Prior & Co., Allen, Australian tenor and musical act
Proske, Captain, tiger act
Pull, Professor Theo., hypnotist
Purvis, Johnny, donkey act

Quigley, Johnnie, newsboy tenor

Rammage and Vincent, banjoists
Ramza and Arno, horizontal bar act
Rankin, Phyllis, imitations
Rarick, Guy & Co., comedy and dance
Raymond, Charles, one-legged clog dancer
Reed and Shaw, ring comedy act
Reeves, Billy, comic drunk
Reilly, Pat, and Reno, crayon sketches
Reme, Amalia, Tyrolean warbler
Renault, Francis, female impersonator
Reynard, Ed F., ventriloquist
Reynolds, Earle, ice skater
Rice, Andy, monologist
Rice, Fannie, puppet turn
Rice Brothers, Dutch act
Rice and Cohen, comedy sketch
Rice and Newton, mental act
Richards, The Great, female impersonator
Ring, Blanche, seriocomic
Rio Brothers, Three, flying ring turn
Ritchie, Adele, singer
Robinson, Charles, eccentric comedian

Rochester, Claire, novelty singer
Rodero and Maley, song and dance
Roemer and Leroux, gymnasts
Rooney, Pat II, comic
Rooney, Pat III, comic
Rosa, Patti, singer
Rose, Julian, Jew comic
Ross and Fenton, travesties
Rouclere, Harry and Mildred, mental act
Roye and Maye, dance act
Rozinos, The, Joe and Wally, novelty acrobats
Ryan and Richfield, Irish comics

St. Felix Sisters, singing and Dutch clog
Sandow, strong man
Santley, Joseph, & Co., song and dance
Schaffer, Sylvester, novelty turn
Schenck Brothers, acrobats
Schilling, Charley, musical novelty
Schultz, Colonel Magnus, performing dogs
Seixas, Captain, and Water Nymphs, tank act
Seldoms, Three, posture act ("Living Pictures")
Sells, Willie, educated mule
Seville, Lily, character songs
Sexton, Al, song and dance
Shattuck, Truly, seriocomic
Shaw and Lee, comedy song and dance
Sheffer and Blakeley, comics
Sherman and Morrissey, song and dance
Sidneys, Four, tight wire
Silbon Co. (4), aerialists
Silk, Frank X., tramp comic
Singer's Midgets
Slayman's Arabs, acrobats
Snow Brothers, acrobats
Spissell Brothers and Mack, knockabout comedy acrobats
Sprague and McNeece, stunt roller skaters
Steele, Harry, novelty comic
Stirk Family, novelty bicycle act
Stone, Belle, novelty acrobat
Stone and Vernon, adagio turn
Strassel's Wonder Seal

Swor Brothers, blackface comics
Sylvester, Everett, contortionist

Tannen, Julius, monologist
Tate, Harry, & Co., "Motoring," sketch act
Telma, Norman, contortionist
Termini, Joe, comedy musician
Thomson, Charles, juggler
Thorn and Darwin, illusionists
Thornton, Bonnie, seriocomic
Toto, clown
Trahan, Al, and Vesta Wallace, song and dance
Travilla Brothers, Three, tank act with seal
Trovollo, ventriloquist
Turnour, Millie, equilibrist
Tuscano Brothers, battle-ax jugglers
Tyson and McWatters, impersonations

Vaidis Sisters, aerial artists
Van, Billy B., comedian
VanAuken, McPhee, and Hill, acrobats
Verdi Ladies' Quartet, singers
Vinton, Ed, and Buster, dog act
Volt, Tom, and Frank Vern, skaters

Wakefield, Ella Holt, pianalogue
Walton and Edwards, Dutch comics
Waterbury Brothers and Tenney, musical act
Waters' Seals, Captain
Wayburn, Ned, trick piano turn
Wayne, Hortense, coon shouter
Webb Brothers, musical clowns
Welch, Francis, & Co., comedy act
Weston, Lucy, seriocomic
Westony, pianist
Whalen and West, song and dance
Wheeler, Bert and Betty, comedy duo
Whelan, Albert, novelty impersonator
White, Frank, and Lew Simmons, blackface act
White, George, and Emma Haig, flirtation dance act
White, Thelma, song and dance
Whiting, Emma, song and dance

Whiting, Stanley, coon shouter
Wichman, George A., clay modeler
Williams and Bernie, novelty acrobats
Williams, Gus, Dutch comic
Wilson, Al, yodeler
Wilson, Alf H., character impersonations
Wilson Sisters, cornetists
Winney, Will, banjoist
Winston's Seals and Diving Nymphs, tank act
Wirth, May, horse act
Withers, Charles, rube comic
Wood and Sheppard, musical act
Woods and Mack, bone and banjo turn
Woodward's Educated Seals
Woosters, Three, tumblers
Wylie, Raymond, stunt singer

Yacopis, The, teeterboard act
York and King, comedy sketch
Young, Frank, soft-shoe dancer

Ziska and King, comedy juggling act

Index

CATALOG OF DOVER BOOKS

Philosophy, Religion

GUIDE TO PHILOSOPHY, C. E. M. Joad. A modern classic which examines many crucial problems which man has pondered through the ages: Does free will exist? Is there plan in the universe? How do we know and validate our knowledge? Such opposed solutions as subjective idealism and realism, chance and teleology, vitalism and logical positivism, are evaluated and the contributions of the great philosophers from the Greeks to moderns like Russell, Whitehead, and others, are considered in the context of each problem. "The finest introduction," BOSTON TRANSCRIPT. Index. Classified bibliography. 592pp. 5⅜ x 8.

T297 Paperbound **$2.00**

HISTORY OF ANCIENT PHILOSOPHY, W. Windelband. One of the clearest, most accurate comprehensive surveys of Greek and Roman philosophy. Discusses ancient philosophy in general, intellectual life in Greece in the 7th and 6th centuries B.C., Thales, Anaximander, Anaximenes, Heraclitus, the Eleatics, Empedocles, Anaxagoras, Leucippus, the Pythagoreans, the Sophists, Socrates, Democritus (20 pages), Plato (50 pages), Aristotle (70 pages), the Peripatetics, Stoics, Epicureans, Sceptics, Neo-platonists, Christian Apologists, etc. 2nd German edition translated by H. E. Cushman. xv + 393pp. 5⅜ x 8.

T357 Paperbound **$1.75**

ILLUSTRATIONS OF THE HISTORY OF MEDIEVAL THOUGHT AND LEARNING, R. L. Poole. Basic analysis of the thought and lives of the leading philosophers and ecclesiastics from the 8th to the 14th century—Abailard, Ockham, Wycliffe, Marsiglio of Padua, and many other great thinkers who carried the torch of Western culture and learning through the "Dark Ages": political, religious, and metaphysical views. Long a standard work for scholars and one of the best introductions to medieval thought for beginners. Index. 10 Appendices. xiii + 327pp. 5⅜ x 8.

T674 Paperbound **$1.85**

PHILOSOPHY AND CIVILIZATION IN THE MIDDLE AGES, M. de Wulf. This semi-popular survey covers aspects of medieval intellectual life such as religion, philosophy, science, the arts, etc. It also covers feudalism vs. Catholicism, rise of the universities, mendicant orders, monastic centers, and similar topics. Unabridged. Bibliography. Index. viii + 320pp. 5⅜ x 8.

T284 Paperbound **$1.75**

AN INTRODUCTION TO SCHOLASTIC PHILOSOPHY, Prof. M. de Wulf. Formerly entitled SCHOLASTICISM OLD AND NEW, this volume examines the central scholastic tradition from St. Anselm, Albertus Magnus, Thomas Aquinas, up to Suarez in the 17th century. The relation of scholasticism to ancient and medieval philosophy and science in general is clear and easily followed. The second part of the book considers the modern revival of scholasticism, the Louvain position, relations with Kantianism and Positivism. Unabridged. xvi + 271pp. 5⅜ x 8.

T296 Clothbound **$3.50**

T283 Paperbound **$1.75**

A HISTORY OF MODERN PHILOSOPHY, H. Höffding. An exceptionally clear and detailed coverage of western philosophy from the Renaissance to the end of the 19th century. Major and minor men such as Pomponazzi, Bodin, Boehme, Telesius, Bruno, Copernicus, da Vinci, Kepler, Galileo, Bacon, Descartes, Hobbes, Spinoza, Leibniz, Wolff, Locke, Newton, Berkeley, Hume, Erasmus, Montesquieu, Voltaire, Diderot, Rousseau, Lessing, Kant, Herder, Fichte, Schelling, Hegel, Schopenhauer, Comte, Mill, Darwin, Spencer, Hartmann, Lange, and many others, are discussed in terms of theory of knowledge, logic, cosmology, and psychology. Index. 2 volumes, total of 1159pp. 5⅜ x 8.

T117 Vol. 1, Paperbound **$2.00**

T118 Vol. 2, Paperbound **$2.00**

ARISTOTLE, A. E. Taylor. A brilliant, searching non-technical account of Aristotle and his thought written by a foremost Platonist. It covers the life and works of Aristotle; classification of the sciences; logic; first philosophy; matter and form; causes; motion and eternity; God; physics; metaphysics; and similar topics. Bibliography. New Index compiled for this edition. 128pp. 5⅜ x 8.

T280 Paperbound **$1.00**

THE SYSTEM OF THOMAS AQUINAS, M. de Wulf. Leading Neo-Thomist, one of founders of University of Louvain, gives concise exposition to central doctrines of Aquinas, as a means toward determining his value to modern philosophy. religion. Formerly "Medieval Philosophy Illustrated from the System of Thomas Aquinas." Trans. by E. Messenger. Introduction. 151pp. 5⅜ x 8.

T568 Paperbound **$1.25**

THE PHILOSOPHICAL WORKS OF DESCARTES. The definitive English edition of all the major philosophical works and letters of René Descartes. All of his revolutionary insights, from his famous "Cogito ergo sum" to his detailed account of contemporary science and his astonishingly fruitful concept that all phenomena of the universe (except mind) could be reduced to clear laws by the use of mathematics. An excellent source for the thought of men like Hobbes, Arnauld, Gassendi, etc., who were Descarte's contemporaries. Translated by E. S. Haldane and G. Ross. Introductory notes. Index. Total of 842pp. 5⅜ x 8.

T71 Vol. 1, Paperbound **$2.00**

T72 Vol. 2, Paperbound **$2.00**

THE CHIEF WORKS OF SPINOZA. An unabridged reprint of the famous Bohn edition containing all of Spinoza's most important works: Vol. I: The Theologico-Political Treatise and the Political Treatise. Vol. II: On The Improvement Of Understanding, The Ethics, Selected Letters. Profound and enduring ideas on God, the universe, pantheism, society, religion, the state, democracy, the mind, emotions, freedom and the nature of man, which influenced Goethe, Hegel, Schelling, Coleridge, Whitehead, and many others. Introduction. 2 volumes. 826pp. 5⅜ x 8.
T249 Vol. I, Paperbound $1.50
T250 Vol. II, Paperbound $1.50

LEIBNIZ, H. W. Carr. Most stimulating middle-level coverage of basic philosophical thought of Leibniz. Easily understood discussion, analysis of major works: "Theodicy," "Principles of Nature and Grace," Monadology"; Leibniz's influence; intellectual growth; correspondence; disputes with Bayle, Malebranche, Newton; importance of his thought today, with reinterpretation in modern terminology. "Power and mastery," London Times. Bibliography. Index. 226pp. 5⅜ x 8.
T624 Paperbound $1.35

AN ESSAY CONCERNING HUMAN UNDERSTANDING, John Locke. Edited by A. C. Fraser. Unabridged reprinting of definitive edition; only complete edition of "Essay" in print. Marginal analyses of almost every paragraph; hundreds of footnotes; authoritative 140-page biographical, critical, historical prolegomena. Indexes. 1170pp. 5⅜ x 8.
T530 Vol. 1 (Books 1, 2) Paperbound $2.25
T531 Vol. 2 (Books 3, 4) Paperbound $2.25
2 volume set $4.50

THE PHILOSOPHY OF HISTORY, G. W. F. Hegel. One of the great classics of western thought which reveals Hegel's basic principle: that history is not chance but a rational process, the realization of the Spirit of Freedom. Ranges from the oriental cultures of subjective thought to the classical subjective cultures, to the modern absolute synthesis where spiritual and secular may be reconciled. Translation and introduction by J. Sibree. Introduction by C. Hegel. Special introduction for this edition by Prof. Carl Friedrich xxxix + 447pp. 5⅜ x 8.
T112 Paperbound $1.85

THE PHILOSOPHY OF HEGEL, W. T. Stace. The first detailed analysis of Hegel's thought in English, this is especially valuable since so many of Hegel's works are out of print. Dr. Stace examines Hegel's debt to Greek Idealists and the 18th century and then proceeds to a careful description and analysis of Hegel's first principles, categories, reason, dialectic method, his logic, philosophy of nature and spirit, etc. Index. Special 14 x 20 chart of Hegelian system. x + 526pp. 5⅜ x 8.
T254 Paperbound $2.00

THE WILL TO BELIEVE and HUMAN IMMORTALITY, W. James. Two complete books bound as one. THE WILL TO BELIEVE discusses the interrelations of belief, will, and intellect in man; chance vs. determinism, free will vs. determinism, free will vs. fate, pluralism vs. monism; the philosophies of Hegel and Spencer, and more. HUMAN IMMORTALITY examines the question of survival after death and develops an unusual and powerful argument for immortality. Two prefaces. Index. Total of 429pp. 5⅜ x 8.
T291 Paperbound $1.65

THE WORLD AND THE INDIVIDUAL, Josiah Royce. Only major effort by an American philosopher to interpret nature of things in systematic, comprehensive manner. Royce's formulation of an absolute voluntarism remains one of the original and profound solutions to the problems involved. Part one, 4 Historical Conceptions of Being, inquires into first principles, true meaning and place of individuality. Part two, Nature, Man, and the Moral Order, is application of first principles to problems concerning religion, evil, moral order. Introduction by J. E. Smith, Yale Univ. Index. 1070pp. 5⅜ x 8.
T561 Vol. 1 Paperbound $2.25
T562 Vol. 2 Paperbound $2.25
the set $4.50

THE PHILOSOPHICAL WRITINGS OF PEIRCE, edited by J. Buchler. This book (formerly THE PHILOSOPHY OF PEIRCE) is a carefully integrated exposition of Peirce's complete system composed of selections from his own work. Symbolic logic, scientific method, theory of signs, pragmatism, epistemology, chance, cosmology, ethics, and many other topics are treated by one of the greatest philosophers of modern times. This is the only inexpensive compilation of his key ideas. xvi + 386pp. 5⅜ x 8.
T217 Paperbound $1.95

EXPERIENCE AND NATURE, John Dewey. An enlarged, revised edition of the Paul Carus lectures which Dewey delivered in 1925. It covers Dewey's basic formulation of the problem of knowledge, with a full discussion of other systems, and a detailing of his own concepts of the relationship of external world, mind, and knowledge. Starts with a thorough examination of the philosophical method; examines the interrelations of experience and nature; analyzes experience on basis of empirical naturalism, the formulation of law, role of language and social factors in knowledge; etc. Dewey's treatment of central problems in philosophy is profound but extremely easy to follow. ix + 448pp. 5⅜ x 8.
T471 Paperbound $1.85

CATALOG OF DOVER BOOKS

MIND AND THE WORLD-ORDER, C. I. Lewis. Building upon the work of Peirce, James, and Dewey, Professor Lewis outlines a theory of knowledge in terms of "conceptual pragmatism." Dividing truth into abstract mathematical certainty and empirical truth, the author demonstrates that the traditional understanding of the a priori must be abandoned. Detailed analyses of philosophy, metaphysics, method, the "given" in experience, knowledge of objects, nature of the a priori, experience and order, and many others. Appendices. xiv + 446pp. 5⅜ x 8.
T359 Paperbound **$1.95**

SCEPTICISM AND ANIMAL FAITH, G. Santayana. To eliminate difficulties in the traditional theory of knowledge, Santayana distinguishes between the independent existence of objects and the essence our mind attributes to them. Scepticism is thereby established as a form of belief, and animal faith is shown to be a necessary condition of knowledge. Belief, classical idealism, intuition, memory, symbols, literary psychology, and much more, discussed with unusual clarity and depth. Index. xii + 314pp. 5⅜ x 8.
T236 Paperbound **$1.50**

LANGUAGE AND MYTH, E. Cassirer. Analyzing the non-rational thought processes which go to make up culture, Cassirer demonstrates that beneath both language and myth there lies a dominant unconscious "grammar" of experience whose categories and canons are not those of logical thought. His analyses of seemingly diverse phenomena such as Indian metaphysics, the Melanesian "mana," the Naturphilosophie of Schelling, modern poetry, etc., are profound without being pedantic. Introduction and translation by Susanne Langer. Index. x + 103pp. 5⅜ x 8.
T51 Paperbound **$1.25**

SUBSTANCE AND FUNCTION, EINSTEIN'S THEORY OF RELATIVITY, E. Cassirer. In this double-volume, Cassirer develops a philosophy of the exact sciences that is historically sound, philosophically mature, and scientifically impeccable. Such topics as the concept of number, space and geometry, non-Euclidean geometry, traditional logic and scientific method, mechanism and motion, energy, relational concepts, degrees of objectivity, the ego, Einstein's relativity, and many others are treated in detail. Authorized translation by W. C. and M. C. Swabey. xii + 465pp. 5⅜ x 8.
T50 Paperbound **$2.00**

*THE ANALYSIS OF MATTER, Bertrand Russell. A classic which has retained its importance in understanding the relation between modern physical theory and human perception. Logical analysis of physics, prerelativity physics, causality, scientific inference, Weyl's theory, tensors, invariants and physical interpretations, periodicity, and much more is treated with Russell's usual brilliance. "Masterly piece of clear thinking and clear writing," NATION AND ATHENAEUM. "Most thorough treatment of the subject," THE NATION. Introduction. Index. 8 figures. viii + 408pp. 5⅜ x 8.
231 Paperbound **$1.95**

CONCEPTUAL THINKING (A LOGICAL INQUIRY), S. Körner. Discusses origin, use of general concepts on which language is based, and the light they shed on basic philosophical questions. Rigorously examines how different concepts are related; how they are linked to experience; problems of the field of contact between exact logical, mathematical, and scientific concepts, and the inexactness of everyday experience (studied at length). This work elaborates many new approaches to the traditional problems of philosophy—epistemology, value theories, metaphysics, aesthetics, morality. "Rare originality . . . brings a new rigour into philosophical argument," Philosophical Quarterly. New corrected second edition. Index. vii + 301pp. 5⅜ x 8
T516 Paperbound **$1.75**

INTRODUCTION TO SYMBOLIC LOGIC, S. Langer. No special knowledge of math required — probably the clearest book ever written on symbolic logic, suitable for the layman, general scientist, and philosopher. You start with simple symbols and advance to a knowledge of the Boole-Schroeder and Russell-Whitehead systems. Forms, logical structure, classes, the calculus of propositions, logic of the syllogism, etc., are all covered. "One of the clearest and simplest introductions," MATHEMATICS GAZETTE. Second enlarged, revised edition. 368pp. 5⅜ x 8.
S164 Paperbound **$1.75**

LANGUAGE, TRUTH AND LOGIC, A. J. Ayer. A clear, careful analysis of the basic ideas of Logical Positivism. Building on the work of Schlick, Russell, Carnap, and the Viennese School, Mr. Ayer develops a detailed exposition of the nature of philosophy, science, and metaphysics; the Self and the World; logic and common sense, and other philosophic concepts. An aid to clarity of thought as well as the first full-length development of Logical Positivism in English. Introduction by Bertrand Russell. Index. 160pp. 5⅜ x 8.
T10 Paperbound **$1.25**

ESSAYS IN EXPERIMENTAL LOGIC, J. Dewey. Based upon the theory that knowledge implies a judgment which in turn implies an inquiry, these papers consider the inquiry stage in terms of: the relationship of thought and subject matter, antecedents of thought, data and meanings, 3 papers examine Bertrand Russell's thought, while 2 others discuss pragmatism and a final essay presents a new theory of the logic of values. Index. viii + 444pp. 5⅜ x 8.
T73 Paperbound **$1.95**

TRAGIC SENSE OF LIFE, M. de Unamuno. The acknowledged masterpiece of one of Spain's most influential thinkers. Between the despair at the inevitable death of man and all his works and the desire for something better, Unamuno finds that "saving incertitude" that alone can console us. This dynamic appraisal of man's faith in God and in himself has been called "a masterpiece" by the ENCYCLOPAEDIA BRITANNICA. xxx + 332pp. 5⅜ x 8.
T257 Paperbound **$1.95**

THE SENSE OF BEAUTY, G. Santayana. A revelation of the beauty of language as well as an important philosophic treatise, this work studies the "why, when, and how beauty appears, what conditions an object must fulfill to be beautiful, what elements of our nature make us sensible of beauty, and what the relation is between the constitution of the object and the excitement of our susceptibility." "It is doubtful if a better treatment of the subject has since been published," PEABODY JOURNAL. Index. ix + 275pp. 5⅜ x 8.
T238 Paperbound $1.00

THE IDEA OF PROGRESS, J. B. Bury. Practically unknown before the Reformation, the idea of progress has since become one of the central concepts of western civilization. Prof. Bury analyzes its evolution in the thought of Greece, Rome, the Middle Ages, the Renaissance, to its flowering in all branches of science, religion, philosophy, industry, art, and literature, during and following the 16th century. Introduction by Charles Beard. Index. xl + 357pp. 5⅜ x 8.
T40 Paperbound $1.95

HISTORY OF DOGMA, A. Harnack. Adolph Harnack, who died in 1930, was perhaps the greatest Church historian of all time. In this epoch-making history, which has never been surpassed in comprehensiveness and wealth of learning, he traces the development of the authoritative Christian doctrinal system from its first crystallization in the 4th century down through the Reformation, including also a brief survey of the later developments through the Infallibility decree of 1870. He reveals the enormous influence of Greek thought on the early Fathers, and discusses such topics as the Apologists, the great councils, Manichaeism, the historical position of Augustine, the medieval opposition to indulgences, the rise of Protestantism, the relations of Luther's doctrines with modern tendencies of thought, and much more. "Monumental work; still the most valuable history of dogma . . . luminous analysis of the problems . . . abounds in suggestion and stimulus and can be neglected by no one who desires to understand the history of thought in this most important field," Dutcher's Guide to Historical Literature. Translated by Neil Buchanan. Index. Unabridged reprint in 4 volumes. Vol I: Beginnings to the Gnostics and Marcion. Vol II & III: 2nd century to the 4th century Fathers. Vol IV & V: 4th century Councils to the Carlovingian Renaissance. Vol VI & VII: Period of Clugny (c. 1000) to the Reformation, and after. Total of cii + 2407pp. 5⅜ x 8.

T904 Vol I	Paperbound $2.50
T905 Vol II & III	Paperbound $2.50
T906 Vol IV & V	Paperbound $2.50
T907 Vol VI & VII	Paperbound $2.50
	The set $10.00

THE GUIDE FOR THE PERPLEXED, Maimonides. One of the great philosophical works of all time and a necessity for everyone interested in the philosophy of the Middle Ages in the Jewish, Christian, and Moslem traditions. Maimonides develops a common meeting-point for the Old Testament and the Aristotelian thought which pervaded the medieval world. His ideas and methods predate such scholastics as Aquinas and Scotus and throw light on the entire problem of philosophy or science vs. religion. 2nd revised edition. Complete unabridged Friedländer translation. 55 page Introduction to Maimonides's life, period, etc., with an important summary of the GUIDE. Index. lix + 414pp. 5⅜ x 8.
T351 Paperbound $1.85

ASTROLOGY AND RELIGION AMONG THE GREEKS AND ROMANS, Franz Cumont. How astrololgy developed, spread, and took hold of superior intellects, from ancient Babylonia through Rome of the fourth century A.D. You see astrology as the base of a learned theology, the influence of the Neo-Pythagoreans, forms of oriental mysteries, the devotion of the emperors to the sun cult (such as the Sol Invictus of Aurelian), and much more. The second part deals with conceptions of the world as formed by astrology, the theology bound up with them, and moral and eschatological ideas. Introduction. Index. 128pp. 5¾ x 8.
T581 Paperbound $1.35

AFTER LIFE IN ROMAN PAGANISM, Franz Cumont. Deepest thoughts, beliefs of epoch between republican period and fall of Roman paganism. Contemporary settings, hidden lore, sources in Greek, Hebrew, Egyptian, prehistoric thought. Secret teachings of mystery religions, Hermetic writings, the gnosis, Pythagoreans, Orphism; sacrifices, nether world, immortality; Hades, problem of violent death, death of children; reincarnation, ecstacy, purification; etc. Introduction. Index. 239pp. 5⅜ x 8.
T573 Paperbound $1.35

History, Political Science, Americana

THE POLITICAL THOUGHT OF PLATO AND ARISTOTLE, E. Barker. One of the clearest and most accurate expositions of the corpus of Greek political thought. This standard source contains exhaustive analyses of the "Republic" and other Platonic dialogues and Aristotle's "Politics" and "Ethics," and discusses the origin of these ideas in Greece, contributions of other Greek theorists, and modifications of Greek ideas by thinkers from Aquinas to Hegel. "Must" reading for anyone interested in the history of Western thought. Index. Chronological Table of Events. 2 Appendixes. xxiv + 560pp. 5⅜ x 8.
T521 Paperbound $1.85

CATALOG OF DOVER BOOKS

THE ANCIENT GREEK HISTORIANS, J. B. Bury. This well known, easily read work covers the entire field of classical historians from the early writers to Herodotus, Thucydides, Xenophon, through Poseidonius and such Romans as Tacitus, Cato, Caesar, Livy. Scores of writers are studied biographically, in style, sources, accuracy, structure, historical concepts, and influences. Recent discoveries such as the Oxyrhinchus papyri are referred to, as well as such great scholars as Nissen, Gomperz, Cornford, etc. "Totally unblemished by pedantry." Outlook. "The best account in English," Dutcher, A Guide to Historical Lit. Bibliography, Index. x + 281pp. 5⅜ x 8.
T397 Paperbound **$1.50**

HISTORY OF THE LATER ROMAN EMPIRE, J. B. Bury. This standard work by the leading Byzantine scholar of our time discusses the later Roman and early Byzantine empires from 395 A.D. through the death of Justinian in 565, in their political, social, cultural, theological, and military aspects. Contemporary documents are quoted in full, making this the most complete reconstruction of the period and a fit successor to Gibbon's "Decline and Fall." "Most unlikely that it will ever be superseded," Glanville Downey, Dumbarton Oaks Research Lib. Geneological tables. 5 maps. Bibliography. Index. 2 volumes total of 965pp. 5⅜ x 8.
T398, 399 Two volume set, Paperbound **$4.00**

A HISTORY OF ANCIENT GEOGRAPHY, E. H. Bunbury. Standard study, in English, of ancient geography; never equalled for scope, detail. First full account of history of geography from Greeks' first world picture based on mariners, through Ptolemy. Discusses every important map, discovery, figure, travel, expedition war, conjecture, narrative, bearing on subject. Chapters on Homeric geography, Herodotus, Alexander expedition, Strabo, Pliny, Ptolemy, would stand alone as exhaustive monographs. Includes minor geographers, men not usually regarded in this context: Hecataeus, Pytheas, Hipparchus, Artemidorus, Marinus of Tyre, etc. Uses information gleaned from military campaigns such as Punic Wars, Hannibal's passage of Alps, campaigns of Lucullus, Pompey, Caesar's wars, the Trojan War. New introduction by W. H. Stahl, Brooklyn College. Bibliography. Index. 20 maps. 1426pp. 5⅜ x 8.
T570-1, clothbound, 2-volume set **$12.50**

THE EYES OF DISCOVERY, J. Bakeless. A vivid reconstruction of how unspoiled America appeared to the first white men. Authentic and enlightening accounts of Hudson's landing in New York, Coronado's trek through the Southwest; scores of explorers, settlers, trappers, soldiers. America's pristine flora, fauna, and Indians in every region and state in fresh and unusual new aspects. "A fascinating view of what the land was like before the first highway went through," Time. 68 contemporary illustrations, 39 newly added in this edition. Index. Bibliography. x + 500pp. 5⅜ x 8.
T761 Paperbound **$2.00**

AUDUBON AND HIS JOURNALS, J. J. Audubon. A collection of fascinating accounts of Europe and America in the early 1800's through Audubon's own eyes. Includes the Missouri River Journals —an eventful trip through America's untouched heartland, the Labrador Journals, the European Journals, the famous "Episodes", and other rare Audubon material, including the descriptive chapters from the original letterpress edition of the "Ornithological Studies", omitted in all later editions. Indispensable for ornithologists, naturalists, and all lovers of Americana and adventure. 70-page biography by Audubon's granddaughter. 38 illustrations. Index. Total of 1106pp. 5⅜ x 8.
T675 Vol I Paperbound **$2.00**
T676 Vol II Paperbound **$2.00**
The set **$4.00**

TRAVELS OF WILLIAM BARTRAM, edited by Mark Van Doren. The first inexpensive illustrated edition of one of the 18th century's most delightful books is an excellent source of first-hand material on American geography, anthropology, and natural history. Many descriptions of early Indian tribes are our only source of information on them prior to the infiltration of the white man. "The mind of a scientist with the soul of a poet," John Livingston Lowes. 13 original illustrations and maps. Edited with an introduction by Mark Van Doren. 448pp. 5⅜ x 8.
T13 Paperbound **$2.00**

GARRETS AND PRETENDERS: A HISTORY OF BOHEMIANISM IN AMERICA, A. Parry. The colorful and fantastic history of American Bohemianism from Poe to Kerouac. This is the only complete record of hoboes, cranks, starving poets, and suicides. Here are Pfaff, Whitman, Crane, Bierce, Pound, and many others. New chapters by the author and by H. T. Moore bring this thorough and well-documented history down to the Beatniks. "An excellent account," N. Y. Times. Scores of cartoons, drawings, and caricatures. Bibliography. Index. xxviii + 421pp. 5⅝ x 8⅜.
T708 Paperbound **$1.95**

POLITICAL PARTIES, Robert Michels. Classic of social science, reference point for all later work, deals with nature of leadership in social organization on government and trade union levels. Probing tendency of oligarchy to replace democracy, it studies need for leadership, desire for organization, psychological motivations, vested interests, hero worship, reaction of leaders to power, press relations, many other aspects. Trans. by E. & C. Paul. Introduction. 447pp. 5⅜ x 8.
T569 Paperbound **$2.00**

THE EXPLORATION OF THE COLORADO RIVER AND ITS CANYONS, J. W. Powell. The thrilling first-hand account of the expedition that filled in the last white space on the map of the United States. Rapids, famine, hostile Indians, and mutiny are among the perils encountered as the unknown Colorado Valley reveals its secrets. This is the only uncut version of Major Powell's classic of exploration that has been printed in the last 60 years. Includes later reflections and subsequent expedition. 250 illustrations, new map. 400pp. 5⅝ x 8⅜.
T94 Paperbound **$2.00**

FARES, PLEASE! by J. A. Miller. Authoritative, comprehensive, and entertaining history of local public transit from its inception to its most recent developments: trolleys, horsecars, streetcars, buses, elevateds, subways, along with monorails, "road-railers," and a host of other extraordinary vehicles. Here are all the flamboyant personalities involved, the vehement arguments, the unusual information, and all the nostalgia. "Interesting facts brought into especially vivid life," N. Y. Times. New preface. 152 illustrations, 4 new. Bibliography. xix + 204pp. 5⅜ x 8. T671 Paperbound **$1.50**

GARDNER'S PHOTOGRAPHIC SKETCH BOOK OF THE CIVIL WAR, Alexander Gardner. The first published collection of Civil War photographs, by one of the two or three most famous photographers of the era, outstandingly reproduced from the original positives. Scenes of crucial battles: Appomattox, Manassas, Mechanicsville, Bull Run, Yorktown, Fredericksburg, etc. Gettysburg immediately after retirement of forces. Battle ruins at Richmond, Petersburg, Gaines'Mill. Prisons, arsenals, a slave pen, fortifications, headquarters, pontoon bridges, soldiers, a field hospital. A unique glimpse into the realities of one of the bloodiest wars in history, with an introductory text to each picture by Gardner himself. Until this edition, there were only five known copies in libraries, and fewer in private hands, one of which sold at auction in 1952 for $425. Introduction by E. F. Bleiler. 100 full page 7 x 10 photographs (original size). 224pp. 8½ x 10¾. T476 Clothbound **$6.00**

Music

A GENERAL HISTORY OF MUSIC, Charles Burney. A detailed coverage of music from the Greeks up to 1789, with full information on all types of music: sacred and secular, vocal and instrumental, operatic and symphonic. Theory, notation, forms, instruments, innovators, composers, performers, typical and important works, and much more in an easy, entertaining style. Burney covered much of Europe and spoke with hundreds of authorities and composers so that this work is more than a compilation of records . . . it is a living work of careful and first-hand scholarship. Its account of thoroughbass (18th century) Italian music is probably still the best introduction on the subject. A recent NEW YORK TIMES review said, "Surprisingly few of Burney's statements have been invalidated by modern research . . . still of great value." Edited and corrected by Frank Mercer. 35 figures. Indices. 1915pp. 5⅜ x 8. 2 volumes. T36 The Set, Clothbound **$12.50**

A DICTIONARY OF HYMNOLOGY, John Julian. This exhaustive and scholarly work has become known as an invaluable source of hundreds of thousands of important and often difficult to obtain facts on the history and use of hymns in the western world. Everyone interested in hymns will be fascinated by the accounts of famous hymns and hymn writers and amazed by the amount of practical information he will find. More than 30,000 entries on individual hymns, giving authorship, date and circumstances of composition, publication, textual variations, translations, denominational and ritual usage, etc. Biographies of more than 9,000 hymn writers, and essays on important topics such as Christmas carols and children's hymns, and many other unusual and valuable information. A 200 page double-columned index of first lines — the largest in print. Total of 1786 pages in two reinforced clothbound volumes. 6¼ x 9¼. The set, T333 Clothbound **$15.00**

MUSIC IN MEDIEVAL BRITAIN, F. Ll. Harrison. The most thorough, up-to-date, and accurate treatment of the subject ever published, beautifully illustrated. Complete account of institutions and choirs; carols, masses, and motets; liturgy and plainsong; and polyphonic music from the Norman Conquest to the Reformation. Discusses the various schools of music and their reciprocal influences; the origin and development of new ritual forms; development and use of instruments; and new evidence on many problems of the period. Reproductions of scores, over 200 excerpts from medieval melodies. Rules of harmony and dissonance; influence of Continental styles; great composers (Dunstable, Cornysh, Fairfax, etc.); and much more. Register and index of more than 400 musicians. Index of titles. General Index. 225-item bibliography. 6 Appendices. xix + 491pp. 5⅝ x 8¾. T705 Clothbound **$10.00**

THE MUSIC OF SPAIN, Gilbert Chase. Only book in English to give concise, comprehensive account of Iberian music; new Chapter covers music since 1941. Victoria, Albéniz, Cabezón, Pedrell, Turina, hundreds of other composers; popular and folk music; the Gypsies; the guitar; dance, theatre, opera, with only extensive discussion in English of the Zarzuela; virtuosi such as Casals; much more. "Distinguished . . . readable," Saturday Review. 400-item bibliography. Index. 27 photos. 383pp. 5⅜ x 8. T549 Paperbound **$2.00**

Dover publishes books on art, music, philosophy, literature, languages, history, social sciences, psychology, handcrafts, orientalia, puzzles and entertainments, chess, pets and gardens, books explaining science, intermediate and higher mathematics mathematical physics, engineering, biological sciences, earth sciences, classics of science, etc. Write to:

Dept. catrr.
Dover Publications, Inc.
180 Varick Street, N. Y. 14, N. Y.